New Perspectives on CALL
for Second Language Classrooms

ESL AND APPLIED LINGUISTICS PROFESSIONAL SERIES
Eli Hinkel, Series Editor

Hinkel/Fotos, Eds. • *New Perspectives on Grammar Teaching in Second Language Classrooms*

Birch • *English L2 Reading: Getting to the Bottom*

Hinkel • *Second Language Writers' Text: Linguistic and Rhetorical Features*

Hinkel • *Teaching Academic ESL Writing: Practical Techniques in Vocabulary and Grammar*

Fotos/Browne, Eds. • *New Perspectives on CALL for Second Language Classrooms*

New Perspectives on CALL for Second Language Classrooms

Edited by

Sandra Fotos
Senshu University

Charles Browne
Aoyama Gakuin University

LEA LAWRENCE ERLBAUM ASSOCIATES, PUBLISHERS

2004   Mahwah, New Jersey   London

Lawrence Erlbaum Associates, Inc., Publishers
10 Industrial Avenue
Mahwah, New Jersey 07430

Cover design by Kathryn Houghtaling Lacey

Library of Congress Cataloging-in-Publication Data

New perspectives on CALL for second language classrooms /
edited by Sandra Fotos, Charles Browne.
p. cm.—(ESL and applied linguistics professional series)
Includes bibliographical references and index.
ISBN 0-8058-4404-X (cloth : alk. paper)
ISBN 0-8058-4405-8 (pbk. : alk. paper)
1. Language and languages—Computer-assisted instruction.
I. Fotos, Sandra. II. Browne, Charles. III. Series.
P53.28.N485 2003
418'.00285—dc22

2003065114
CIP

Printed in the United States of America
10 9 8 7 6 5 4 3 2

Contents

Preface

Spurred by the rapid development of technology from the early 1980s, *computer-assisted language learning* (CALL) has now become an important component of second and foreign language learning pedagogy. Originally viewed as a supplement to classroom instruction, communicative interaction-based CALL activities are now used to promote learner autonomy and to encourage involvement with the target language both inside and outside of the classroom. CALL publications have evolved from explanations of computers and software to broad explorations of CALL-based pedagogy for a variety of instructional needs. In this direction, the present volume is designed to be a practical handbook for language teachers, teacher trainers, and students who want to learn more about their options for using CALL as well as to develop an understanding of the theory and research supporting these options.

Chapters in this collection synthesize previous CALL theory and research and describe practical applications of CALL to both second and foreign language classrooms, including procedures for evaluating these applications. The implementation of CALL at the institutional level is also addressed, including designing multimedia language laboratories and creating collaborative CALL-based projects between educational institutions. Although many chapters locate their descriptions of CALL activities and projects within the ESL/EFL (English as a second or foreign language) setting, the principles and activities described are equally useful for other languages as well.

The book does not require prior knowledge of CALL, computers, or software. As an assistance to the readers, a glossary of CALL terms and an appendix of World Wide Web addresses are provided. Because CALL is developing rapidly, the book has an accompanying Web site (http://www.erlbaum.com/callforL2classrooms.htm) presenting chapter abstracts, author contact information, and regularly updated links to pedagogical, research, and teacher development sites.

ORGANIZATION OF THE BOOK

The book is organized into five sections, each with a section header introducing the chapters. Part I discusses theoretical and descriptive approaches to CALL by reviewing literature and trends in the field and includes three overview chapters. In their introductory chapter, Fotos and Browne describe the development of CALL models and summarize general types of CALL activities. The second chapter, by Warschauer, presents current developments and future directions of the Internet, and in the final chapter of section one, Liddell and Garrett chart the evolution of the language laboratory and its future as a center for research.

Part II contains six "how-to" chapters for the second and foreign language classroom. As an introduction, the first chapter by Hubbard describes learner training to maximize the CALL experience. The second chapter by Pennington reviews the impact of CALL on second language writing and is followed by two chapters describing CALL-based writing activities. Braine discusses local area network-based second and foreign language writing classes, and Fotos continues the emphasis on CALL as a resource for communicative language use by describing an e-mail project for foreign language students. Taylor and Gitsaki present a pedagogical framework for the use of the Web for language learning, and the final chapter by Iwabuchi and Fotos describes teacher development of course-specific CD-ROM software. These chapters position CALL within current teaching pedagogy combining formal instruction with communicative language use.

Part III addresses CALL within the institutional setting. Chapters in this section include Browne and Gerrity's description of the nuts and bolts of setting up a CALL lab, O'Connor and Gatton's case study of the introduction of multimedia-based languages classes in the foreign language setting, and Opp-Beckman and Kieffer's blueprint for working with other institutions to create a collaborative model for online activities.

Part IV presents models for evaluating CALL, with Reeder, Heift, Roche, Tabyanian, Schlickau, and Gölz discussing criteria for assessing CALL software, and Susser and Robb outlining procedures for Web site evaluation.

In Part V, the concluding chapter by Chapelle and Hegelheimer sums up the contributions of the book to CALL theory and practice by relating the chapters to current research and pedagogy.

This collection of articles attempts to integrate theoretical issues, research findings, and practical guidelines on different aspects of CALL to provide teachers with multiple levels of resources for their personal development, their needs-based creation of specific CALL activities, their curriculum design, and their implementation of institutional and inter-institutional CALL projects.

—Sandra Fotos
—Charles Browne

INTRODUCTION TO CALL

The chapters in Part One provide an introduction to three general aspects of CALL: Its models and instructional options, the Internet as a language learning and communication tool, and the evolution of traditional language laboratories into today's multimedia and research centers. The three chapters each begin with a historical background, trace current developments, and then speculate about the future, identifying CALL as an integral part of language teaching and learning.

The first chapter, "Introduction: The Development of CALL and Current Options," by Fotos and Browne, reviews the history of CALL and the stages in its development, noting benchmark publications. It discusses the changing models of CALL in response to changes in language-learning pedagogy, and considers the current model, Integrative CALL, presenting research on its effectiveness in developing fluency and accuracy in the second language (L2) as well as in promoting learner autonomy, motivation, satisfaction and self-confidence. A variety of CALL activities are introduced, and the book is then positioned within the growing field of CALL literature as a handbook for teachers and practitioners who want to learn about options for, as well as the theory and research behind, using CALL in the classroom at the institutional level, and for cooperative inter-institutional projects.

In the second chapter, "Technological Change and the Future of CALL," Warschauer argues that information and communication technologies will have an increasingly ecological effect on society. He describes key areas where the Internet can be expected to influence communication and language learning in the 21st century, including the nature of electronic genres, the relationship of English and the Internet to identity, the changing nature of reading and writing, the increased role of online audio and audio-visual communication, and the new roles of teachers and learners. Reviewing CALL models and noting their tendency to become increasingly learner-centered, Warschauer relates the development of L2 accuracy and fluency to the concept of agency, meaning that students can use the computer not only to learn a second language, but also to make their mark on the world. Based on these trends, he outlines a future role for computers in L2 teaching and learning.

The final chapter in this section, "The New Language Centers and the Role of Technology: New Mandates, New Horizon," by Liddell and Garrett, charts the evolution of language laboratories from early facilities characterized by behavioral approaches to L2 learning that were often based on drilling via tape recorders into today's multipurpose "language resource centers" that strongly emphasize information technology. The authors point out that the fundamental changes which have occurred were not so much due to specific technological innovations as they were driven by a growing awareness within the centers of what it means to support the needs of teachers of foreign languages. Liddell and Garrett suggest that the future of such multimedia centers will depend upon their placement within their institutions, the presence of an academic director who will represent their interests, and their development as a locus for research.

The Development of CALL
and Current Options

Sandra Fotos
Senshu University

Charles Browne
Aoyama Gakuin University

Computer-assisted language learning (CALL[1]) has been defined as "the search for and study of applications on the computer in language teaching and learning" (Levy, 1997, p. 1) and is now used routinely in a variety of instructional situations. As a result, language teachers are increasingly required to possess CALL expertise that includes both practical skills and a thorough understanding of information technology (IT) theory. Teachers may need to design, implement, and evaluate CALL activities in their classrooms, they may be asked to supervise an institution-wide project or to work with other institutions to develop CALL-based exchange programs, or they may be put in charge of setting up and operating a multimedia language laboratory. It is thus becoming essential for teachers to be familiar with CALL options within the classroom, at the institutional level, and at the broader level of inter-institutional collaboration.

In this introductory chapter we review the rise of CALL and its applications by considering the historical context of computers and their changing role in second language (L2) learning. We note the growing body of research demonstrating CALL's effectiveness in promoting both fluency and accuracy in the target language as well as improving motivation and learner autonomy. We then consider the changes in CALL models concomitant

---

[1]Chapelle (2001) reported that use of the term CALL for computers in language learning was agreed on by early practitioners who met at the 1983 Teachers of English to Speakers of Other Languages (TESOL) conference.

with changes in language-learning pedagogy in general. We also present a broad classification of CALL activities, indicating the chapters in this volume that discuss these activities from the practitioner's perspective.

AN OVERVIEW OF COMPUTER USE IN L2 LEARNING

Developed in the mid 1940s from earlier work in the 1930s and early 1940s, large mainframe computers were used during World War II for missile guidance and cryptography and were thus involved with language processes from the very start. Mechanical translations appeared in the 1940s as a spin-off from cryptography but proved to be inadequate; as a result, U.S. government funding for computer research initially decreased after the war (Last, 1992). However, because of the improved systems and programming languages that were developed throughout the 1950s, by the 1960s linguists were using computers to create concordances for text analysis. The first electronic corpus, the Brown Corpus of Standard American English was developed during this period. It consisted of about 1 million words, the minimum number required to provide a stable word-frequency list.[2]

Until the invention of microcomputers, language learners had to work noninteractively with mainframe computers by punching their data on cards, running the program, then waiting for the results. Despite these limitations, simple CALL programs for drill and testing appeared as early as the 1950s, and a number of pioneer CALL projects existed by the 1960s (see Chapelle, 2001; Levy, 1997, for descriptions). Early programs required the learner to choose one of two answers and the score was presented after the data had been processed. This linear type of program was the first generation of CALL software, and both researchers and educators acknowledged its limitations. The challenge was to create a learner interface that presented the computer as an interactive tutor evaluating the student and providing subsequent activities, a model characterizing CALL from its inception (Kern & Warschauer, 2000; Levy, 1997; Taylor, 1980).

This first phase of CALL has been termed behavioristic CALL (Kern & Warschauer, 2000; Warschauer, 1996a). It dominated the 1960s and 1970s and replicated the teaching techniques of structural linguistics and the audio-lingual method, a behaviorist model of language learning based on habit formation (Richards & Rodgers, 2001). Emulating techniques used in language laboratories at the time, CALL consisted mainly of drill-and-practice

---

[2]Although the creation of the million-word Brown corpus was considered a feat at the time, the sophistication and power of modern computers is demonstrated by the greatly increased size and complexity of modern corpora such as the Cobuild Bank of English, which as of 2002 consisted of more than 450 million words.

programs and was regarded as a supplement to classroom instruction rather than its replacement. However, it should be noted that even today numerous drill programs still exist for vocabulary study and grammar practice because repeated exposure to such material has been shown to promote its acquisition, and the computer provides both immediate feedback and presents material at the learner's pace, thereby encouraging learner autonomy (Chapelle, 2001; Ellis, 2002; Fotos, 2001; Healy, 1999).

By the end of the 1970s, however, behaviorist approaches to language learning were challenged by communicative approaches based on meaning-focused language use rather than formal instruction (Richards & Rodgers, 2001). The emergence of increasingly powerful microcomputers in the 1980s presented a greater range of possibilities for learner interaction, and pioneer books on CALL methodology, such as Higgins and Johns' influential *Computers in Language Learning* (1984), Underwood's seminal *Linguistics, Computers and the Language Teacher* (1984), and Ahmad, Greville, Rogers, and Sussex's *Computers, Language Learning and Language Teaching* (1985) began to appear.[3] This period also witnessed the establishment of key professional organization such as the Computer Assisted Language Instruction Consortium (CALICO) in the United States and the European Association for Computer Assisted Language Learning (EuroCALL) in Europe, and publication of their journals, *CALICO Journal* and *ReCALL*. In addition, language teachers themselves began to write language-learning software using programs such as Hypercard, which were based on a nonlinear concept of interactivity—one of the key concepts driving the subsequent development of the Internet (Levy, 1997). This next generation of CALL software was characterized as communicative CALL (Kern & Warschauer, 2000; Underwood, 1984; Warschauer, 1996a) because it emphasized communicative use of the language rather than mastery of isolated forms. Programs consisted of language games, reading and writing practice, text reconstruction, cloze tests, and puzzles. However, once again the prevailing model was the computer as tutor for the student, a "teacher in the machine" (Levy, 1997), and some researchers evaluating CALL questioned whether this technology was truly compatible with communicative methodology (see Dunkel, 1991; Underwood, 1984).

In reaction to criticisms that CALL was limited to mechanistic drills and lacked the ability to give learners essential feedback, the early 1990s was characterized by a different model, the computer as stimulus (Kern & Warschauer, 2000; Warschauer, 1996a). Here, software followed a cognitive model of language learning that aimed to stimulate students' motivation,

---

[3]See early works by Ahmad et al. (1985) and Higgins and Johns (1984), as well as Levy (1997) and Chapelle (2001) for full discussions of the history of early CALL.

critical thinking, creativity, and analytical skills rather than merely the achievement of a correct answer or the passive comprehension of meaning. A related learning model was the use of the computer as a tool providing the means for students to become active learners (Levy, 1997; Taylor, 1980). Software in this category, such as word processors, spelling and grammar checkers, desktop publishing programs, and concordancers, did not supply language-learning activities but facilitated the students' understanding and manipulation of the target language (Warschauer, 1996a).

The present stage of CALL, integrative CALL, arose in the mid 1990s and has been made possible by the development of powerful desktop computers that support rapid use of the Internet, local area networks (LANs), multimedia, and linked resources known as hypermedia (Warschauer, 1996a). Currently, a typical multimedia language program might allow students to do a reading assignment in the target language, use a dictionary, study grammar and pronunciation related to the reading, perhaps access support materials and translations in the students' first language (L1), view a movie of the reading, and take a comprehension test on the reading content, receiving immediate feedback, all within the same program. This is a highly interactive and individualized approach, with the main focus on content supported by modules instructing learners on specific skills (Kern & Warschauer, 2000).

Much of the theory underlying integrative CALL is derived from the Vygotskyan sociocultural model of language learning (Wertsch, 1985) in which interaction is regarded as essential for the creation of meaning. Thus, person-to-person interaction is a conspicuous feature of many current CALL activities. The rise of LANs to teach writing interactively and e-mail exchange programs among students, classes, and institutions are examples of interactive language learning activities, as are multiplayer role-playing games and interactive online real-time learning situations such as MOOs (multiple-user-domain object oriented) and simulation games played by different users. The rise of the Internet has promoted the use of CALL for information retrieval, creating the concept of computer literacy, a term referring to the development of skills for data retrieval, critical interpretation, and participation in online discourse communities (see Felix, 1999, 2002; Hawisher & Self, 2000; Murray, 2000; Warschauer, 1999). Learner autonomy—the influential concept from general education suggesting that students learn better when they discover things through their own efforts rather than when they receive knowledge passively through instruction—is an important goal of the current view of CALL (Healy, 1999).

A second feature of integrative CALL is the movement away from language-learning software and CD-ROMs to Web-based activities that allow learners flexible, self-paced access to information (Felix, 1998, 1999, 2000; Lin & Hsieh, 2001; Schcolnik, 2002; Warschauer, 1999). Thus, both teachers and students increasingly view computers and CALL as means to an end—the end being authentic, Web-based communication for meaningful purpose—rather than merely as a tool for language learning.

Regarding the future of CALL and the direction of educational technology in general, the point has been made repeatedly that no one knew what a powerful communication tool the telephone would eventually become, how the car would transform transportation, or how important television would become as a global medium. In the same way, from our current vantage point at the start of the computer era, it is impossible to visualize the changes that will occur as a result of its future development. Some researchers caution against the destruction of human relationships and the fragmentation of human society as a result of computer-mediated communication (CMC) preempting face-to-face interaction, warning that "improved tools are still projecting an unimproved and thoroughly unrevolutionary agenda" (Brown, 1997, p. 245). Other researchers (e.g., Ogden, 1995; Warschauer, 1999) predict that we are heading toward a world without borders, with the rise of knowledge brokers and information literates as the new aristocracy and power elite. However, still others caution that the expensive technology and infrastructure required for online activities tend to privilege the culture and educational pedagogies of the advanced nations, creating a hegemonic "digital divide" between technological haves and have-nots (e.g. Crystal, 2001; Hawisher & Self, 2000; Hoffman & Novak, 2001; Murray, 2000; Warschauer, 2003). However, Murray (2000) observed that the new communication technologies such as video conferencing and e-mail have not yet replaced the old forms such phone calls and letters, but rather complement them, so the direction of the relationship between language learning and technology is still unclear.

Nonetheless, most researchers agree that a major shift is taking place (see discussions in Crystal, 2001; Murray, 2000; Warschauer, 2003)—a shift in the use of general technology and a shift in education away from the teacher-centered classroom toward a learner-centered system where the learner is in control of the lesson content and the learning process. CALL has historically been rooted in educational technology, and findings from the general field of education will continue to be influential in determining its future directions. The general differences between education in the pre-computer industrial society and education in the computer-based information society are summarized in Table 1.1. The most effective uses of CALL support this new model of education, and language teachers need to be able to respond by creating CALL-based activities for their particular instructional situation. A quote that has made the rounds of language teaching e-mail lists and online journals during the past several years states the situation clearly: "Technology will not replace teachers; teachers who use technology will replace those who don't!" Teachers must therefore find op-

TABLE 1.1
Education in the Pre-Computer Society Versus
Education in the Information Society[a]

	Education in the Pre-Computer Society	*Education in the Information Society*
School	Isolated from society	Integrated in society
	Information on school functioning is confidential	Information on school functioning is openly available
Teacher	Initiates and controls instruction	Empowers students to find appropriate instruction for their particular learning styles and strategy preferences
	Teacher-fronted instruction of the whole class	Teacher as facilitator guides the students' independent learning; students often work in groups or pairs or singly
	Evaluates students	Helps students evaluate their own progress
	Low emphasis on communication skills	High emphasis on communication skills
Student	Mostly passive learning	Actively in charge of own learning
	Learning mostly at school	Learning at school and outside of school
	Little teamwork	Much teamwork
	Answers questions from textbooks or teacher	Asks questions; learns to find answers to questions
	Low interest in learning	High interest in learning

[a]Adapted from Pelgrum (2001, p. 164).

portunities to gain CALL skills by taking courses in computer technology, teaching themselves, and using their colleagues and the World Wide Web as resources, this last option suggested to be especially significant in skills development (Egbert, Paulus, & Nakamichi, 2002).[4]

EFFECTIVENESS OF CALL

An important question at this point concerns the effectiveness of CALL: Does its use really promote language learning and student development? A large number of books describing and evaluating CALL, summarizing research on CALL effectiveness, and presenting CALL-based activities shown to promote language learning have been published recently, including Boswood (1997), Chapelle (2001), Crystal (2001), Debski and Levy (1999), Egbert and Hanson-Smith (1999), Felix (1998, 2002), Hanson-Smith (2000), Levy (1997), Warschauer and Kern (2000), and Warschauer, Shetzer, and Meloni (2000). These works strongly emphasize the significant role of

---

[4]See Levy's (1997, chap. 5) survey of language teachers' use of CALL.

CALL in developing linguistic proficiency and communicative competence in L2 learners as well as promoting increased levels of learner autonomy, motivation, satisfaction, and self-confidence. For example, mid-1990s summaries of CALL research noted positive results from its use, indicating that CALL permitted students to control the pace of their learning and their interaction with others, and encouraged them to become better writers because they had an authentic audience and a purpose for writing (Pennington, 1996; Pennington & Stevens, 1992; Warschauer, 1995; Yates, 1996). The use of CALL and distance learning activities was found to create classroom discourse communities and encouraged shy students to participate more fully (Palloff & Pratt, 1999; Warschauer, 1996b). Students also reported that CALL activities helped them develop their ideas and promoted learning from their classmates. In addition, developing expertise in using computers gave students feelings of pride and achievement and greatly encouraged their autonomy as learners (see summaries in Warschauer, 1996b, 1999; Shetzer & Warschauer, 2000). Thus, CALL has been shown to produce a number of favorable learning outcomes.

CALL ACTIVITIES

CALL has been divided into seven general types of activity (Warschauer 1996a). One of the most important is writing (see Pennington, chap. 5, this volume). This includes word processing, text analysis, and desktop publishing, often combined with communication over a LAN. Though student use of spell checkers and grammar checkers is common in these types of activities, much more sophisticated and interactive approaches are also possible. Many L2 teachers, for example, now request their students to use computers to write essays then to e-mail each other what they have written or to post their essays on a LAN. The students then discuss and correct each other's writing (in this volume, see Braine, chap. 6; Pennington, chap. 5), engaging in meaningful discourse and creating knowledge through interaction.

A second type of CALL is communicating. This includes e-mail exchanges (see Fotos, chap. 7, this volume), student discussions with each other or with their teacher on LANs (see Braine, chap. 6, this volume), MOOs (sites on the Internet where student do role-playing games and talk with each other), and real-time chat. These activities are particularly useful for foreign language teaching where students share the same L1 because they create the need to use the foreign language for authentic communication.

Another CALL activity is use of multimedia. This includes courseware presented on CD-ROM or online for study of specific skills such as pronunciation or grammar, and integrated skills-based or communicative practice where hyperlinks allow students to access a range of supplementary material for learning support (in this volume, see Hubbard, chap. 4; Opp-Beckman & Kieffer, chap. 12; Reeder et al., chap. 13; Taylor & Gitsaki, chap. 8). Often teacher-created programs are course-specific and are designed to quiz students over material covered in class (in this volume, see O'Connor & Gatton, chap. 11; Iwabuchi & Fotos, chap. 9).

Other CALL activities involve the Internet, such as Web searches for information and student construction of home pages. Related to this is the field of information literacy, a concept similar to computer literacy and referring to the ability to obtain information from the Internet and process it selectively and critically (in this volume, see Taylor & Gitsaki, chap. 8; Susser & Robb, chap. 14; Warschauer, chap. 2). The tremendous amount of online resources means that teacher evaluation of Web sites and L2 learning materials has now become an important aspect of Internet-based activities (in this volume, see Chapelle & Hegelheimer, chap. 15; Reeder et al., chap. 13; Susser & Robb, chap. 14).

An additional use of CALL is concordancing and referencing, or using a corpus to examine the range of usages for grammar and vocabulary items, and using online dictionaries for definitions and usage information.

Yet another significant use of CALL is distance learning. In the United States, United Kingdom, and Europe, many college professors now teach some or all of their courses online.[5] Research on distance learning and courses with online components suggests that online students make the same gains as those achieved by students receiving a regular "brick-and-mortar" lecture (McIntyre & Wolff, 1998). Although it began only recently, distance learning via the Internet has already developed into an important field, with a rapidly increasing number of publications on its implementation and evaluation (e.g., Abbey, 2000; Belanger & Jordan, 2000; Lau, 2000; Palloff & Pratt, 1999; White & Weight, 2000). In fact, an article in the *Chronicle of Higher Education* (November 16, 2001) titled "The Deserted Library" suggests that U.S. college students are doing most of their research online as well.

An additional aspect of distance learning is the teacher creation of Web pages to disseminate their lesson plans, course material, research papers, and other material. Many teachers now routinely take attendance online and post course outlines, specific activities, tests, drills, and so on, on their home pages. Veteran teachers may recall when there was often a filing cabi-

---

[5]Many university review committees now consider the development of electronic teaching materials as a legitimate part of a candidate's tenure or promotion portfolio, and increasingly, university hiring search committees search for candidates who have experience teaching with technology. A discussion of this issue is found in the spring 2002 issue of *TEXT Technology* (11:1), especially the opening paper by Siemens (2002) on the credibility of electronic publishing.

net of time-tested activities, lessons, and tests in the teachers' office for instructors to browse through and copy. Now this "filing cabinet" has moved online to hundreds of sites, including listening laboratories, Test of English as a Second Language (TOEFL) practice, reading and writing activities and exercises, tests, holiday-related and other types of cultural activities, Web page design, and so forth (see the Appendix for a list of links). Again, teachers are required to be able to evaluate sites and online materials (in this volume, see Chapelle & Hegelheimer, chap. 15; Reeder et al., chap. 13; Susser & Robb, chap. 14; Taylor & Gitsaki, chap. 8).[6]

Another important use of CALL is test taking. There is extensive research on computer-assisted language testing (CALT), suggesting that computer-based tests, particularly those that respond to learners' choices by presenting subsequent items at varying levels of difficulty, are effective in building language skills because they provide immediate feedback and multimedia support by access to dictionaries, grammatical explanations, and audio and video material for study of test items (see Chalhoub-Deville, 1999; Chapelle, 2001). Because the TOEFL is now administered by computer, students routinely use CD-ROM TOEFL practice tests and other self-tests. Furthermore, many teachers have developed their own tests, checked them for reliability and validity, and posted them on home pages for others to use, or have developed freeware for course-specific test creation (see the Appendix for links to test sites).

Thus, CALL is now an integral part of L2 classrooms and is likely to assume increasing importance as technology improves (see Chapelle & Hegelheimer, chap. 15, this volume). This book serves as a practical handbook for those who would like to develop an understanding of the wide range of issues, research, and applications of CALL to the 21st-century L2 classroom. In the near future it is likely that many L2 teachers will need to be prepared to: (a) use classroom CALL and perhaps put part or all of their courses online, (b) evaluate CALL materials and Web sites (in this volume, see Reeder et al., chap. 13; Susser & Robb, chap. 14), (c) participate in institution-wide CALL projects (see O'Conner & Gatton, chap. 11, this volume) as well as inter-institutional partnerships (see Opp-Beckman & Kieffer, chap. 12, this volume), and (d) use or administer multimedia language laboratories (in this volume, see Liddell & Garrett, chap. 3; Browne & Gerrity, chap. 10). These issues are addressed in the chapters that follow. In chapter 15, Chapelle and Hegelheimer observe, "The need has never been greater for teachers with basic technological skills who understand the capabilities and limitations of technology in teaching and who accept responsibility for critically examining the options and their implications" (p. 313). Teachers must therefore meet

---

[6]Many L2 textbooks now have a Web-based component for students to perform activities on the book Web site, submit tests for scoring, and participate in chat sessions or post messages to bulletin boards.

the challenge of this continually evolving technology and embrace CALL as a powerful instructional partner.

REFERENCES

Abbey, B. (Ed.). (2000). *Instructional and cognitive impacts of web-based education.* London: Idea Group.

Ahmad, K., Greville, C., Rogers, M., & Sussex, R. (1985). *Computers, language learning and language teaching.* Cambridge, England: Cambridge University Press.

Belanger, F., & Jordan, D. (2000). *Evaluation and implementation of distance learning: Technologies, tools and techniques.* London: Idea Group.

Boswood, T. (Ed.). (1997). *New ways of using computers in language teaching.* Alexandria, VA: Teachers of English to Speakers of Other Languages.

Brown, D. (1997). *Cybertrends: Chaos, power and accountability in the information age.* London: Penguin.

Bruce, J., Peyton, K., & Batson, T. (Eds.). (1993). *Network-based classrooms: Promises and realities.* Cambridge, England: Cambridge University Press.

Chalhoub-Deville, M. (Ed.). (1999). *Development and research in computer adaptive testing.* Cambridge, England: University of Cambridge Examinations Syndicate/Cambridge University Press.

Chapelle, C. (2001). *Computer applications in second language acquisition.* Cambridge, England: Cambridge University Press.

Crystal, D. (2001). *Language and the Internet.* New York: Cambridge University Press.

Debski, R. (1997). Support of creativity and collaboration in the language classroom: A new role for technology. In R. Debski, J. Gaskin, & M. Smith (Eds.), *Language learning through social computing: Applied Linguistics of Australia Occasional Papers Number 16* (pp. 39–65). Melbourne, Australia: University of Melbourne Printing Services.

Debski, R., & Levy, M. (Eds.). (1999). *WORLDCALL: Global perspectives on computer-assisted language learning.* Lisse, Netherlands: Swets & Zeitlinger.

The deserted library. (2001, November 16). *Chronicle of Higher Education,* pp. A35–A38.

Dunkel, P. (1991). Research on the effectiveness of computer-assisted instruction and computer-assisted language learning. In P. Dunkel (Ed.), *Computer assisted language learning and testing* (pp. 5–36). New York: Newbury House.

Egbert, J., & Hanson-Smith, E. (Eds.). (1999). *CALL environments: Research, practice, and critical issues.* Alexandria, VA: Teachers of English to Speakers of Other Languages.

Egbert, J., Paulus, T., & Nakamichi, Y. (2002). The impact of CALL instruction on classroom computer use: A foundation for rethinking technology in teacher education. *Language Learning and Technology, 6*(3), 108–126. Retrieved December 27, 2002, from http://llt.msu.edu/vol6nu,3/egbert/

Ellis, N. (2002). Frequency effects in language processing: A review with implications for theories of implicit and explicit language acquisition. *Studies in Second Language Acquisition, 24*(2), 143–188.

Felix, U. (1998). *Virtual language learning: Finding the gems amongst the pebbles.* Melbourne, Australia: Language Australia.

Felix, U. (1999). Web-based language learning: A window to the authentic world. In R. Debski & M. Levy (Eds.), *WORLDCALL: Global perspectives on computer-assisted language learning* (pp. 85–98). Lisse, Netherlands: Swets & Zeitlinger.

Felix, U. (Ed.). (2002). *Beyond Babel: Language learning online* (pp. 29–58). Melbourne, Australia: Language Australia.

Fotos, S. (2001). Structure-based interactive tasks for the EFL grammar learner. In E. Hinkel & S. Fotos (Eds.), *New perspectives on grammar teaching in second language classrooms* (pp. 135–154). Mahwah, NJ: Lawrence Erlbaum Associates.

Hanson-Smith, E. (Ed). (2000). *Technologically enhanced learning environments.* Alexandria, VA: Teachers of English to Speakers of Other Languages.

Hawisher, G., & Self, C. (Eds.). (2000). *Global literacies and the World-Wide Web.* London: Routledge.

Healy, D. (1999). Theory and research: Autonomy and language learning. In J. Egbert & E. Hanson-Smith (Eds.), *CALL environments: Research, practice, and critical issues* (pp. 391–402). Alexandria, VA: Teachers of English to Speakers of Other Languages.

Higgins, J., & Johns, T. (1984). *Computers in language learning.* London: Collins.

Hoffman, D., & Novak, T. (2001). The growing digital divide: Implications for an open research agenda. In E. Brynjolfsson & B. Kahin (Eds.), *Understanding the digital economy: Data, tools and research* (pp. 245–260). Cambridge, MA: MIT Press.

Kern, R., & Warschauer, M. (2000). Introduction: Theory and practice of network-based language teaching. In M. Warschauer & R. Kern (Eds.), *Network-based language teaching: Concepts and practice* (pp. 1–19). Cambridge, England: Cambridge University Press.

Last, R. (1992). Computers and language learning: Past, present and future. In C. Butler (Ed.), *Computers and written text* (pp. 227–245). Oxford, England: Blackwell.

Lau, L. (Ed.). (2000). *Distance learning technologies: Issues, trends and opportunities.* London: Idea Group.

Levy, M. (1997). *Computer-assisted language learning: Context and conceptualization.* New York: Oxford University Press.

Lin, B., & Hsieh, C. (2001). Web-based teaching and learner control: A research review. *Computers & Education, 37,* 377–386.

McIntyre, D., & Wolff, F. (1998). An experiment with WWW interactive learning in university education. *Computers & Education, 31,* 255–264.

Murray, D. (2000). Protean communication: The language of computer-mediated communication. *TESOL Quarterly, 34,* 397–422.

Ogden, F. (1995). *Navigating in cyberspace: A guide to the next millennium.* Toronto, Canada: MacFarlane Walter & Ross.

Palloff, R., & Pratt, K. (1999). *Building learning communities in cyberspace: Effective strategies for the online classroom.* San Francisco: Jossey-Bass.

Pelgrum, W. (2001). Obstacles to the integration of ICT in education: Results from a worldwide educational assessment. *Computers & Education, 37,* 163–178.

Pennington, M. (1996). *The computer and the non-native writer: A natural partnership.* Cresskill, NJ: Hampton Press.

Pennington, M., & Brock, M. (1992). Process and product approaches to computer-assisted composition. In M. Pennington & V. Stevens (Eds.), *Computers in applied linguistics: An international perspective* (pp. 79–109). Clevedon, UK: Multilingual Matters.

Pennington, M., & Stevens, V. (1992). *Computers in applied linguistics: An international perspective.* Clevedon, UK: Multilingual Matters.

Richards, J., & Rodgers, T. (2001). *Approaches and methods in language teaching* (2nd ed.). Cambridge, England: Cambridge University Press.

Schcolnik, M. (2002). Advanced EFL online: How can it help? In U. Felix (Ed.), *Beyond Babel: Language learning online* (pp. 29–58). Melbourne, Australia: Language Australia.

Shetzer, H., & Warschauer, M. (2000). An electronic literacy approach to network-based language teaching. In M. Warschauer & R. Kern (Eds.), *Network-based language teaching: Concepts and practices* (pp. 171–185). New York: Cambridge University Press.

Siemens, R. (2002). The credibility of electronic publishing: Introduction and overview. *TEXT Technology, 11*(1), 2–16.

Taylor, R. (Ed.). (1980). *The computer in the school: Tutor, tool, tutee.* New York: Teachers College Press.

Underwood, J. (1984). *Linguistics, computers and the language teacher: A communicative approach.* Rowley, MA: Newbury House.

Warschauer, M. (1995). *Computer-mediated collaborative learning: Theory and practice* (Research Note 17). Honolulu, HI: University of Hawaii, Second Language Teaching and Curriculum Center, University of Hawaii Press.

Warschauer, M. (1996a). Computer-assisted language learning: An introduction. In S. Fotos (Ed.), *Multimedia language teaching* (pp. 3–20). Tokyo: Logos International.

Warschauer, M. (1996b). Motivational aspects of using computers for writing and communication. In M. Warschauer (Ed.), *Telecollaboration in foreign language learning. Proceedings of the Hawaii Symposium. Technical Report 21* (pp. 29–46). Honolulu: University of Hawaii Press.

Warschauer, M. (1999). *Electronic literacies.* Mahwah, NJ: Lawrence Erlbaum Associates.

Warschauer, M. (2003). *Technology and social inclusion: Rethinking the digital divide.* Cambridge, MA: MIT Press.

Warschauer, M., & Kern, R. (Eds.). (2000). *Network-based language teaching: Concepts and practice.* Cambridge, England: Cambridge University Press.

Warschauer, M., Shetzer, H., & Meloni, C. (2000). *Internet for English teaching.* Alexandria, VA: TESOL.

Wertsch, J. (1985). *Vygotsky and the social formation of the mind.* Cambridge, MA: Harvard University Press.

White, K., & Weight, B. (Eds.). (2000). *The online teaching guide: A handbook of attitudes, strategies and techniques for the virtual classroom.* San Francisco: Allyn & Bacon.

Yates, S. (1996). Oral and written linguistic aspects of computer conferencing: A corpus-based study. In S. Herring (Ed.), *Computer-mediated communication: Linguistic, social and cross cultural perspectives* (pp. 29–46). Amsterdam: John Benjamins.

Technological Change and the Future of CALL

Mark Warschauer
University of California, Irvine

The future of CALL depends on many factors, including research in applied linguistics, change in the status of languages and language learning, and sociological changes in schools and education. One important factor that will influence the future of CALL is technological change. To discuss this point, it is first necessary to clarify the relationship between technology change and other types of changes.

Technological determinism refers to the idea that the introduction of new technology automatically brings certain results (see discussions in Chandler, 1995; Feenberg, 1991). Deterministic outlooks underlie many common beliefs about educational technology; note, for example, the frequent discussion of the alleged impact of computers on learning without regard to how the computers are actually used. Dede (1995, 1997) has described this as based on a fire metaphor, that is, the notion that computers generate learning the way a fire generates warmth.

Technological determinism does have a certain logic because there is sometimes a correlation between the presence or use of particular technologies and other outcomes. But correlation does not imply causation. Levinson (1997) made a useful distinction between hard determinism and soft determinism. The former implies strict causation, and it is a concept rejected by most scholars. The latter more sensibly suggests that although technological development does not automatically cause outcomes, it does enable new processes and outcomes. For example, in teaching and learning there are obviously many types of classroom (or distant) interaction that are enabled by computers and the Internet that simply couldn't have occurred previously.

Furthermore, in thinking about the possible pedagogical changes enabled by new technologies, it is important to look broader than the classroom itself. Technology can create new social contexts that shape how learning takes place. For example, the earlier development of the printing press had a profound effect on Europe, thus contributing to a process by which notions of teaching and learning were dramatically altered (Eisenstein, 1979). This was not so much an "impact," with the printing press causing change (and, indeed, the earlier invention of movable type in Asia brought little change at all); rather, there was a co-constituitive shaping of technology and society as social conditions in Europe provided a ripe context for emergence of the printing press as an important factor in further societal change. There is thus a broad ecological effect; as Postman (1993) has noted, 50 years after the introduction of the printing press, there was not a Europe plus a printing press, but a transformed Europe. Today, information and communication technologies (ICTs) are poised to have a similarly strong ecological effect on society, especially taking into consideration Castells's (1998) observation that "information technology, and the ability to use it and adapt it, is the critical factor in generating and accessing wealth, power, and knowledge in our time" (p. 92).

The role of ICTs in enabling change must also be examined at the individual level. Vygotsky's work (e.g., 1962) clarified the mediating role of any tool or technology at the level of human activity, ultimately reshaping how we communicate and even think. Ong (1982), who has studied the relationship between orality and literacy, similarly noted the relationship between technology and human consciousness, especially with technologies of the word.

With this as a backdrop, let us examine 10 developments that will take place—and indeed, are already taking place at a rapid pace—in ICT. I briefly review 10 developments under way and then discuss the types of changes these may enable in CALL.

DEVELOPMENTS IN ICT

The first important change is from phone-based to wireless communication because of improved technology and telephone–Internet relay facilities. It has been suggested that low-weight solar-powered electric planes (like those pictured at <http://www.aerovironment.com/area-telecom/telecom.html>) will serve as communications relay platforms facilitating low-cost wireless communication from anywhere on earth.

A second change will be a move from dial-up Internet connections to permanent, direct online connections. For example, according to Telecommunications Research International (see <http://cyberatlas.Internet. com/big_picture/geographics/article/0,1323,5911_352761,00.html#table>), cable modem access in the US grew by some 44% in the first quarter of 2000, whereas high-speed digital forms of access using existing phone lines grew by 183%.

A third change will be from the use of mainly personal computers to the use of portable computing and online devices. One step in this process is the likely convergence of the laptop computer, personal digital assistant, and cellular telephone into powerful handheld computing and (tele)communication devices.

A fourth change will be from narrowband (referring to the speed at which information passes over communication lines) to broadband. Cable modem connections currently deliver 10 megabits per second, shared among many users. The next version of broadband ("broaderband") is expected to provide up to 40 megabits per second for each user, or 26 times the bandwidth of the fast T1 connections (1.5 megabit per second) used by most institutions today, facilitating extremely rapid Internet connection.

A fifth change will be from expensive personal computing systems to widely affordable computers and other hardware, first in developed countries and then in developing countries. In Egypt, for example, the cost of purchasing a personal computer has fallen by half in recent years, and Internet access is now free.

Related to this, a sixth development is that the Internet will change from being an exclusive form of communication and information, mostly limited to people in developed countries, to becoming a mass form of communication accessible to most of the planet. Recent statistics indicate that more than 10% of the world's population is online.

A seventh development will be a movement from text-based information and communication to audiovisual forms of information and communication, as exemplified by the growing popularity of digital photography and home video production facilitated by new technology and the increasing trend for Internet news sites to offer multimedia presentations of news.

An eighth change will be from use of English as the main online language to multilingual Internet use. By 2005, the number of Web pages in English is expected to drop to 41% of the world's total (Computer Economics, 1999). At the same time, however, it is suggested that a much higher percentage of the commercial web pages will be in English. A present indication of this trend is the large percentage of English language secure servers used for Internet commerce (see the discussion in *The Default Language*, 1999). This will create a situation of diglossia, where people using their native languages for local or regional communication and commerce use English for international communication and commerce on the Internet.

A ninth change will be from "non-native" to "native" users of information technology. This concept does not refer to language use but rather to comfort and skill in using computers. Children who grow up with computers and the Internet will be able to access information and communicate online with "nativelike" fluency, as opposed to older generations, many of whom have had difficulty making the transition from print to screen.

A 10th change will be the movement of CALL from the language laboratory to the classroom. Computers and other online devices will be found in every classroom in developed countries, not only in computer laboratories. For example, the Maine Department of Education has made computers available to all seventh-grade students in the state, together with wireless access points in most schools.

TECHNOLOGY AND ENGLISH TEACHING

What is the expected effect on English teaching of these likely future developments? Five areas are examined: new contexts, new literacies, new genres, new identities, and new pedagogies.

New Contexts

The projected developments of ICT will have a profound influence on the context in which English is taught. Largely because of the increased use of English in new globalized media and commerce there has been a major expansion in the number of L2 English speakers around the world. According to recent estimates (see Crystal, 1997), there are now more than 375 million native speakers of English (i.e., the "inner circle" of English-speaking countries such as the United States, Australia, and England; Kachru, 1986), an equal number of English as a second language (ESL) speakers of English (ESL speakers in Kachru's, 1986, "outer circle" of countries such as India and Nigeria), and some 750 million English as a foreign language (EFL) speakers in countries such as China, Japan, Egypt, and Israel. This represents a significant growth in the number of non-native speakers of English and suggests there will be a fundamental change in the relationship between native and non-native speakers. Extrapolating from the work of Graddol (1999), it can be estimated that a century ago there were about three native speakers of English for every proficient non-native speaker of the language. However, a century from now this proportion will be reversed. Indeed, the very distinction among native English speaker, ESL speaker, and EFL speaker will change as millions of people throughout the world use English to communicate globally and access international media.

For example, according to a recent study (Warschauer, El Said, & Zohry, 2002), Egyptian colloquial Arabic is used in most informal e-mail. However, nearly all formal communication by e-mail—even between one Egyptian and another—is conducted in English.

Continuing to examine the impact of improved ICT and the changed context of English use, one U.S. study suggests that e-mail is now the main form of business communication in many US industries, surpassing both face-to-face and telephone communication (American Management Association International, as cited in Warschauer, 2000). This fact necessitates a reconsideration of the relationship of computers and the Internet to ESL and EFL teaching. Just 10 years ago, for example, it was common for teachers involved in CALL to say that "a computer is just a tool; it is not an end in itself but a means for learning English" (cited in Warschauer, 2002, p. 136). Yet recently, one EFL teacher in Egypt noted, "English is not an end in itself; it's just a tool for being able to use computers and get information on the Internet." The juxtaposition of these two very different views of CALL illustrates how teachers' concepts about English teaching and the Internet are evolving now and will change in the future. Effective CALL is no longer a matter of using e-mail and the Internet to help teach English but is increasingly directed at teaching English to help people learn to write e-mail and use the Internet.

New Literacies

This leads to another likely result of ICT developments, the emergence of important new literacies (see discussion in Warschauer, 1999, 2003). In the era of print, the act of reading consisted of an attempt to understand the meaning of a single author. In contrast, reading in the online era has become an attempt to interpret information and create knowledge from a variety of sources. Although all reading and research skills include selecting the right questions, choosing the right tools, finding information, archiving and saving information, interpreting information, and using and citing information, there is a great difference between reading a book in the library and assuming that the information in it is reliable because it has been vetted twice—once by the publisher and again by the librarian who purchased the book—and conducting research online, where the very act of reading cannot be done without making critical decisions at every step. Online readers must constantly determine whether to scroll down a page, pursue an internal link, try an external link, or quit the page and conduct a new search. In the past, "critical literacy" was presented as a special category of language education; however, in the online future, virtually all literacy will necessitate critical judgment.

New Genres

Similar changes are occurring with respect to writing. It has been suggested that the essay will increasingly become a marked form. Although essays may still be studied as a literary form, it has been suggested (Faigley, 1997) that few people will actually write them because they will be replaced by multimedia presenting concepts through multiple technologies. This affects the way English writing must be taught in the future. For examples of possible types of student writing of the future, teachers should consider some of the educational Web sites being developed by students in the ThinkQuest competition (http://www.thinkquest.org). In these sites, students demonstrate mastery not only of multimedia but also of electronic communication, which may represent the future of writing instruction.

The importance of teaching new types of writing through electronic communication can also be illustrated by a situation that occurred in an ESL writing course (Warschauer, 1999). A graduate student from China had previously conducted research with coresearchers from Sweden and agreements had been reached about the rights of authorship using the data collected. However, the student was surprised to learn by e-mail that his Swedish co-researchers were going to publish the data under their own authorship. He attempted to write them an e-mail message protesting the situation:

> Dear Svet:
> How about your decision for your mothers treatment. I am sorry I can not give advice. . . . Zhongshan hospital has special wards for foreign guests. If you can tell me and Hengjin in detail, we can supply more information about hospital and doctors.

The first draft of his e-mail message failed to convey his point because it focused principally on the health of the Swedish colleague's mother and only discussed the disagreement in a vague manner at the end of the message. The student worked with his teacher intensively by e-mail to complete two more drafts of the message until it effectively communicated what he wanted to say:

> Dear Svet:
> When I received your email message of Nov 4, I was very surprised to see that you went ahead with your paper on maternal health care. As you must be aware after our discussion in Shanghai last September-October, when we distributed all the topics among us, the topic of maternal health care was incumbent on me for analysis and publication. . . .
> In conclusion, I am afraid the only satisfactory solution I can see is to publish my paper with me as the first author.

This problem was resolved in a satisfactory manner through the speed of electronic communication and a needs-based collaborative approach to writing instruction.

Although most ESL and EFL students do not perform sociological research with international scholars, many will find that they need to carry out some form of collaborative long-distance inquiry and problem solving as part of their jobs and community activities. It is thus incumbent on ESL and EFL teachers to help these students develop the online writing skills necessary for these tasks. Such instruction includes both the pragmatics of written online interaction and the hypermedia authoring and publishing skills needed for effective presentation of material (see discussion in Shetzer & Warschauer, 2000; Warschauer, 1999).

New Identities

The increased importance of online communication is also contributing to new kinds of identities. As an example, consider the case of Almon, a Hong Kong immigrant to the United States (discussed in Lam, 2000). Though Almon had lived in the United States for several years, he performed poorly in English class and had little confidence in his academic English ability. Yet he developed his own "J-Pop" Web site about a Japanese popular singer and spent several hours each day e-mailing and chatting with other J-Pop fans around the world who were attracted to his site. Although most of the fans were Chinese or Japanese, all communication, as well as the site itself, was in English. Through this process Almon developed self-confidence in his English communication ability as part of a global youth movement that uses English and new media to share ideas. This case does not suggest that teachers should downplay academic literacies, but it does imply that students who use new media can develop a wide range of literacies and identities, and these skills must be taken into account in English teaching.

New Pedagogies

We must now consider the new pedagogies that these changes will elicit. The progress of CALL has been based on evolution from the mainframe computer to the personal computer to the networked, multimedia computer, and corresponding changes have occurred in CALL-based pedagogy. Table 2.1 illustrates some of the changes that have occurred and are occurring in CALL since its inception in the 1960s. The stages have not occurred in a rigid sequence, with one following the other, from "bad CALL" to "good CALL" because any of these may be combined for different purposes. However, there has been a general transformation in CALL over the years, with new ideas and uses of computers being introduced.

TABLE 2.1
The Three Stages of CALL

Stage	1970s–1980s: Structural CALL	1980s–1990s: Communicative CALL	21st Century: Integrative CALL
Technology	Mainframe	PCs	Multimedia and Internet
English teaching paradigm	Grammar transla- tion and audio- lingual	Communicate lan- guage teaching	Content based, Eng- lish for Specific Purposes/English for Academic Pur- poses
View of language	Structural (a formal structural system)	Cognitive (a men- tally constructed system)	Sociocognitive (de- veloped in social interaction)
Principal use of computers	Drill and practice	Communicative ex- ercises	Authentic discourse
Principal objective	Accuracy	Fluency	Agency

Note. Based on Kern and Warschauer (2000), Warschauer (1996, 2000a).

The first phase of CALL development was structural CALL, an approach used during the 1960s and 1970s that followed the teaching techniques of structural linguistics. Here, CALL primarily took the form of drill-and-practice programs. However, by the end of the 1970s, such behavioristic approaches to language learning had given way to communicative approaches focusing on the meaning of language in use rather than on its form, and this was reflected the changed nature of CALL activities.

Following a cognitive view of language learning that held that learners develop language as an internal mental system primarily through interaction, communicative CALL took the form of communicative exercises performed as a way of practicing English. The content of the interaction was not seen as important, nor was the learners' own speech or output. Rather, the provision of input was seen as essential for learners to develop their mental linguistic systems. In contrast, the current paradigm of integrative CALL is based on a sociocognitive view of language learning. From this viewpoint, learning a second or foreign language involves apprenticing into new discourse communities. The purpose of interaction is seen as helping students enter these new communities and familiarize themselves with new genres and discourses, so the content of the interaction and the nature of the community are extremely important. It is no longer sufficient to engage in communication merely to practice language skills.

The following example illustrates the primary difference between communicative CALL and integrative CALL. An English teacher was frustrated because, although his students used the Internet once a week to practice English, they tended to waste time chatting in their own language and did not engage in meaningful English usage. This situation highlights a critical limitation of the communicative approach to CALL, that is, viewing Internet only as a medium of simple (and perhaps purposeless) communication practice. It was suggested that the students should perform real-life tasks on the Internet and solve real-life problems in a community of peers or mentors. For example, the students could conduct an international research project on an issue they were interested in (see Warschauer, Shetzer, & Meloni, 2000) or perform a service for their communities such as creating an English Web site for a local organization (Warschauer & Cook, 1999). Here, the use of English for communication would be incidental to the main task, but as a result of carrying out the activity, the students would be learning important new English genres and engaging in new discourses.

Agency

Performance of meaningful activities online is related to the objectives of integrative CALL and, indeed, to the general goals of second or foreign language learning which have evolved from a primary focus on accuracy to a focus on accuracy plus fluency. In the 21st century, however, it is necessary to add a new objective: accuracy plus fluency plus agency. Agency has been defined as "the satisfying power to take meaningful action and see the results of our decisions and choices" (Murray, 1997, p. 126) and "the power to construct a representation of reality, a writing of history, and to 'impose reception of it' by others" (Kramsch, A'Ness, & Lam, 2000, p. 97, quoting Bourdieu). Incorporating the objective of agency in CALL activities enables the computer to provide students with a powerful means to make their mark on the world. As an example, we should consider the difference between writing a paper (i.e., writing a text for the teacher) and creating a multimedia document that will be displayed on the Internet. In the latter, students are involved in creatively bringing together several media to share with a wide international audience, and perhaps even helping to create the very rules by which multimedia is created, given the current creative explosion of new forms of online expression. By assisting their students in carrying out such authoring—fulfilling a meaningful purpose for a real audience—teachers are helping them exercise their agency. The purpose of studying English thus becomes not just to acquire it as an internal system but to be able to use English to have a real impact on the world.

CONCLUSION

In the late 1970s a computer-assisted instructional manual (Patrikis, 1997, p. 171) suggested that the advantage of computer-based instruction was that it was completely removed from "real life." Students could therefore learn English without having to participate in the real world, although, of course, they had to come back to the real world to use what they had learned.

In contrast, let us consider a more current expression of the value of computers in instruction, that of Shneiderman (1997), who said, "We must do more than teach students to 'surf the net,' we must also teach them how to make waves" (p. vii). Thus, teachers will make the best use of computers in the classroom when students are encouraged to perform the most real tasks possible, taking advantage of the power of modern ICTs to try to change the world in ways that suit students' own critical values and the interests of humankind.

Of course, this is not a new idea. Freire and Macedo (1987) expressed the same perspective when they noted that literacy is not only about "reading the word," but also about "reading the world," and not only about reading the world but also writing it and rewriting it (p. 37). These concepts have been an important part of critical pedagogy throughout the 20th century, but today new forms of ICTs provide a powerful new means of achieving them.

Changes in ICTs can thus enable students to read, write, and rewrite the world in their English classes as never before, but only if we too enable our students to use the full power of these technologies. As Pimienta (2002) suggested, we need to view our students as being "in front of a keyboard" rather than "behind a screen." In the end, the most important developments may not be those that occur in the technological realm, but rather those that take place in our own conceptions of teaching and learning.

ACKNOWLEDGMENTS

This chapter draws from an earlier paper, "The Death of Cyberspace and the Rebirth of CALL," which was first presented at the CALL for the 21st Century IATEFL and ESADE conference in July 2000, and then appeared in *English Teachers Journal* (53), fall 2000, published by the Ministry of Education of Israel.

REFERENCES

Castells, M. (1998). *End of millennium.* Malden, MA: Blackwell.
Chandler, D. (1995). Technological or media determinism. [Online article]. Retrieved November 20, 2002, from http://www.aber.ac.uk/media/Documents/tecdet/tecdet.html

Computer Economics, I. (1999). *Computer Economics projects worldwide Internet users to approach 350 million by year 2005.* Retrieved January 1, 2000, from http://www.computereconomics.com/new4/pr/pr990118.html

Crystal, D. (1997). *English as a global language.* Cambridge, England: Cambridge University Press.

Dede, C. (1995). *Testimony to the US Congress, House of Representatives, Joint Hearing on Educational Technology in the 21st century.* Retrieved January 4, 2002, from http://www.virtual.gmu.edu/SS_research/cdpapers/congrpdf.htm

Dede, C. (1997). Rethinking how to invest in technology. *Educational leadership, 55*(3), 12–16.

The default language. (1999, May 15). *Economist,* pp. 67–67.

Eisenstein, E. L. (1979). *The printing press as an agent of change: Communications and cultural transformations in early-modern Europe.* Cambridge, England: Cambridge University Press.

Faigley, L. (1997). Literacy after the revolution. *College Composition and Communication, 48*(1), 30–43.

Feenberg, A. (1991). *Critical theory of technology.* New York: Oxford University Press.

Freire, P., & Macedo, D. (1987). *Reading the word and the world.* Hadley, MA: Bergin & Garvey.

Graddol, D. (1999). The decline of the native speaker. In D. Graddol & U. H. Meinhof (Eds.), *English in a changing world: AILA Review 13* (pp. 57–68). Guildford, England: Biddles.

Kachru, B. (1986). *The alchemy of English: The spread, functions, and models of non-native Englishes.* Urbana: University of Illinois Press.

Kern, R., & Warschauer, M. (2000). Theory and practice of network-based language teaching. In M. Warschauer & R. Kern (Eds.), *Network-based language teaching: Concepts and practice* (pp. 1–19). New York: Cambridge University Press.

Kramsch, C., A'Ness, F., & Lam, E. (2000). Authenticity and authorship in the computer-mediated acquisition of L2 literacy. *Language Learning & Technology, 4*(2), 78–104.

Lam, E. (2000). Second language literacy and the design of the self: A case study of a teenager writing on the Internet. *TESOL Quarterly, 34,* 457–482.

Levinson, P. (1997). *The soft edge: A natural history and future of the information revolution.* London: Routledge.

Murray, J. H. (1997). *Hamlet on the holodeck: The future of narrative in Cyberspace.* New York: The Free Press.

Ong, W. (1982). *Orality and literacy: The technologizing of the word.* London: Routledge.

Patrikis, P. C. (1997). The evolution of computer technology. In R. Debski, J. Gassin, & M. Smith (Eds.), *Language learning through social computing* (pp. 159–178). Parkville, Australia: Applied Linguistics Association of Australia.

Pimienta, D. (2002). *The digital divide: The same division of resources?* Unpublished paper, Santo Domingo, Dominican Republic.

Postman, N. (1993). *Technopoly: The surrender of culture to technology.* New York: Vintage Books.

Shetzer, H., & Warschauer, M. (2000). An electronic literacy approach to network-based language teaching. In M. Warschauer & R. Kern (Eds.), *Network-based language teaching: Concepts and practice* (pp. 171–185). New York: Cambridge University Press.

Shneiderman, B. (1997). Foreword. In R. Debski, J. Gassin, & M. Smith (Eds.), *Language learning through social computing* (pp. v–viii). Melbourne, Australia: Applied Linguistics Association of Australia.

Vygotsky, L. S. (1962). *Thought and language.* Cambridge, MA: MIT Press.

Warschauer, M. (1996). Computer-assisted language learning: An introduction. In S. Fotos (Ed.), *Multimedia language teaching* (pp. 3–20). Tokyo: Logos International.

Warschauer, M. (1999). *Electronic literacies: Language, culture, and power in online education.* Mahwah, NJ: Lawrence Erlbaum Associates.

Warschauer, M. (2000). The changing global economy and the future of English teaching. *TESOL Quarterly, 34,* 511–535.

Warschauer, M. (2003). *Technology and social inclusion: Rethinking the digital divide.* Cambridge, MA: MIT Press.

Warschauer, M., & Cook, J. (1999). Service learning and technology in TESOL. *Prospect, 14*(3), 32–39.

Warschauer, M., El Said, G. R., & Zohry, A. (2002). Language choice online: Globalization and identity in Egypt. *Journal of Computer Mediated Communication, 7*(4). Retrieved November 21, 2002, from http://www.ascusc.org/jcmc/vol7/issue4/warschauer.html

Warschauer, M., Shetzer, H., & Meloni, C. (2000). *Internet for English teaching.* Alexandria, VA: Teachers of English to Speakers of Other Languages.

3

The New Language Centers and the Role of Technology: New Mandates, New Horizons

Peter Liddell
University of Victoria

Nina Garrett
Yale University

Where second language acquisition (SLA) theory and technology-enhanced language learning (TELL[1]) practice are concerned, it is tempting to see a direct cause-and-effect relationship between the situation that existed in the late 1980s and the substantial changes that took place in the 1990s. There is no doubt that the infrastructure of language learning changed markedly in the 1990s and that the changes did bring learning theory and classroom practice closer together. But the role of TELL is still not at all clear in this new environment, in the sense that the new technologies, with their greatly increased capacity to improve communication, have not yet been exploited in any systematic, theoretically well-founded way. Without that link, technology remains an adjunct activity, as can be seen by the varying degrees of infrastructural separation between the new language centers and the language "labs."

The term *language lab* (often associated with rows of students seated in front of audiotape recorders) has given way to *language resource center* or *language media center,* and in many cases the change in name has been accompanied by a major expansion and improvement in the kind of technological resources they bring to language learners and teachers. A language lab

---

[1]TELL refers to all technologies, including analog, that have been or are still being used to support language learning. Because these technologies are rapidly settling onto a computer-based platform, CALL has become the preferred acronym. CALL is used in this chapter in the strict sense (i.e., when computers are the sole technology involved).

is thought of as a room full of tape cassette players, whereas a language media center is thought of as housing at least some computers and video equipment, if not in all cases a fully digital multimedia operation. But these changes have for the most part neither proceeded from nor contributed to significantly different ways of relating technology to pedagogy, for reasons that are outlined in the following sections of this chapter: Language teaching and learning have traditionally had little status in the Western academy, and the technology has from the outset been seen as ancillary, aiding only the most mechanical and routine aspects of instruction.

THE PROBLEMATICS OF THE LATE 1980s: TIES THAT BIND

Traditions in Philology: The Influence of the Classical Tradition

Insofar as the humanistic roots of the Western university can be traced to the Renaissance, they are inseparably linked to the philological tradition of that movement. To understand the thought and the literature of the classical world, it was argued, scholars must be able to read the original texts, hence must learn the languages of antiquity. Most traditional university language programs in North America and the United Kingdom grew out of that philological tradition, with reading and writing abilities being given clear priority over speaking and listening skills.

Because pattern-recognition and cognitive skills are fundamental to text decoding and accuracy, it is not surprising that, in the past almost 100 years since language learning was first enhanced by recording machines, the media used to foster these skills consistently focused on speech modeling and the drilling of patterns. Unfortunately, this tendency continued to dominate TELL long after the importance of other, less paradigmatic motivating factors had been recognized in classroom pedagogy. Small wonder that the research literature of mediated learning overwhelmingly discovers "no significant difference" in learning achievements that are attributable to the technology alone (other variables influence the outcome in most cases).[2]

---

[2]The No Significant Difference Web site, which surveys the literature on technology-enhanced learning over eight decades, is, rightly, considered to be misleading, precisely because its citations focus on the contribution of technology alone, as if that could be divorced from the context of its use and its users. In recent years, the site has a companion list that cites literature that does register a difference. Similar reservations can be made about this site, too.

Traditions in TELL

Technology in the more modern sense has been used to support language learning in North America for almost a century. From recording native speakers on wire to recording them on tape or CD, not much changed, methodologically speaking, until recently. Technically, of course, the changes were substantial: The fidelity, volume, and speed of the medium; its storage capacity; and the convenience of rapid, selective access to a wider array of models and practice exercises. But most of the media that were co-opted to support language skills had been invented for entirely different, far less cognitive purposes—such as recording or relaying authentic information and entertainment in a linear, uninterrupted, untruncated stream. By contrast, the exercises devised on those media for language learning tended to be overwhelmingly synthetic, abstracted, repetitive slices of language designed to exemplify and reinforce the recognition and acquisition of structural principles. As the methodology evolved, language lab technology was not only at odds with the classroom practice, it consisted of misappropriating media that had a far more stimulating other life. In essence, by the late 1980s, there was a growing dichotomy between the face-to-face classroom, with its mixture of cognitive learning and simulated realistic interactivity on the one hand, and the computer- and tape-based language laboratory on the other. Yet, in North America and certain jurisdictions such as the United Kingdom, providing facilities for TELL is less of an option now than it ever was: All North American first-year textbooks for the "major" languages, and many second-year texts, now espouse TELL. They routinely include audio, video, and computer drills, both for home use and for instructional use. Newer texts include online Web access to CALL drills that are automatically scored. The substantial costs of these ancillary items are included in the price of textbooks; therefore, institutions are morally obliged to ensure that students can use them. Technological facilities are not an option, in other words, whether *in situ* or available online for remote access (if copyright can be protected).

Communicative Needs, Conservative Methods

A new fact of university-level language-learning life began to arise in the decades leading up to the 1990s in North America, Europe, and other regions. It contrasted sharply with the classical, "philological" tradition, so met with varying degrees of welcome in the language and literature departments. Social policy, greater population mobility, and SLA theory itself underpinned a demand, by the mid-1980s at the latest, for more pragmatic, more career-related, and more oral language-learning skills. University language and literature departments and publishers that embraced the trend to greater orality were able to capitalize on the communicative approach to enhance students' acquisition of speaking and listening skills. Frequently, however, that clashed with the methods of the philological tradition and the technologies that had been co-opted to support it.

Europe. In Europe, the communicative approach to language learning originated with the need for greater mobility of skilled and service workers, and was often called "contact threshold" learning (van Ek, 1975). The learners were most often training for, or already employed in, specific manual and service industry careers, and were typically not enrolled in general undergraduate studies at academic institutions. The need for labor mobility led to a multitude of programs for learning languages for special purposes—some of them very specialized indeed, such as the sophisticated program developed with European funding to train English- and French-speaking Channel Tunnel rail drivers in each others' language (Bangs, 1994; Bangs & Shield, 1999). As with many of these training programs, the "Chunnel-train" drivers learned through a combination of classroom instruction, TELL, and real-life immersion (e.g., exchanges, home stays).

Continental European language-learning centers at academic institutions have concentrated on language pedagogy for specialists, such as doctors, engineers, lawyers, or journalists. Learning a foreign language may be a requisite of the professional program, but in Germany and France, for example, the language courses have often been treated as ancillary to the main program. Technology has also not played a significant role for the most part. In programs that require reading and writing skills, the language lab is often employed for acquiring vocabulary and mastering structural patterns, with oral skills being honed in the classroom, using the services of native-speaking assistants. In such cases—as in North America—the pedagogy of the program often sees no role for technology other than as an infinitely patient, cognitive assistant. There are indications that this may change, again with the assistance of major European funding. The government of the state of Bavaria, for example, has initiated a program called *Sprachchancen* with the aid of significant European funding (see http://www.sprachchancen.de/). The purpose of the program is to encourage the increased use of online learning resources for courses being delivered in academic language centers. In the case of less commonly taught languages (LCTLs) that are needed for special purposes, this may be the only viable option.

In smaller northern and northwestern European countries such as Sweden or the Netherlands the pattern differs, particularly where English is concerned. Students there typically enter university with 9 years of school English and with a relatively high degree of oral proficiency that is reinforced by movies and television shows that are normally broadcast in English (with or without subtitles). In those countries, English may be the language of instruction in many courses, particularly in the professional faculties. The role of technology is therefore often to improve specialized vocabulary and the idiomatic use of English, by using concordancers and other sophisticated exploratory tools (centers at Stockholm and Umeå are good examples).

North America.   In North America, Krashen and Terrell's (1983) natural approach coincided with similar methodological and pedagogical needs in the mid- to late-1980s, with an increasing focus on socially contextualized, stepped, curriculum goals, or learner outcomes.

One group of learners who added significantly to the communicative pressures of other learners was students of the professional faculties (e.g., nursing, engineering, medicine, and business). These students had highly pragmatic L2 needs, but their programs rarely allowed time for sufficient language electives of the traditional sort. What many students of this group required, in as short a time as possible, were specific, professional, nonacademic, interactive oral skills, so that they could conduct technical discussions, teach, or interview clients or patients. The standard minimum four semesters of the typical "generic" language, literature, and culture (LL&C) department programs did not meet their needs specifically enough.

Many of the professional students wanted to learn to communicate in LCTLs for work with people who could not be expected to have English or another major L2. For universities with traditional disciplinary structures, this caused severe administrative problems: Instructors in the LL&C departments generally lacked either the skill or the incentive or the opportunity to concentrate on such specialized courses. Frequently, instructors had to be hired into the respective professional faculties, where there were no comparable colleagues and no technical infrastructure. Often, these instructors were native speakers with some background in the respective professional field but no training in, or readily available support for, SLA pedagogy. As is seen in the second part of this chapter, the needs of language teachers in professional faculties may have been one catalyst for administrative innovation, but it was rarely the only structural and academic or pedagogical problem that language centers were intended to resolve.

Summary: The "Technology Gap"

In communicative curricula, simulations of real-life situations became the preferred classroom activity, but they could not be emulated well with technology, only stimulated, by video reenactments, for example. Where the technology was found to be useful, however, was in making up for class time formerly dedicated to practicing cognitive skills, usually with pattern drilling on a computer (early CALL programs). Despite some attempt to motivate further practice at the computer with automated responses, such as right–wrong comments, score-keeping, and built-in reference tools (grammatical explanations and paradigms, dictionaries), the "intelligence" of the technology in no way matched the nuanced quality of a live instructor. Thus, where classroom teaching adapted to both affective and cognitive styles of learning, the technology of the language labs remained firmly in the cognitive camp. By the late 1980s, signs of strain in the infrastructure of language learning at the postsecondary level could be roughly summed up as: methodological, technological, professional, and structural.

Methodological. The traditional, academic needs of philology students in the liberal arts often clashed with the needs of students training in the professions and other students with more interest in the communicative skills.

Technological. The usage of technology was growing, computer exercises were successful at giving practice in cognitive learning, and other media (especially if coordinated through a computer) provided simulations, illustrations, and motivation, but overall, TELL was inadequate, both for the communicative aspirations of a growing body of learners and for the methodological and pedagogical needs of the teacher. Having a significant body of poorly supported, lone instructors scattered across the professional faculties only exacerbated the situation, at larger institutions in particular. Lack of cohesion and common purpose made the situation ripe for change. Many of the weaknesses were found to be systemic, deriving from the traditional role assigned to language teaching in the traditional LL&C departments, or as marginalized support for professional programs. Without structural change there appeared to be little chance to break the cycle.

Professional. The status of language teaching in the university reward system (promotion, salary increases) in several jurisdictions often discourages involvement by mainstream academics. One criticism of language teachers is that they lack the research connection of the teaching researchers of LL&C (who are usually members of the same department). In European language centers this is partially offset by affiliation with teacher training and expertise in classroom (rarely in CALL) pedagogy. Contractually, too, there are entrenched weaknesses. Until the past 5 years or so, and despite actual course assignment patterns, candidates' ability to teach language classes was rarely mentioned as a significant requirement in North American tenure-track job advertisements for positions involving research and teaching in the LL&C (philology) departments. Graduate training reflects this still. The dominant North American pattern has been that almost all tenure-track faculty members in LL&C departments were trained exclusively in literary criticism but might do as much as two thirds of their teaching in language classes. Their preparation for this consisted of little more than being language teaching assistants in their graduate school years, often with little or no formal training. Because of the bias in their own L2 learning experience toward reading and writing skills, the aspiring graduate students who were not native speakers often lack the necessary oral fluency for the new curriculum.

Structural. Before the situation that we have just described could change, some administrative innovation was required. Language labs, and even language media centers, typically do not have the resources or the credentials to undertake major initiatives to change the context in which they operate. Language lab directors are often thought of as staff, not faculty, and are seen as managers of student workers and providers of the routine services demanded of them by teachers (though they often teach language classes themselves as part of their responsibilities). Direct access to higher administrators or senior faculty in the LL&C departments may be problematical. In short, they may lack a strong political voice at the academic table.

A second source of structural weakness may exist within the institution's technological infrastructure. The language labs that grew out of the classical humanistic tradition may be situated outside the main campus technology support system. Thus, they may exist as stand-alone units and be vulnerable to elimination or to takeover by academic computing; in either case they lose their disciplinary integrity and may no longer serve as training grounds or resources for language teachers or as a supportive home for language programs.[3]

In seeking solutions to this cycle of problems, many universities in the United States and a small number in Europe examined their support systems and made significant innovations during the 1990s. What follows is a synopsis of the changes as they were instituted at a number of North American universities, with some reference to Europe and other jurisdictions.

THE NEW LANGUAGE CENTERS: A NEW MANDATE

There are centers, and there are centers, and as they proliferate, their functions and structures proliferate as well.
—P. Patrikis (personal communication, April 1999)

Within the past decade several institutions have developed a new kind of unit, a center for language study, established by administrators or influen-

---

[3]For an in-depth discussion of trends and challenges in the development of language technology centers and their directors' positions, see Garrett, "Language Media" (1997).

tial language faculty to strengthen the institution's language programs across the board through a combination of new resources—political, theoretical, pedagogical, and technological. A number of these centers have grown up in North American universities to address the common problems of their language programs in the changing academic scene outlined in the earlier part of this chapter. The new mandate of these centers usually includes the following goals:

- To provide an intellectual home for language teaching, often including the so-called LCTLs housed in professional faculties[4] and, in some cases, for SLA theory and research.
- To validate language teaching and learning across the entire curriculum; to raise the general campus awareness of the complexity and value of language study in a genuinely international curriculum.
- To provide new resources and expertise for the support of language programs in departments and programs where the senior faculty may not have the necessary professional focus.
- To provide substantive education in pedagogy and technology for graduate students, especially recognizing the need for such education in today's job market.
- To support the integration of technology into language learning and teaching.
- To collect data on how language education is handled across the institution as a basis for recommendations for parity among language faculty, coherence of policy, and professional standards.
- To coordinate and rationalize assessment at all levels and for all curricular purposes—the foreign language requirement, placement, advanced achievement and certification, fellowships, or professional certification.
- To manage more efficiently the administration of programs in the small-enrollment LCTLs (and in some cases ESL) that have no logical departmental home (this mandate may include effecting savings in these areas).
- To meet local needs in the spirit of the local academic culture (the source of many of the differences). For this reason, they often depend on the diplomatic skills and academic respect of the director, in particular among departments viewing themselves as stakeholders.

---

[4]Several universities first considered creating a language center to house LCTLs (definitions of these varies—often it includes Asian languages, Arabic, African, and some European languages, including ESL). The demand for instruction or testing in these languages typically arises either from students wanting to satisfy language requirements or from professional schools wanting to broaden the options for students entering or graduating from their programs.

The new breed of language center was typically put into place by high-level faculty or administrators who perceived the need for a powerful infra-structure if language programs are to serve the needs of students graduating into the 21st century and global engagement. Such a center is the natural home of a new breed of CALL practice and practitioners as well, because it is easy to understand that technology can and should play a major role in achieving almost every one of these goals. Even though the heaviest emphasis is on the strengthening of learning and teaching across all skills and for many different purposes (and this strengthening may not itself directly include technology use at every point), technology is seen as one of the most efficient instruments for creating community, for presenting the intersection of teaching and research, for collecting data (whether empirical or administrative), for managing testing, and for forging professional connections and networks generally. With some humor, Nina Garrett (2000) described her position as director of the Yale Center for Language Study at the Web site of a colloquium on language centers, which she organized in 2000, as being "to support, strengthen, coordinate, equalize, make more efficient, evaluate, develop administrative policies relating to, develop a professional community for, provide resources for, develop materials for, build up the use of technology in, integrate into the overall curriculum (and often save money on) the learning of languages." On the same Web site Richard Levin (2000), president of Yale, defined the mandate of the Yale center more elegantly as ensuring that language teaching is as excellent, and language teachers as respected, as those in any other area at Yale.

The New Language Centers—Defining the Roles and Mandate

As the new centers arise, technology plays an important part, but it cannot be divorced from the overall cultural relations between the existing departments of the institution. Experience in both the United States and Europe suggests that a language center built mainly out of components of the former traditional LL&C departments is likely to fail, where language instruction is structurally divorced from those departments. Two options that have been tried and shown to be unsatisfactory are realignment and independence.

Realignment (Say, With Linguistics). Realignment may separate the languages psychologically, but especially in curriculum, from "their" literatures and cultures. Consequently, unless sufficient (usually new) funds are made available to secure their professional status (e.g., through research, conferences, or bringing in outside experts), language teachers may become entrenched in a worse second-class role than in the previous structure.

Independence. Independence is not a preferred solution either. With the possible exception of Middlebury College, no major North American university has successfully created a language center as a separate entity. In Europe, according to D. Bickerton (personal communication, April 1999), "It is very difficult to make an independent Language Center work." To survive they usually need to generate their own revenue or offer graduate programs.

The New Language Centers—Features in Common

Technology. In most of the eight language centers convened at the colloquium at Yale University in March 2000 (Garrett, 2001), the language technology unit has been completely integrated. Typically the person in charge of the technological side of the operation is the associate director of the center, in some cases the director. Where a center does not take over the language lab per se, the center usually has its own technological facility for training language teachers and graduate student teaching assistants. The relation between a language center and the campus academic computing unit can be problematic, but academic computing can also be one of the center's most powerful allies. In today's networked campus and world, it is simply no longer possible for the language technology effort to remain autonomous and unconnected.

Given authority and appropriate resources, language centers can begin to develop uses of technology to support radically new approaches to language teaching and learning. With staff who have a solid background both in computing and in foreign languages (even, optimally, in language teaching), centers can encourage the development of multimedia materials that are not just computerized versions of conventional pedagogical activities. Because teachers tend to teach as their teachers have taught, or as the textbook and methodology books tell them to, and very few have any exposure to SLA theory, it is extremely difficult for them to imagine uses of the technology that have no precedent in non-technology-based methods; they tend to suspect that any such use is technology driven, that is, motivated more by the gadgetry than by sound pedagogy. But expert programmers in language centers can develop templates for innovative language materials, which interested teachers can then flesh out with the content of their own language.

Relations With Stakeholder Departments. A key group of academic stakeholders whose support is vital may be the traditional LL&C departments, particularly if their courses are affected. Three factors influence their attitude where establishment of an autonomous language center is concerned. Typical fears are: (a) that it may increase the likelihood (if it has not already occurred) of amalgamation of departments; (b) that student enrollment numbers will be lost to the new center if it is responsible for courses, affecting funding and staffing; and (c) that the disciplinary hegemony of LL&C departments in the university's power structure will be (further) diluted. These concerns cannot be ignored, obviously.

Academic Leadership. In the first phase, the new centers tend to depend on the leadership skills of the academic director. As a new component of the institution's structure, this individual requires a multiplicity of academic, pedagogical, and diplomatic skills in this initial phase. The directors of the new centers, whether or not they have tenure, tend to have a kind of status roughly equal to that of department chairs or assistant deans; they have more input into campus policy and more access to campus resources than language lab directors. They can therefore serve as advocates and spokespersons for the language teaching faculty, and because they are not balkanized in individual departments, as teachers are, they can serve also as advocates and spokespersons for the language teaching enterprise generally, insisting on its importance in any truly international curriculum. And even outside their work on behalf of language learning and teaching, they can provide the infrastructure for the development of fully fledged multilingual computing for the campus as a whole. For example, librarians, area studies councils, anthropology, religious studies, history, political science, and environmental studies often need the ability to do word processing, printing, e-mail and web browsing in a wide variety of languages. Likewise, academic computing staff are seldom knowledgeable enough about computing with non-Roman orthographies to provide the necessary support.

A common feature of the new centers is their director's research reputation. Parity with other academics is important during the initial phase; indeed, it is consistently cited by the directors as the single most important basis for a new center's academic respectability among its institutional peers.[5] Directors usually have a background in philology or applied linguistics, or other discipline-specific or interdisciplinary studies. However, for the long-term future of the center, and of the institution, a less personality-driven, more institutionally integrated solution is preferable, given that such centers are providing a unique, sustainable benefit, of course.

Research Into SLA and CALL. Despite the academic reputation of the directors of new centers, research into SLA is usually not one of the stated mandates of language centers in North America or Europe. This is partly

---

[5]In an e-mail survey conducted in September 2000 by the first author, directors of several centers who had been invited to the colloquium at Yale were asked to define their preferences for such positions. This information forms the basis of this section of the chapter.

because the emphasis is on the pragmatic improvement of teaching and learning and partly because in the past language teachers were seldom trained in appropriate research methods or the theoretical basis for research hypotheses. (Materials development projects are sometimes referred to as research but are seldom rewarded as such; see the Statement on CALL research developed by EuroCALL, CALICO, and IALL at http://www.eurocall-languages.org/research/research.htm.) However, as more language teachers are now being trained in graduate programs providing SLA theory and research methods, their interest in research is expected to contribute to their higher status in the job market.[6] Here again the center can play a major role. Language teachers who are not tenured or tenure track—as the majority are not—may be unable to apply for major grants, because funding agencies typically see lecturers or adjuncts as peripheral nonpermanent employees of the institution. With the center director as principal investigator to anchor the grant proposal and to provide the theoretical expertise where appropriate, and with the center staff to provide the technological support, teachers can propose and be the principal staff on major grants whose value to the institution can be further multiplied by their generalizability across languages.

New Horizons—A Sustainable Future

These benefits of language centers do not come cheap. The institutions attending the Yale colloquium were primarily larger, wealthier research universities in the United States. They, and other language centers that sprang up there in the past decade, serve an administrative, coordinating function, with a pedagogical mandate and academically respected leadership, both of which can attract significant funding.[7] With the acquisition of both equipment and personnel the old adage applies: You get what you pay for. Language technology specialists tend to command good salaries outside the academic world, and academic searches for center directors are often very difficult, especially if the search committees are made up of

---

[6]Curiously, there is as yet little awareness of the enormous potential of the computer for data collection and analysis in both SLA and pedagogical research. The papers from an extraordinarily interesting meeting some 6 or 8 years ago called CALC—Computers in Applied Linguistics Conference—were never published, and even now very little of the research presented at conferences on applied linguistics or SLA uses the computer environment for language learning in theoretically interesting ways.

[7]American foundations and granting agencies such as Culpeper, Mellon, Luce, Title VI, FIPSE, and the Consortium for Language Teaching and Learning reinforce these last two roles with substantial resources. The European Union, as mentioned in the case of Bavaria, may be setting similar trends in motion with major funding of online resources.

literature faculty who have little idea what they should be looking for or how or where to look. Nonetheless, the benefits are real even where they cannot be quantified.

At most campuses where centers have been established, both the morale and the professional competence of the language faculty have risen dramatically, as has the campus understanding both of the intellectual value of language learning and of its value to contemporary international education. Furthermore, the integration of sophisticated technology use into language learning is not a trendy add-on; it is the essential basis for the most important developments in our field. As a "branch of moral philosophy" (Goodman, as cited in Postman, 1993), technology always has the ability to call institutional assumptions into question, even though in the cases reviewed here it was not the primary motivator of innovation.

This chapter focused on the evolution and sustainability of the new language centers. We have argued that they most certainly have the potential to bring about significant change and consolidate the progress made so far, particularly once they become independent of the necessarily pioneering efforts of their initial academic leader. Whether the institutions that have led the way will become models elsewhere depends not on individual contributions, nor on the successful exploitation of technology, but ultimately and fundamentally on the conviction that the research into and practice of language learning are vital to human understanding.

ACKNOWLEDGMENTS

The first author is grateful to the editor of *ZIFU* for permission to use portions of a previously published article by Liddell (2001).

REFERENCES

Bangs, P. (1994). En train de Parler. In U. Beck & W. Sommer (Eds.), *Learntec '93*. Berlin: Springer-Verlag. Retrieved June 30, 2003, from http://members.aol.com/bangspaul/paulspubs.htm

Bangs, P., & Shield, L. (1999). Why turn authors into programmers? *ReCALL, 1*(11), 20.

Garrett, N. (1997). Language media: Our professional future. *IALL Journal of Language Learning Technologies, 29,* 23–35.

Garrett, N. (2000). Language Centers Colloquium. Retrieved December 16, 2000, from http://www.yale.edu/cls/centerscolloquium/

Garrett, N. (2001). Language centers: Mandates and structures. *ADFL Bulletin, 32,* 3.

Krashen, S. D., & Terrell, T. D. (1983). *The natural approach.* New York: Alemany Press.

Levin, R. (2000). Language Centers Colloquium. Retrieved December 16, 2000, from http://www.yale.edu/cls/centerscolloquium/

Liddell, P. (2001). The infrastructure of language learning centres [Electronic version]. *Zeitschrift für Interkulturellen Fremdsprachenunterricht, 6*(2). Retrieved June 30, 2003, from http://www.spz.to-darmstadt.de/projekt_ejournal/jg-06-2/beitrag/liddell.htm

Postman, N. (1993). *Technopoly. The surrender of culture to technology.* New York: Random House.

van Ek, J. A. (1975). *The threshold level.* Strasbourg, France: Council of Europe.

II

PERSPECTIVES ON CLASSROOM CALL

The six chapters in Part II address the use of CALL in the L2 classroom by integrating theory, research, and case studies with practical options for the teacher. Although some chapters describe the successful implementation of different forms of CALL-based instruction in the English as a foreign language (EFL) setting, the projects and activities are useful for all L2 classrooms, and are designed to increase student engagement with the target language, a goal that is particularly important in the foreign language context.

In the first chapter, "Learner Training for Effective Use of CALL," Hubbard observes that the typical second language student has received little training in how to exploit CALL effectively for language acquisition. Noting that CALL learners are often required to take responsibility for their own learning, Hubbard introduces the concept of CALL learner training and argues that it should be a central part of the field. He reviews developments in learner training presented in the research literature, including learner control, interactivity, motivation, and authenticity of communication. He then focuses on effective use of tutorial software and meaning technologies, concluding with a discussion of the role of CALL practitioners, researchers and software publishers in developing this area further.

Pennington's chapter, "Electronic Media in Second Language Writing: An Overview of Tools and Research Findings," gives a detailed introduction to the use of CALL for L2 writing instruction. First presenting a review of research on the use of electronic media, she then moves to consideration of CALL-based writing. Focusing on the writing process in the contexts of word processing, networked computers, and hypermedia, Pennington examines trends in literacy and communication that suggest the use of Local Area Networks (LANs), and e-mail exchanges computer will play a key role in future models of language learning and teaching. Her chapter thus provides an important theoretical introduction to the two chapters on CALL-based writing projects that follow.

In the next chapter, "Teaching Second and Foreign Language Writing on LANs," Braine discusses the development of LANs and presents research on their use in L2 writing classes, noting both the pros and cons of using LANs. Describing the differences between second and foreign language learning contexts, he uses findings from his research on ESL and EFL writing over LANs to suggest that LAN-based writing instruction motivates students to interact more freely, as well as helps them to share ideas and feedback from their classmates and teacher simultaneously. Braine also notes that teacher-centered classes are often transformed into classes where the students dominate interactions. Finally, he presents teachers with a range of instructional options for using LAN-based projects to improve student writing quality.

In her chapter, "Writing as Talking: E-mail Exchange for Promoting Proficiency and Motivation in the Foreign Language Classroom," Fotos discusses the differences between writing and speech, reviewing research that suggests that e-mail is similar to speech in written form and can thus be considered a new discourse genre. She describes an e-mail exchange program between university EFL students and American student keypals, noting that the e-mail project provided authentic L2 resources, promoted overall L2 proficiency gains, and led to increased levels of intercultural awareness and motivation to study the target language. Such e-mail exchange programs are suggested to be especially useful in the foreign language context since they provide exposure to the target language outside the classroom. Suggestions for teachers on how to set up their own projects are also provided.

Taylor and Gitsaki note that the growth of information and resources on the Internet is rapidly transforming CALL into WELL (web-enhanced language learning) in their chapter "Teaching WELL and Loving IT." They review changes in CALL that have led to WELL, finding that problems in adapting WELL to the classrooms frequently arise because of the Web's lack of structure and overabundance of material. Noting that the challenge is to select online material when there is no underlying syllabus, the authors offer a pedagogical framework for the use of the Web for language learning, providing activities and teacher guidelines for implementing each stage of the framework. The chapter concludes with a discussion of the results of a classroom-based research project in the university EFL setting measuring student attitudes and beliefs towards the use of CALL and WELL.

In the final chapter of this section, "Creating Course-Specific CD-ROMs for Interactive Language Use," Iwabuchi and Fotos discuss teacher creation of program-specific materials on CD-ROMs. Noting that many parts of the world lack the advanced technology and infrastructure required to support LANs or web-based L2 learning, the authors suggest that CD-ROMs are still a robust source of multimedia providing students with authentic L2 material that can be used outside the classroom, an important consideration in the foreign language setting. The results of a survey suggest that the students who used the courseware especially appreciated the provision of supplementary material such as dictionaries and translation into the students' first language (L1) on CD ROMs. The chapter presents guidelines, checklists, and evaluative procedures for teacher development of courseware providing a communicative review of content, structure, and vocabulary taught in the L2 classroom.

Learner Training for Effective Use of CALL

Philip Hubbard
Stanford University

The past decade has seen remarkable developments in CALL applications on CD-ROMs and over the Internet. Unfortunately, the typical language student using these applications has received little, if any, training toward developing a foundation in how to utilize them effectively for language acquisition. A fundamental quandary in CALL is that learners are increasingly required to take a significant amount of responsibility for their own learning, whether that learning is taking place through the programmed teaching presence in tutorial software or the unstructured spaces of the World Wide Web. They are expected to do this despite the fact that they know little or nothing of how languages are learned compared to an appropriately trained teacher. And they are expected to do this within a domain—that of the computer—that is still relatively unfamiliar as a language-learning environment to most of them.

The goal of this chapter is to introduce the concept of CALL learner training and to provide guidance for making it a more central part of CALL than has thus far been the case. Although CALL learner training clearly has a much wider scope, the focus here is on the classroom teacher who is training students within the confines of his or her own class. Like any other addition to the curriculum, learner training takes both preparation time and class time, and teachers wishing to implement it need to consider the obvious costs and weigh them against the potential benefits. These considerations will have to take into account the particular classroom environment, the teacher's own training and language teaching approach, the objectives of the course, and the proficiency level and readiness of students to take control. Before they can make these judgments appropriately, however, teachers need to understand what learner training is and how they can go about doing it.

The chapter begins by reviewing developments in some related areas of CALL and language learning in general, including computer literacy training, training for specific applications, learner control issues, learner strategy training, and learner autonomy. It then introduces a set of five general principles for CALL learner training. In the next section it discusses three areas in which learner training based on these principles can take place—computer-mediated communication, use of authentic materials from the Web, and use of tutorial programs—and emphasizes the importance of training in the effective use of meaning technologies such as captioning and hypertext dictionaries, for all three. In the following section, it presents an example of learner training for a specific course in academic listening for advanced ESL students. The chapter concludes with a brief discussion of the scope and limitations of learner training and the role of CALL teachers, researchers, and software developers in cultivating this area further.

LEARNER TRAINING RESEARCH AND PRACTICE

Before beginning the discussion of learner training, I would like to clarify the scope of CALL for this chapter because CALL means different things to different people. A convenient classification for CALL applications has been provided by Levy (1997) in his distinction of tutorial versus tool uses of computer technology. According to Levy, a computer functioning in a tutorial role acts as a temporary teacher, providing instruction or guided practice, whereas a computer functioning in the tool role does not have these teaching attributes (p. 181). A typical example of a tutorial application would be a grammar practice or vocabulary learning program; a typical tool application would be a web search engine, an e-mail program, or a word processor. In discussing learner training here, I include both tutorial and tool uses, as well as intermediate applications, such as online dictionaries, which arguably function as either tutors or tools depending on the task and intent of the learner.

In reviewing the research and practice literature, this section begins with training and related issues, such as control, specifically in CALL environments. It then looks at two general areas of learner training with obvious relevance to CALL: learner strategy training and learner autonomy.

General Computer Training

The majority of published studies with a training component, particularly from the early years of CALL, involve training in the technology itself. An excellent recent review of both the techniques and pitfalls in providing basic computer skills (what used to be called *computer literacy*) can be found in Beller-Kenner (1999). More recently, such training has focused on introducing students to the Internet and the World Wide Web, such as how to make an Internet connection and how browsers and web directories operate.

There are few examples of providing training to students that would help them explicitly link that technology to language pedagogy. This is not surprising. Before the spread of the Macintosh and Microsoft Windows operating systems, the machines were harder to learn to operate. Even the skill of keyboarding was an important one to teach to many students before they could begin using word processing efficiently. Until recently, computers have not been considered a natural part of the language education environment, and many of today's practicing teachers did not grow up with them.

Clearly, students need to understand how to operate a computer effectively and what the more common controls of any application do. As more and more students come into language classes already computer proficient and as interfaces continue to move toward either standard or intuitive forms, we can expect training of this sort to be less critical and more often done on an individual, remedial basis.

Training for Specific Applications

A number of books and articles have emphasized the importance of training the learner in how to use specific applications, both CALL and non-CALL, so as to avoid frustration or simply to be able to complete an assigned task (e.g., Huntley, 1997; Morrison, 1997). Most recently, this has involved Internet applications such as web browsers and search engines (Ryan, 1997), e-mail (Gaer, 1999), and MOOs and MUDs (multiuser domains; Falsetti, Frizler, Schweitzer, & Younger, 1997). Jones (2001, p. 2) observes that "learners' lack of technical competence" is a major constraint on successful CALL practice, and that technical training for some Internet projects can take hours away from other communicative activities. It is also worth noting that learner training for specific applications goes beyond the learner-computer interaction. Levy (1997, p. 200) cites a report on collaborative e-mail projects by Eck, Legenhausen, and Wolff (1994) as recognizing "the considerable demands placed on learners, who, as well as needing technical know-how, have to conduct extensive planning and long-term coordination."

Tutorial programs often include their own operational tutorials or detailed instructions in the layout of the user interface and functions of available controls (for a quiz on how nonintuitive these controls can be, see Beller-Kenner, 1999). Unfortunately, students (and sometimes teachers) anxious to get into the main parts of the program find it easy to bypass this important orientation step.

As with general computer skills, there is no question that knowing how to use an application is a prerequisite for knowing how to use it effectively. Although much of this chapter is oriented toward pedagogical issues in learner training, it remains the case that this type of basic operational instruction is still needed for students to succeed in CALL activities. There is also another aspect of familiarizing learners with specific applications that may need to be addressed: Learner anxiety. Lewis and Atzert (2000) report on the computer-related frustration and anxiety found in students doing collaborative web projects that required them to publish over the Internet. They offer suggestions for rechanneling that anxiety in productive ways through critical reflection.

Learner Control

It is a widely held view that giving learners control of their learning is a good thing. This is a central assumption of the learner autonomy movement (see the following discussion), but it has been debated in CALL, and computer-assisted instruction in general, since the spread of tutorial programs began in the 1980s. It has often been presented as a clash of ideals: Higgins (1984) captured the polarity with his metaphor of computer as magister (the master teacher followed unquestioningly by the students) versus pedagogue (the helpful slave who tutors the student at the student's whim). Although software evaluation checklists often mention learner control as a desirable or even necessary feature, it is still common to find programs that are largely linear—"magisterial" in Higgins's sense.

Tool-oriented CALL applications by definition offer the learner a wide range of control, though the teacher can attempt to limit that by being heavily directive in how to use the tool for a particular task. Tutorial programs, on the other hand, generally reflect the designer's bias with respect to the control issue. Some programs can be quite freely navigated while others only allow the user to proceed through a predetermined path. An attempt at a balanced view on the subject is provided by Boling and Soo (1999), who cite a number of studies demonstrating that a high degree of learner control does not always promote effective learning. Acknowledging the variety of issues control involves, they argue that novice learners may be more comfortable with software which embodies "high teacher control," where the objectives and the paths to them are clearly laid out. More proficient learners may be better suited to moderate teacher control and higher learner control. Pennington (1996) cites several studies showing another issue of control for novice learners, noting that software such as grammar checkers can exert control over these learners by providing useless or even incorrect advice which the learners may follow with negative consequences.

The issue of learner control is of particular interest here because software which does allow a lot of learner control requires a different sort of training from that which does not. Learners certainly need to understand the range of options as well as how to actually use the control features. However, more importantly, they also need to be able to judge when using a particular control, such as turning on or off text support in a multimedia program, will help them with a particular learning task.

Learner Strategy Training

Much has been written on the value of training learners to use effective language learning strategies. Clearly, to the extent that strategy training works well in other areas of language learning, it should have at least as valuable a place in CALL. Training in learner strategies for listening (Morley, 1991; Peterson, 1991) and reading (Anderson, 1999; Carrell, Pharis, & Liberto, 1989) in particular have been widely discussed. Many of these proposed strategies assume a cognitive model of comprehension driven by top-down processes involving schema theory, prediction, and so on (Carrell, 1984; Mandler, 1984). Software has been developed that is compatible with these views, such as the listening exercises found on the Cyber Listening Lab Web site of Davis (2002), which includes prelistening activities for schema activation. A recent handbook by Brown (2002) is a self-training manual for language students largely built on instilling effective learner strategies. Books such as those by Oxford (1990) and McDonough (1995) are teacher-oriented works discussing learner training for effective strategy use in detail. McDonough presents some important cautionary notes relevant not only to strategy training but to the type of learner training advocated in this chapter. He points out that research has shown only weak relationships between formal strategy training and improvements in proficiency, that ingrained cultural behaviors may limit the effectiveness of strategy training, and that research has not yet shown the persistence of strategy training over time (pp. 101–102).

Training for Learner Autonomy

Although it has grown relatively independently, the learner autonomy movement can be seen as an extension of learner strategy training to the entire domain of language learning. While formal definitions vary, learner autonomy is generally taken to involve the ability of a learner to acquire a language deliberately and systematically (as opposed to incidentally) outside the confines of a formal classroom, sometimes with guidance from an instructor, manager, tutor, or peer, and sometimes without such guidance. Among the significant publications in the field are volumes edited by Pemberton, Li, Or, and Pierson (1996) and Benson and Voller (1997).

There have also been some direct applications of autonomy to CALL recently. Warschauer, Schetzer, and Meloni (2000) listed autonomous learning as one of the five learning goals that should be connected with use of the Internet (p. 86), Averill, Chambers, and Dantas-Whitney (2000) discuss learner training in an individualized computer learning environment, and a monograph on autonomy by Benson (2001) includes an entire chapter on technology and autonomy. Healey (1999, p. 400) notes that in developing autonomy for CALL purposes, learners need to know how to control "the time, the pace, the path to the goal, and the measurement of success." She cites Good and Brophy (1987), who give a set of preconditions for motivation in the classroom setting, noting that these are relevant for managers of autonomous learning as well. Among the five, two stand out for their potential in CALL learner training—appropriate level of challenge or difficulty and a variety of teaching methods—since these are areas that CALL learners in particular need to become proficient in handling, not just for motivational purposes but for sound pedagogical reasons. Healey claims, "The facilitator in an autonomous setting has a substantial role to play in encouraging learners to use a variety of materials and methods and in explaining how to go about it" (p. 399). As we will see, such training is not limited to autonomy per se but is relevant to learner training for any CALL activity independent of the teacher, including homework assigned in a typical class setting.

Why Train?

As noted previously, while there is some literature on training for general computer competency and for using various tutor and tool applications (Averill et al., 2000; Beller-Kenner, 1999; Falsetti et al., 1997; Gaer, 1999; Huntley, 1997), there seems to be little in the way of literature showing that learner training in the pedagogical uses of CALL software is taking place.

In fact, the two threads that seem to come through the research and practice involving learner use of CALL applications, both for tutorial and tool purposes are

1. that learners left alone will gravitate naturally toward the uses of technology most helpful to them;

2. that training may be useful at beginning stages, but need not be sustained—Once the learner knows how to operate the software, effective use will follow.

These assumptions are rarely made explicit, but the dearth of counterevidence, in the form of pedagogical training procedures, argues for their widespread acceptance by the field. I believe that both of these assumptions are open to challenge. Despite the cost in time and effort, I am convinced that most students will profit from some formal, sustained training in how to take *operational* competence in a given computer application and transfer that into *learning* competence. We should not release our students into powerful learning environments unprepared: It is our responsibility as teachers to see that they are able to make informed decisions about how to use computer resources effectively to meet their learning objectives.

FIVE PRINCIPLES FOR LEARNER TRAINING

This section offers five principles to guide teachers who want to engage in CALL learner training. The content here, when not cited, is drawn from my experience over the last two decades using the computer in both tutor and tool roles in my ESL courses. The first of these principles promotes the idea that we as teachers should get some firsthand CALL experience as learners before attempting to guide our students. The second offers a corollary for learners: For them to make rational decisions on how to use computers in their language learning, they need to be informed about some of the basic findings in the field of L2 acquisition. The third states that for training to be valuable it must continue over time, not be something that is done at the beginning of a computer experience and then taken for granted thereafter. The fourth stresses the importance of collaborative debriefings. The final principle emphasizes the value of training students to exploit content for additional practice—both programmed content in language-learning software and authentic content from computer-mediated communication and the Web.

Principle 1: Experience CALL Yourself

When we teach in a classroom using a board, books, and tapes, we are teaching in an environment we have learned in. But while most language teachers have learned one or more foreign languages themselves to at least some degree of proficiency and therefore can speak from the learner's perspective in general, considerably fewer have done this through the medium of computers. It is of course possible to train learners without having known CALL from the learner's perspective; however, it is arguably a useful experience, one that may lead to a sense of empathy and otherwise uncaptured insights.

There are several ways to get such an experience without investing a lot of time or money.

1. If you have a reasonable degree of proficiency in a language, visit a Web site in that language. Go there to find information and remain to exploit the material for language learning. Try to notice some specific elements of grammar and identify a few unknown words or phrases. For most languages, you can find an online dictionary through www.babylon.com

2. Try to learn a bit of a new language from scratch, especially if you work with beginners. You can pick a commonly taught one and use a search engine to find a host of online materials. The Rosetta Stone (www. RosettaStone.com) has online sample lessons available in many uncommonly taught languages as well. This is an excellent way to get a sense of what learning is like for your students using tutorial software. You may even decide you want to continue.

3. Try a foreign language MOO or chat room for a language you have some degree of fluency in. Turbee (1999) recommends spending 20 to 40 hours in a MOO before introducing it to students: Why not spend some of that time in a foreign language environment to get a clearer picture of what your students will experience? You can go beyond simply using the language to noticing any new elements of the communication styles of the native speakers there. If you are a bit hesitant, it is certainly acceptable to "lurk" and eavesdrop before joining in and interacting.

Principle 2: Give Learners Teacher Training

In a significant article two decades ago, Richards and Rodgers (1982) introduced a framework for characterizing language teaching methods in terms of approach, design, and procedure, a framework that has turned out to be useful in identifying the considerations necessary for any kind of coherent language teaching. In this framework, *approach* (a term they take from Anthony, 1963) is used to refer to theories of what language is and how languages are learned; *design* entails the roles of the teacher, learner, and materials as they relate to the syllabus model and learning objectives; and *procedure* covers the techniques and processes that take place within the classroom in pursuit of those objectives. I have found this framework adaptable for CALL (Hubbard, 1988, 1992, 1996; see Levy, 1997, for a discussion of the limitations of these adaptations for tool uses of CALL) and have introduced it for a number of years as an instructional foundation in teacher training courses. If, as is claimed here, the CALL language learner has taken on more of what in traditional settings were teacher responsibilities, then it stands to reason that some teacher training is called for if learners are to become successful in that new role. An introduction to the core concepts of Richards and Rodgers' model, or something equivalent in scope, provides a basis for understanding the elements of directed language learning.

While it is of course not practical to give language learners the level of training we give language teachers, it is possible to provide them with some general knowledge about the field so that they can incorporate it into their own learning practices. In particular, we can provide at least the seed of a language-learning approach, helping them internalize a reasoned conception of what language is and what processes are involved in learning a second one.

It is useful to begin by giving learners some general advice on the importance of setting objectives, planning, and recognizing and maintaining motivation. Next, you can share with the learners some generalizations from your own training, professional development, and experience relevant to the area or areas of language they are learning. Finally, the learners need to understand the importance of making a connection between a particular CALL activity and some desired learning outcome or progress toward it. A lot of articles on learner autonomy note the importance of setting clear objectives and selecting appropriate material. What they generally fail to do is to provide examples of how to link those objectives to the materials with specific procedures and to stress the importance of the learner gaining control over the selection of that path. Toward this end, it is sometimes useful to get students part way into an exercise and then stop and ask them to figure out why they are doing it.

Principle 3: Use a Cyclic Approach

We are not normally expected to learn a sport or any other complex skill from a single training session followed by experience, yet that appears to be a common procedure for CALL activities. Using a cyclic approach to training instead has two advantages. First, it allows new ideas to be accreted one at a time in a focused manner. Second, it gives the opportunity to remind students of points they may easily forget over time. Beller-Kenner (1999) notes the importance of this in general computer training in her advice to teach the technical aspects of CALL in small chunks, with review in successive sessions (p. 371). Clearly, it is important in pedagogical training as well.

An implication of the cyclicity principle is that training in effective use of a CALL application needs to come after learners have achieved a certain comfort level with it. Letting learners play with a lesson or two in a tutorial program before talking about how to use it appropriately allows them to have the foundation to understand and interpret suggestions for effective use. Pretraining and then simply turning them loose even with a relatively simple program is likely to cause overload. Similarly, in e-mail, chat, or web activities, it is helpful to let them "play" with a new application a bit before having to be concerned about the language-learning potential of different ways to use it.

Principle 4: Use Collaborative Debriefings

Collaborative learning has become something of a buzzword in language instruction and rightfully so. It adds a social dimension that is important for both motivational purposes and for increasing target language contact, particularly production and the requisite negotiation of meaning (Pellettieri, 2000). Since much of CALL is done in either a socially isolated or degraded environment, the value of returning to a physical social space and discussing the experience is even higher than for traditional class activities. This is because in using tutorial software individually or even doing projects involving the Web or CMC, learners may lose track of what they are doing and why they are doing it. In addition to you as the teacher using a cyclic training approach, it is important for the learners to share these otherwise isolated experiences with one another from time to time.

Collaborative debriefings can be done either at the end of a CALL class session or at the beginning of a class following CALL activities done as homework. The purpose is to help learners maintain a balance between the task objectives and language-learning objectives so that the latter do not get mislaid. It can be enormously enlightening to have a 10- to 15-minute class session in which students are given a simple set of questions such as "What did you do?" "What did you learn?" "What language did you practice?" and are asked to discuss them in pairs or small groups. It can help both learners and teachers in checking learner understanding of objectives, progress toward them, and strategies and tactics used to approach them. Even more importantly, it allows the learners to discover how their peers have dealt with the same activity, leading them to reflect on whether they are getting what they need from the activity and what they might do differently in the future. In the event that physical proximity is not possible, an alternative would be a scheduled online chat session or electronic discussion board. There is some evidence that this might even be more effective for some students. Pellettieri (2000) cites a number of studies supporting the widely held view that in chat sessions "learners report reduced anxiety about participating and increased motivation for using the target language" (p. 63). A bonus for the instructor is that some chat software allows record keeping, as do all discussion boards, making details of the student interactions more accessible for review.

Principle 5: Teach General Exploitation Strategies

In addition to specific training for individual applications, there are some general CALL-oriented strategies that students should be introduced to. In keeping with the third principle, they can be introduced to these gradually over time at appropriate junctures rather than in one overwhelming session, as well as being reminded repeatedly of their value with specific examples from current class activities and assignments.

1. Mine language material for other uses. This is something done for students in almost every language textbook, but there is little evidence that students typically do this when they are working on their own, except in response to specific assignments. Since familiar material is generally easiest to learn from (Skehan, 1998), once a CALL task is completed, it is important to show students how they can use that material for other learning purposes. For example, they can get vocabulary items out of read material or out of transcripts from material listened to. They can review native speaker material for information on specific grammatical points, such as tenses, prepositions, or uses of articles. They can also review the transcripts of their chat sessions, e-mails or discussion board entries, to see whether they can notice any of their own errors in grammar or word choice.

2. Make difficult material easier. One of the major problems with introducing learners to the authentic material on the Web is that we are often pushing them into dealing with material far beyond their acquired proficiency level. Computers have provided us with some very neat tools for helping make sense out of these, tools which can be collectively termed *meaning technologies* (Hubbard, 2001a). These are discussed in more detail in the following section. The key is to train learners in the use of meaning technologies in both tool and tutor domains so that they know when and how to wield them in the accomplishment of learning goals rather than simply finding them a convenient shortcut to the completion of an instructor's assignment.

3. Make easy material more difficult. Despite the desired objective of making CALL tutorials adapt to the individual, software to date does not do this very effectively. While researchers and methodologists grapple with ways to make software more adaptive, it is also possible to train the learners on how to adapt to the software by changing the way they approach it if it is too easy. This can be a difficult thing for students to understand, since the apparent objective for most tutorial programs is to "get the right answer"

rather than the intended "learn something or improve a skill." For a typical multimedia program, for example, the challenge can be increased in a number of ways. First, learners can turn off all meaning technologies that they have control over (text, glossary, translation, etc.) so that they do not automatically appear. Similarly, programs which allow control over pace or difficulty can be set to their highest level. Second, if the software has audio, they can turn down the volume to reduce the signal's clarity. Third, they can be encouraged to push themselves to read text material faster or make their response faster. Fourth, in any dictation activity, they should wait until the end of the prompt before putting in the missing material rather than typing it in as they hear it, as this may promote more accurate processing of larger chunks of language. Fifth, by using scroll options, closing their eyes, or simply holding a piece of paper over parts of the screen, they can turn multiple-choice questions into open-ended ones, hide graphics that provide visual support, or hide text support that they cannot turn off. These are just a few suggestions. Students who buy into this idea will be able to come up with ways of their own to produce an appropriate level of challenge for CALL material that is too easy.

AREAS FOR GENERAL TRAINING

Besides the specific CALL tasks or exercises a teacher may assign as part of a class, students are often anxious for sources of authentic materials and opportunities to practice communication with native speakers or other learners. This is especially true if they are looking for ways to continue learning once the course has ended. If you have a self-access language lab with dedicated computer materials, be sure to familiarize yourself with what is there so that you can make appropriate recommendations. For information on what is available on the Web for English, both native speaker material and specialized material for language learning, see the listings in Windeatt, Hardisty, and Eastment (2000) and Warschauer et al. (2000). For other links and other languages, simply type an appropriate term such as "French listening" into a major search engine such as Google (www. google.com), and information on useful current Web sites will become instantly available.

This section begins with a discussion of meaning technologies, or technology-based meaning aids, which are seen to be important to all areas of CALL learner training. It then looks at three general areas where useful training can take place. It should be noted in advance that these choices are meant to be representative: There are, no doubt, other areas in which training is valuable beyond these. Furthermore, much of what is presented here is speculative. It is meant to suggest general directions rather than to provide any specific roadmap for training, and notably, these suggestions are not yet supported directly by learner training research.

Meaning Technologies

The term *meaning technologies* refers to "features of language learning materials that are based on technology and make the meaning of a language item accessible to a learner" (Hubbard, 2001a, p. 82). There are a number of these already widely available, including text captions, machine translations, hypertext dictionaries and glossaries, text-to-speech applications, and auto summarizers. They can either have been specifically programmed as meaning aids (as in the case of the assistance in most tutorial programs and the captioning found on the Web) or be automated as stand-alone applications, such as the machine translation programs available on the Web. Some of them are exceedingly popular among students because they make getting the meaning of language much easier than traditional options such as paper dictionaries. In fact, it is their ease of use which raises concerns: They can make it possible to give the appearance of comprehension to the learner, while in fact without their mediation, the language would continue to be incomprehensible. To put it more bluntly, they can be used either naively or deliberately by a student as a shortcut that subverts the real learning objectives.

We cannot do much about their deliberate abuse, but we can train learners in the effective use of a meaning technology, including both mastery of the operation of the application itself and an understanding of how to apply it both strategically for particular purposes and tactically to solve a specific meaning problem. There are two general reasons for using a meaning technology: (a) to get at meaning solely for understanding and (b) to get at meaning to link a particular form to it. In the first case, meaning technologies are used like more traditional meaning aids (translations, dictionaries, glossaries, printed transcripts, etc.). Once the meaning is clear, there is no particular reason to retain the form (text, translation, definition, etc.), so any learning that takes place is entirely incidental. In the second case, however, meaning technologies play an important role in helping to isolate items for learning.

There is little research yet on the optimal use of meaning technologies to support learning, but the following is some general advice that learners can be given:

- Use meaning technologies freely when comprehension is the main goal, rather than language learning or practice.
- Be aware that using a meaning technology can interrupt flow and interfere with text cohesion: Try to go through material at a natural pace

at least once without interruption, using meaning technologies before or after.

- Let a strong skill support a weak one, but don't let it displace the weak one; for example, be careful of overusing text support (scripts or captions) for audio or video or you may end up improving reading rather than listening.
- Take advantage of the computer's ability to capture information you look up; especially, copy and paste word definitions into a personal file for later review.

CMC

A growing area of CALL is that of computer-mediated communication (CMC). CMC typically involves two basic parameters: time (synchronous [real time] or asynchronous [delayed]) and medium (text or voice, both audio and audiovideo). Combining these two parameters yields the following types of applications:

- Synchronous text (e.g., chat and instant messaging).
- Asynchronous text (e.g., e-mail and discussion boards).
- Synchronous voice (e.g., Internet telephony and audio or video conferencing).
- Asynchronous voice (e.g., voicemail and voice discussion boards).

Note that it is possible to blend text and voice: while in principle this could be done synchronously, in current practice for language learning this seems limited to asynchronous applications.

Much has been written in recent years on supporting language learning through CMC, particularly e-mail and chat, along with its cousins, MUDs and MOOs (Falsetti et al., 1997; Turbee, 1999). The focus here is on training learners in how to employ these applications more effectively for conscious language learning. In this section, due to space limitations, I will limit the discussion to two of these areas—synchronous text and asynchronous voice—as these two capture the widest range of features.

Synchronous text interchanges are thought by many to mimic elements of spoken conversation (Holliday, 1999, p. 188). There are at least two key points for learner training in this area, based on insights found in Pellettieri (2000). She stated that synchronous tasks "should be goal-oriented, with a minimum of possible outcomes" (p. 83). Extending her idea into training, this suggests that learners should be given practice in how to prepare themselves for such interactions, especially if the teacher is not prepared to heavily monitor the sessions. Learners should understand as part of their language-learning approach that if they are ready for the interaction, and have a reason for doing the task, they will get more value from it. Second, Pellettieri provides evidence that learners can and do negotiate meaning during CMC sessions. This can be extended into the realm of learner training as instruction in CALL-specific negotiation strategies. For example, presented with an unknown item in an interaction, a learner could use a quick copy and paste of that item into the response followed by a question mark, implicitly prompting for a definition or recast.

Turning now to asynchronous voice, while the technology involved is more complex, there are a number of ways to send such messages.

- Regular e-mail: sending a short voice recording as an attachment.
- Voicemail services, such as OneBox (www.onebox.com).
- Language learning services, such as Wimba (www.wimba.com).

Regardless of the application used, it is important to begin by having the learners try to send and receive a voice message, either to you or to a partner in class, purely to test their ability to use the system. Once they are comfortable with the system, including use of the pause button to collect their thoughts in the middle of a message if such a feature is available, the following are some areas in which useful training can take place.

1. If the objective is to build speaking fluency, the message should be neither memorized nor written out and simply read. If students are unable or unwilling to speak without support, train them in using an outline, much as you would for an oral presentation.

2. If students are communicating with "voicepals" (the spoken equivalent of penpals or keypals), it is helpful to train them to use forms of the language that naturally lend themselves to extended monologues. Three particularly good areas for this are stories, descriptions, and opinions. Personal stories are a good place to start, as they are useful in building social relationships and have a natural discourse structure based on chronological order. To build their confidence, let students practice a story in class a few times before sending it out as a spoken message.

3. If learners have access to multiple partners through voice, they can be trained to send a similar message to several of them requesting the same information or opinion (e.g., "How do you celebrate New Year?" or "Do you think computers can replace teachers?"). This approach allows a more in-depth view of a particular question and embodies both the variety and redundancy that assist motivation and language learning.

4. In listening to their partner's messages, learners should attend to meaning first. However, they can be trained to then mine the message for

new words and expressions, particularly if they are interacting with native speakers or more advanced learners. They can also do a dictation of all or part of the message and send it back to the partner (or the teacher) for checking.

Selecting and Exploiting Authentic Materials on the Web

If learners need to select appropriate materials for specific tasks, the objective is really determined by the task. If, however, they are looking for materials to help them specifically improve their language proficiency, then training learners in some general guidelines for locating such material is important.

The following are some suggested directions. To turn these into training activities, teachers not only need to present them but also need to send their students out on tasks that reflect these guidelines, holding one or more debriefing sessions as part of the package.

1. Select materials with familiar content, for example, a news story in the target language about the student's native culture.

2. Select a set of materials with related content. It has long been recognized in content-centered instruction that building coursework around a single theme provides valuable redundancies and can heighten motivation. A special issue of *TESOL Journal* in 2001 was devoted to the most recent manifestation of this approach: sustained-content language teaching (Murphy & Stoller, 2001)

3. Select materials that are conceptually simple. As noted by Skehan (1998), among others, material which is both linguistically and conceptually challenging can provide too great a cognitive load for effective processing

4. Select materials that are close to one's actual level. In keeping with Krashen's (1982) input hypothesis, material which is close to a learner's acquired level of proficiency seems to make better fodder for acquisition than material that is far beyond that level.

5. Select materials with meaning technology support. There are a number of sites, such as PBS's Online News Hour, which include text along with audio or video versions of authentic material. These are especially useful for learners who want to improve listening but whose reading skill outstrips their listening abilities.

6. Mine materials selectively. In keeping with the final principle from the previous section, authentic material on the Web can be used to learn about grammar and discourse patterns or to build vocabulary. However, it is important to do this in a pragmatic and efficient manner. For example, while a number of words might be looked up using an online or hypertext dictionary, only those which seem useful need to be recorded for later review.

Interactional Sequences in Tutorial CALL

From multimedia CD-ROMs to web-based drills and quizzes, the CALL world is full of material claiming to help students learn language forms and rules or produce and understand better. However, this material rarely includes any instruction in how to use it effectively. In some cases, learners can follow a set of predetermined pathways more or less blindly. In others, learners are given considerable freedom to choose pathways and support materials but may have very little idea of how to go about using these options to support learning.

Hubbard (2001b) offers a framework for classifying interactional sequences in tutorial CALL applications based on a review of more than 30 published programs for ESL and several other languages. The great majority of exercises in that review fit into the interrogation mode, where the user is presented with an item that is an implicit or explicit question and expected to make some response to it, as in a multiple choice vocabulary quiz or a set of comprehension questions following a reading or video presentation. A simplified version of that framework can be used to help students understand the elements they can control in a tutorial application. The key concepts for an individual item are *deliberation* following the computer prompt and *consolidation* following the program's feedback.

To understand the roles of deliberation and consolidation more clearly, consider the following simple example. In a vocabulary tutorial program, the learner is presented with a response domain consisting of a set of four pictures of animals (frog, horse, lion, bird). The task is to click on the picture representing the best response to a prompt. The learner then sees the prompt "Which of these can fly?" Deliberation refers to the processes that go on in the learner's mind beginning with comprehending the response domain (the pictures in this case) and the prompt (both decoding the text and assigning it lexical and sentence meaning). Deliberation then moves to linking the comprehended information to long-term knowledge about animals and flying and then reaching a decision (click on the bird). If there is a problem (e.g., What does *fly* mean?), deliberation also includes deciding whether to guess, skip the item, or ask for help, depending on the resources the program makes available. For familiar items, deliberation is automatic; for less familiar ones, it may be quite controlled and conscious. The input to deliberation may also include feedback from the computer following a previous attempt. Essentially, then, deliberation refers to whatever happens cognitively on the learner's side during a tutorial interaction.

Consolidation also refers to cognitive processes on the part of the learner. In this example, it refers to what happens after the computer program has presented its final round of feedback for an item before the next item is considered. In particular, if something new has been presented (such as the meaning of *fly*), consolidation is the process through which the learner reflects briefly on the experience of that single item. Ultimately, the effectiveness of this process determines the degree to which some new experience or bit of information is learned or forgotten. Consolidation can include raising questions, raising awareness, or associating new material with existing knowledge structures, and it can involve specific acts on the learner's part, such as writing down a new word for later study.

There are two important points here. One echoes the earlier notion of getting the learner to adapt appropriately to the tutorial software (rather than the more ideal but unrealistic other way around). Tutorial software often includes a number of controls that the learner can either preset or activate during the lesson. If the learners have been given or can create specific learning objectives, then they are more likely to use these controls to support deliberation and consolidation appropriate to those objectives. If not, then it is easy for learners to see controls as either shortcuts to the answer (irrespective of their learning value) or as complications to be ignored. The second point is for learners to be trained to understand the value of the deliberation and consolidation processes themselves (metacognitive training). To this end, it is helpful to introduce the notion of a learning journal, where learners write notes, including both new items and questions, as they go through a program. These can be handed in to the teacher or used during a collaborative debriefing session. Above all, learners need to be trained that the real objective is not just to get through material or make a high score. Completion and scores are only indirect measurements of what has or has not been internalized.

IMPLEMENTING LEARNER TRAINING IN A LISTENING CLASS

So far, I have presented a rationale for learner training, a set of guidelines for implementing it, and some general areas in which it can be implemented. In this section, I briefly describe how I used some of these principles for learner training in an ESL academic listening class in autumn 2001. While a second listening course was available in the winter, for more than half of the students this would be their last formal English course with a significant listening component. Thus, one of the course objectives was to prepare them for learning on their own after the course.

During the second week of the course, I gave students an overview of what listening is and how it relates to language learning. In it, I distinguished the need for building proficiency in three areas:

1. Improving the ability to extract and interpret meaning, particularly from academic lectures, including the importance of schema activation, recognition of discourse markers, prediction, note taking, and so on.

2. Increasing language knowledge, including understanding the sound system, reviewing and activating grammar, and especially building vocabulary.
3. Increasing processing accuracy and automaticity, both phonological (with rapid speech and reduced forms) and grammatical (recognizing grammatical markers and improving "chunking" ability).

Although this division is necessarily oversimplified, it provides the basis of a language-learning approach in a form that seems both comprehensible and useful to these students.

Beginning the third week, students had required homework in the language lab using Macintosh-based materials developed originally for this course: HyperACE Intermediate (Hubbard, Gordon, & Rylance, 1995), which includes practice in number processing along with picture identification exercises, and MicroReport (Hubbard & Tenney, 1996), in which students get intensive comprehension and note-taking practice followed by a dictation activity. Training for these began at the end of the second week with a session in the lab where the two programs were introduced and students had a chance to play with them a bit. Students had a week to complete a homework set consisting of three of these exercises (about 60–90 minutes of lab time) and fill out a report rating each exercise as to how much time they spent and how easy and how useful they thought it was, followed by any comments.

In a debriefing session the following week, we discussed some of the patterns of use. The objective of this was to lead students toward the following generalization. The goal of the activity is not to get the right answer; rather, it is to process the language intensively. Thus, there is no reason for them to guess as they would in a testing situation. The software lets them listen as many times as they want before making a choice. They can keep listening until they are sure they know the answer or until they are sure they won't be able to determine it. In keeping with the cyclicity principle, this has more impact after they have already had a session or two on their own.

I let them go the next week without a debriefing session. The following week, I noted that in their weekly reports, some students indicated that the material in one or more of the activities was too easy (this always happens). I then gave them 10 minutes or so to discuss in pairs or triads why it was easy and what they could do to make it more challenging. This was followed by 10 minutes of whole-group discussion where we exchanged ideas about how to make the material more challenging. I repeated to them the message that the goal is not just to get the right answer but to improve language processing or potentially learn new language while doing so.

Just before the midpoint of the quarter, I introduced them to an online site English, Baby! (www.englishbaby.com). I assigned them to try one of the listening exercises (either the movie review or "eavesdropping") and come prepared the next class to discuss the experience.

The last two weeks of the quarter were oriented even more toward developing in students the ability to continue as independent learners. Learning techniques and strategies that had been presented throughout the quarter were reviewed, and I introduced the students to a second online site: Randall's Cyber Listening Lab (www.esl-lab.com). In introducing it, I first went through an exercise as a whole-class activity and then asked them to pick another one to do at home. As part of that assignment, they had to describe how easy and how useful they found their chosen exercise to be, explain exactly how they went through it, and come prepared to discuss ways they could do it differently the next time. In the following class, we held an extended collaborative debriefing, with students sharing their experiences in small groups before coming together for a whole-class discussion. Two other segments of this final part of the course were to review various ways of mining material for language items or processing practice and to present a web page with annotated links to various useful ESL and native speaker Web sites. Students were given an outline for planning an individual course for the intersession using this material and strongly encouraged to follow through and create one.

CONCLUSION

I began this chapter by identifying the following dilemma:

1. Technology has given learners more of the responsibility formerly held by teachers to direct and evaluate their own language learning.
2. Learners are generally ill-prepared to take on that responsibility.

I argued that the solution to this is to engage in some form of training for learners so that their effectiveness in this area could be improved. Toward that end, I reviewed the limited history of CALL training and offered a set of five principles for CALL teachers, summarized as follows:

1. Experience CALL as a learner before training your students.
2. Give learners some language teacher training.
3. Use a cyclic approach.
4. Hold collaborative debriefings.
5. Teach general exploitation strategies.

I then discussed some areas representing both tutorial and tool domains of CALL where learner training would be useful, and I described the learner training I did in a specific academic listening course.

Throughout this chapter, I have tried to remain relatively neutral about how best to accomplish the goals of learner training. Rather, I have focused on general guidelines out of an awareness that this is a relatively unexplored field and that the language teaching approaches, the environments teachers teach in, the level of the learners, and the readiness of the learners to take on this role vary greatly. Clearly, learner training is an area ripe for action research by instructors interested in trying out new techniques and sharing the results with others in the field.

I have provided a relatively broad, though not particularly deep, view of CALL learner training here. In doing so, I do not mean to suggest that such an approach is good for an individual class. I would recommend rather that it is better to start with one or two useful areas for your class and try them out, keeping in mind how they relate to your students' short-term and long-term needs.

While the thrust of the discussion was toward classroom teachers, the concepts are relevant to others. At the program or institutional level, administrators of self-access centers can develop both workshops and training materials based on some of the preceding recommendations for generalized learner training. Commercial software developers should seriously consider putting learner training into their products and find ways to encourage learners to go through that training reflectively and cyclically. As with all areas of CALL, research is needed and researchers are encouraged to challenge or elaborate on the claims made here. At the moment, we are far from a theory which can tell us much about how best to train learners for more independence in CALL. And as with all other aspects of CALL, the technology is changing at a rapid pace in sometimes unpredictable directions so that today's research may tell us little about tomorrow's learning environments. However, we can be relatively certain that both tool and tutor applications of CALL will grow, and that we will continue to need to train students to effectively harness the learning power that technology brings.

REFERENCES

Anderson, N. (1999). *Exploring second language reading: Issues and strategies.* Boston: Heinle & Heinle.

Anthony, E. (1963). Approach, method, and technique. *English Language Teaching, 17,* 63–67.

Averill, J., Chambers, E., & Dantas-Whitney, M. (2000). Investing in people, not just flashy gadgets. In E. Hanson-Smith (Ed.), *Technology-enhanced learning environments* (pp. 85–98). Alexandria, VA: Teachers of English to Speakers of Other Languages.

Beller-Kenner, S. (1999). CALL issues: Introducing students to computers. In J. Egbert & E. Hanson-Smith (Eds.), *CALL environments: Research, practice, and critical issues* (pp. 362–385). Alexandria, VA: Teachers of English to Speakers of Other Languages.

Benson, P. (2001). *Teaching and researching autonomy in language learning.* London: Longman.

Benson, P., & Voller, P. (Eds.). (1997). *Autonomy and independence in language learning.* London: Longman.

Boling, E., & Soo, K.-S. (1999). CALL issues: Designing CALL software. In J. Egbert & E. Hanson-Smith (Eds.), *CALL environments: Research, practice, and critical issues* (pp. 442–456). Alexandria, VA: Teachers of English to Speakers of Other Languages.

Brown, H. D. (2002). *Strategies for success: A practical guide to learning English.* New York: Addison Wesley Longman.

Carrell, P. (1984). Evidence of formal schema in second language comprehension. *Language Learning, 34,* 87–112.

Carrell, P., Pharis, B. G., & Libreto, J. C. (1989). Metacognitive strategy training for ESL reading. *TESOL Quarterly, 23,* 647–678.

Davis, R. (2002). *Randall's cyber listening lab.* Retrieved December 7, 2002, from http://www.esl-lab.com

Eck, A., Legenhausen, L., & Wolff, D. (1994). Assessing telecommunications projects: Project types and their educational potential. In H. Jung & R. Vanderplank (Eds.), *Barriers and bridges: Media technology in language learning* (pp. 45–52). Frankfurt, Germany: Peter Lang.

Falsetti, J., Frizler, K., Schweitzer, E., & Younger, G. (1997). Getting started with MOOs: MOO and YOO—What to DOO. In T. Boswell (Ed.), *New ways of using computers in language teaching* (pp. 112–120). Alexandria, VA: Teachers of English to Speakers of Other Languages.

Gaer, S. (1999). Classroom practice: An introduction to e-mail and World Wide Web projects. In J. Egbert & E. Hanson-Smith (Eds.), *CALL environments: Research, practice, and critical issues* (pp. 65–78). Alexandria, VA: Teachers of English to Speakers of Other Languages.

Good, T. L., & Brophy, J. E. (1987). *Looking in classrooms.* New York: Harper & Row.

Healey, D. (1999). Theory and research: Autonomy and language learning. In J. Egbert & E. Hanson-Smith (Eds.), *CALL environments: Research, practice, and critical issues* (pp. 391–402). Alexandria, VA: Teachers of English to Speakers of Other Languages.

Higgins, J. (1984). Learning with a computer. In S. Holden (Ed.), *Teaching and the teacher* (pp. 83–87). Oxford, England: Modern English Publications.

Holliday, L. (1999). Theory and research: Input, interaction, and CALL. In J. Egbert & E. Hanson-Smith (Eds.), *CALL environments: Research, practice, and critical issues* (pp. 181–188). Alexandria, VA: Teachers of English to Speakers of Other Languages.

Hubbard, P. (1988). An integrated framework for CALL courseware evaluation. *CALICO Journal, 6,* 51–72.

Hubbard, P. (1992). A methodological framework for CALL courseware development. In M. Pennington & V. Stevens (Eds.), *Computers in applied linguistics* (pp. 39–66). Clevedon, England: Multilingual Matters.

Hubbard, P. (1996). Elements of CALL methodology: Development, evaluation, and implementation. In M. Pennington (Ed.), *The power of CALL* (pp. 15–32). Houston, TX: Athelstan.

Hubbard, P. (2001a). The use and abuse of meaning technologies. *Contact, 27,* 82–86. Available online at http://www.stanford.edu/~efs/phil/MT.pdf

Hubbard, P. (2001b, March). *Understanding interactional sequences in tutorial CALL.* Paper presented at the 35th annual TESOL Convention, St. Louis, MO. Retrieved December 6, 2002, from http://www.stanford.edu/~efs/phil/Hubbard-TESOL01.htm

Hubbard, P., Gordon, C., & Rylance, C. (1995). HyperACE Intermediate [Computer software]. Houston, TX: Athelstan.

Hubbard, P., & Tenney, K. (1996). MicroReport: Who, what, and where in the USA [Computer software]. New York: Gessler.

Huntley, H. (1997). Word processing mastery. In T. Boswell (Ed.), *New ways of using computers in language teaching* (pp. 5–6). Alexandria, VA: Teachers of English to Speakers of Other Languages.

Jones, J. (2001). CALL and the teacher's role in promoting learner autonomy. *CALL Electronic Journal Online, 3*. Retrieved November 4, 2001, from http://www.clec.ritsumei.ac.jp/english/callejonline/6-1/jones.html

Krashen, S. (1982). *Principles and practice in second language acquisition.* Oxford, England: Pergamon.

Levy, M. (1997). *Computer-assisted language learning: Context and conceptualization.* Oxford, England: Oxford University Press.

Lewis, A., & Atzert, S. (2000). Dealing with computer-related anxiety in the project-oriented CALL classroom. *CALL Journal, 13,* 377–395.

Mandler, J. (1984). *Stories, scripts, and scenes: Aspects of schema theory.* Hillsdale, NJ: Lawrence Erlbaum Associates.

McDonough, S. (1995). *Strategy and skill in learning a foreign language.* London: Edward Arnold.

Morley, J. (1991). Listening comprehension in second/foreign language instruction. In M. Celce-Murcia (Ed.), *Teaching English as a second/foreign language* (2nd ed., pp. 81–106). Boston: Heinle & Heinle.

Morrison, B. (1997). How do you use it? In T. Boswell (Ed.), *New ways of using computers in language teaching* (pp. 7–10). Alexandria, VA: Teachers of English to Speakers of Other Languages.

Murphy, J., & Stoller, F. (2001). Sustained-content language teaching: An emerging definition. *TESOL Journal, 10,* 3–7.

Oxford, R. (1990). *Language learning strategies: What every teacher should know.* Boston: Heinle & Heinle.

Pellettieri, J. (2000). Negotiation in cyberspace: The role of chatting in the development of grammatical competence. In M. Warschauer & R. Kern (Eds.), *Network-based language teaching: Concepts and practice* (pp. 59–86). New York: Cambridge University Press.

Pemberton, R., Li, E. S. L., Or, W. W. F., & Pierson, H. D. (Eds.). (1996). *Taking control: Autonomy in language learning.* Hong Kong: Hong Kong University Press.

Pennington, M. (1996). The power of the computer in language education. In M. Pennington (Ed.), *The power of CALL* (pp. 1–14). Houston, TX: Athelstan.

Peterson, P. (1991). A synthesis of methods for interactive listening. In M. Celce-Murcia (Ed.), *Teaching English as a second/foreign language* (2nd ed., pp. 106–122). Boston: Heinle & Heinle.

Richards, J., & Rodgers, T. (1982). Method: approach, design, and procedure. *TESOL Quarterly, 16,* 153–168.

Ryan, K. (1997). Using search engines for academic research. In P. Lewis & T. Shiozawa (Eds.), *CALL: Basics and beyond* (pp. 41–46). Tokyo: Japan Association of Language Teaching.

Skehan, P. (1998). *A cognitive approach to language learning.* New York: Oxford University Press.

Turbee, L. (1999). Classroom practice: MOO, WOO, and more—Language learning in virtual environments. In J. Egbert & E. Hanson-Smith (Eds.), *CALL environments: Research, practice, and critical issues* (pp. 346–361). Alexandria, VA: Teachers of English to Speakers of Other Languages.

Warschauer, M., Shetzer, H., & Meloni, C. (2000). *Internet for English teaching.* Alexandria, VA: Teachers of English to Speakers of Other Languages.

Windeatt, S., Hardisty, D., & Eastment, D. (2000). *The Internet.* Oxford, England: Oxford University Press.

5

Electronic Media in Second Language Writing: An Overview of Tools and Research Findings

Martha C. Pennington
University of Luton

The invention of writing is perhaps the most significant event in the history of human affairs. According to Coulmas (1989), writing developed in prehistoric times out of systems for keeping records of economic transactions and other events and has made possible the complex social and economic organization of cities as well as history, science, and technology of all kinds. As it has gradually taken on a range of functions far beyond its original purposes, writing has provided the foundation for amassing a great store of human knowledge and for developing the cognitive capacities of literate individuals:

> Writing has evolved as a system for recording language in its externalized form, as speech, and in its internalized form, as ideas. In the latter capacity, it has no doubt helped to promote the (at least partly independent) development of the cognitive side of language—and indeed, our cognitive abilities more generally—by making possible complex constructions of ideas built on a mountain or chain of "captured" thoughts, which, when written down, can be increasingly probed and built upon. . . . Writing became a means of capturing our thoughts, and the thoughts of others, of storing them and holding them constant for later reflection, contemplation and development. In this way, writing made it possible to greatly expand our ability to process our own thoughts and the thoughts of others. That is, writing expanded our *cognitive world,* our access to other cognitive worlds and our ability to create new cognitive worlds. (Pennington, 2000b, p. 6)

Today our access to information resources on computers, CD-ROM databases, Internet search tools, multimedia utilities, and people made accessible through e-mail and Web sites expands our cognitive worlds and resources to a virtually unlimited degree. At the same time, these electronic media are changing our modes of interaction with information and with each other (Pennington, 2003).

The new media are participating in an evolutionary trend that is moving human experience away from face-to-face interaction and toward modes of representation and communication that make greater use of visual media and that allow information to be created, transmitted, and received at a distance (Pennington, 2000a, 2000b, 2001). The possibilities of communication across physical distances, historical periods, and communities ushered in by writing were greatly enhanced by the invention of printing and later by the telegraph, which allowed written messages to be transmitted by wire. Transmission by wire was further expanded to include voice (telephone) and later visual images (television). As telemedia took hold in human communications, the first typing machines were produced in the drive to automate work processes. The confluence of automation and the transmission of information by wire have resulted in the various computer tools and media available today. These include the following:

- composing and revising text (word processors).
- correcting text (spell checkers and grammar checkers).
- storing and reproducing text (disks and printers).
- sending text electronically (e-mail and Internet).
- creating new kinds of computer text (hypertext and web pages).

The computer utilities that aid in the production and transmission of written text can be combined with other media tools to give the computer user access to virtually any mode or combination of modes of information capture, storage, creation, and dissemination by electronic means. By making it possible to transform information into a computerized form such as hypertext or digitized images and sound, and to create new computerized forms such as Web pages or computer-generated art and musical compositions, these new tools are expanding our symbolic repertoire and creative resources and, in the process, are changing our practices of literacy and expression. Kress (1998) has observed a major shift away from the purely textual transmission of information toward other modes of representation and communication, especially visual modes. He notes:

> After a period of some two to three hundred years of the dominance of writing as *the* means of communication and representation, there is now, yet again, a deep shift taking place in the system of media and modes of represen-

tation and communication, and in the system of evaluating these. The change is of great significance in its social and political ramifications. To call it a "tectonic shift" may not be an exaggeration, because the landscape of communication and representation, the semiotic landscape, is indeed being remade. Where before there was the single, central mountain range of written language, now another alpine system is being thrust up by forces of a complex kind: in part, social, political, technological, and, as yet less recognised, by economic forces as well. (Kress, 1998, pp. 58–59)

The resources of electronic media are helping to drive this shift in the way information is presented and communicated to others. Today, thanks to a variety of electronic media, our semiotic resources have been expanded and interlinked in ways that promote new information sharing. In addition, the group within which we communicate has grown far beyond the bounds of our original home community to that potentially including the entire human family. This expansion and development of information resources and access is taking place at the same time as the rapid expansion of the English language as the *lingua franca* for the creation and sharing of knowledge.

Given the rapid development and pervasive influence of electronic media in contemporary life, it is important for teachers and others involved in teaching L2s or foreign languages to have a good understanding of these media and the ways in which they impact language learning and teaching. In what follows, I review the main media that are available for writing in an L2 or foreign language in the context of CALL. I begin with a discussion of word processing and then describe other forms of electronic writing aids, including networking and hypermedia options. Throughout the discussion, I seek to make connections with larger trends in literacy and communication, arguing that language teachers today should actively involve themselves and their students in these developments (see also Pennington, 2003).

THE WORD PROCESSOR: THE BASIC CALL WRITING TOOL

Features of Word Processing

Word processors, which generally include a spell checker and sometimes a grammar checker as well, are the basic CALL writing tool. As compared to a pen, a word processor offers both a suite of advanced writing tools and a facilitative environment for generating ideas and producing text, both as drafts and finished copy. After learning to type on a computer keyboard and mastering computer commands for word processing, most students go on to become regular computer users. The value of word processors for writing is generally considered to be their capacity to ease the mechanical processes of generating text; revising text by deletions, additions, substitutions, and block moves; and producing clear and attractive finished copy (for reviews and discussions of research, see Bangert-Drowns, 1993; Bruce & Rubin, 1993; Cochran-Smith, 1991; Pennington, 1991, 1993b, 1993c, 1993d, 1996a, 1996b, 1996c, 1996d, 1999a, 1999b; Snyder, 1993). Beyond these writing and revision tools, the attributes and capabilities of the computer writing environment that aid the writing process include the following (Pennington, 1991, 1996b):

- the physical ease of making keypresses and typing text.
- the focusing of attention by the clear and restricted amount of text that is visible on the computer screen.
- the marking of the point where text is being produced by the blinking cursor, which also acts as a prompt to the writer to keep writing.
- the writer's awareness of the possibility of saving or changing text at any time.

These features of word processing assist the writing process even as they change it. Several researchers (e.g., Bernhardt, Edwards, & Wojahn, 1989; Haas, 1989; Pennington, 1996a, 1996b, 1996c, 1996d; Williamson & Pence, 1989) have observed a unique mode of writing in a computer context. As Chadwick and Bruce (1989) remark:

> Computers change the writing process in that their various text manipulation features allow writers to jump backwards and forwards in their texts, revise and rephrase, delete and insert and at the same time provide the writer with a hard copy at any stage. Once the first draft is completed the student can read and reread, make any number of changes without the generation of non-productive labor or fear of spoiling the presentation of the text. The student no longer faces the frustrating dilemma of whether to rewrite the whole, involving meaningless copying, or leave changes with he[or she] knows should be made but wants to avoid. . . . The student can therefore exhaust his[or her] own intuitions about what is good or bad, what needs changing or leaving alone, before requesting feedback from a tutor [or teacher]. (p. 18)

Effects such as these that the word processor can have on L2 students' writing are potentially very significant. Starting with the most basic effect of positive attitudes, I trace a chain of word processing effects that might ultimately lead to high-quality written products. At each step, I attempt to relate the research findings to characteristics of the medium and the way it is used.

Attitudes Related to Computer Use

The capability of the computer to facilitate the writing process has been linked to the development of positive attitudes toward writing since the fear of making errors and having to recopy text is greatly reduced (e.g., Cochran-Smith, Paris, & Kahn, 1991; Cross, 1990; Dalton & Hannafin, 1987; Etchison, 1989; Hawisher, 1987; Roblyer, Castine, & King, 1988; Teichman & Poris, 1989; Williamson & Pence, 1989). The mechanical capacities of a word processor are especially valuable for L2 learners, for whom the physical and cognitive processes of generating and revising text require greater effort and attention (Jones & Tetroe, 1987) than when writing in their L1. For L2 writers, many of whom lack confidence in their writing ability (Betancourt & Phinney, 1988), a sense of empowerment gained through use of the machine may be as important as the actual capabilities of the machine to aid their writing process. The use of a word processor may help to close the gap between writing in L1 and L2 in part by relieving the anxiety that many writers feel about writing in their L2, especially when producing academic work (Pennington, 1999a; Phinney, 1989).

Similar to what has been shown for students in general, many studies conducted on word processing with ESL and EFL writers have found positive attitudes associated with writing in the context of CALL (e.g., Akyel & Kamisli, 1999; Neu & Scarcella, 1991; Pennington & Brock, 1992; Phinney, 1991a, 1991b; Phinney & Mathis, 1990; Rusmin, 1999). For example, in a longitudinal investigation of the introduction of word processing in a class of mature writers in Hong Kong (Rusmin, 1999), although the pattern of responses varied from the beginning to the end of term, all but 2 of the 27 students had positive overall attitudes toward the computer and used it by choice in their written work. The positive attitudes associated with word processing extend beyond the computer to writing, English language, and language learning. In their comparison of word processing and pen-and-paper composing in English by Turkish university students, Akyel and Kamisli (1999) note:

> In addition to having a positive attitude to the writing instruction offered, the student writers in the computer group developed an overall positive attitude to using the computer as a writing medium. Learning how to use the computer as a tool to express their ideas and feelings improved their attitudes to writing and built up their confidence about their ability to write in English, thus encouraging them to write more. . . . For these students, learning how to use the computer started a process of self-empowerment and confidence-building. Even those subjects who did not like writing started to have different feelings about writing. Thus Student Writer 1 commented:

Although I do not like writing a composition, it is much better writing on the computer. Writing on the computer is more fun than writing by hand. (p. 42)

Text Length and Characteristics

Production of longer texts is a general effect of word processing (Bangert-Drowns, 1993; Schramm, 1989). In ESL and EFL as well, the writer working in an electronic medium tends to write less self-consciously and more freely, often for longer periods, resulting in longer texts (Brock & Pennington, 1999; Chadwick & Bruce, 1989; Li & Cumming, 2001; Pennington & Brock, 1992). Writing for longer periods and producing longer texts are effects of the physical and mental facilitation of a computer-based writing process. These "facilitative effects on writing are the most basic type of outcome of word processing and the starting point for any other types of effects on a computer user's writing process or written products" (Pennington, 1999b, p. 4).

The physical easing of the writing process can lead to a relaxation of coherence and writing conventions, resulting in "unconstrained and experimental, . . . 'train of thought' or 'spaghetti writing'—long strings of loosely connected strands of ideas" (Pennington, 2000b, p. 14). Text produced with a computer is less likely to be written according to set rhetorical modes and the standards of formal written language than text produced by traditional means. If judged by the same criteria, it may fall short of the usual standards for the form and content of written work. In some cases, a text produced in one sitting on a word processor is properly viewed not as finished work but as a draft that provides the basis for revision to a finished work that can achieve a high standard (Pennington, 1993b, 1993c, 1996b, 1996c, 1996d). In other cases, a computer-generated text is properly viewed as a new type of work. The products of word processing are not entirely equivalent to those produced by the earlier writing technologies of pen and typewriter; even less are the products of writing in other CALL contexts such as the electronic environments of networks, hypertext, and Web pages (see the following sections).

Revision

The word processing environment facilitates revision, and surface-level editing for spelling and mechanics is facilitated by the availability of a spell checker, and possibly a grammar checker as well. The small size of the text visible on the computer screen in word processing may promote intensive revision at word, phrase, and sentence level (Pennington, 1993b, 1993c, 1996b, 1999b). In addition, the ease of searching individual words and of deleting, adding, or moving whole sections of text means that the word processor can naturally function as a macro-level revision tool. Research on revision using a word processor (for reviews, see Cochran-Smith, 1991; Hawisher, 1989) shows a high quantity of revision in computer contexts as well as diversity and breadth of revisions (e.g., Cochran-Smith, 1991; Dalton & Hannafin, 1987; Oliver & Kerr, 1993). Other research stresses the benefits of word processing for correction of surface errors and local editing (e.g., Cochran-Smith, 1991; Harris, 1985; Lutz, 1987), some studies draw attention to positive effects at the level of sentences or larger discourse units (e.g., Hill, Wallace, & Haas, 1991; McAllister & Louth, 1988; Robinson-Staveley & Cooper, 1990), and others specifically link the computer's ability to stimulate revision to positive effects in the quality of students' writing (e.g., Oliver & Kerr, 1993; Robinson-Staveley & Cooper, 1990). Classroom research has also demonstrated the value of CALL-based pedagogy for increasing students' awareness of and ability to apply revision strategies in their own writing (e.g., Steelman, 1994).

Some studies of ESL and EFL writers have yielded favorable effects for revision on a word processor, as students devoted more time to revising, revised more actively, and made more revisions on computer than when writing by traditional means (Chadwick & Bruce, 1989; Li & Cumming, 2001; Phinney & Khouri, 1993). Some research with ESL and EFL learners has also demonstrated that word processing promotes revisions beyond the surface level. Thus, Chadwick and Bruce's (1989) computer-using group of Hong Kong university students made more meaning-level changes in their English compositions than did a pen-and-paper comparison group. In a comparative study of word processing and pen-and-paper composing by Turkish university students (Akyel & Kamisli, 1999), the computer group revised more in the categories of organization, sentence structure, word form, and spelling. In a longitudinal study of one L2 writer, Li and Cumming (2001) report more syntactic and discourse-level revisions in computer-assisted writing than in pen-and-paper writing. In addition, a study of French L2 writers (Bisaillon, 1999) has shown that teaching revision strategies for use with word processing can increase the quantity of revision in the areas of sentence-level coherence and organization in the L2.

There is evidence that meaning-level revision is stimulated by word processing aligned to a process approach (Daiute, 1985; Pennington, 1996b; Susser, 1993a), which often includes peer feedback. In a case study of ESL writers in Hawaii (Pennington & Brock, 1992), the students who used a combination of peer feedback and word processing made more meaning-level changes than did students working with word processing and only a grammar-checking program (Pennington & Brock, 1992). A more extensive study of a group of Hong Kong students (Brock & Pennington, 1999) determined that those writing on computer with peer feedback made more revisions overall and more content-level revisions on each of their class assignments than did a comparison group using only computer aids. Whereas word processors and spell checkers have definite value for ESL and EFL writers, grammar checkers have little value for L2 or novice writers because the feedback they give is highly inaccurate and inflexible, making them frustrating to use (Brock, 1990, 1993, 1995; Pennington, 1992, 1993a).

Researchers have also noted that revision activity in a CALL writing environment tends to be highly intensive and concentrated (Pennington, 1993b, 1993c; 1996b, ch. 2; Piolat, 1991), that it is more interactive and continuous than when writing by pen-and-paper means (Owston, Murphy, & Wideman, 1992; Phinney & Khouri, 1993; Williamson & Pence, 1989), and that it involves more "tinkering" to try out changes in small bits of text which may or may not survive to final drafts (Cochran-Smith, 1991; Marcoul & Pennington, 1999; Williamson & Pence, 1989). Composing with a word processor typically involves continuous revision and repeated tinkering in which changes are made physically and temporally near the point of generation of text, rather than being made in a separate step following the generation of a draft.

Planning and Overall Approach to Writing

When composing with pen and paper, the desire to limit the drudgery of rewriting leads to a long first step of intensive planning, followed by a less cognitively demanding second step of generating text according to the writing plan. If revision is attempted at all, it will generally be postponed until after an entire draft or section of a composition has been completed. The revision process may lead back into a new phase of planning and then generation of new text on that basis, but more typically it is carried out according to the original plan or outline. In place of a prestructured and staged writing macrocycle in which an entire text is generated, experienced computer writers compose in a series of drafting episodes comprising linked microcycles of text generation and revision (Pennington, 1996b, ch. 3; 1996c, 1996d). Instead of writing text to fit an already worked-out writing plan or outline, computer writers typically jump right into the writing process, or they may do a limited amount of planning, usually of an informal kind, before beginning to write. Most commonly, computer writers do most of their planning and decision making as they are writing, whether in L1 (Haas, 1989) or in L2 (Akyel & Kamisli, 1999; Li & Cumming, 2001). Rather than developing a structure for a composition and then fitting words and sentences to it top down, in a computer context, the structure of a composition evolves bottom up, from the nature of the content generated, as an outgrowth of lexical relations and the natural subdivisions of the content (Pennington, 1996b).

The "bureaucratic" look-before-you-leap approach to writing involving careful planning of ideas and conservation of text, which is encouraged by the pen-and-paper medium, does not make effective use of word processor utilities. It will therefore tend to be replaced in a computer environment by an "entrepreneurial" jump-right-in approach to writing involving rapid generation of ideas and innovation of text. Such an approach, which is encouraged by the capabilities of a word processor, is a more linear, real-time mode of producing written work and is thus a simpler and more natural way of composing a text than the forward-planning approach of pen-and-paper writers. An effortful cognitive mode of *pre-reflection* focused on advance planning and structuring of a composition before writing naturally gives way over time in a computer writing environment to a cognitive mode of *post-reflection* and *in-process reflection* focused on continuous revision and planning as text is being generated.

In addition to saving effort by "automating some of the more burdensome aspects of text production and revision" (Kozma, 1991, p. 35), the attributes of the word processor encourage a restructuring of the writing task into a less cognitively demanding process involving smaller episodes of text generation and revision, and smaller and more concrete units of planning and reflection. This natural computer writing style, in being less cognitively demanding than a process that requires the writer to plan the structure of a text in advance, may have particular value for L2 writers (Pennington, 1996b, 1996c, 1996d). The continuous process of generating and revising text using a word processor may furthermore result in "a cumulative alteration of textual cohesion and coherence" (Owston et al., 1992, p. 272) and therefore a more developed final draft. Thus, word processing in an L2 context appears to have substantial potential for improving students' revision and their writing overall.

Text Quality

The most important test of the value of word processing is whether it results in a high-quality written product. According to the results of many research studies (e.g., Bruce & Rubin, 1993; Dalton & Hannafin, 1987; Owston et al., 1992; Robinson-Staveley & Cooper, 1990; Snyder, 1990), word processing has passed this essential test, as student compositions produced by word processing in contrast to pen and paper received higher holistic marks or analytic ratings for content, organization, and language. Added to the accumulated positive findings for word processing are three meta-analytical reviews of comparative studies using traditional measures of writing quality (Bangert-Drowns, 1993; Roblyer et al., 1988; Schramm, 1989). The picture is clouded, however, by the existence of other research presenting negative findings for the quality of word-processed as compared with pen-and-paper compositions (e.g., Greenleaf, 1994; Harris, 1985) and by some studies showing no advantage either way (e.g., Dunn & Reay, 1989; Etchison, 1989; Hawisher & Fortune, 1989; Teichman & Poris, 1989). A similar mixed pattern can be seen in the L2 research findings, including both positive results (e.g., Lam & Pennington, 1995; McGarrell, 1993) and negative or neutral results (e.g., Benesch, 1987; Chadwick & Bruce, 1989) for word processing.

The studies in which word-processed compositions received significantly lower ratings than pen-and-paper compositions are, in fact, few in number and represent a declining proportion of the research evidence. Compared with the early reports of research on word processing, when the negative findings loomed large in a relatively small number of studies, the weight of the evidence is increasingly favorable. Clearly, the computer offers many advantages over the typewriter or pen. Equally clearly, there are factors in the context of computer writing, such as the characteristics of the students and the instructional approach taken, that can have a determining effect as to whether the results are positive (Pennington, 1999a, 1999b). Like any other medium or tool, the effects of the computer are ultimately determined by the way it is used.

Final Remarks on Word Processing

The research on word processing has been relatively extensive, demonstrating strongly positive effects for student writers, including L2 writers in general and ESL and EFL writers in particular, in terms of (a) attitudes and (b) length of texts, along with more modest positive effects in terms of (c) overall writing quality and (d) quantity of revision; there are also suggestive findings in a positive direction for (e) quality of revision. Added to the accumulated evidence of positive effects of word processing on students' writing are the many observations by researchers of changes in the nature of writing processes and products in a computer context. Such changes in writing processes and products are presumably inevitable in the context of new technologies. Even writing with a fountain pen rather than a quill and ink, or a ballpoint pen rather than a pencil, makes a definite difference in the fluidity of writing that may change the writer's mindset and hence the process and outcomes of writing. The technology of the printing press and later the typewriter makes possible a highly uniform kind of text and allows writers more time and freedom for original creation rather than meticulous hand copying. These changes in writing processes and outcomes are precursors of those we see today in computer-produced texts.

I have argued that the advantages of word processors are especially important for L2 writers. The word processor may help these writers to compensate for their lack of full proficiency in the L2 and to develop a more effective and efficient writing process, and so to begin to close the gap between them and L1 writers. At the same time as I believe the research supports these conclusions about the effects of word processing, these findings have less importance than they did 5 or 10 years ago, for two reasons. One reason is that the word processor is the writing tool of choice for all people in the modern world, and writing teachers no longer have any realistic option besides writing in a computer context. The second reason is that autonomous word processing is no longer the main arena of computer-based developments, as is reviewed in the next section.

BEYOND WORD PROCESSING: THE WIDER CONTEXT OF WRITING IN CALL

Expanding the CALL Writing Context Through Networks

The domination of teachers in traditional classrooms is well known. As characterized by researchers at the University of Birmingham (Coulthard & Brazil, 1992; Sinclair & Brazil, 1982; Sinclair & Coulthard, 1975), the pattern of interaction in classrooms the world over tends to be organized around a relatively restricted, three-move pattern of: (a) a teacher's *initiation* move (most commonly by asking a question and calling for a response), followed by (b) a *response* from one or more students, and then (c) teacher *follow-up* to the student response (most commonly by an evaluation such as "good" or "correct"). However, teaching and learning in a writing class where CALL is used promotes a different communicative dynamic, with more collaboration, more time spent writing, and more active participation by students than in a traditional classroom (Daiute, 1985; Snyder, 1990; Sudol, 1985; Williamson & Pence, 1989). Where students can communicate with each other over a network, the level of participation by individual students is increased and additional opportunities for collaboration made available (Warschauer, 1997, 1999). Networks also bring many different kinds of tools and sources of information within the reach of student users. These potentials of CALL and computer networks both increase the learner's access to resources and add a new dimension to the ESL and EFL writing class.

Linking Writers in LANs and WANs

L2 student writers can gain partners and input on their writing via a LAN (or intranet), such as in a computer lab, or a wide area network (WAN), such as a university or a school district computer network, or the worldwide network of the Internet (Howard, 1992). A departmental or university-wide network can be used as a means of giving out assignments and turning in completed written work (e.g., as an attachment to an e-mail message) without the need for hard copy, and as a way of maintaining contact between teachers and students, and among the students themselves, outside of class time. These networks also allow the sharing and joint production of work by students as well as teachers.

Through a class LAN or computer lab, students can be linked to classmates or others, including their teachers, to send and receive e-mail and other types of messages about their ideas and their writing (Mabrito, 1991), and to comment on each others' work (Palmquist, 1993). They can also participate in "team editing" (Kaufer & Neuwirth, 1995) and other types of collaborative projects facilitated by the network environment (Bruce, Peyton, & Batson, 1993; Bruce & Rubin, 1993). One researcher studying the use of networks for teaching writing in Hong Kong (Hoffman, 1996) noted that "a LAN in a writing lab can support . . . prewriting and invention, collaborative drafting and peer review, efficient revising and editing, and the sharing of texts with a variety of real audiences" (p. 61). Positive effects for use of computer labs with networking have been reported for ESL and EFL classes in terms of course efficiency and effectiveness, student writing activity and learner motivation, experimentation, and independence from the teacher (Hoffman, 1993, 1994, 1996; Kamisli, 1992; Markley, 1992; Sullivan & Pratt, 1996; Susser, 1993b).

E-Mail Exchanges

The audiences and participants for writing are expanded in a larger network or by Internet access, which also makes possible e-mail "penpals" and other types of electronic exchange across classes or among individual students. L2 students may be linked to L1 students within the same institution (Nabors & Swartley, 1999) or across institutions in the same country (Esling, 1991) as well as in different countries (Sayers, 1989; Slater & Carpenter, 1999; Woodin, 1997). In a study in which English-speaking learners of Spanish established e-mail contact with partners in Spain who were learning English, Woodin (1997) found that e-mail functioned "as a bridge between the language classroom and the natural setting" (p. 31), providing opportunities for authentic communication with speakers of the target language. Students were able to communicate naturally on any topic they wished and their motivation to communicate with their partners was high. In a study providing e-mail partners for ESL students on an American university campus, Nabors and Swartley (1999) also found that the use of e-mail with "freedom of topic" promoted students' creative communication with their partners. These researchers speculated that the students' ability to select their own topics was a key aspect for establishing effective e-mail partnerships since they could indicate where shared knowledge could be assumed or should be built up. In an e-mail exchange between students in France and England (Slater & Carpenter, 1999), in contrast, the careful structuring of e-mail contact around provided topics and tasks resulted in a less positive experience for the students involved. The conclusion is that for network partnerships to be effective, they must be designed to make appropriate use of the medium.

Communication in Networks

Some researchers have remarked on positive features of communication in networks and their effects on students' writing. In a study of four EFL teachers in Hong Kong who used e-mail with their students (Hoffman, 1993, 1994), both students and teachers commented on the efficiency, the flexibility, and the "warmth" of communication given over the network. In addition, according to Hoffman (1996):

> Electronic mail provided students with more timely, more complete, and more usable information about their writing and assignments than written comments on work returned to them. They also found, on occasion, that e-mail feedback was more face-saving and less stressful than face-to-face communication. (p. 65)

Placing L2 students in a computer network encourages a more equal social structure that results in a more participatory form of education, with the particular benefit for language learners of more speaking time in the L2. Sullivan and Pratt (1996), for example, discovered that a far greater proportion of turns (85%) were taken by ESL students during large-group discussions in writing lessons in a computer-networked classroom as compared with a traditional oral classroom, where approximately two thirds of the turns were taken by the teacher. In addition, whereas only half of the students in the traditional classroom participated in large-group discussions related to writing, 100% of the students in the computer writing classroom participated in such discussions.

Sullivan and Pratt (1996) further found that the feedback given by ESL student peers over the computer network was especially focused and included suggestions for revision which tended to be reinforced by several students. In the face-to-face discussions, in contrast, once a point was made it might be agreed by other group members in simple responses such as "yeah" or "uh-huh" but would not usually be repeated by another student. It might be assumed that a computer network would be more effective as a feedback environment for writing than face-to-face L2 conversation, where a greater amount of information must be handled and where maintaining solidarity takes precedence over transactional tasks and informational goals. As in the case of word processing, however, the simple fact of linking student writers in a peer network does not ensure a good result in their writing, and network-based peer feedback is not necessarily more that effective than peer feedback given in face-to-face interaction. Thus, EFL student writers in Hong Kong who engaged in face-to-face peer interaction in a classroom setting made greater gains and received higher holistic scores on their final drafts than did students who engaged in peer discussion via a LAN (Braine, 2001).

New Voices, New Perspectives

Students writing on networks have been described as participating in "a communal process of knowledge making" (Barker & Kemp, 1990, p. 26). At the same time as it can bring writers together to increase shared knowledge and create a unified voice, a computer network offers a context in which a diversity of voices can be expressed. Sirc and Reynolds (1993) describe an electronic network for interaction as "a multivocal, multicultural word processor . . . the technology of polyphony, of heterotopia" (p. 156). An L2 writer who engages with this "technology of polyphony" gains new perspectives and may be able to define an individual voice through contrast and comparison with other writers' voices and points of view. Barclay (1995) has maintained that the cognitive activities involved in computer-mediated interaction are similar to processes involved in composing and revising formal arguments and are "often associated with reading in a literary way— 'dialogization (heteroglossia),' 'defamiliarization,' 'refraction of the implied author's intent,' and 'multiple reading' " (p. 24). The communicative environments provided by networking may therefore have value in helping student writers to develop perspective and objectivity, to build their arguments, and to create an individual writer's voice.

Increasingly, computer networks are being used for interactive writing of different kinds—in particular, *synchronous*, near-immediate or real-time, interaction. These include not only e-mail but newsgroups and various types of Internet and Web-based discussion groups, chat sites, and simulations (see Windeatt, Hardisty, & Eastment, 2000, for descriptions and sample classroom activities). Such writing environments seem to encourage a high degree of creativity and novelty. Barclay (1995) maintains that computer-mediated written discussion is characterized by the elements of "clowning, ridicule, play, masks, rough-and-tumble, mixed genres, appropriated forms, interruption, and parodic revoicing" (p. 24). Moran and Hawisher (1998) note "our new tendency to use on-line space as a space for creating alternative selves, experimenting with roles we might not have assumed in face-to-face, 'live' communication" (p. 98). By promoting experimentation and creativity, interactive writing environments may enhance the language-learning process and so be especially beneficial for L2 writers.

New Language

Although the network context may have value for L2 writers, it also changes some of the attributes of writing to those of speech (Baron, 1998, 2000; Collot & Belmore, 1996; Spears & Lea, 1992). It has even been suggested (Baron, 1998, 2000) that e-mail is creating a "creole" form of communication blending features of speech and writing. Similar to e-mail, but apparently to an even greater extent, students writing in real-time (synchronous) interactive network environments such as chat rooms are creating new language to fit the new medium and their new identities as communicators within that medium. Cantonese-English bilingual university students in Hong Kong, for example, are localizing the language in which they write by using L1 expressions translated into English or rendered by informal romanized transcription, along with (romanized) Cantonese sentence particles to convey pragmatic meaning (for an example, see Bolton, 2000, p. 282).

HYPERTEXT, HYPERMEDIA, AND THE WORLD WIDE WEB

Hypertext is medium for representing information as a network of linked informational "chunks" that exists online and can be accessed in any order by mouse clicks. In the characterization of Snyder (1998):

> Hypertext is essentially a network of links between words, ideas and sources, one that has neither a centre nor an end. We "read" hypertext by navigating through it, taking detours to "footnotes", and from those "footnotes" to others, exploring what in print culture would be described as "digressions" as long and complex as the "main" text. Any other document can be linked to and become part of another text. The extent of hypertext is unknowable because it lacks clear boundaries and is often multi-authored. (pp. 126–127)

When expanded to include not only text but other forms of electronic visual and audio media, hypertext is usually referred to as hypermedia or multimedia.

The World Wide Web is a very large set of hypertext links accessible on the Internet. As Warschauer (1999) observes:

> The impact of hypertext becomes more profound when a single computer's files are linked with other files around the world, as on the World Wide Web. First, the Web places an unprecedented amount of information at the hands of individual users all around the globe. Second, it makes any computer user around the world a potential international author, without having to go

through the costly expense of printing and distributing information on paper. Third, the Web further complicates the process of both writing and reading by allowing the author to make links (and the reader to thus pursue links) to any other work created anywhere in the world on the Web. The Web can thus be expected to have a deep impact not only on how we gather and share information, but also how we conceptualize reading and writing. (pp. 7–8)

New Literacies

Hypermedia tools for combining media in multilayered presentations such as Web pages are helping to shape new forms of expression and new canons of literacy involving text in combination with other visual media:

> When text is combined with other modes of expression in a unified presentation such as on a Web page . . . it may . . . shift from being the primary focus of the page to assuming a secondary purpose of supporting other media. Instead of text illustrated by pictures or graphics one may end up with a multimedia presentation captioned or illustrated by text. (Pennington, 2000a, p. 23)

New domains of communication and literacy are emerging in the context of hypermedia and the Web as part of a historical trend identified by Kress (1998) away from a definition of literacy uniquely in terms of written text and toward a new orientation to visual and combined-media literacy:

> In the present technological context of electronic, multimodal, multimedia textual production, the task of text-makers is that of complex orchestration. Further, individuals are now seen as the remakers, transformers, of sets of representational resources—rather than users of stable systems, in a situation where multiple representational modes are brought into textual compositions. All these circumstances call for a new goal in textual (and perhaps other) practice: [that of] *design.* . . . Design takes for granted competence in the use of resources, but beyond that it requires the orchestration and remaking of these resources in the service of frameworks and models that express the maker's intentions in shaping the social and cultural environment. . . . Design shapes the future through deliberate deployment of representational resources in the designer's interest. Design is the textual principle for periods characterised by intense and far-reaching change. (Kress, 1998, p. 77)

Teachers must acknowledge that the present generation of students is aware of the shift in emphasis from issues of text and language to issues of design, and is developing new values and standards for their computer practices. This awareness is illustrated in a study of computer use in relation to Web sites of junior high school students in Mexico (Romano, Field, & de

Huergo, 2000) by one student's observation that "sites of excellence for my age require pictures and mail" (p. 209). In a study that examined L2 French student texts produced in hypertext mode for a Web-based student newspaper (Marcoul & Pennington, 1999), attention to design features and content took precedence over correct language. Whereas the goal of writing in traditional academic tasks and genres is to present a logical analysis of a subject as a progression of explicitly linked ideas, when writing in hypermedia, the writer attempts to create a highly expressive and compact form, aiming at a more artistic, evocative or iconic goal, similar to writing poetry, composing a piece of music, or creating a picture. The primary mode of expression in web-based composition is thus easily transformed from analytic linguistic terms to holistic imagistic terms.

Web-Based Communication

Web-based communication is often in a dialectic or reflexive form presenting contrasting views of topics or issues, typically by making links between one's own and other Web sites. The "contestive" potential of communication on the World Wide Web helps to counter the dominance of Western culture and commerce that pervades all media in the present day. As observed by Hawisher and Selfe (2000):

> The Web as a complicated and contested site for postmodern literacy practices. This site is characterized by a strongly influential set of tendential cultural forces, primarily oriented toward the values of the white, western industrialized nations that were responsible for designing and building the network and that continue to exert power within it. Hence, this system of networked computers is far from world-wide; it does not provide a culturally neutral conduit for the transmission of information; it is not a culturally neutral or innocent communication landscape open to the literacy practices and values of all global citizens. But the site is also far from totalizing in its effects . . . [as] the Web also provides a site for transgressive literary practices that express and value difference; that cling to historical, cultural, and racial diversity; and that help groups and individuals constitute their own multiple identities through language. (p. 15)

EFL students in Mexico realized the potential of the World Wide Web to engage with those outside their context and to give an accurate view of their own world at the same time (Romano et al., 2000). A similar interaction of global and local viewpoints can be seen in Australians' use of the Web, leading McConaghy and Snyder (2000) to remark: "Perhaps, in the final analysis, the possibilities for engaging the local in the global through the World Wide Web represent the new medium's greatest potential" (p. 89).

A Future Scenario

As a further development of the potentials of these media, Ashworth (1996) speaks of a "marriage of hypermedia and electronic networks" (p. 94) through which "people will communicate in real time over a network, supporting their arguments and illustrating their points with video clips, sound quotes, background music, and the like" (p. 95). This is in fact close to the reality of how Internet and Web-based communication tools are being used in some business contexts, pointing the way for the next step in the series of computer revolutions impacting educational contexts. It is possible to imagine a time in the not-too-distant future when computers will be giving independent input—for example, locating information in databases to support, illustrate, or challenge points being made—in these real-time interactions. Such a scenario, in which the computer takes a role as a participant in electronic interactions with humans, can be seen as part of the evolution of an ever larger and more diverse universe of discourse—the logical outcome of an ever-expanding supply of information coupled with an increasingly abstract, nonphysical, and diversified concept of communication (Pennington, 2001, 2002a, 2002b).

CONCLUSION

The computer offers a range of new media and tools that can assist the L2 student writer. At the same time, the new technologies change the processes and products—indeed, the very nature—of writing as well as language and communication more generally:

> The result of writing in an electronic medium may not be the written products of a pen-and-paper age but more ephemeral forms of *think-text* and *talk-text*. These electronic writing products may be further transformed or linked with the aid of the computer to other "texturizing" or representational forms, such as graphics, hypertext, pictures, and indeed video or sound. They may also be linked to and transformed by the ideas and the language of other computer users, as the computer makes it easier to write as a joint or distributed activity among a number of writers. The products of writing in a computer age will necessarily be new and different from those of another age, and they will answer to new values and standards. . . . Doing literacy in an electronic era means learning skills and producing works which challenge long-standing writing processes and values. (Pennington, 2000b, p. 21)

While making possible much greater choice and creativity in expression of ideas, the contexts of communication provided by electronic media are at the same time becoming sites for contesting long-standing literacy practices and developing new practices. The new electronic literacies respond to the needs of an increasingly fast-moving and enlarging information state and an increasingly interconnected universe of discourse in which communication increasingly occurs at a physical and social distance among communicators who inhabit literally different worlds.

Teachers in L2 education cannot realistically meet their students' needs if they ignore these developments or seek to force-fit the use of electronic media to traditional modes of communication or pedagogy. Rather than attempting to maintain the status quo, those teaching L2 or foreign languages need to engage with the new media, giving not only word processing but also networking, hypermedia, and the Internet and World Wide Web a place in L2 learning pedagogy.

REFERENCES

Akyel, A., & Kamisli, S. (1999). Word processing in the EFL classroom: Effects on writing strategies, attitudes, and products. In M. C. Pennington (Ed.), *Writing in an electronic medium: Research with language learners* (pp. 27–60). Houston, TX: Athelstan.

Ashworth, D. (1996). Hypermedia and CALL. In M. C. Pennington (Ed.), *The Power of CALL* (pp. 79–95). Houston, TX: Athelstan.

Bangert-Drowns, R. L. (1993). The word processor as an instructional tool: A meta-analysis of word processing in writing instruction. *Review of Educational Research, 63,* 69–93.

Barclay, D. (1995). Ire, envy, irony, and ENFI: Electronic conferences as unreliable narrative. *Computers and Composition, 12,* 23–44.

Barker, T. T., & Kemp, F. O. (1990). Network theory: A postmodern pedagogy for the writing classroom. In C. Handa (Ed.), *Computer and community: Teaching composition in the twenty-first century* (pp. 1–27). Portsmouth, NH: Boynton/Cook.

Baron, N. S. (1998). Letters by phone or speech by other means: The linguistics of e-mail. *Language & Communication, 18,* 133–170.

Baron, N. S. (2000). *Alphabet to email: How written English evolved and where it's heading.* London: Routledge.

Benesch, S. (1987). *Word processing in English as a second language: A case study of three non-native college students.* Paper presented at the conference on College Composition and Communication, Atlanta, GA. ERIC Document No. ED 281383.

Bernhardt, S. A. (1993). The shape of text to come: The texture of print on screens. *College Composition and Communication, 44,* 151–175.

Bernhardt, S. A., Edwards, P. G., & Wojahn, P. R. (1989). Teaching college composition with computers: A program evaluation study. *Written Communication, 6,* 108–133.

Betancourt, F., & Phinney, M. (1988). Sources of writing block in bilingual writers. *Written Communication, 5,* 461–478.

Bisaillon, J. (1999). Effects of the teaching of revision strategies in a computer-based environment. In M. C. Pennington (Ed.), *Writing in an electronic medium: Research with language learners* (pp. 131–157). Houston, TX: Athelstan.

Bolton, K. (2000). The sociolinguistics of Hong Kong and the space for Hong Kong English. *World Englishes, 19,* 265–285.

Braine, G. (2001). A study of English as a foreign language (EFL) writers on a local-area network (LAN) and in traditional classes. *Computers and Composition, 18,* 275–292.

Brock, M. N. (1990). Can the computer tutor? An analysis of a disk-based text analyzer. *System,* *18*, 351–359.

Brock, M. N. (1993). Three disk-based text analyzers and the ESL writer. *Journal of Second Language Writing, 2*, 19–40.

Brock, M. N. (1995). Computerized text analysis: Roots and research. *Computer Assisted Language Learning, 8*, 227–258.

Brock, M. N., & Pennington, M. C. (1999). A comparative study of text analysis and peer tutoring as input to writing on computer in an ESL context. In M. C. Pennington (Ed.), *Writing in an electronic medium: Research with language learners* (pp. 61–94). Houston, TX: Athelstan.

Bruce, B., Peyton, J. K., & Batson, T. (Eds.). (1993). *Network-based classrooms: Promises and realities.* New York: Cambridge University Press.

Bruce, B. C., & Rubin, A. (1993). *Electronic quills: A situated evaluation of using computers for writing in classrooms.* Hillsdale, NJ: Lawrence Erlbaum Associates.

Chadwick, S., & Bruce, N. (1989). The revision process in academic writing: From pen & paper to word processor. *Hongkong Papers in Linguistics and Language Teaching, 12*(April), 1–27.

Cochran-Smith, M. (1991). Word processing and writing in elementary classrooms: A critical review of related literature. *Review of Educational Research, 61*, 107–155.

Cochran-Smith, M., Paris, C. L., & Kahn, J. L. (1991). *Learning to write differently: Beginning writers and word processing.* Norwood, NJ: Ablex.

Collot, M., & Belmore, N. (1996). Electronic language: A new variety of English. In S. Herring (Ed.), *Computer mediated communication: Linguistic, social, and cross-cultural perspectives* (pp. 13–28). Philadelphia: John Benjamins.

Coulmas, F. (1989). *The writing systems of the world.* Oxford, England: Blackwell.

Coulthard, M., & Brazil, D. (1992). Exchange structure. In M. Coulthard (Ed.), *Advances in spoken discourse analysis* (pp. 50–78). London: Routledge.

Cross, G. (1990). Left to their own devices: Three basic writers using word processing. *Computers and Composition, 7*(2), 47–58.

Daiute, C. (1985). *Writing and computers.* Reading, MA: Addison-Wesley.

Dalton, D. W., & Hannafin, M. J. (1987). The effects of word processing on written composition. *Journal of Educational Research, 80*, 338–342.

Dunn, B., & Reay, D. (1989). Word processing and the keyboard: Comparative effects of transcription on achievement. *Journal of Educational Research, 82*, 237–245.

Esling, J. H. (1991). Researching the effects of networking: Evaluating the spoken and written discourse generated by working with CALL. In P. Dunkel (Ed.), *Computer-assisted language learning and testing: Research issues and practice* (pp. 111–131). New York: Newbury House/HarperCollins.

Etchison, C. (1989). Word processing: A helpful tool for basic writers. *Computers and Composition, 6*(2), 33–43.

Greenleaf, C. (1994). Technological indeterminacy: The role of classroom writing practices and pedagogy in shaping student use of the computer. *Written Communication, 11*, 85–130.

Haas, C. (1989). How the writing medium shapes the writing process: Effects of word processing on planning. *Research in the Teaching of English, 23*, 181–207.

Harris, J. (1985). Student writers and word processing: A preliminary evaluation. *College Composition and Communication, 36*, 323–330.

Hawisher, G. E. (1987). The effects of word processing on the revision strategies of college freshmen. *Research in the Teaching of English, 21*, 145–160.

Hawisher, G. E. (1989). Research and recommendations for computers and composition. In G. E. Hawisher & C. L. Selfe (Eds.), *Critical perspectives on computers and composition instruction* (pp. 44–69). New York: Teachers College Press.

Hawisher, G. E., & Fortune, R. (1989). Word processing and the basic writer. *Collegiate Microcomputer, 7*, 275–284, 287.

Hawisher, G. E., & Selfe, C. L. (2000). Introduction: Testing the claims. In G. E. Hawisher & C. L. Selfe (Eds.), *Global literacies and the World-Wide Web* (pp. 1–18). London: Routledge.

Hill, C. A., Wallace, D. L., & Haas, C. (1991). Revising on-line: Computer technologies and the revising process. *Computers and Composition, 9*(1), 83–117.

Hoffman, R. (1993). The distance brings us closer: Electronic mail, ESL learner writers and teachers. In G. Davies & B. Samways (Eds.), *Teleteaching* (pp. 391–399). International Federation for Information Processing, University of Trondheim, and the Norwegian Computer Society.

Hoffman, R. (1994). The warm network, electronic mail, ESL learners, and the personal touch. *On-CALL: The Australian Journal of Computers and Education, 8*(2), 10–13.

Hoffman, R. (1996). Computer networks: Webs of communication for language teaching. In M. C. Pennington (Ed.), *The power of CALL* (pp. 55–77). Houston, TX: Athelstan.

Howard, T. (1992). WANs, connectivity, and computer literacy: An introduction and glossary. *Computers and Composition, 9*(3), 41–57.

Jones, S., & Tetroe, J. (1987). Composing in a second language. In A. Matsuhashi, (Ed.), *Writing in real time: Modelling production processes* (pp. 34–57). Norwood, NJ: Ablex.

Kamisli, S. (1992). *Word processing and the writing process: A case study of five Turkish English as a second language (ESL) students.* Unpublished doctoral dissertation, Columbia University.

Kaufer, D. S., and Neuwirth, C. (1995). Supporting online team editing: Using technology to shape performance and to monitor individual and group action. *Computers and Composition, 12,* 113–124.

Kozma, R. B. (1991). Computer-based writing tools and the cognitive needs of novice writers. *Computers and Composition, 8*(2), 31–45.

Kress, G. (1998). Visual and verbal modes of representation in electronically mediated communication: The potentials of new forms of text. In I. Snyder (Ed.), *Page to screen: Taking literacy into the electronic era* (pp. 53–79). London and New York: Routledge.

Lam, F. S., & Pennington, M. C. (1995). The computer vs. the pen: A comparative study of word processing in a Hong Kong secondary classroom. *Computer Assisted Language Learning, 7,* 75–92.

Li, J., & Cumming, A. (2001). Word processing and ESL writing: A longitudinal case study. In R. Manchon (Ed.), *International Journal of English Studies, 1*(2), 127–152.

Lutz, J. (1987). A study of professional and experienced writers revising and editing at the computer with pen and paper. *Research in the Teaching of English, 21,* 398–421.

Mabrito, M. (1991). Electronic mail as a vehicle for peer response. *Written Communication, 8,* 509–532.

Marcoul, I., & Pennington, M. C. (1999). Composing with computer technology: A case study of a group of students in computer studies learning French as a second language. In M. C. Pennington (Ed.), *Writing in an electronic medium: Research with language learners* (pp. 285–315). Houston, TX: Athelstan.

Marcus, S. (1993). Multimedia, hypermedia and the teaching of English. In M. Monteith (Ed.), *Computers and language* (pp. 21–43). Oxford, England: Intellect Books.

Markley, P. (1992). Creating independent ESL writers and thinkers: Computer networking for composition. *CAELL Journal, 3*(2), 6–12.

McAllister, C., & Louth, R. (1988). The effect of word processing on the quality of basic writers' revisions. *Research in the Teaching of English, 22,* 417–427.

McConaghy, C., & Snyder, I. (2000). In G. E. Hawisher & C. L. Selfe (Eds.), *Global literacies and the World-Wide Web* (pp. 74–92). London: Routledge.

McGarrell, H. M. (1993, August). *Perceived and actual impact of computer use in second language writing classes.* Paper presented at the Congress of the Association de Linguistique Appliquee (AILA), Frije University, Amsterdam.

Moran, C. (1995). Notes toward a rhetoric of e-mail. *Computers and Composition, 12,* 15–21.

Moran, C., & Hawisher, G. E. (1998). The rhetorics and languages of electronic mail. In I. Snyder (Ed.), *Page to screen: Taking literacy into the electronic era* (pp. 80–101). London and New York: Routledge.

Nabors, L. K., & Swartley, E. C. (1999). Student email letters: Negotiating meaning, gathering information, building relationships. In M. C. Pennington (Ed.), *Writing in an electronic medium: Research with language learners* (pp. 229–266). Houston, TX: Athelstan.

Neu, J., & Scarcella, R. (1991). Word processing in the ESL writing classroom: A survey of student attitudes. In P. Dunkel (Ed.), *Computer-assisted language learning and testing: Research issues and practice* (pp. 169–187). New York: Newbury House/HarperCollins.

Oliver, R., & Kerr, T. (1993). The impact of word processing on the preparation and submission of written essays in a tertiary course of study. *Higher Education, 26,* 217–226.

Owston, R. D., Murphy, S., & Wideman, H. H. (1992). The effects of word processing on students' writing quality and revision strategies. *Research in the Teaching of English, 26,* 249–276.

Palmquist, M. E. (1993). Network-supported interaction in two writing classrooms. *Computers and Composition, 10,* 25–57.

Pennington, M. C. (1991). Positive and negative potentials of word processing for ESL writers. *System, 19,* 267–275.

Pennington, M. C. (1992). Beyond off-the-shelf computer remedies for student writers: Alternatives to canned feedback. *System, 20*(4), 423–437.

Pennington, M. C. (1993a). Curriculum on a shaky foundation: An assessment of the research base supporting computer-assisted text analysis for second language writing. *Computer Assisted Language Learning, 5*(3), 167–177.

Pennington, M. C. (1993b). A critical examination of word processing effects in relation to L2 writers. *Journal of Second Language Writing, 2,* 227–255.

Pennington, M. C. (1993c). Exploring the potential of word processing for non-native writers. *Computers and the Humanities, 27*(3), 149–163.

Pennington, M. C. (1993d). Modeling the student writer's acquisition of word processing skills: The interaction of computer, writing, and language media. *Computers and Composition, 10,* 59–79.

Pennington, M. C. (1996a). The power of the computer in language education. In M. C. Pennington (Ed.), *The power of CALL* (pp. 1–14). Houston, TX: Athelstan.

Pennington, M. C. (1996b). *The computer and the non-native writer: A natural partnership.* Cresskill, NJ: Hampton Press.

Pennington, M. C. (1996c). Writing the natural way: On computer. *Computer Assisted Language Learning, 9,* 125–142.

Pennington, M. C. (1996d). The way of the computer: Developing writing skill in an electronic environment. In S. Fotos (Ed.), *Multimedia language teaching* (pp. 93–113). Tokyo: Logos International.

Pennington, M. C. (1999a). The missing link in computer-assisted writing. In K. Cameron (Ed.), *CALL: Media, design & applications* (pp. 271–292). Lisse, Switzerland: Swets & Zeitlinger.

Pennington, M. C. (1999b). Word processing and beyond: Writing in an electronic medium. In M. C. Pennington (Ed.), *Writing in an electronic medium: Research with language learners* (pp. 1–26). Houston, TX: Athelstan.

Pennington, M. C. (2000a, June). *Computers and the human experience.* Town and Gown Lecture, University of Luton.

Pennington, M. C. (2000b, July). *Writing minds and talking fingers: Doing literacy in an electronic age.* Plenary address at the CALL for the 21st Century conference cosponsored by IATEFL and ESADE, Barcelona.

Pennington, M. C. (2001, March). *Changing relationships between context and communication from pre-language to post-language.* Invited presentation, University of California at Berkeley, Davis, and Santa Barbara campuses.

Pennington, M. C. (2003). The impact of the computer in second language writing. In B. Kroll (Ed.), *Exploring the dynamics of second language writing* (pp. 287–310). New York: Cambridge University Press.

Pennington, M. C., & Brock, M. N. (1992). Process and product approaches to computer-assisted composition. In M. C. Pennington & V. Stevens (Eds.), *Computers in applied linguistics: An international perspective* (pp. 79–109). Clevedon, England: Multilingual Matters.

Phinney, M. (1989). Computers, composition, and second language teaching. In M. C. Pennington (Ed.), *Teaching languages with computers: The state of the art* (pp. 81–96). La Jolla, CA: Athelstan.

Phinney, M. (1991a). Computer-assisted writing and writing apprehension in ESL students. In P. Dunkel (Ed.), *Computer-assisted language learning and testing: Research issues and practice* (pp. 189–204). New York: Newbury House/HarperCollins.

Phinney, M. (1991b). Word processing and writing apprehension in first and second language writers. *Computers and Composition, 9,* 65–82.

Phinney, M. (1996). Exploring the virtual world: Computers in the second language writing classroom. In M. C. Pennington (Ed.), *The power of CALL* (pp. 137–152). Houston, TX: Athelstan.

Phinney, M., & Khouri, S. (1993). Computers, revision, and ESL writers: The role of experience. *Journal of Second Language Writing, 2,* 257–277.

Phinney, M., & Mathis, C. (1990). ESL student responses to writing with computers. *TESOL Newsletter, 24*(2), 30–31.

Piolat, A. (1991). Effects of word processing on text revision. *Language and Education, 5,* 255–272.

Robinson-Staveley, K., & Cooper, J. (1990). The use of computers for writing: Effects on an English composition class. *Journal of Educational Computing Research, 6,* 41–48.

Roblyer, M. D., Castine, W. H., & King, F. J. (1988). *Assessing the impact of computer-based instruction: A review of recent research.* New York: Haworth.

Romano, S., Field, B., & de Huergo, E. W. (2000). Web literacies of the already accessed and technically inclined: Schooling in Monterrey, Mexico. In G. E. Hawisher & C. L. Selfe (Eds.), *Global literacies and the World-Wide Web* (pp. 189–216). London: Routledge.

Rusmin, R. S. (1999). Patterns of adaptation to a new writing environment: The experience of word processing by mature second language writers. In M. C. Pennington (Ed.), *Writing in an electronic medium: Research with language learners* (pp. 183–227). Houston, TX: Athelstan.

Sayers, D. (1989). Bilingual sister classes in computer writing networks. In D. M. Johnson & D. H. Roen (Eds.), *Richness in writing: Empowering ESL students* (pp. 120–133). New York: Longman.

Schramm, R. M. (1989). The effects of using word-processing equipment in writing instruction: A meta-analysis (Doctoral dissertation, Northern Illinois University). *Dissertation Abstracts International, 50,* 2463A.

Sharples, M. (1997, March). The new writing environment: Expanding the notion of writing. Workshop on second language writing in computer environments, The Language Centre, University of Brighton.

Sinclair, J., & Brazil, D. (1982). *Teacher talk.* Oxford, England: Oxford University Press.

Sinclair, J., & Coulthard, M. (1975). *Towards an analysis of discourse: The English used by teachers and pupils.* Oxford, England: Oxford University Press.

Sirc, G., & Reynolds, T. (1993). Seeing students as writers. In B. Bruce, J. K. Peyton, & T. Batson (Eds.), *Network-based classrooms: Promises and realities* (pp. 138–160). New York: Cambridge University Press.

Slater, P., & Carpenter, C. (1999). Introducing e-mail into a course in French as a second language In M. C. Pennington (Ed.), *Writing in an electronic medium: Research with language learners* (pp. 267–283). Houston, TX: Athelstan.

Snyder, I. A. (1990). *The impact of word processors on students' writing: A comparative study of the effects of pens and word processors on writing context, process and product.* Unpublished doctoral dissertation, Monash University.

Snyder, I. (1993). Writing with word processors: A research overview. *Educational Research, 35,* 49–68.

Snyder, I. (1998). Beyond the hype: Reassessing hypertext. In L. Snyder (Ed.), *Page to screen: Taking literacy into the electronic era* (pp. 125–143). London and New York: Routledge.

Spears, R., & Lea, M. (1992). Social influence and the influence of the "social" in computer-mediated communication. In R. Spears & M. Lea (Eds.), *Contexts of computer-mediated communication* (pp. 30–65). New York: Harvester Wheatsheaf.

Steelman, J. D. (1994). Revision strategies employed by middle level students using computers. *Journal of Educational Computing Research, 11,* 141–152.

Sudol, R. R. (1985). Applied word processing: Notes on authority, responsibility, and revision in a workshop model. *College Composition and Communication, 36,* 331–335.

Sullivan, N., & Pratt, E. (1996). A comparative study of two ESL writing environments: A computer-assisted classroom and a traditional oral classroom. *System, 29,* 491–501.

Susser, B. (1993a). ESL/EFL process writing with computers. *CAELL Journal, 4*(2), 16–22.

Susser, B. (1993b). Networks and project work: Alternative pedagogies for writing with computers. *Computers and Composition, 10*(3), 63–89.

Teichman, M., & Poris, M. (1989). Initial effects of word processing on writing quality and writing anxiety of freshman writers. *Computers and the Humanities, 23,* 93–103.

Warschauer, M. (1997). Computer-mediated collaborative learning: Theory and practice. *Modern Language Journal, 81,* 470–481.

Warschauer, M. (1999). *Electronic literacies: Language, culture, and power in online education.* Mahwah, NJ: Lawrence Erlbaum Associates.

Williamson, M. M., & Pence, P. (1989). Word processing and student writers. In B. Britton & S. M. Glynn (Eds.), *Computer writing environments: Theory, research, and design* (pp. 93–127). Hillsdale, NJ: Lawrence Erlbaum Associates.

Windeatt, S., Hardisty, D., & Eastment, D. (2000). *The Internet.* Oxford, England: Oxford University Press.

Woodin, J. (1997). E-mail tandem learning and the communicative curriculum. *ReCALL, 9*(1), 22–33.

Teaching Second and Foreign Language Writing on LANs[1]

George Braine
The Chinese University of Hong Kong

The use of computers in writing classes has seen a rapid change within the past decade. What began with asynchronous applications, such as word processing, has developed into real-time LANs for collaborative writing. Traditional classroom interactions are usually linear; when the teacher or a student speaks, the others listen. With the introduction of LANs into writing classes, students have begun to interact freely, sharing ideas and receiving feedback from classmates and the teacher simultaneously. Teacher-centered classes have been transformed into classes where the students often dominate interactions.

INTRODUCTION

The first application of LANs in writing classes was for deaf students at Gallaudet University in Washington, D.C. In a typical classroom, a LAN consists of a number of computer terminals linked through a server. The network allows real-time conferencing, the simultaneous contribution to a discussion by all participants connected by the network. The real-time conferencing capability is especially beneficial to discussions because the

---

[1]This is a greatly revised version of a chapter published previously as "Teaching Writing on Local Area Networks" appearing in *Computers and Language Learning* (1998) published by the SEAMEO Regional Language Centre, Singapore. Used with permission.

lack of turn taking allows all participants to pick up and comment on any topic mentioned in the discussion. The simultaneity also eliminates interruptions, which means that students who want to think over and revise their ideas are no longer at a disadvantage. By permitting the teacher to quickly access the writing of all the students in a class, LANs also encourage immediate feedback. The teacher and students thus interact freely, sharing ideas, receiving feedback, and taking part in small-group discussions.

In fact, LAN classes have further advantages over traditional[2] lecture-style writing classes. Social context cues such as skin color, gender, and age, which tend to privilege some students over others during face-to-face meetings, have little effect on LAN discussions. Furthermore, students who are at a disadvantage because they are less articulate orally than in writing, take more time to verbalize their thoughts, and are reluctant to interrupt others are also not disadvantaged. LANs also eliminate the anxiety caused by accents, thereby removing a prime obstacle to free interaction in L2 and foreign language classes. Overall, because LANs minimize the negative effects of accent, skin color, gender, or age, what is written becomes more important than who wrote it. For ESL and EFL teachers who value learner-centered instruction and collaborative learning, but often face the daunting task of motivating their students to participate more actively in the learning process, LANs appear to be the ultimate solution.

HOW LAN SOFTWARE FUNCTIONS

LAN software programs are marketed under a number of brand names such as RealTime Writer, DIWE, CT Classroom, and CommonSpace. DIWE (also known as Daedalus), which in 1999 was used at more than 575 secondary and tertiary institutions in the United States and at 35 two- and four-year tertiary institutions in other countries (S. Meigs, personal communication, February 9, 1999), is used here to illustrate how LANs function in writing classes. DIWE is capable of displaying two "windows" on each computer screen (see Fig. 6.1) for private writing (the composing area) and public viewing (the transcript area). The teacher and students write in the private writing and composing areas of their computers and the writing then appears on the public viewing and transcript area on every computer screen in the classroom. The writing that appears on the public viewing window is called the main conference. Because the writing appears sequentially (see Fig. 6.2) and can be scrolled on the computer screen, the teacher and students can be in-

---

[2]Traditional here means a class in which instruction is provided mainly through a teacher-fronted lecture style, discussions are conducted orally, and students either write by hand or word process their papers.

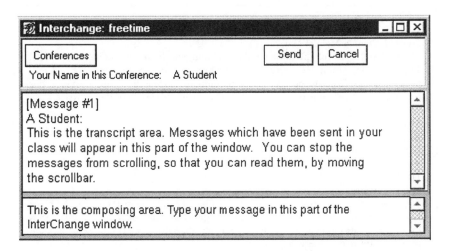

FIG. 6.1. InterChange window. This conference on InterChange is titled "freetime"; the name appears on the top left corner of the window. The student has signed on with a pseudonym, as "A Student." The transcript area and message area functions are explained in the texts that appear on the window. Used with permission of the Daedalus Group Inc.

volved in a simultaneous, real-time discussion. The software program is also capable of running subconferences, a third window that allows smaller groups of students, with or without the teacher, to hold simultaneous discussions separately from the main conference, with the option of joining the main conference at any time. In writing classes, subconferences are especially appropriate for the peer review of papers in small groups of three or four students. Thus, at any given time, the class could be involved in discussions on the main conference and a number of subconferences.

WHAT THE RESEARCH SHOWS

Although the quantity of writing generated by LANs is impressively high, the measure of the effectiveness of an expensive pedagogical tool such as LANs, especially in a non-ideological and pragmatic contexts, such as in L2 and foreign language writing classes, ought to be the enhancement of writing quality. However, according to Eldred and Hawisher (1995), no empirical study indicates that computer networks enhance writing quality. Although not explicitly stated, the research surveyed by them appears to cover writing classes for native speakers of English.

For ESL writers, at least four empirical studies have compared students' writing in LAN-based and traditional writing classes to determine which

11:39:58
Msg #51 Cheung Meimei May:
Although the writer tells his unhappy story in Cambodia, he writes it quite interestingly. The story is quite funny. However, I think the deep meaning in this paper not only tells us his story. It reflects the poor situation in Cambodia during the Communist rule. It is so sad to know that a nine year old boy always has to lie and steal in order to survive.

11:40:08
Msg #52 Judy Chan:
George, does the ILC have this film?

11:40:52
Msg #53 Ashley Ip:
The thesis is also very attractive to me because I have been living in a very peaceful place since I was born. It is very difficult for me to imagine how I can live if there is a war. And, I think this is also some experience that only few students have. Therefore I think the paper is attractive to everyone.

11:41:28
Msg #58 Cora Limleena:
"surviving in Cambodia" is an interesting paper.
First of all, the thesis statement is clearly stated in the first paragraph-"I survived through the entire four years by knowing how to lie and how to steal." This attract readers attention as we are all curious to know how and why!
Examples quoted are the writer's first hand experience and so it is more believable. However I am sorry that it is really a hard time for a nine-year-old boy to lie and to steal!

11:41:50
Msg #55 May Ho:
Although the paper 'Surviving in Cambodia' only contains four paragraphs, especially the second and third paragraphs are quite long, I feel interested to read this paper. It is because the whole paper only talks about the personal experiences of the writer. He describes it clearly and in details.
    Besides, the introduction and the conclusion are coordinated which makes the paper to be well organized.
    Actually, I really feel the conflicts of the writer. Because of survival, he needed to do many immoral things that he knew it is incorrect. Although he did many immoral things, I accept his behaviour.
    I enjoy to read this paper.

11:41:56
Msg #56 Felix Chan:
Ponh Lan's paper is kind of interesting one with implicit implication behind it. On the one hand, he indicated his acts were not ethical ones with sarcastic sense, but he also reflected about how he survived through the hardship in an adventurous way. Readers will find it fascinating in exploring the thesis of his paper.

FIG. 6.2.   Excerpt from a LAN discussion in an EFL writing class.

context is more effective in enhancing writing quality. Ghaleb (1993) compared two first-year ESL writing classes in the United States, one writing on a LAN and the other in a traditional setting. Writing quality was determined by the holistic scores awarded by three raters on a scoring guide designed by the author. The first drafts in the LAN class were of a higher quality. However, the final drafts in the LAN class showed only a mean improvement of .2, whereas papers in the traditional class showed a mean improvement of .8. Ghaleb attributed the lower improvement rate of the LAN class to the students' first drafts being closer to their maximal performance.

Sullivan and Pratt (1996) also compared two groups of student writers in Puerto Rico, one writing on a LAN and the other in a traditional setting. Again, writing quality was measured by the holistic scores of two raters on a scale designed by the authors. At the beginning of the semester, the mean score of papers in the traditional class were of a higher quality, but by the end of the semester, the mean scores decreased significantly (−.46). In the LAN class, the mean scores of papers increased by .07, which the authors attributed to the LAN.

Braine (1997) compared four first-year ESL writing classes in the United States, two writing on a LAN and the other two in a traditional class, over two academic quarters. The first and final drafts of student essays were scored holistically by three raters using the TOEFL Test of Written English (TWE) Scoring Guide, which uses a 6-point scale. The mean scores of first and final drafts in LAN classes were of a higher quality, although papers in the LAN classes improved less (.3) than papers in the traditional classes (.4).

Braine (2001) also compared EFL student writers working on a LAN with those in traditional writing classes at a Hong Kong university. The study was conducted over a three-week period during three semesters and compared the holistic scores of first drafts and final versions of students' papers using three raters and the TOEFL TWE Scoring Guide. Although first drafts in LAN classes (4.45) were qualitatively higher than the papers produced in traditional classes (4.12), the final drafts in the traditional classes were of a higher quality (4.54). Furthermore, the drafts in traditional classes showed more improvement. The overwhelming quantity of writing produced and the disjointed nature of LAN discussions were seen as obstacles to the enhancement of EFL students' writing on LANs. (See Table 6.1 for a comparison of these studies.)

As for the effectiveness of LANs in the enhancement of writing quality, the results of these studies are at best inconclusive. In Ghaleb (1993) and Braine (2001), final drafts in traditional writing classes were of a higher quality than final drafts in LAN classes. In Braine (1997), final drafts in LAN classes were of a higher quality. In Ghaleb (1993) and Braine (1997, 2001), papers in traditional classes showed more improvement from first

TABLE 6.1
Changes in Writing Quality Measured by Holistic Scores

	LAN Classes		Traditional Classes	
	Draft 1	Draft 2	Draft 1	Draft 2
Ghaleb (1993)	3.4	3.6 (+.2)	3.1	3.9 (+.8)
Sullivan & Pratt (1996)	3.19	3.26 (+.07)	3.41	2.95 (−.46)
Braine (1997)	5.3	5.6 (+.3)	4.8	5.2 (+.4)
Braine (2001)	4.25	4.45 (+.2)	4.12	4.54 (+.42)

Note. In Ghaleb (1993) and Braine (1997, 2001), papers were scored on a 6-point scale. In Sullivan and Pratt (1996), papers were scored on a 5-point scale.

draft to final version. In Sullivan and Pratt (1996), the opposite was observed: Papers written in the traditional class actually declined in quality whereas papers in the LAN class improved; nevertheless, the first drafts in the traditional class were of a higher quality than both first and final drafts in the LAN class. Furthermore, even the final drafts in the LAN class were of a lower quality than the first drafts in the traditional class, thereby bringing into question Sullivan and Pratt's claim that use of the LAN was responsible for the improvement in writing quality.

Would prolonged use of LANs ensure enhancement in writing? In the case of most ESL and EFL writers, their use of LANs may be limited to required writing courses offered by English departments or intensive ESL or EFL programs. At one American university, despite my repeated invitations to teachers from other disciplines—especially to those who taught writing-intensive writing across the curriculum (WAC) courses—not one agreed to teach on LANs.

ADVANTAGES OF USING LANS IN WRITING CLASSES

Figure 6.2 is an excerpt from a LAN discussion as it appeared in the public viewing window. The discussion was conducted by students enrolled in an EFL writing class at The Chinese University of Hong Kong. Fourteen students, four male and ten female, all Cantonese L1 speakers, participated in this discussion, their first meeting on the LAN. The total meeting time was 105 minutes, and the 14 students contributed 99 messages during this period. The female students sent 52 messages and the males sent 25. The balance 22 messages were from the teacher, which included six instructions, 12 responses to student comments, three explanations, and one prompting. The most number of messages sent by a female and male student was right, and the least was one. All LAN interactions are quoted verbatim.

This excerpt, obtained midway through the discussion of a paper titled "Surviving in Cambodia" from the class text, illustrates a number of features of the DIWE program. Because each student signs onto the program from his or her computer terminal, every message carries the student's name at the beginning. Thus, six students, four females and two males, have participated in this segment of the discussion. Cheung May's contribution, which appears at the beginning of the segment, is actually the fifty-first message sent to the discussion.

As can be seen from the transcript, Cheung May's message was sent at 11:39 a.m. and Felix Chan's at 11:41 a.m. Within two minutes, six students writing simultaneously had contributed more than 375 words to the discourse. Except for Judy Chan's question directed at the teacher, the other messages are fairly long and thoughtful, especially in the context of their spontaneity.

The great number of student contributions is a common feature of LAN discussions in L2 and foreign language writing classes, and has been documented repeatedly. As Fig. 6.3 indicates, a number of studies (Braine, 1997, 2001; Ghaleb, 1993; Markley, 1992; Sullivan, 1993) have shown that students' contributions over the LAN, as measured by a word count, is unusually high for ESL and EFL classes. In fact, in Braine's (2001) study, where students were focused on an intensive writing activity (peer reviews in small groups), they averaged 480 words in a 100-minute period, an extremely high output under any circumstance. In contrast, Ghaleb (1993) noted that

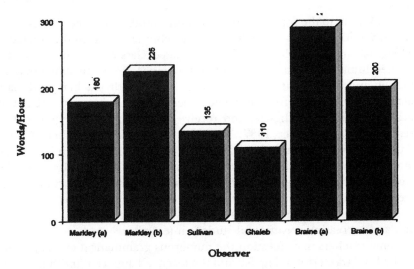

FIG. 6.3. Quantity of writing per student in LAN classes. The word count has been prorated to 60 minutes for comparison. The duration of these classes ranged from 40 to 100 minutes. Braine (a) refers to the 1997 study; Braine (b) refers to the 2001 study.

students in a traditional writing class wrote an average of only four words per 50-minute class meeting. Research indicates that the only way to learn writing is by writing, and that quantity often equals quality in writing development (see Horning, 1987; Shaughnessy, 1977). In LAN writing classes, most discussions, analyses of student papers, and feedback on in-class writing occur on the LAN. Instead of the teacher lecturing about writing, the students actually write, prolifically.

But prolific writing alone is not the objective of writing instruction. Writing as thinking is also a fundamental aspect of the process approach, and transcripts of LAN peer reviews show numerous examples of insightful comments and suggestions. A brief analysis of the transcript in Fig. 6.4 is relevant here. Three students—Joan Yip, Natalie Li, and Sharon Chow—are conducting a peer review for the first student. Joan Yip, when commenting on Sharon Chow's paper, not only suggests the need for clarification but also points out some references that Sharon could use. Natalie Li, when offering suggestions to Chow, tactfully says that "some parts of the paper" are somewhat confusing because Chow does not differentiate between the four types of elderly care services. She also points out that the topic (the title?) does not match the contents of the paper. Furthermore, she provides explicit instructions on how the paper's conclusion could be improved. Natalie Li, when providing feedback to Joan Yip, first compliments the writer and then points out the numerous grammatical errors in Yip's paper. Yip, in response, explicitly seeks the help of her classmates in improving her paper.

In addition to the high quantity of writing, another notable feature in an L2 LAN writing class is the reduction of teacher talk. The studies included in Fig. 6.3 indicated that students dominated class discussions in all the studies, initiating at least 75% of the interactions. Research shows that authentic and appropriate classroom interactions with teachers and classmates provide L2 and foreign language learners with the most opportunities to practice, hypothesize, and receive advice on their language skills (e.g., see Ellis, 1984; Pica, 1987). However, 65% to 75% of the speech in traditional foreign language classes is attributed to teachers, who initiate most interactions through direct questions and matters relating to classroom discipline and management, thereby giving students fewer opportunities for meaningful interaction (Chaudron, 1988; Nunan, 1989). Thus, the use of LANs may be one of the most effective ways of reducing dominant teacher talk and increasing meaningful student interaction.

Some teachers may question the numerous grammatical errors present in the LAN transcript in Fig. 6.2 and the teacher's apparent indifference to these errors. The grammatical errors may at least partly due to the students' attempts to contribute quickly to a fast-paced, rapidly growing discussion. The teacher's apparent indifference may be explained through research

1:12:50
Msg #2 Joan Yip:
Comments on Sharon's paper: Besides old people's home: the general picture of elderly care in Hong Kong
1. I enjoy this paper as it has a clear organization and precise ideas.
2. Before I analyze your paper, I want to express my opinion on the improvements of this paper. I consider you can distinguish the content of which service is considered as residential care and other is community support services. Are they regarded as one thing which is told in the paper. I think you would clarify this subject first. (Then, I suggest you can look the White Paper on Social Welfare' Services in 86' and 91' to give more statistic figure as the evidence. I think they will help much more.) Besides, I think it may useful for the readers to have the definitions of residential care and community support services. What is the main difference between them?)
. . .

1:13:32
Msg #3 Natalie Li:
Besides old people's home:
I enjoy reading some parts of the papers. I think Sharon has done a good job in collecting relevant information for writing this paper. However, I find some parts of the paper to be a bit confusing because Sharon does not explain clearly about the differences between the four types of elderly care services. On the whole, I think the paper is well-organized as Sharon has used clear thesis statement and topic sentences to guide the readers to read through the whole article. Nevertheless, I feel a little bit disappointed when I try to compare the topic with the content of this paper. From reading the topic, I expect that I would have better ideas about the different aspects of elderly services in Hong Kong. But it turns out that Sharon has only introduced four types of services. It seems to me that some other important and relevant information like the prices and criteria for application are missing. Concerning the introduction of this paper, I think it is quite effective because Sharon has used some figures to arouse the interest of the readers. However, I think the conclusion is not as good as the introduction because some of the sentences are not well written. For example, the second last sentence of the conclusion is not completed. Thus, Sharon needs to revise the conclusion carefully because both introduction and conclusion are important in giving the readers the general impression of the paper! One very last question. Sharon, what do you mean by "non-acute elderly impaired persons" in the 5th paragraph?
. . .

1:39:04
Msg #5 Joan Yip:
Comments on Natalie's paper: The Gender Choice Centre: Parents can decide
1. I enjoy this paper as it is not an interesting topic to write the paper.
3. the introduction is effective esp. the first sentence can arise the attention or interest of the readers but the thesis statement is not clearly stated in this paper.
7. Natalie can make the appropriate definition of the technical
terms e.g. " insemination technique". However, except the clear definition of some technical terms, you can add analogy to make the factual content more interesting.
10. the conclusion is clear, precise and effective. It can conclude the main ideas of the paper.
12. I think you would add the some transitional sentences between the 3rd and 4the paragraph because it can make the structure of the paper more systematic.
. . .

FIG. 6.4. *(Continued)*

1:43:04
Msg #7 Natalie Li: Nostalgia Restaurants in Hong Kong: Reinventing the Past, I enjoy reading this paper. I think Joan is successful in giving the readers a clear picture about the settings and concept of reinventing the past for the new "Dai Pai Dong". You know what, I really want to go to the new "Dai-Pai Dong" to have a nice lunch today after reading your paper! . . . However, there are still some places that need to be improved. First, I think the whole paper should be revised carefully because there are some grammatical mistakes. Also, I think Joan can explain more clearly about how the new Dai Pai Dong reinventing the beverages sold there.

1:44:08
Msg #8 Joan Yip:
Response to Sharon's comments
Actually, I know the introduction of my paper is too long, it is difficult for me to cut off the points in the 1st para. Everything in the 1st para. seems to me is very important, I do not know how to cut off some informations in the 1st para. Can you or Natalie give me some suggestions?

Besides, I agree the Sharon's comments on the word, "Nostalgia". Yes, I take it for granted that the readers will its meanings but I am wrong. Thank you for your comments! I will improve it.

FIG. 6.4.   LAN discussion showing examples of insightful comments and suggestions.

findings and anecdotal reports that suggest that grammar-based approaches do little to improve writing ability (see Keim, 1989; Lauer, 1980; Reber, 1967), and consequently grammar should not be the focus of L2 and foreign language writing classes (Raimes, 1991; Zamel, 1985). In fact, some reports (e.g., Perl, 1979; Reber, 1967) have even described the adverse effects of using grammar-based approaches in writing classes.

A significant difference between L2 classes, such as ESL classes in the United States, and foreign language classes, such as EFL classes overseas, is that the former consist of students speaking a variety of L1s. For instance, students speaking 10 languages, from Icelandic to Urdu, were enrolled in the classes considered for Braine's (1997) study. When speakers of such diverse languages are brought together, they are compelled to converse in the target language. On the other hand, foreign language classes are mainly monolingual, the students usually being speakers of a local language that they often use to converse with each other, even during English classes. Hence, when LANs are used for interaction in foreign language classes, the use of the students' L1 is minimized.

Language teachers have long recognized errors as a natural part of the learning process. According to some researchers (Dulay & Burt, 1974; Horning, 1987; Krashen, 1982), a learner acquires a language in a preset sequence, irrespective of the rules that are imposed or taught. When the learner is ready to perceive the rule, errors will be self-corrected. Thus, errors are a natural part of the language-learning process and indicate the stage the learner has reached in that process. Frequent error correction could therefore have a negative effect, especially among beginning writers, and may prevent the writer from saying anything at all (Perl, 1979; Rose, 1980; Shaughnessy, 1977). When allowed to participate without being stifled by rules, students are free to think and express their ideas through writing.

FOR THE TEACHER

Like all software programs, LAN applications are not suitable for all contexts. The success of the software depends on a number of factors, such as the students' familiarity with word processing, their level of proficiency in the target language, the teacher's attitude to collaborative learning, the teacher's beliefs on the role of grammar in writing instruction, and the classroom activity in which the application is used.

LANs are not the exclusive property of writing classes. In fact, they are more common in business, laboratory, and industrial settings, where personnel within one organization at a single location need to be connected electronically for the sharing of information. Although the sharing of computer files at such locations demand some expertise in LAN management, DIWE and other software programs have simplified the process for students and teachers so that writing classes can be managed with no expertise in computers and without the confusion and frustration that LANs can cause. However, a basic knowledge of typing or word processing is a prerequisite to the successful operation of LANs in writing classes. Students with faster typing or word processing skills are likely to overwhelm others in LAN discussions.

The students' proficiency in the target language is another crucial factor for the successful operation of LANs. Although not designed with ESL and EFL students in mind, LANs have been successfully used in ESL classes with heterogeneous L1 speakers in the United States as well as in EFL classes with homogeneous L1 speakers in Puerto Rico, Taiwan, Japan, and Hong Kong. Nevertheless, beginning writing classes, where a low proficiency in the target language limits the students' ability to write more than basic sentences, would severely limit the prolific writing that LANs usually generate.

The participants' attitude to collaborative learning is another important requirement for the success of LANs in writing classes. Some teachers, long accustomed to complete domination of their classes, are afraid of "losing control" in student-centered contexts. Such attitudes would only constrain student participation and inhibit the full utilization of LAN potential. Despite years of proven success, some L2 and foreign language writing teachers still regard the process approach to writing with some suspicion. For instance, they equate peer reviews of students' papers and collaborative writing with plagiarism. Papers written on LANs are often read by many students in the class, which should be seen in a positive light because it brings student writing closer to real-world readership. Although not all students are keen to collaborate, teachers with the correct attitude can foster collaboration in place of individualism in their classes.

As mentioned earlier, grammar instruction and error correction do not appear to enhance L2 writing instruction. To exploit the advantages of LANs to the fullest, students must be allowed to express their ideas freely, without the constraints of grammar rules. The smooth flow of student writing shown in Fig. 6.2 may have been slowed if they had been instructed to ensure grammatical accuracy their writing. Although grammar plays a vital role in the acquisition of a language, grammatical accuracy could be postponed to the final drafts of student papers. If not, the discussion on a LAN could be as slow and stilted as in most face-to-face discussions, caused by the students' fear of making mistakes and the self-consciousness created by accents.

Perhaps the most critical factor in the use of LANs in writing classes is the activity for which LANs are used. This is best illustrated by Fig. 6.2, which shows that just five students wrote nearly 400 words within 2 minutes on a LAN discussion. The total amount of writing generated by an entire class could be staggering and simply overwhelm the discussion in a sea of words. When a discussion gets lively, new messages are added so rapidly that many students are unable to keep up with the discussion, creating a confusing, disjointed discourse that nullifies the collaborative nature of LANs.

This phenomenon is best illustrated in Fig. 6.5, which is another excerpt from the LAN discussion described in Fig. 6.2. The discussion is now coming to end and the teacher has asked the students to indicate their research paper topics. Although in Message 88 Cora Limleena has indicated that she is leaving the discussion, Message 89 from Cheung May is directed at Cora; each message was written simultaneously, without an awareness of the other's contents. Message 91 from Ng Lei-Ling is a commentary on a paper discussed before "Surviving in Cambodia" was discussed and is therefore out of context. Message 92 from Shirley Yau indicates her inability to keep up with the discussion; she assumes that the computer is malfunctioning, although her confusion may be caused by incoming messages flooding the computer screen. In Message 93, Judy Chan responds to a questions posed earlier (in Message 76) by the teacher on "battered husbands." Hence, Chan's message at this stage would make little sense to the other students. Message 96 from Tang Kwokkuen on "Surviving in Cambodia" adds further confusion and indicates the extent to which he is lagging in the discussion.

12:01.02
Msg #88 Cora Limleena:
Bye everybody! See you all next time!

12:01.24
Msg #89 Cheung Meimei May:
Cora Limleena, we are lucky to live in Hong Kong. Therefore, we don't immigrate to other Asian countries as we cannot enjoy our women's rights.

12:02.04
Msg #90 Chong Ka-Yan:
I have chosen quite a different topic from the others. It's about multilevel marketing.

12:02.08
Msg #91 Ng Lei-Ling:
In my opinion, when the writer want to cite some examples or personal experiences, he had better present it clearly or give preparation for the readers to change their minds from the present situation in Russia.
Actually the data or information provided in this passage is quite abundant and valuable. But it seems that it can't concentrate on the core subject.

Msg #92 Shirley Yau:
Sorry, I can't receive your message.! I knew you had sent messages to other students! Are there any problems in my computer? James has the same problem too!

12:02.46
Msg #93 Judy Chan:
George, I think the problem is not serious in HK, but it is now of more concern because the media is interested in this topic. you know how powerful media is. I'm not sure about the exact situation, maybe battered husbands feel shameful and made no report. But I think it is far less a serious than battered wives.

12:02.50
Msg #94 Jessie Leung:
The paper indicates the author has a profound knowledge over nuclear issues inside the country and its impact across borders. Actually, this paper is more difficult to read than the serious since there are more professional terms and vocabulary. Instead of writing
. . .

12:03.00
Msg #95 May Ho:
It is a enjoyable experience top have a lesson in the computer writing lab. I hope we can have another chance.

12:03.04
Msg #96 Tang Kwokkuen:
This time comes to the passage "Surviving in Cambodia" . It seems to me that the author stressed on the idea that lying and stealing are the keys to survival . . .

FIG. 6.5. Excerpt of a noncohesive LAN discussion in an EFL writing class.

Thus, LANs are more effective in small-group discussions, such as peer reviews of student papers, rather than in large classes. Using the sub-conference capability of DIWE, for instance, a number of discussions can be run simultaneously, each discussion limited to three or four students in the group. Although more intense, such discussions would also be more cohesive.

CONCLUSION

When L2 students write in the target language, they have to think about the contents in an active manner instead of passive memorizing and textbook underlining. Active thinking requires the understanding of concepts, the analysis of information, the evaluation of evidence, and the construction and testing of hypothesis. These are higher level intellectual skills, and to develop these skills, language students must write. LANs are probably the ideal medium to promote writing because they provide a supportive, anxiety-free, motivating environment; sufficient exposure to examples of the target language that are varied, comprehensible, and have "real" communicative value; and practice in using the target language in real communicative situations.

REFERENCES

Braine, G. (1997). Beyond word processing: Networked computers in ESL writing classes. *Computers and Composition, 14*, 45–58.

Braine, G. (2001). A study of English as a foreign language (EFL) writers on a local-area network (LAN) and in traditional classes. *Computers and Composition, 18*, 275–292.

Chaudron, C. (1988). *Second language classrooms: Research on teaching and learning.* Cambridge, England: Cambridge University Press.

Dulay, H., & Burt, M. (1974). Errors and strategies in child second language acquisition. *TESOL Quarterly, 8*, 129–136.

Eldred, J., & Hawisher, G. (1995). Researching electronic networks. *Written Communication, 12*, 330–359.

Ellis, R. (1984). *Classroom second language development.* Elmsford, NY: Pergamon Press.

Ghaleb, M. (1993). *Computer networking in a university freshman ESL writing class: A descriptive study of the quantity and quality of writing in networking and traditional writing classes.* Unpublished doctoral dissertation, The University of Texas at Austin.

Horning, A. (1987). *Teaching writing as a second language.* Carbondale: Southern Illinois University Press.

Keim, W. (1989). The writing-grammar battle: Adventures of a teacher/administrator. *English Journal, 78*, 66–70.

Krashen, S. (1982). *Principles and practice in second language acquisition.* Oxford, England: Pergamon Press.

Lauer, J. (1980). The rhetorical approach: Stages of writing and strategies for writers. In T. R. Donovan & B. W. McClelland (Eds.), *Eight approaches to teaching composition* (pp. 53–64). Urbana, IL: National Council of Teachers of English.

Markley, P. (1992). Creating independent ESL writers & thinkers: Computer networking for composition. *CAELL Journal, 3,* 6–12.

Nunan, D. (1989). *Understanding language classrooms.* London: Prentice Hall.

Perl, S. (1979). The composing process of unskilled college writers. *Research in the Teaching of English, 13,* 317–336.

Pica, T. (1987). Second language acquisition, social interaction, and the classroom. *Applied Linguistics, 8,* 3–21.

Raimes, A. (1991). Out of the woods: Emerging traditions in the teaching of writing. *TESOL Quarterly, 19,* 220–258.

Reber, A. S. (1967). Implicit learning of artificial grammars. *Journal of Verbal Learning and Verbal Behaviour, 6,* 855–863.

Rose, M. (1980). Rigid rules, inflexible plans, and the stifling of language: A cognitivist analysis of writer's block. *College Composition and Communication, 31,* 389–401.

Shaughnessy, M. (1977). *Errors and expectations.* New York: Oxford University Press.

Sullivan, N. (1993). Teaching writing on a computer network. *TESOL Journal, 3,* 34–35.

Sullivan, N., & Pratt, E. (1996). A comparative study of two ESL writing environments: A computer-assisted classroom and a traditional oral classroom. *System, 29,* 491–501.

Zamel, V. (1985). Responding to student writing. *TESOL Quarterly, 19,* 79–101.

7

Writing as Talking: E-Mail Exchange for Promoting Proficiency and Motivation in the Foreign Language Classroom

Sandra Fotos
Senshu University

Linked to the development of telecommunications and the availability of personal computers for home and office, a new form of discourse has emerged, Computer-Mediated Communication (CMC). Defined as any type of human-to-human communication mediated by a computer (Murray, 2000, p. 398), the different forms of CMC have been characterized by their immediacy (Warschauer, 1995a), with the most immediate being synchronous communication, such as real-time video conferencing and online chatting using Internet Relay Chat (IRC), chat rooms, MOOs (Multiple-user-domain-Object-Oriented), or LANs (Local Area Networks; see Braine, chap. 6, this volume), where people are reading and writing at the same time. Delayed-time or asynchronous forms are read after they are written and include e-mail, electronic bulletin boards, postings to e-mail lists, and the World Wide Web.

Because of the various functions performed by CMC, there is no single well-defined rhetorical structure (Crystal, 1995, 2001; Murray, 1995, 2000). However, one type of CMC, e-mail, is suggested to possess stable discourse features (Moran & Hawisher, 1998), particularly when used for personal correspondence, chatting, or participation in discussion groups. E-mail is certainly written language—it is input from a computer keyboard and read off the screen of the recipient—yet numerous studies have established that e-mail discourse has features that combine both the spoken and written mode of communication (Crystal, 2001; Heim, 1987; Kern, 1996; McIntyre & Wolff, 1998; Murray, 1995, 2000; Warschauer, 1996a, 1999). In fact, one researcher (Baron, 2000, p. 257) suggests that it resembles contact languages such as creoles or pidgins since it emerged abruptly in the mid-1990s, came from new social circumstances (computer technology), has bilingual users (people who use both speech and writing), has a constantly widening range of users and uses, and is still evolving. However, in his recent analysis of the language of the Internet, Crystal (2001) proposes that e-mail is a "third medium," distinct from speech or writing, and is characterized by the evolution of new roles to suit its requirements. Referring to CMC as "netspeak," he reminds us to, "remember that 'speak' here involves writing as well as talking, and that any 'speak' suffix also has a receptive element, including 'listening and reading' " (2001, pp. 17–18).

Warschauer (1999) also argues that e-mail is a truly unique form of communication since interaction is text-based but can be nearly as rapid as spoken language, and can take place between two people, from one person to many people, or from many people to many people independently of time and place (p. 5). Thus, for the first time in history, speech-like communication occurs through text that can be transmitted and stored. E-mail and hypertext are promoting new forms of literacy and communication at the global level and can be expected to have a significant cognitive impact, functioning as an "intellectual amplifier" (Shetzer & Warschauer, 2000, p. 173).

This chapter discusses discourse as meaning creation, presents differences between speech and writing in relation to e-mail discourse, reviews research on e-mail as an important communicative activity for the L2 classroom, and describes an e-mail exchange project between Japanese university EFL students and American university student keypals. It is suggested that the exchange promoted significant English proficiency gains, gave the EFL students increased motivation to study English, and provided a way for them to use the target language for authentic communication—very difficult to achieve in the foreign language situation. Teacher guidelines for setting up and evaluating an e-mail exchange project are also presented.

DISCOURSE AS THE CREATION OF MEANING

Several decades years ago educational psychologist Jerome Bruner (1973; also 1990) established that communication is an essential prerequisite for the development of knowledge and understanding. This view has dominated general educational pedagogy since its articulation and has given rise to the powerful cooperative/collaborative learning paradigm where students work in groups to complete interactive learning tasks. Cooperative learning has restructured the classroom from a traditional teacher-centered format, with its unidirectional knowledge flow, to a group participation pattern allowing learners to interact with each other. Implicit in the collaborative learning paradigm is the view of knowledge as a continuing and dynamic process rather than a fixed product, and one of the most influential arguments for the socially constructed nature of knowledge is the sociocultural theory of Vygotsky (Wertsch, 1985).

Vygotsky (1896–1934), a Russian psychologist who investigated mental development in children, suggested that to develop cognitively, children must construct meaning interactively through discourse from their earliest years. From the interactionist perspective, social interaction is seen as essential for cognition and the creation of meaning throughout the individual's life.

This chapter suggests that e-mail provides opportunities for such collaborative, meaning-based discourse to occur regardless of the distance of the interlocutor. A particular feature of e-mail, the scaffolding effect provided by the embedded text that the writer is replying to, is suggested to be especially significant in enabling the creation of new knowledge in the Vygotskian sense, including increased knowledge of the target language.

WRITING VERSUS SPEECH

Because e-mail has been suggested to have features of both speech and writing (Crystal, 2001; Murray, 1995, 2000), it is useful to consider the two forms of communication. There have been many studies on the differences between speech and writing (e.g., Brown & Yule, 1984, Crystal, 1995; Halliday, 1985; Murray, 1995; Nunan, 1993, Tannen, 1982), and writing has been found to be mainly transactional because it conveys information. Although transactional forms of speech exist, such as formal presentations, speech is also interactional, or speaker oriented, and is often used to establish and maintain social relationships. Such speech is frequently characterized by a casual register[1] and short turns during the con-

---

[1]Register (in this case referring to language variety rather than voice quality) is an important concept for language learners. Defined as "the linguistic features of the text that reflect the social context in which it is produced" (McCarthy, 1991, p. 32), the type of register indicates the choice of lexicon and other linguistic and paralinguistic features. A classic example is "motherese" or "caretaker speech," the simplified, redundant language that people use to

versation as compared with formal speech, where a single speaker may talk uninterruptedly for many minutes. However, the difference between speech and writing is not perceived as bimodal but is represented as an oral-literate continuum, with casual speech at one end and formal academic written discourse at the other. Speech and writing thus merge and may share features depending on the genre and speech function (Murray, 1995; Tannen, 1982).

A number of specific differences between these two forms of communication have been described, and the following discussion is based on the work of Brown and Yule (1994), Crystal (1995), and Murray (1995):

1. Speech has simplified grammar and vocabulary. The grammar of the spoken sentence is less structured than writing. There are often no embedded clauses and, if regular sentence grammar exists, it is often limited to declarative sentences. However, many spoken utterances are not complete sentences; subjects, verbs, pronouns, and other elements are often omitted.

Speech vocabulary also tends to be simplified and often refers to previous topics or shared information. Consequently, speech is characterized by vague terms, ellipsis and anaphora; for example, "a lot of," "things," "they," and "it." Specialized terms are often used and, unless the speakers share the same background knowledge, they do know what these terms mean. In fact, the role of specialized interactive speech in establishing and maintaining discourse communities has been widely demonstrated (see references in Brown & Yule, 1994).

2. Speech has shorter turns. Whereas written language generally consists of unbroken discourse, speakers usually take turns speaking. Turns may be quite short or may even overlap, and listeners often nod or give other forms of feedback to indicate understanding. When they do not understand or have questions, they often interrupt the speaker and request clarification. This has been called "negotiation of meaning" and is seen as important in the L2 acquisition process (see Chapelle, 2001; Fotos, 2001).

Written language usually builds coherence by use of connecting forms such as "nonetheless," "however," or "therefore" that show the relationships between parts of the discourse. However, casual speech lacks such formal

---

babies. Another example of register is the use of different levels of politeness in speech according to the situation, the topic, and the interlocutor. Ignorance of when it is socially appropriate to use these difference levels operates against the full development of pragmatic competence in foreign language learners, most of whom have few opportunities for authentic use of the target language.

discourse markers; the relationship between current and past speech is usually established by the context of the talk or by casual discourse markers such as "well" or "uh."

3. Speech is accompanied by paralinguistic information. Speech is often accompanied nonverbal or paralinguistic cues such as body language, gestures, and facial expressions that convey meaning.

4. Speech has repetition and redundancy. Repetition and redundancy help the listener process what is being said by repeating information and by supplying breaks in the propositional content.

5. Speech uses multiple registers, sometimes within the same discourse. A variety of registers (see note 1) are used according to the social context, the topic and interlocutors. For example, "women's register" (Tannen, 1994) is characterized by more tag questions, rising intonation and plural pronouns than standard speech. Thus, the register of spoken language is variable. However, written language is usually in standard form and cannot be adjusted according to the situation, the topic, or the reader.

Such differences between speech and writing are significant for L2 instruction. For example, it has been observed that the standard grammar of English—and therefore the type of English generally taught in ESL and EFL classes—is based on the structure of written English, not on the structure of speech even though the two forms are quite different (Nunan, 1993). Consequently, the development of materials and their use in communicative language classrooms are oriented towards the written form of the language, and the provision of authentic speech-like material is difficult because many commercial textbooks and CD-ROM materials use conventions of written English, even for dialogues. The same consideration applies to instructional material used for other language teaching situations as well; provision of actual speech-like discourse is rare.

E-MAIL DISCOURSE: SPEECH, WRITING AND MORE

Considering these differences, it is understandable that researchers have suggested that e-mail is a new discourse genre. It is different from both speech in written form and writing, although it often has characteristics of both, as well as other features suggested to be unique. (Baron, 2000; Crystal, 2001; Heim, 1987; Maynor, 1994; Moran & Hawisher, 1998; Murray, 1995, 2000; Warschauer, 1999). The time constraints of composing online and the frequent need for a quick reply are seen as reasons for this combination of features.

Characteristics of E-mail

Murray's (1995) research suggests that e-mail generally uses a simplified speech-like register and simple vocabulary even when complicated topics are being discussed. There is frequent use of anaphora and contractions, and greetings or closings are often omitted. In terms of grammar, sentences may be quite speechlike, and subjects and verb parts are sometimes omitted. There are frequently spelling and grammar errors in people's messages because of time constraints and the fact that not all e-mail software has spell-check functions (Yates, 1996).

Abbreviations and acronyms (BTW = by the way; IMO = in my opinion) are common (see Crystal, 2001, p. 85, for a list), spelling is often simplified (please = pls; thanks = tnx; F2F = face-to-face), and there are even ways of supplying paralinguistic information to provide clues to the emotional state of the speaker. Little figures called emoticons are constructed from keyboard characters and, when viewed by tilting the head to the left, show winks [;-)], smiles [:-)] or frowns/sadness [:-<] (see Crystal, 2001, p. 37, for a list). Asterisks stress important information or indicate italics, and rising question intonation is shown by multiple vowels ("sooo?"). Capital letters express emphasis or shouting, and multiple question marks or exclamation marks also show emphasis and the emotional condition of the writer. Note-taking symbols are common, such as the ampersand and plus or minus signs (for more discussion, see Murray, 1995).

However, despite the apparent simplicity of e-mail text, the level of literacy needed to decode it is quite high (Crystal, 2001; Maynor, 1994; Murray, 1995, 2000). In e-mail, simplicity does not indicate low levels of language proficiency but is rather a feature of the genre.

Creation of Meaning Through the Scaffolding Effect of Embedded Text

A particularly interesting feature of e-mail discourse is the use of embedded text. When replying to an e-mail message, most people use the reply function of their e-mail software. This leaves in the original message, preceded by angle brackets, lines or other symbols to the left side of each line, depending on the software used, permitting writers to retain the part of the original text to which they are replying, inserting their own comments above or underneath the original text. The original text is thus embedded in the reply, and it is common to have multiple embedding as people reply to replies.

Discourse analysis in developmental psychology and L2 acquisition research has identified an important phenomenon for the collaborative creation of meaning during social interaction. This is scaffolding, a term indicating that people supply part of an utterance for their interlocutors, who then use it to build their own utterances. In SLA theory, scaffolding is considered to be an important process where learners can expand their own knowledge by modeling grammar structures or borrowing forms from the previous utterance, thereby extending their linguistic development (Appel & Lantolf, 1994; Mercer & Fisher,1997; Tannen, 1993; Trenches, 1996; Warshauer, 1995a). In e-mail, the retention of the original text allows writers to use it as a scaffold for constructing meaning. The original message thus becomes part of a dialogue to which the writer reacts.

Example 7.1 below shows student use of the teacher-provided L2 title in several places and Example 7.2 depicts expansion of a provided L2 scaffold.

Example 7.1: Scaffolding on a subject title provided by the teacher:

Subject: Re: <u>Your summer vacation plans</u>

<u>My summer plans</u> is that I will travel Europe with my friends from 3 September to 10 September. We have <u>planed</u> about this travel for a year. So we are looking forward to <u>summer vacation</u>.

Example 7.2: Learner extension of the L2 from a scaffold. The provided subject has been deleted and a new subject title has been constructed by the student:

Subject: <u>Great my summer vacation !!!</u>

How was your <u>summer vacation</u> ? <u>My summer vacation was great !!!!!</u> I want to tell you one of my <u>great</u> experiences which I got in <u>summer vacation</u>.

The speed of e-mail and its speech-like features can enable the creation of meaning—previously restricted to speech—to occur in written language. It may also be that the scaffolding provided by embedded e-mail text serves a significant function in extending both cognition and language profi-

ciency for L2 learners and this possibility is explored in the following discussion.

USING E-MAIL IN THE LANGUAGE CLASSROOM

E-mail is considered an important form of CALL, and a number of teacher
guides on its use by itself or as part of an Internet-based CALL curriculum
have been published recently (see Boswell, 1997; Hanson-Smith, 2000;
Teeler & Gray, 2000, Warschauer, 1995a, 1995b, 1995c; Warschauer, Shetzer, & Meloni, 2000). One book in this area, Warschauer's *E-mail for English
Teaching* (1995b), stresses the role of e-mail exchange for developing linguistic proficiency, cultural knowledge, and communicative competence in
L2 learners.

Theoretical support for this positive view of e-mail comes from the
interactionist perspective discussed previously. Here, language is viewed as
a tool for learning, a way of constructing knowledge collaboratively
through a "text-mediational" view treating text as a "thinking device" for
the generation of new meaning (Warschauer, 1995a, pp. 4-5). The features
of e-mail such as embedded text, the use of simple grammar, and non-
attention to surface errors, together with the speed of e-mail exchange, can
lend themselves not only to meaning-focused language use by L2 learners
but to the development of cognition itself.

Results from studies made as early as the 1980s on the use of e-mail in
English composition classrooms (see reviews in Kern, 1996; Warschauer,
1995a; and Shetzer & Warschauer, 2000; also see Pennington, chap. 5, this
volume) indicate that e-mail exchanges not only enabled L2 students to
control their own learning and interaction but also to spend more time on
the learning task and become better writers because they had an authentic audience and a communicative purpose for writing. E-mail exchange
facilitated the establishment of classroom communities, and many L2 researchers note that shy learners, who rarely spoke in face-to-face situations, actively participated in e-mail exchanges with their teachers and
other students (see Braine, chap. 6, this volume; Markley, 1998).

A survey of ESL learner attitudes toward CMC reported similar findings
(Warschauer, 1996, p. 36). Participation in e-mail projects helped the students develop their thoughts and ideas, enabled them to learn about different cultures and helped them to improve their English proficiency, giving them feelings of accomplishment and enjoyment. These positive
results also produced enhanced motivation to study the target language
(Hanson-Smith, 2000; Kern, 1996; Ushioda, 2000). Additional studies

have noted improved accuracy produced by L2 students' linguistic adjustments to the rhetorical style of keypals from various cultures (see Davis & Thiede, 2000).

Researchers also suggest that e-mail exchange encourages students to recognize that the L2 is more than just a focus for study but is actually a powerful medium for communication. (Beauvois, 1998; Gu & Zhe, 1999; Shetzer & Warschauer, 2000; Warschauer, 2003). Recent statistics showing that e-mail is becoming more important for global communication than the phone, fax, or direct conversation demonstrate that the ability to use e-mail successfully is now a necessary communication skill. This raises the important consideration that L2 teachers "must not only use e-mail to promote English teaching, but also teach English to help people learn to communicate effectively by e-mail" (Warschauer, 2002, p. 455).

Such findings have led to the creation of a number of Web sites where L2 students can find keypals (a new form of penpals because a keyboard is used for correspondence rather than a pen) for e-mail exchanges, explore links to language learning activities, and access information on study-abroad programs.

AN E-MAIL EXCHANGE PROGRAM IN THE FOREIGN LANGUAGE SETTING

The following section presents the favorable results obtained from an e-mail exchange project conducted between Japanese university EFL students and American university students working at the University of Oregon's American English Institute (AEI), a training center for ESL students. The project took the form of 2 one-semester elective EFL classes for developing computer skills and participating in an e-mail exchange using the target language. The foreign language students volunteered for the classes, took proficiency tests at the beginning and end of the semester, and completed a questionnaire about the class. The second semester group also completed a motivation questionnaire.

Establishing Goals

Before beginning the project, a number of goals were identified. The first was to improve the students' fluency and accuracy in reading and writing English. A specific writing skill targeted was contrastive and comparative writing. An additional goal was to increase the students' confidence in using English for authentic communication and to develop pragmatic competence in various communicative acts such as greetings, closings, describing things, giving opinions, and asking questions, and agreeing or disagreeing. It was believed that the speech-like nature of e-mail would promote the students' skills in these areas.

A more technical goal was to develop the students' expertise in the functions of e-mail such as reading messages in English, composing original messages and replies and sending e-mail. An additional goal was the development of skill in using browser software for accessing English Web sites, and for participating in group conferencing and discussions.

Selecting the Participants

This project consisted of 2 elective one-semester CALL classes that met once a week for a 90-minute period. The participants were Japanese university second year EFL students majoring in international economics who had volunteered to take the class.

The students in the first semester class were 20 volunteers who were released from a class of 46 students taking a required reading class on current economic affairs. The remaining 26 students did regular reading assignments and served as a control for the e-mail project. This was not an experimental design because the sample was self-selected, with intervening variables of high motivation and interest—the students who volunteered were obviously those who were interested in the project—and some members of the CALL group spent extra time during the semester participating in the e-mail exchange.

In cooperation with staff members at the AEI, 5 American students working as teaching assistants in the AEI program were hired as "tutors" and were asked to correspond with 4 Japanese students each for the 2 semesters of the project. Because the tutors and students were free to exchange e-mail about any topic they were interested in, each pair developed their e-mail communications over the semester. The L2 students were told not to be concerned with the accuracy of their English but rather to focus on understanding and being understood by their keypals.

Initial Training in Computer Use

Only 2 of the 20 students in the first group had ever used a computer, so the first 3 class meetings were spent on basic skills. None of the students

TABLE 7.1
Pre- and Posttest Scores on TOEFL-Type Proficiency Test

	N	Pretest*	Posttest**	Significance (paired t tests)
E-mail class	20	54.4	69.6	$p < .05$ ($t = -7.778$, 19 df)
Reading class	26	52.4	55.7	$p < .05$ ($t = -4.500$, 19 df)

*The difference between the pretest scores of the e-mail class and the reading class was not significant at $p < .05$ ($t = .482$, 19 df) using an unpaired t test.

**The difference between the posttest scores of the e-mail class and the reading class was significant at $p < .05$ ($t = 3.540$, 19 df) using an unpaired t test.

had used English word processing programs or had e-mailed in English, so they needed additional training in these areas, particularly in typing. The remainder of the classes was spent on e-mail exchanges with the tutors. All students completed at least 7 e-mail exchanges and many entered the CALL lab during their free time to compose additional e-mail, thus spending more time on their activities than the students in the regular reading class.

Measuring Proficiency Gains

At the beginning of the first semester, the entire current affairs class, including the 20 students who were participating in the e-mail project, was given a TOEFL-type pretest and was tested again at the end of the semester. The test had reading and vocabulary sections identical to the Institutional TOEFL, but no listening section. The mean pre- and posttest scores in Table 7.1 indicate that although both groups made significant gains during the semester, the e-mail group gained more than 15 points, whereas the control group gained about 3 points on the posttest. Although both groups' gains were statistically significant, the e-mail group's gain was significantly higher than that of the control group ($t = -7.778$, $p < .05$). Thus, participation in the e-mail project appeared to have promoted a larger gain in English proficiency than would have occurred through normal study (Fotos & Iwabuchi, 1999).

These gains must be interpreted cautiously, however. As mentioned, some of the e-mail group spent extra time participating in the project, and the gain might be due to this fact alone. Still, most of the regular students were enrolled in extra English classes as well, so they too received additional English training yet did not make gains equivalent to the e-mail group. Future research will have to control for this point.

Scaffolding as a Promoter of Proficiency Gains?

To understand how the e-mail students' proficiency might have increased during the relatively short period of 1 semester, it is necessary to consider scaffolding. As shown by Example 7.3, the students often used their tutor' original text to construct their replies, sometimes building on them as a base for more elaborate constructions or copying them, including the (incorrect for the context) verb.

> Example 7.3: Tutors' Text as Scaffolding for L2 Students' Replies (The tutor's original text and the tutor's text used in the student's reply are underlined)
>
> A. Student: In addition to this, I have to answer some questions. You write "Have you ever traveled outside of Japan?" Yes, I have ever traveled outside of Japan. I went to United States once when I was a high school student.
> B. Tutor: Can you read news about basketball in Japan? Recently the NBA has some serious problems… It is the first time for the NBA to cancel some games. The problem is about the amount of money which the NBA players receive.
> Student: I had heard the news in Japan. The most important problem is exactly money. The NBA games are canceled is very disappointed with many fans. I think almost players receive enough money but they still want more money.
> C. Tutor: I also lòve *Raising Arizona*. I think we have similar tastes.
> Student: I think you and I have similar tastes, as you say!
> D. Tutor: Does your family visit you at all?
> Student: My family sometimes visit me. When they visit me, I am glad.

It is possible that such scaffolding on the tutors' embedded text may have contributed to the L2 students' writing ability and promoted overall proficiency gains.

Questionnaire Results: First Semester Student Attitudes Toward the E-Mail Project

At the end of the first semester, an English questionnaire consisting of 9 open-ended questions was administered to the e-mail class participants (see Appendix). Seventy-five percent of the students used the words "enjoyed", "enjoyable" or "pleasant" when describing their e-mail exchange. In fact, 3 students wrote that they enjoyed studying English for the first time in their lives!

In addition, 60% use the words "conversation" or "talk" when describing their e-mail exchanges rather than the term "writing." This suggests that, despite the time lag, they considered e-mail to be closer to speech than to writing (cf. Crystal, 2001, who feels that the lag may decrease the speech-like nature of e-mail exchange). This result is in line with research suggesting that e-mail represents speech-like discourse within the written environment (Murray, 1995, 2000). One student wrote, "It was very enjoyable to have a lot of friendly *conversation* with Oregon students." Another commented, "It was very good for me to be able to have *conversation* with American students." Such remarks suggest that they felt as though they were engaging in conversation with their tutors.

Sixty-five percent said that the natural style of communication used in the e-mail exchange improved their English proficiency. This result was important because many foreign language students believe that formal study of the L2, such as memorization of grammar structures, rules, and vocabulary, is the best way to learn the target language. However, by participating in the e-mail exchange these foreign language students also appeared to recognize the importance of meaning-based authentic communication for developing proficiency.

In addition, 85% reported that they became more confident in their English ability because they could understand their tutors' messages and could make themselves understood in English. This is important in the foreign language learning situation because few students have opportunities for meaningful discourse in the target language.

The e-mail exchange class with peer native speakers of the target language was suggested to have the following advantages (Fotos & Iwabuchi, 1999):

1. *Reading and writing for authentic purposes.* In the e-mail exchange, L2 students used the target language for authentic purposes, something difficult to achieve in the foreign language situation.

2. *Face-saving and low concern for errors.* As mentioned, research has found that e-mail provides a safe and nonthreatening way to interact with others. Within the e-mail environment, the EFL students were able to communicate with English native speakers without the risk of a face-to-face exchange. In addition, because it was stated at the beginning of the exchange that errors were not important, the students were not overly concerned with the accuracy of their L2 production, only that their communication would be understood by their keypals.

3. *Proficiency gains in the target language.* The 20 foreign language students in the e-mail group made a significant proficiency gain of 15 points on the reading and writing portion of the Institutional TOEFL whereas the control group of 26 students taking the regular L2 reading class gained only 3 points. Such a large gain achieved during a 1-semester time frame is particularly interesting when it is recalled that there was no significant dif-

ference between the 2 groups' initial foreign language proficiency nor was any instruction or homework given to the e-mail group during the project. Therefore, the significant proficiency gains appear to have been achieved solely through participation in the e-mail exchange.

MOTIVATION GAINS THROUGH E-MAIL EXCHANGE

A second e-mail exchange project took place the following semester and was organized in the same way as the first project. The participants were 17 second-year Japanese university EFL students who volunteered to take the elective CALL course, with the remainder of the students taking the regular L2 reading class. The class met for 1 90-minute period a week for one semester. As with the previous group, the first 3 class meetings were spent on training in use of computers, e-mail software, Web browsers and typing.

At the beginning and end of the semester a TOEFL-type test consisting of the reading and vocabulary section of a practice TOEFL minus the listening section was administered to the e-mail students. Their average score on the TOEFL test at the beginning of the program was 58.0 points, and their average posttest score at the end of the semester was 68.3 points, a significant gain of more than 10 points ($t = -3.444$, $p < .05$) as measured by a paired t test. This gain was similar to the 15 point gain made by the students in the first semester class.

Motivation

Although it was understood that the L2 students already had considerable motivation to study the target language because they volunteered to take the e-mail class, a research goal during the second semester was to investigate whether the students' motivation to study the L2 increased as a result of their participation.

A few years ago Fotos and Iwabuchi (1997) designed and administered a 50-item motivation questionnaire in Japanese to Japanese university EFL students. The questionnaire had 44 statements followed by a 5-point Likert scale, ranging from strongly disagree to strongly agree. In addition to the traditional integrative and instrumental items, there was an international category, a travel category and 3 categories that addressed intrinsic motivation.

The same questionnaire was administered to the e-mail class students at the beginning of the semester and again at the end. For this report, motivation was not broken down into individual types; rather, the students' scores on each item were added to give a total motivation score for each student. The average motivation score for the e-mail students at the beginning of the project was 185.4 out of a possible total of 250 points. At the end of the class, the average score had risen about 5 points to 190 points. Eleven of the 17 students gained in motivation, with an average gain of 17.1 points, which was nearly significant (t = –2.047, p < .0797) using a paired t test.

By comparison, a previous study of EFL student motivation gains made over an academic year (Fotos & Iwabuchi, 1997) compared initial and final motivation for students in two elective EFL classes and one required current economic affairs class of first and second year students from the same university and department as the students participating in the e-mail project. The average final motivation score for one elective class was 151.7 points, the second was 163.8 points and the required class had an average gain score of only 143.1 points. However, the e-mail group's average score at the end of the project was more than 190 points. Thus, not only was the e-mail group's initial motivation score of 184.5 points higher than the highest final scores reported for the previous motivation study, but the e-mail group's final score was nearly 50 points higher then the regular students taking the required reading classes.

It appears that the self-selected group came into the class with high initial levels of motivation, and the satisfying nature of the e-mail exchange increased this motivation. The 7 students who showed no increase already had very high levels of motivation, at an average of 195.4 points, and other research has reported similar findings for self-selected participants with high initial motivation (Ushioda, 2000).

Questionnaire Results: Second Semester Student Attitudes Toward the E-mail Project

This group also completed the English questionnaire consisted of 9 open-ended questions measuring their attitudes towards the project (see the Appendix), and the results were quite similar to the first semester group's response. Nearly 80% used the words enjoyed, pleasant or much fun when describing their exchange of e-mail with American students. Although in the foreign language situation there are few chances for students to use the target language communicatively, again most students used words like conversation and talk to describe their e-mail exchange, and 50% wrote that they felt as if they were "talking face-to-face." In addition, 60% said that having an American keypal encouraged them to use English, and 100% said they now wanted to go abroad to study—another indication of an increase in motivation. Also, 60% said that they were less afraid of making mistakes in English and 40% said they felt "less uneasy" when speaking English. One of the project's goals was to improve the students' confidence in using English communicatively, and such comments suggest that this goal was achieved.

As for writing, 50% said that they felt more relaxed when writing e-mail than when speaking face-to-face with native English speakers, and noted that their English came out more smoothly in e-mail. The e-mail exchange thus gave the L2 students a way to make a personal connection with a native English speaker and to use the target language naturally in communication. In fact, several students did not want the project to end. One wrote. "In this class, this is the last e-mail between you and me, my teacher said. But I would like to continue e-mail with you. If you agree me, is it OK?"

SIGNIFICANT PROFICIENCY AND MOTIVATION GAINS THROUGH E-MAIL EXCHANGE

A one-semester course is very short, especially when it meets for only 1 90-minute period a week. However, both classes of foreign language students made significant proficiency gains as measured by a TOEFL-type test, and these gains were not achieved through teacher-fronted instruction or homework, but through the students' self-paced e-mail exchange with their tutors. As the questionnaire responses indicate, this activity was perceived as very enjoyable. Both groups of students also commented that they felt as if they were conducting an oral conversation with their tutors. One student wrote, "I have almost no sense of distance for I felt like my tutor is standing just in front of me."

It can be suggested that an e-mail exchange program provides an enjoyable way for L2 students to use the target language communicatively in meaning-focused contexts, even if the students are studying within the foreign language situation.

TO THE TEACHER: SETTING UP AN E-MAIL EXCHANGE PROJECT

The following is a list of considerations to guide teachers who wish to set up their own e-mail exchange project.

Before the project:

1. *Course structure, time frame, and assessment.* After determining the needs of the students who will participate in the e-mail exchange, the teacher

should establish the course structure, curriculum goals, specific objectives (these may include developing expertise in using computers and software) and assessment procedures. A syllabus for the course should be prepared, including the course content, time frame, and type of assessment to be conducted. Assessment should include proficiency pre- and posttests, as well as postproject questionnaires and interviews soliciting student opinions and suggestions for improving the project.

2. *Keypals.* If the goal is for foreign language students to exchange e-mail with target language native speaker peers, it is best to use paid keypals if possible because it is difficult for volunteer-based projects to be sustained over an extended period. In the case described in the previous section, a sister school relationship already existed between the American and Japanese universities, funds were available to hire American students as tutors for the entire year, and staff at both institutions closely supervised the project. This represents an optimum set of conditions. If funds are not available, teachers can use keypal sites (see the Appendix for a list of sites) but should not expect to establish a systematic program requiring regularity of replies (see Nozawa, 2002, for a discussion of problems with keypal exhanges). If keypals are not available, an option that is increasingly being used is structured content-based class or group exchanges (see Kern, 1996) where one L2 class or group writes to another on specified topics for predetermined objectives. This option provides both intra- and inter-group interaction.

3. *Hardware, software and staffing requirements.* Teachers should determine the availability of computer systems and e-mail software, developing their own expertise before the start of the program and arranging for computer availability at free times for students who are unable to complete their e-mail exchanges during class time. In the two-semester case study described, it was necessary to apply for student access to the computer lab so that they could complete their e-mail outside of class if necessary. In addition, staffing requirements must be determined, and the availability of teachers to supervise the program and support staff ascertained.

4. *Selecting students.* The teacher should choose students who are interested in the project and who are able to work independently.

5. *Training.* Students should be trained in the use of computers and e-mail software and should understand the nature of the project and the teacher expectations regarding their participation. If support staff are involved, they should also understand the project requirements and their expected role. In the case study presented, most of the L2 students did not know how to type using an English keyboard and needed training in this skill as well.

During the project:

1. *Weekly assessment.* The teacher should keep track of the students' progress each week by being copied when the students send their e-mail to their keypals. This also allows monitoring to insure that the e-mail content is appropriate for the class objectives.

2. *Targeting specific structures for instruction.* Teachers should keep track of problematic forms, pragmatic usages, and other target language concerns. These can periodically be addressed in class and will help promote accuracy gains and facilitate cultural understanding.

After the project:

1. *Evaluation.* The teacher should administer proficiency tests and questionnaires to the participants to elicit their feelings about participation in the project, to measure changes in attitudes towards the L2 and the L2 culture, and to measure changes in proficiency levels.

ACKNOWLEDGMENTS

Part of the literature review was published as an inhouse research report for the author's university in 1998. A brief summary of the first semester e-mail project was reported in Fotos and Iwabuchi (1999). The author thanks Professor Takashi Iwabuchi of Senshu University for his administration of the e-mail project.

REFERENCES

Appel, G., & Lantolf, J. (1994). Speaking as mediation: A study of L1 and L2 text recall tasks. *Modern Language Journal,* 78, 437–452.

Baron, N. (2000). *Alphabet to email: How written English evolved and where it's heading.* New York: Routledge.

Beauvois, M. (1998). E-talk: Computer-assisted classroom discussion—attitudes and motivation. In J. Swaffar, S. Romano, P. Markley, & K. Arens (Eds.). *Language learning online: Theory and practice in the ESL and L2 computer classroom* (pp. 99–120). Austin, Texas: Labyrinth.

Boswell, T. (Ed.). (1997). *New ways of using computers in language teaching.* Alexandria, VA: Teachers of English to Speakers of Other Languages.

Brown, G., & Yule, G. (1994). *Teaching the spoken language.* New York: Cambridge University Press.

Bruner, J. (1973). *Beyond the information given: Studies in the psychology of knowing.* New York: Norton.

Bruner, J. (1990). *Acts of meaning.* Cambridge, MA: Harvard University Press.

Chapelle, C. (2001). *Computer applications in second language acquisition.* Cambridge, England: Cambridge University Press.

Crystal, D. (1995). *The Cambridge encyclopedia of the English language* (2nd ed). Cambridge, England: Cambridge University Press.

Crystal, D. (2001). *Language and the Internet.* New York. Cambridge University Press.

Davis, B., & Thiede, R. (2000). Writing into change: Style shifting in asynchronous electronic discourse. In M. Warschauer & R. Kern (Eds.), *Network-based language teaching: Concepts and practices* (pp. 87–120). *New York: Cambridge University Press.*

Fotos, S. (2001). Cognitive approaches to grammar instruction. In M. Celce-Murcia (Ed). *Teaching English as a second or foreign language.* (3rd ed.) (pp. 267–284). Boston, MA: Heinle & Heinle.

Fotos, S., & Iwabuchi, T. (1997, March). Activities for success; Building intrinsic motivation in language class. Presentation at the annual convention of Teachers of English to Speakers of other Languages (TESOL), Orlando, FL.

Fotos, S. & Iwabuchi, T. (1999). Using e-mail to build communicative competence. *TESOL EFL-IS Newsletter,* 19, 2, 8–9.

Gu, P., & Zhe, Z. (1999). Improving EFL learning environment through networking. In R. Debski & M. Levy (Eds.). World CALL: Global perspectives on computer- assisted language learning (pp. 169–184). Lisse, Netherlands: Swets & Zeitlinger.

Halliday. M.A.K. (1985). *Spoken and written language.* Burwood, Victoria: Deakin University Press.

Hanson-Smith, E. (Ed). (2000). *Technologically enhanced learning environments.* Alexandria, VA: Teachers of English to Speakers of Other Languages.

Heim, M. (1987). *Electric language.* New Haven, CN: Yale University Press.

Kern, R. (1996). Computer-mediated communication: Using e-mail exchanges to explore personal histories in two cultures. In M. Warschauer (Ed.), *Telecollaboration in foreign language learning. Proceedings of the Hawaii symposium* (pp. 105–119). Technical Report # 21. Honolulu: University of Hawaii Press.

Markley, P. (1998). Empowering students: The diverse roles of Asians and women in the EFL computer classroom. In J. Swaffar, S. Romano, P. Markley & K. Arens (Eds.). *Language learning online: Theory and practice in the ESL and L2 computer classroom* (pp. 81–96). Austin, TX: Labyrinth.

Maynor, N. (1994). The language of electronic mail: Written speech? In G. Little & M. Montgomery (Eds.) *Centennial Usage Studies* (pp. 48–53). Tuscaloosa: Alabama University Press.

McCarthy, M. (1991). *Discourse analysis for language teachers.* Cambridge, England: Cambridge University Press.

McIntyre, D., & Wolff, F. (1998). An experiment with WWW interactive learning in university education. *Computers and Education,* 31, 255–264.

Mercer, N., & Fisher, E. (1997). Scaffolding through talk. In R. Wegerif & P. Scrimshaw (Eds.), *Computers and talk in the primary classroom* (pp. 196–210). Clevedon, England: Multilingual Matters.

Moran, C., & Hawisher, G., (1998). The rhetorics and languages of electronic mail. In I. Snyder (Ed.). *Page to screen: Taking literacy into the electronic era* (pp. 80–101). London: Routledge.

Murray, D. (1995). *Knowledge machines.* Singapore: Longman.

Murray, D. (2000). Protean communication: The language of computer-mediated communication. *TESOL Quarterly,* 34, 397–422.

Nozawa, K. (2002). Keypal exchange for writing fluency and intercultural understanding. In P. Lewis (Ed.), *The changing face of CALL: A Japanese perspective* (pp. 187–202). Lisse, The Netherlands: Swets & Zeitlinger.

Nunan, D. (1993). *Introducing discourse analysis.* London: Peguin English.

Shetzer, H., & Warschauer, M. (2000). An electronic literacy approach to network-based language teaching. In M. Warschauer & R. Kern (Eds.), *Network-based language teaching: Concepts and practices* (pp. 171–185). New York: Cambridge University Press.

Tannen, D. (1982). The oral-literature-continuum in discourse. In D. Tannen (Ed.), *Spoken
and written language: Exploring orality and literacy.* (pp. 1–6). Norwood, NJ: Ablex.

Tannen, D. (1993). *Framing in discourse.* Oxford: Oxford University Press.

Tannen, D. (1994). *Gender and discourse.* New York: Oxford University Press.

Teeler, D., & Gray, P. (2000). *How to use the Internet in ELT.* Hong Kong: Longman.

Trenches, M. (1996). Writing strategies in a second language: Three case studies of learners
using electronic mail. *Canadian Modern Language Review, 52*(3). 464–497.

Ushioda, E. (2000). Tandem language learning via e-mail: From motivation to autonomy. *Re-
CALL, 12,* 121–128.

Vygotsky, L. (1978) *Mind in society: The development of higher psychological processes.* Cambridge:
Harvard University Press.

Warschauer, M. (1995a). *Computer-mediated collaborative learning: theory and practice* (Research
Note 17). Honolulu: University of Hawaii Press.

Warschauer, M. (1995b). *E-mail for English teaching.* Alexandria, VA: Teachers of English to
Speakers of Other Languages.

Warschauer, M. (Ed.). (1995c). *Virtual connections: Online activities and projects for networking language learners.* Honolulu: University of Hawaii Press.

Warschauer, M. (1996). Motivational aspects of using computers for writing and communica-
tion. In M. Warschauer (Ed.), *Telecollaboration in foreign language learning. Proceedings of the
Hawaii symposium* (pp. 26–46). Technical Report #21. Honolulu: University of Hawaii
Press.

Warschauer, M. (1999). *Electronic literacies.* Mahwah, NJ: Lawrence Erlbaum Associates.

Warschauer, M. (2002). A developmental perspective on technology in language education.
TESOL Quarterly, 36(3), 453–475.

Warschauer, M. (2003). *Technology and social inclusion: Rethinking the digital divide.* Cambridge,
MA: MIT Press.

Warschauer, M., Shetzer, H., & Meloni, C. (2000). *Internet for English Teaching.* Alexandria, VA:
Teachers of English to Speakers of Other Languages.

Wertsch, J. (1985). *Vygotsky and the social formation of the mind.* Cambridge, MA: Harvard University Press.

Yates, S. (1996). Oral and written linguistic aspects of computer conferencing: A corpus based
study. In S. Herring (Ed.), *Computer mediated comunication: Linguistic, social and crosscultural
perspectives* (pp. 29–46). Amsterdam: John Benjamins.

APPENDIX

Student Attitude Questionnaire

1. How did you feel about exchanging e-mail with American students?

2. What impression did you have about writing e-mail in English?

3. Did your keypal help you improve your English? If yes, how?

4. How much did this project affect your desire to go abroad?

5. How do you feel now about making mistakes in writing English?

6. How did you feel about communicating by writing as compared with face-to-face communication?

7. Would you like to continue to be in this project? Why?

8. How much progress did you make using the English keyboard?

9. Did your attitude change about using computers to study English? If yes, how did it change?

8

Teaching WELL and Loving IT

Richard P. Taylor
Christina Gitsaki
Nagoya University of Foreign Studies

Over the past 30 years CALL has been through three main stages: behaviorist CALL, communicative CALL, and integrative CALL (Warschauer & Healey, 1998). When people think of CALL, they traditionally think of it in terms of software and CD-ROMs, but recently the widespread availability of the Internet and its application in educational institutions have helped reshape the use of computers for language learning. Increasingly, L2 educators are finding ways to use the infinite number of resources available on the Web to help their students improve their communication and language skills. The Internet is thus transforming CALL into WELL (web-enhanced language learning).

Despite its advantages as a resource for teaching L2 and foreign languages, however, the Internet lacks structure and contains considerable irrelevant and useless material. In terms of language pedagogy, it does not provide a syllabus for language tasks to be completed. Therefore, the main challenge for the teachers who want to use the Web for L2 instruction is how to expose their students to the Web when there is no underlying language-learning syllabus.

This chapter redefines the role of the computer in foreign language teaching by considering WELL and the role of the teacher and the learner in this new paradigm, outlines a pedagogical framework for the use of the Web for language learning, and describes sample activities for implementing each stage of the framework. By integrating WELL into the existing language curriculum, teachers can make the Web a true asset for language learning.

The chapter also presents the results of a survey designed to measure Japanese university students' attitudes and beliefs toward the use of the Internet and web-based activities for learning EFL after they have been exposed to the previously mentioned pedagogical framework.

PHASES OF CALL

When CALL first started in the 1960s and 1970s it was based on a behaviorist learning model and consisted of repetitive language drills and practice exercises (often referred to as drill-and-kill exercises) mainly because such exercises were easy to program on the computer because of their "systematic and routine character" and "their lack of open-endedness" (Kenning & Kenning, 1990, p. 53). During this phase, CALL made self-paced instruction possible for large groups of students. The student was a passive recipient of language because he or she merely responded to drill exercises, whereas the computer was a mechanical tutor who never became tired (Warschauer & Healey, 1998, p. 57).

During the next decade, the 1970s to the 1980s, CALL reflected the then-current language teaching methods—community language learning (Curran, 1976), total physical response (Asher, 1977), and communicative language teaching approach—which put emphasis on the interdependence of language and communication. This pedagogical orientation gave rise to a variety of CALL activities, vocabulary games, gap filling, text reconstruction, speed reading, and simulation. The computer remained a tutor but it was criticized as being inadequate for teaching communicative competence. During this era—although the process of learning was very important—CALL still measured only outcomes (Chapelle, 1989, pp. 7–9). The teacher assumed the role of coordinator and planner trying to integrate CALL into the existing curriculum (Warschauer & Healey, 1998).

During the 1980s and 1990s, a sociocognitive view of language teaching (see Graus, 1999) sought to "integrate the various skills and integrate technology more fully into the language learning process" (Warschauer & Healey, 1998, p. 58). The multimedia networked computer promoted interactivity with materials, people, and learning environments beyond the immediate classroom (Chapelle, 1994), while CALL became "a matrix of diverse activities" (Levy, 1997, p. 41), for example, e-mail, web browsers, video conferencing, and multimedia packages. During this phase, the computer was viewed as a tool for communication, with learners defining their needs and preferences and the teacher acting as a facilitator, assuming a minimal or central role depending on the type of the CALL program (for an extensive account of the three phases of CALL, see Levy, 1997; Warschauer & Healey, 1998).

At the start of the 21st century, the use of the Web became more prominent. "Part library, part publishing house, part telephone, part interactive television, the Web represents one of the most diverse and revolutionary media in human history" (Warschauer & Healey, 1998, p. 64). From a pedagogical point of view, the Web contains unlimited resources for authentic material used in real-life situations while it enables learners to choose the information they want to read (Warschauer, Turbee, & Roberts, 1994). It is thus interactive, motivating, easy to use, and fun because Web sites have colors, pictures, sounds, animation, and video clips (Shneiderman, 1998). Use of the Web also helps students develop strategies to cope with authentic L2 use.

In this new era of WELL, the learner is more autonomous and is able to direct learning into the areas he or she is interested in. Learners can become creative because they can publish on the Web, and communicate directly with the teacher through e-mail, and ask for feedback or advice. Levy (1997, p. 172) listed five interaction types available through the Web: (a) the students can interact with a Web site (look at a Web site or publish one on the Web), (b) they can interact with a "form field" (fill in an interactive form on the Web), (c) they can interact with a teacher or a student (e.g., exchange e-mail with their teacher or with keypals or work on a LAN), (d) they can interact with a group (students participate in a LAN-based discussion group), or (e) they can use it as a learning environment (e.g., a MOO). The computer thus becomes a tool for communication, publishing, and accessing research, and a conduit for information exchange (Heimans, 1995). The teacher has an active role to play in WELL as a facilitator who provides guidance to students, organizes collaborative projects, and ensures that the technology available can support the successful completion of the projects, for example, by checking that the computer lab is in working order, and be able to take troubleshooting action.

As the computer becomes a tool, it is up to the teacher and the learner to determine whether the use of the tool is appropriate and how to make the best use of it. Teachers must show students how use the Web as a tool for learning L2 and foreign languages (Barson, 1998; Felix, 1999). Furthermore, the teacher must become a researcher who explores the Web for resources and a framer who establishes a frame through which the students can enter the Web (Heimans, 1995).

Table 8.1 summarizes the different phases of CALL in terms of the CALL programs used in each phase and the roles performed by the computers, the teachers and the learners in each phase.

FRAMEWORK FOR TEACHING WELL

Despite the numerous advantages of the Web, many teachers are still skeptical about using it for L2 instruction for several reasons: (a) the Web lacks structure, (b) it contains an overwhelming amount of information and con-

TABLE 8.1
Summary of CALL Programs and Computer,
Teacher, and Learner Roles

Phase	1960s–1970s	1970s–1980s	1980s–1990s	21st Century
CALL Programs	Drills and repetitive practice exercises	Text reconstruction, gap filling, speed reading, simulation vocabulary games	E-mail, web browsers, video conferencing, multimedia packages	Web-based materials for language learning
Computer	Mechanical tutor	Stimulus for talk	Tool for communication	Research tool, publisher, conduit for information exchange
Teacher	(No role)	Coordinator/ planner	Facilitator	Researcher and framer
Learner	Passive recipient of language	Communicator	Active	Autonomous and creative

siderable irrelevant and useless material, and (c) there is no underlying language-learning syllabus—the Web does not provide a framework for language tasks to be completed. It is therefore up to the teacher "to prepare the way for the use of the computer" (Levy, 1997, p. 203).

It is not surprising that many teachers do not know where to start. To make the Web a true asset for L2 learning, there must be careful planning of how to integrate WELL into the existing curriculum. Although access to the Web is essential for students to explore and use its resources, letting them simply surf the Web with no specific task in mind will not teach them much about the target language (see Dodge, 1997; Frizler, 1995; Meskill, 1999; Trickel & Liljegren, 1998; Willis, 1997; Yang, 1998). The Web is like an ocean offering an abundance of information, but without navigation tools students can get lost. Teachers therefore need to guide students through different stages that will introduce students to the use of the Web and the computer, and help them use the Web and learn the target language at the same time. Adapted from a model for the educational use of Internet technologies by Willis (1997), the framework presented in Fig. 8.1 offers a guideline for teachers to help them introduce WELL to their students in carefully planned stages.

The first stage of the framework is electronic communication. Students are introduced to online interactions such as e-mail (one to one or group), online discussions, video conferencing, and chat. The basic skills taught in this stage are how to write and send e-mail messages; how to reply to e-mail

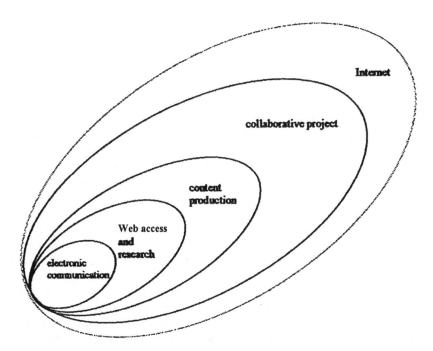

FIG. 8.1. Framework for Teaching WELL (adapted from the WELL framework by Willis (1997)). Permission to reproduce Fig. 8.1 was obtained from Willis (1997).

messages; how to store, save, and delete messages; and how to participate in synchronous communication.

During the second stage, Web access and research, students conduct research on the Web and collect information on a specific topic. In this stage, students learn how to use a search engine; how to browse through search results looking for specific information; how to download information, being careful of copyright concerns; and how to copy and print resources. In the third stage, content production, students learn how to create and publish a home page and how to publish a project on the Web. In the final stage, collaborative project, students work collaboratively to produce a web-based project. Some of the basic skills that students learn are teamwork, project management, negotiating, and dividing duties and tasks.

Implementation of the Framework

The following section presents a number of activities that we have designed and used with our students to use the WELL for teaching EFL.

Stage 1: Electronic Communication.   To introduce L2 students to the use of e-mail, it is a good idea to begin by showing them how to create their own e-mail account on the Web. This involves filling in an interactive form in which students have to register and choose a user name and a password for their new account. After that students can practice sending and replying to e-mail messages by carrying out a simple survey. For example, students can develop a simple questionnaire of five or six items, send it to their other classmates or to a group of classmates, reply to their classmates' question-naires, receive and collate the answers to their own questionnaire, write a small report, and e-mail the report to the teacher. After the students have practiced using the e-mail program, they are ready to become involved in keypal projects and, later on, in online chat rooms and video conferencing, provided the necessary hardware is available.

Stage 2: Web Access and Research.   In this stage the students are involved in web-search projects. First, they are introduced to a topic (e.g., planning a trip abroad). Second, they are involved in brainstorming activities that will help them review relevant vocabulary (e.g., vacation destinations, vacation activities, etc.). Third, the students formulate a research question (e.g., they choose where they would like to go for the vacation and what they would like to do there). Fourth, the students search the Web and complete a chart with the information they find. Finally, the students share their in-formation with their classmates; for example, they interview each other or role play a travel agent and customer situation where the travel agent tries to sell his or her vacation package to the customer (for more topics and web-search projects, see Gitsaki & Taylor, 2000a).

Stage 3: Content Production.   Creating a home page can help students use their web-searching experience by presenting the uniform resource loca-tors (URLs) of the Web sites they visited and noting the things that they liked about the sites. The students can publish a web page that people from other countries around the world can access; they can be creative and prac-tice the L2 at the same time.

For home-page creation, students can use one of the numerous web-publishing software packages available today, or they can use basic hyper-text markup language (HTML) tags. Using HTML for creating a home page has certain advantages: (a) no special software is needed (just a basic text editor and a web browser), (b) the students become aware of how web pages are constructed, (c) they can use the format of other web pages by viewing the HTML source code, and (d) they can continue working on their home page and using the L2 outside the classroom.

There are considerable resources on the Internet teaching basic HTML tags and home page construction. The following three sites were used for our project:

- PageTutor.com: HTML Tutorials for the rest of us
  http://www.pagetutor.com/
- So You Want to Learn HTML ...
  http://www.edb.utexas.edu/resta97/aisd/students/turnbull/
  HTMLtutr/index.html
- University of New Hampshire: A Basic Guide to Using HyperText
  Markup Language (HTML)
  http://www.stereo.sr.unh.edu/tof/WebLesson/printlesson.html

There are three stages for the teacher in the creation of student home pages: (a) sorting out what HTML tags the students need, (b) training the students to use the selected tags, and (c) helping the students to develop their web page. A small set of about 30 HTML tags is sufficient for a basic home page (for a suggested list of HTML tags see Gitsaki & Taylor, 1999, p. 157). This basic set of tags should cover: (a) starting an HTML document, (b) formatting text (using different fonts, font sizes, font types, etc.), (c) making lists (e.g., ordered lists, unordered lists), (d) creating tables, (e) drawing lines, and (f) adding links and pictures.

Teaching these tags to the students is the next step. First, the students start their HTML document. Then, they type a paragraph of text and learn how to format the text using different fonts and sizes. After that, they learn how to display information in lists and tables and how to use lines to separate the different sections of their home page. Finally, they learn how to add pictures to their page and create links to their favorite Web sites.

During the training stage of this project, small tasks are used to help students practice the different HTML tags. For example, students can experience the different font sizes by creating a rollercoaster (see www.pagetutor.com) or they can create lists (for a complete photocopiable handout of HTML training activities, see Gitsaki & Taylor, 2000b, p. 100).

After the training stage, the students can start creating their home page. Depending on their L2 proficiency and their web-surfing experience, they can include a number of different topics in their home page (see Table 8.2). The students should also add a link to their e-mail addresses so that people can get in touch with them. After the home pages are completed, they are proofread by the teacher and then published on the Web.

Stage 4: Collaborative Project. In this stage, the students work together to produce a newspaper. First, the working teams are assigned. Depending on class size, students form groups of five or six, and the role of each person in the group is decided. Next, the students are introduced to the different parts of a newspaper (e.g., news stories, feature articles, fashion, book reviews, music and CD reviews, cooking, traveling, entertainment guides, ad-

TABLE 8.2
Suggested Topics for a Basic Home Page

Topic	Language Practice
Background Information	Students write a self-introduction, talk about their family, describe their hometown, describe their daily routines, etc.
School Information	Students give information about their school and the course they are studying.
Web Surfing Experience	Students write about their favorite movie, movie star, musician, food recipe, holiday destination, online shop, etc., and they can add links to their favorite Web sites.
Past Experiences	Students write about places they visited, concerts they attended, movies they saw, etc.
Plans for the Future	Students write about their plans for the future (travel plans, dream job, house, car, etc.).

vertisements, comic strips, classified ads, horoscopes, crosswords, word games, puzzles, weather information, etc.).

The groups have to decide on a preliminary title for their newspaper; decide which parts to include; determine which parts each group member is responsible for; and set deadlines for first drafts, final drafts, and for putting the newspaper together.

Once the students have decided what they are going to write about, they should search the Web for information about their stories. They can download information and pictures from different sites and edit the text, synthesize information, and write their own ideas and opinions. Students should also be asked to reference any information and pictures they download from the Web by acknowledging the Web sites they used to collect information and listing their URLs. At this point, students should be cautioned about copyright issues and the legal implications of plagiarizing.

After the students have finished writing their articles, each team has to put together the different pieces by merging the files, making sure that interesting and informative headlines have been chosen, and printing the newspaper or publishing it on the Web.

In the collaborative project, students work in teams and they develop skills for project management and efficient use of time. They also practice speaking the L2 as they negotiate who writes what, what headlines to use, when to submit drafts, and so forth.

Summary

The framework outlined here is in accordance with modern pedagogical theories that emphasize student-centered classrooms, learner autonomy, and project-based learning. The web-based activities described here foster the seven qualities of meaningful learning presented by Jonassen (1995): active, constructive, collaborative, intentional, conversational, contextualized, and reflective.

- The Web-based activities described here promote active learning where learners are engaged in "mindful processing of information where they are responsible for the result" (Jonassen, 1995, p. 60). Learners conduct research on the Web, gather information, and produce reports.
- Learners integrate new knowledge with prior knowledge and collaborate with their classmates in project-based L2 learning.
- Learners intentionally work toward an objective either in groups or on their own.
- During the activities described here, the learners engage in L2 conversations with their classmates through sharing the information they found on the Web and role playing or negotiating L2 content.
- Learners are involved in real-world, meaningful tasks (e.g., using the Web to plan a vacation, creating a home page, reading news online, searching for restaurants, creating a newspaper, etc.).
- Finally, learners can reflect on the decisions and processes involved in the learning process (Jonassen, 1995, pp. 60–61).

REPORT ON A QUESTIONNAIRE

In the first section of this chapter, we presented the principles of a theoretical framework that can be translated into guidelines for designing WELL materials to help students use computers, surf the Web, and learn the L2 at the same time. Just because the Web lacks structure does not mean that what teachers do with the Web should also lack structure! In this section, we briefly report the results of a survey conducted to investigate EFL students' attitudes toward the use of the Internet and web-based activities. The survey was based on a study by Osuna and Meskill (1998), who investigated the use of the Web to integrate Spanish language learning and study of the target language culture.

Participants

The participants in this pilot study were 106 Japanese university freshmen, aged 18 to 19, majoring in medicine, pharmacy, and social studies and taking EFL. Most of the students were computer novices, but all had access to computer labs outside classroom time. The project took place during one semester of the academic year.

Materials

The participants were at a pre-intermediate level of English proficiency and were taught English communication skills using web-based activities and projects found in *Internet English* (Gitsaki & Taylor, 2000a). The students attended one 90-minute class per week, and although this was a Web-based course, the 90-minute class was taught in a traditional classroom (i.e., in a computerless classroom) with the computer work assigned as homework. The students were thus required to spend time outside of the EFL classroom to complete their assignments.

Assessment

During the first 3 weeks of the semester, the students were introduced to basic computer, e-mail, and Internet skills. Classroom activities and simple computer tasks carried out as homework taught them basic computer terminology, how to create an e-mail account on the Web, how to send and reply to e-mail, how to use a search engine, how to use effective keywords, and how to skim and scan search results looking for specific information (see Stage 1 previously discussed). After the students had mastered these basic skills, they were introduced to Web-based projects. Each project was completed in two 90-minute class sessions. During the first class session, the students were introduced to a topic (e.g., famous people), they were involved in vocabulary activities related to the topic, and they were asked to choose what information they would like to find on the Web (e.g., find biographical information about their favorite famous person and create a report). The students had one week to complete their web-search task outside of the classroom. During the second 90-minute class session, the students interviewed each other about the information they found on the Web and participated in group activities where they presented their report or performed a role play (see Stage 2 previously discussed). A survey of student attitudes was conducted at the end of the first semester, after 14 weeks of instruction. By then, students had completed five Web-search projects.

Questionnaire

The questionnaire used was based on a survey that Osuna and Meskill (1998) developed for their study. It consisted of 23 statements measuring the students' perception of the Web as a learning tool, their attitudes and beliefs toward the use of the Web for the course, and their assessment of the web-based tasks used in the course. The students evaluated each statement on a 6-point Likert scale (1 = *strongly disagree* to 6 = *strongly agree*). At the end of the survey there were two open-ended questions asking the students to report what they liked about the course and what they did not like. The questionnaire is given in the Appendix.

Results

Almost all of the students agreed that the Web was a valuable learning tool and that its use was necessary. Of the students, 95% agreed that they learned more computer skills, but only 66% agreed that the Web helped them learn more English.

With regard to English language skills, 81% of the students agreed that they learned more about English (American) culture through using the Web and 59% found that the information on the Web helped them learn English vocabulary, but only 27% reported that the information on the Web helped them learn grammar. The course included many activities to help students practice speaking the target language, and 72% of the students agreed that they talked to their classmates more because of use of the Web. Also, 85% found that the Web provided more up-to-date information than textbooks and magazines, and even though they were computer novices, the students found that the web browser they used was an easy program to learn. Very important, 80% of the students agreed that they continued to use the Web after their assignments were completed. Because one of the aims of the course was to teach students how to use the Web as a tool for language learning, this result suggests that this goal was accomplished. With regard to students' attitudes and beliefs toward the use of the Web, they unanimously agreed that being able to use the Web was a valuable skill.

Regarding use of the Web for language courses, they reported liking using the Web for their English course (85%) and found that the use of the Web made the course more interesting (87%). Also, 71% of the students agreed that they would like to take another course that included a web-based component. With regard to reading information on the Web, 59% agreed that it was easier to read information on the Web than to read English textbooks. Also, 88% of the students thought that they would get better grades in this course because they used the Web, even though their course outline informed them that assessment was based on other criteria.

Overall, the students agreed that they were comfortable using the Web to find information (83%), and they felt more confident using computers now than before they took the course (88%). Moreover, 92% agreed that they would continue to use the Web even after the end of the course.

With regard to students' responses to task technicalities, only 56% of the students found that the activity instructions were easy to follow (all instructions were in English), and 68% agreed that access to the Web was possible at all times. Finally, 73% of the students reported taking more than one hour to complete each of their assignments, indicating significant exposure to the target language outside of the classroom, an important point for the foreign language setting where out-of-class exposure to the L2 is difficult to achieve.

When asked to report what they liked about the course, the students unanimously agreed that they liked learning English and computer skills at the same time. They also appreciated the opportunity to speak to their classmates in the L2 about their research. Finally, the students reported that they liked learning how to use the Web in English and enjoyed learning how to use e-mail in different ways (i.e., sending Web cards to their friends, submitting reports through e-mail, asking their teacher questions about their homework, etc.).

According to the students' comments written in the open-ended section of the survey, the use of the web-based activities made this course: "very interesting," "very fun," "helpful for me." The web activities helped students acquire both English and computer skills: "I became able to use computers," "I learned English and computer skills at the same time," "Because of this course I got my e-mail address. I have friends in U.S. and Tokyo. From now on I can send e-mail to them," "In this class . . . I got used to talking in English," "What I liked about this course was to use the Web a lot and to learn English culture. Thanks to this course, I liked English more," "I learned English using the Web," "I can talk about things I researched," "I can use the Web better than before," "I learned many computer skills because of homework," "I got to know about many English cultures," "I got listening and speaking practice," "I liked that we can study English through the computer. It is a new type of study," "I knew other country's cultures in English," "Thanks to this course, I can use the computer better and I learned more computer skills. And I learned foreign culture more because of this course," "I liked using the Web and speaking English with classmates," "I could talk with classmates who I hardly talked with," "Thanks to this class I could have chances to use computers and speak English," "I liked talking with my classmates in English and learning computers."

The students' main complaint was that they had too much homework to do and that it took them a long time to complete their reports. However, because one of the objectives of the course was to increase the time students spent working with the L2 outside the classroom, this result was not particularly worrisome. A few students reported that they felt shy when they had to do group presentations, and others would have liked more interaction with the teacher to model correct English pronunciation.

Summary

Overall, the students found that the Web was a valuable learning tool although they did not report that large amounts of L2 learning had taken place. This perception concerning language gains can be explained by the fact that L2 students "generally associate language learning with explicit morphosyntactic teaching" (Osuna & Meskill, 1998, p. 77), so when asked if the Web had helped them learn L2 grammar and vocabulary, only a few responded positively. Because this course did not teach L2 grammar explicitly, it is not surprising that students felt that they did not learn much grammar. This result could also indicate that web-search projects may be better for teaching certain aspects of the target language (e.g., culture and vocabulary) but not others (e.g., grammar). Even though the students were exposed to authentic language used in real-life situations, and some implicit language learning may have taken place, SLA research has shown that implicit language learning is difficult to assess (DeKeyser, 1995; Green & Hecht, 1992; Shaffer, 1989).

The students reported that they were satisfied with the medium and this result outweighed any dissatisfaction due to technical difficulties or initial unfamiliarity with CALL. They found that the use of the Web made the course more interesting because the Web offered current and varied information. Finally, the students reported that they would continue to use the Web even after the end of the course. Satisfaction with using the Web as a learning tool is an encouraging result for L2 teachers who are looking for activities that will increase time on task and promote as much out-of-class exposure to the L2 as possible (see Cholewka, 2002; Gu, 2002; Kung & Chuo, 2002; Osuna & Meskill, 1998).

FOR THE TEACHER

To use WELL there are certain steps that must be taken. First, teachers need to familiarize themselves with the software and the computer lab that their students will be using. Next, teachers need to surf the Web for sites to be used in class or to recommend sites to students (for an extensive list of language-learning Web sites, see Felix, 2001). Building a database of useful L2 sites and other resources on the Web is essential. Once the database has been built, teachers can either direct students to sites especially designed for L2 practice (grammar, reading, vocabulary, listening, etc.) or they can design activities based on specific Web sites. The major drawback of such activities is that Web sites are dynamic and may change or disappear, leaving teachers and students with dead links. Therefore, before sending students to a Web site, teachers need to make sure their links are updated and the Web site they are recommending to their students is accessible.

The most creative and motivating way to use web resources is to have students carry out web-search projects. Teachers have a choice: They can either use commercially produced web-based materials or design their own. Textbooks are written by experienced writers, they are based on a teaching approach, and the materials they contain have been piloted before publication. However, many teachers prefer to design their own materials because they find that commercially produced materials are deficient, or they do not want to violate copyright through inappropriate use of commercial activities.

Designing web-search materials for L2 is not an easy task. A number of things have to be considered. The following are five basic principles for designing such projects:

- Choose a topic that is relevant to the specific group of students (e.g. famous people, movies, restaurants, shopping, job hunting, news online, etc.). The Web contains resources to cover almost any topic. Select a topic that will appeal to your students and will motivate them to accomplish their task.

- The task must be specific and the teacher needs to clearly define what the students will do on the Web. Before allowing students to surf the Web for specific information, make sure they have formulated a research question. For example, if your students are going to plan a summer trip abroad, make sure they have decided where they would like to go and what they would like to do there: For example, I'd like to go to the United States, attend a language school, and see a play.

- Make the task outcomes measurable. How will the student know that he or she has accomplished the task? For example, students can be asked to complete a chart with the information they find on the Web. Use of a chart indicates what kind of information they need to find and indicates when they have accomplished their task. For the summer trip project, students can be given a table to complete with the information they find on the Web about flights, accommodation, costs, language courses, sightseeing information, and so on.

- Provide web-search advice to the students; suggest keywords to use for their search, how to combine effective keywords, how to use Internet directories, and so on.

- Finally, give students a time frame in which to accomplish their task; otherwise, they may become sidetracked. As Meskill (1999, p. 157) asserted, "The impetus to complete a task in a given time frame ensures task focus and task persistence."

Teachers must also keep in mind that web-based activities must be curriculum driven. Web-based activities should therefore be integrated into the existing language curriculum (Barson & Debski, 1996) and should have a language focus. Furthermore, web-based activities should help students acquire strategies that will help them use the Web as a tool for further L2 practice (for more on project-oriented CALL, see Debski, 2000).

CONCLUSION

In this chapter we outlined a framework for teaching WELL—how to use the Web resources to expose students to authentic language used in real-life situations and help them become involved in real-world meaningful tasks so that they can practice speaking the L2 with their classmates. We also provided evidence of our students' positive reactions to our web-based course.

Knowing that our students are now well equipped with skills that will help them use L2 Web sites even after the course is over, and having survey reports of how much they enjoyed learning the L2 and computer skills, we feel that the Web has been a true asset for our EFL course. Traditional CALL has been only partially adopted in the foreign language teaching context and it has tended to remain an add-on instead of becoming an integral part of the curriculum (Haworth & Cowling, 1999, p. 167). However, WELL is now having a considerable impact in language pedagogy; it is becoming widespread because it is easy to incorporate into the existing curriculum and it is rewarding to use.

REFERENCES

Asher, J. (1977). *Learning another language through actions: The complete teacher's guidebook.* Los Gatos, CA: Sky Oak Productions.
Barson, J. (1998, July). *Dealing with double evolution: Action-based learning approaches and instrumental technology.* Keynote address at the inaugural WorldCALL Conference, Melbourne, Australia.
Barson, J., & Debski, R. (1996). Calling back CALL: Technology in the service of foreign language learning based on creativity, contingency and goal-oriented activity. In M. Warschauer (Ed.), *Telecollaboration in foreign language learning* (pp. 49–68). Honolulu: University of Hawaii, Second Language Teaching & Curriculum Center.
Chapelle, C. (1989). CALL research in the 1980s: Setting the stage for the 1990s. *CALL Digest, 5*(7), 7–9.
Chapelle, C. (1994). CALL activities: Are they all the same? *System, 22*(1), 33–45.
Cholewka, S. (2002). Increased effectiveness of ESL programs through the incorporation of web-based technology into the ESL curriculum. *CALL 2002 Conference Proceedings,* 31–47.
Curran, C. (1976). *Counseling-learning in second languages.* Apple River, IL: Apple River Press.

Debski, R. (2000). Project-oriented CALL: Implementation and evaluation [Special issue]. *Computer Assisted Language Learning Journal, 13*(4–5).

DeKeyser, R. (1995). Learning second language rules: An experiment with a miniature linguistic system. *Studies in Second Language Acquisition, 17*, 379–403.

Dodge, B. (1997). Some thoughts about webquests. *The Distance Educator, 1*(3), 12–15.

Felix, U. (1999). Web-based language learning: A window to the authentic world. In R. Debski & M. Levy (Eds.), *WorldCALL: Global perspectives on computer-assisted language learning* (pp. 85–98). Amsterdam: Swets & Zeitlinger.

Felix, U. (2001). *Beyond Babel: Language learning online.* Melbourne, Australia: Language Australia.

Frizler, K. (1995). *The Internet as an educational tool in ESOL writing instruction.* Unpublished master's thesis, San Francisco State University.

Gitsaki, C., & Taylor, R. P. (1999). Bringing the WWW into the ESL classroom. In K. Cameron (Ed.), *CALL and the learning community* (pp. 143–159). Exeter, England: Elm Bank.

Gitsaki, C., & Taylor, R. (2000a). *Internet English: WWW-based communication activities. Student book.* Oxford, England: Oxford University Press.

Gitsaki, C., & Taylor, R. (2000b). *Internet English: WWW-based communication activities. Teacher's book.* Oxford, England: Oxford University Press.

Graus, J. (1999). *An evaluation of the usefulness of the Internet in the EFL classroom.* Unpublished master's thesis, University of Nijmegen, The Netherlands.

Green, P. S., & Hecht, K. (1992). Implicit and explicit grammar: An empirical study. *Applied Linguistics, 13*(2), 169–184.

Gu, P. (2002). Web-based project learning and EFL learners: A Chinese example. *Teaching English with Technology: A Journal for Teachers of English, 2*(4), 1–14.

Haworth, W., & Cowling, D. (1999). The WELL project: Local participation and national evaluation. In K. Cameron (Ed.), *CALL and the learning community* (pp. 161–168). Exeter, England: Elm Bank.

Heimans, S. (1995). The Internet & ESL: Resources and roles. *ON-CALL Journal* [Special Article]. Retrieved from www.cltr.uq.oz.au/oncall/article.htm

Jonassen, D. H. (1995). Supporting communities of learners with technology: A vision for integrating technology with learning in schools. *Educational Technology, 35*(4), 60–63.

Kenning, M. M., & Kenning, M. J. (1990). *Computers and language learning: Current theory and practice.* New York: Horwood.

Kung, S. C., & Chuo, T. W. (2002). Students' perceptions of English learning through ESL/EFL websites. *TESL-EJ, 6*(1), 1–14.

Levy, M. (1997). *Computer-assisted language learning: Context and conceptualization.* Oxford, England: Oxford University Press.

Meskill, C. (1999). Computers as tools for sociocollaborative language learning. In K. Cameron (Ed.), *Computer assisted language learning (CALL): Media, design and applications* (pp. 141–162). Lisse, Switzerland: Swets & Zeitlinger.

Osuna, M. M., & Meskill, C. (1998). Using the World Wide Web to integrate Spanish language and culture: A pilot study. *Language Learning and Technology, 1*(2), 71–92.

Shaffer, C. (1989). A comparison of inductive and deductive approaches to teaching foreign languages. *Modern Language Journal, 73*(5), 395–402.

Shneiderman, B. (1998). Relate-create-donate: A teaching/learning philosophy for the cybergeneration. *Computers & Education, 31*(1), 25–39.

Trickel, K., & Liljegren, K. (1998, October). *Using multimedia computers effectively in the ESL classroom: Use the computers. Don't let them use you.* Paper presented at the 1998 Southeast Regional TESOL Conference, Louisville, KY.

Warschauer, M., & Healey, D. (1998). Computers and language learning: An overview. *Language Teaching, 31*, 57–71.

Warschauer, M., Turbee, L., & Roberts, B. (1994). *Computer learning networks and student empow-erment.* Research note #10. Honolulu: University of Hawaii, Second Language Teaching & Curriculum Center.

Willis, D. (1997). A suggested framework for the educational use of Internet technologies and the development of students' learning abilities to critically evaluate materials. Retrieved April 1999, from wfs.eun.org/support/edumodel/ppframe.htm

Yang, P. J. (1998). Networked multimedia and foreign language education. *CALICO Journal, 15*(1–3), 75–88.

APPENDIX

QUESTIONS INCLUDED IN THE QUESTIONNAIRE
AND PERCENTAGE OF STUDENTS AGREEING
WITH EACH OF THE STATEMENTS

1. Overall, the Web is a valuable learning tool.	93%
2. Being able to use the Web is a valuable skill.	95%
3. The use of the Web is unnecessary.	8%
4. I liked using the Web for this course.	85%
5. Use of the Web in this course made it a more interesting course.	87%
6. I learned more computer skills because of using the Web.	95%
7. I learned more English because of using the Web.	66%
8. The information on the Web has helped me learn English grammar.	27%
9. The information on the Web has helped me learn English vocabulary.	59%
10. The information on the Web has helped me learn more about the English culture.	81%
11. I talked to my classmates (through e-mail or in person) more because of the use of the Web in the course.	72%
12. The Web provided more up-to-date information for the course than textbooks or magazines.	85%
13. It is easier to read information on the Web than it is to read English textbooks.	59%
14. I will get a better grade in this course because using the Web was part of this course.	88%
15. I would like to take another course that includes the use of the Web.	71%
16. I am comfortable using the Web to find information.	83%
17. I feel more confident using computer technology now than before I took this course.	88%
18. The web browser I used (e.g., Netscape, Internet Explorer) is an easy program to learn.	79%
19. Activity instructions were easy to follow.	56%
20. Access to the Web was possible at all times.	68%
21. I completed my assignment in 1 hour or less.	27%
22. I used the Web even after my assignment was completed.	80%
23. I will continue using the Web even after the end of this course.	92%

Creating Course-Specific CD-ROMs for Interactive Language Learning

Takashi Iwabuchi
Sandra Fotos
Senshu University

One of the earliest forms of CALL was the drill or pattern-practice exercise, an activity that reflected the structural orientation of L2 pedagogy in the late 1970s and 1980s. Although current language teaching practices emphasize meaning-focused language use, and learners are encouraged to process target structures in authentic discourse, the effectiveness of structure-based computer software tutorials for improving learner accuracy in the drilled structure has been noted from the earliest reviews of CALL effectiveness (see Dunkel, 1991) and continues up to the present (e.g., Marzio, 2000). The challenge, therefore, is to retain those elements that promote the development of accuracy while providing meaning-focused use of the target structure to enhance SLA.[1] This challenge is met by today's language-learning software. Whereas early CALL software was text based and was characterized by low interactivity, today's hypermedia programs provide students with instruction on and practice in using target forms, listening exercises, dictionary assistance, pronunciation exercises, translation, and communicative usages of the forms through authentic texts, sound, and video clips software (Cummins, 2002; Wachman, 1999).

The term *hypermedia* refers to the combination of *hypertext* (clickable text linked to further information in the form of text, sound, graphics, video, or animation) and *multimedia* (a combination of text, video, sound, and graph-

---

[1]For discussions relating SLA theory to CALL activities, see Chapelle (2001) and Chun and Plass (2000).

ics; Ashworth, 1996). Most language-learning software today consists of hypermedia and, because of the large amount of memory required if such programs are not network or Web based, they are produced on CD-ROMs. In addition to an abundance of commercial programs, it is possible for teachers to use multimedia authoring software to develop their own course-specific material.

Although some CALL practitioners—especially in the technology and infrastructure-rich Western nations—might consider CD-ROMs to be dated technology compared with what network and Web-based instruction offer, such a view is not accurate. As one CALL researcher noted, "The reports of the demise of the CD-ROM have proved to be a little premature . . . it remains the case that the CD-ROM is still capable of rich and significant exploitation" (Chesters, 2001, p. 145). Taking the perspective that CD-ROM software is an extremely useful form of CALL, especially for the many instructional situations in the world that lack abundant and up-to-date hardware, language laboratory facilities, LAN capabilities, and a speedy connection to the Internet, this chapter reviews the development of CALL software in relation to the pedagogic model of the time, then describes the development of two course-specific CD-ROMs that incorporate hypermedia features.

CHANGING VIEWS OF CALL SOFTWARE

Many classifications for CALL software have been suggested. Early views focused on the role of the computer as tutor, tool, or tutee (Taylor, 1980), or as magister or pedagogue (Higgins, 1988), whereas more recent accounts take a historical perspective, examining the changing perception of CALL in relation to changes in language-learning pedagogy (see Chapelle, 2001; Kern & Warschauer, 2000). Still others evaluate CALL activities according to the presence of features promoting SLA (Chapelle, 2001; Egbert, Chao & Hanson-Smith, 1999) or its use in L2 research (Chapelle, 2001; Chapelle, Jamieson, & Park, 1996). However, one of the most succinct definitions is used by Levy (1997): the *tutor–tool* framework. Here computer software either *tutors* students through drills, games, pronunciation lessons, or other practice activities, or serves as a *tool* to support learning, for example, word processing and database management software, CMC software, dictionaries, concordancers, translations, and the like.

In this chapter, we approach courseware development from both perspectives: Course-specific hypermedia should both tutor students and support their learning activities through the provision of supplementary services.

FEATURES OF COMMUNICATIVE CALL

Although repetitive language drill-and-practice programs are often regarded as relics from the era of behaviorism and structural linguistics, such activities are actually robust, as their conspicuous use until the present testifies. Computer-based drill-and-practice exercises provide students with repeated exposure to instructed target forms, a process suggested to promote their acquisition.[2]

This is particularly important in the foreign language setting, where the students' only exposure to the target language is in the classroom or the language laboratory. In many EFL settings, for example, the development of accuracy is often paramount because of requirements to pass the English section of school entrance examinations, achieve high scores on English proficiency tests such as the TOEFL for study abroad, or demonstrate English skills through scores on measures such as the TOEIC (Test of English for International Communication) as a condition of employment (Fotos, 2001a). In such settings, CALL-based practice exercises provide immediate feedback on the correctness of the students' answers, and the material is presented at the students' pace, allowing them to control their learning, thus promoting autonomy. In addition, these activities can be done outside of the classroom, providing additional opportunities for target language practice. The success of various commercial CD-ROMs for test preparation attests to the effectiveness of this type of learning format.

However, in 1984—shortly after the introduction of desktop computers and the rise of communicative approaches to L2 learning—Underwood, a major CALL researcher, criticized drill-based structural CALL and advocated a communicative approach providing meaning-focused language use. Underwood (1984, p. 52) described five features of communicative CALL:

1. Emphasis on use of the form for communication rather than on the features of the form
2. Implicit grammar teaching through communicative activities rather than explicit presentation of rules
3. Little or no evaluation of the correctness or incorrectness of student responses because this disrupts the focus on meaning; thus, rather than a single right or wrong answer, a variety of student responses should be encouraged
4. Use of the target language as the language of instruction on the computer screen

---

[2]See Biber and Reppen (2002), Ellis (2002), and Gass and Mackey (2002) for research on the relationship of frequency effects to SLA.

5. Use of qualitatively different CALL activities rather than the mere replication on the computer screen of pen-and-paper exercises

Communicative CALL activities were to be a source of inspiration, providing new experiences for the students and promoting their autonomy as learners. Such considerations have led to the present view of CALL software as a stimulus for student discussion, writing, and critical thinking, and much current CALL software follows Underwood's (1984) five principles.

CONSIDERATIONS FOR COURSEWARE DEVELOPMENT

The CD-ROMs described here were designed to combine structure-based drill activities providing repeated exposure to instructed forms and vocabulary with the communicative features described previously. They were developed to supplement a content-based EFL reading course on current economic affairs for Japanese university students. Following Hubbard's (1996) development-evaluation-implementation framework for software design, three components were considered in planning the software contents: (a) the theoretical approach to the course material to be covered; (b) the design, referring to the goals and objectives of the course syllabus; and (c) the procedure, referring to the type of activities needed, their contents, and how they would be presented by the software.

Theoretical Approach and Course Design

In 1989 the Japanese Ministry of Education mandated a major reform of English language teaching. Before this, as in many foreign language settings, EFL was taught mainly through a structural syllabus and focused on mastery of grammar points, development of translation skills, and memorization of vocabulary items. However, the curriculum reform recommended a revised English syllabus emphasizing communicative skills and the development of knowledge of the L2 culture to promote international understanding. In compliance with these directives for English teaching, our aim was to develop foreign language courseware for reading that went beyond simple comprehension of the reading texts and memorization of discrete vocabulary items, and aimed for the development of overall communicative competence, the development of academic English skills, and an appreciation of English as an international language. The primary goal was for students to improve their reading ability of authentic L2 content-based material through both traditional grammar translation methods involving bottom-up processing of items, and communicative methods involving predicting, inferencing, tolerance of ambiguity, and top-down processing. Two additional goals were for students to acquire vocabulary related to the course content, current economic affairs, and to develop cultural knowledge of Western economic systems and business practices. An important overall goal was development of the students' ability to learn independently and to self-assess and self-monitor, skills found to be promoted by CD-ROM courseware (Cummins, 2002; Kaltenböck, 2001).

However, a problem with many university-level EFL students is that they have studied the target language mainly to pass college entrance examinations. Consequently, after they enter university, they often forget what they studied. Considering the findings of Biber and Reppen (2002) regarding improved vocabulary retention through repeated exposure, we believed that the best way to maintain and even improve the students' vocabulary was to provide multiple communicative opportunities for them to encounter vocabulary taught during grammar-translation exercises in the reading classroom, as well as to encounter other course-related vocabulary. By using the computer as a teaching assistant—the-computer-as-tutor paradigm—we believed that this goal could be achieved and that the students' general reading ability would also be improved. In addition, it would also be possible for the students to spend out-of-class time exposed to communicative English—exposure to the target language being a constant concern in the foreign language situation. Therefore, an additional aim was to maximize individual out-of-class practice in target language reading and vocabulary building. Our first CD-ROM was intended to improve skills in reading authentic language news articles, and our second CD-ROM presented content-based vocabulary within communicative contexts.

Overview of Procedures and Course-Specific Contents

English versions of Japanese newspaper and magazine articles about current economic affairs were collected to provide authentic material in the target language[3] without copyright violations, and a database was made. A core list of topics and vocabulary words was created, and 10 reading topics and 20 vocabulary words were selected from these. Using the database, 10 newspaper articles were selected for each reading topic and five articles were selected for each word. In designing this material, we started from the premise that a meaning-based approach to teaching reading and vocabulary required frequent interaction with large amounts of reading material.

---

[3]A useful discussion of what constitutes an authentic task and authentic language use in the CALL context is found in Chapelle (1999).

CD-ROMs were thus seen as a useful and inexpensive way to provide large amounts of material that would have been difficult and expensive to prepare as hard copies—cost being an important consideration for many instructional situations.

The most important feature of the software presented here is that it is course specific. Although commercial CD-ROM materials are abundant, they do not address the needs of specific courses. A second feature is interactiveness leading to student autonomy. A custom-made CD-ROM takes advantage of three powerful characteristics of CALL: (a) the computer reacts to the choices made by students; (b) the students can practice at their own pace; and (c) the material used comes from authentic English, with considerable support in the form of dictionaries, pronunciation guides, and explanations in the students' L1, a practice highly recommended to provide the scaffolding necessary for learners to understand target language text that otherwise would be incomprehensible (Cummins, 2002, p. 105).

As a model for teachers who wish to create their own courseware, the next section describes the production of two course-based CD-ROMs.

COURSEWARE DEVELOPMENT

The challenge was to develop materials that would motivate the students to invest considerable time in study outside of the classroom. Although courseware creation was time consuming, we believed that investing the time resulted in the production of durable and interesting material that could be used by class after class of L2 students until the reading and vocabulary topics became out of date. We began software development by considering seven principles recommended for CALL software design (Boling & Soo, 1999, p. 443) and closely followed them throughout the design process:

1. The interface and terminology are consistent from screen to screen.
2. The layout of each screen makes good use of space.
3. Legibility and readability are high.
4. The software makes good use of contrast, repetition, alignment, and proximity.
5. There are no serious navigational errors.
6. Undesired actions can be easily reversed.
7. Audio and video playback is of good quality.

Although there are other authoring programs,[4] the first CD-ROM was made with Macromedia Director Version 5 for the Macintosh (a Windows version also exists). Like the earlier Macintosh authoring software, Hyper-Card, Director is a user-friendly application producing "card-based" materials. Consequently, teachers who have had experience with HyperCard will find Director easy to use. The name of the software, Director, came from the movie term *director* because the user produces a "movie" on the "stage" screen. Text, graphics, sounds, and videos are inserted as "cast" members on the stage screen. The commands are similar to natural English, for example, "get," "put," "set," and "go," and prepositions such as "into," "to," and "with," and the program uses normal syntax such as "If . . . , then." The CD-ROM material developed thus consisted of texts, graphics and sounds, with links to additional support material.

Steps in Creating the CD-ROMs

After collecting authentic L2 reading materials, being careful of copyright considerations, the first paragraph of each article was input using a word processing program. Because the first paragraph of an article is usually a summary of the details to follow, it is a succinct and readable presentation of the passage contents. The second step was to copy the paragraphs onto the Director "stage." Linkages with other pages were created by writing commands in the "scores." Font sizes, colors, and locations were selected. It was also possible to insert commands at any place, similar to the earlier program HyperCard. The final stage of developing the material was to change it into a movie to be played on computers lacking the Director software, and then to burn the CD-ROMs.

Director Version 7 was used to create the second CD-ROM. Again, authentic material containing target vocabulary items was input by a word processor, then imported into the authoring program. As with the earlier version of the software, the programming language was similar to natural English: "set," "put," and "go" were the most frequently used commands. If a mistake in programming was made, the software indicated the location and type of the mistake, allowing for easy correction.

The following sections describe how the students interacted with the two sets of courseware. Before they were given the CD-ROMs they were taken to

---

[4]Some other multimedia programs are Hyperstudio, Authorware, and Shockwave, the last being a browser plug-in from MacroMedia that allows the creation of Web-based interactivity. Software used on Web sites for Director-type interactivity includes common gateway interfaces, programs written in such languages as Perl, C++, Applescript, and Javascript.

the language laboratory and were taught how to operate the computers, load the CD-ROMs, and operate the programs.

Reading Courseware Overview

The reading CD-ROM contained 10 topic units with 10 reading passages in each unit, making 100 passages and related activities. The passages were supported by notes about the words, translations of the passage in the students' L1, and grammar and content explanations. For example, while reading a passage, the students could click on unfamiliar words to access a page defining the word in the L1 and explaining it in simple English. It was also possible to print out the page, along with the passage, for future study. By clicking the back button, the students could return to the original passage.

The students began by loading the CD-ROM. When the introductory screen appeared, they wrote their student number and user name, then clicked the start button, which led to the table of contents (Fig. 9.1). A list of 10 newspaper headlines representing the 10 topics appeared on the screen. The students clicked on a headline and went to the first reading

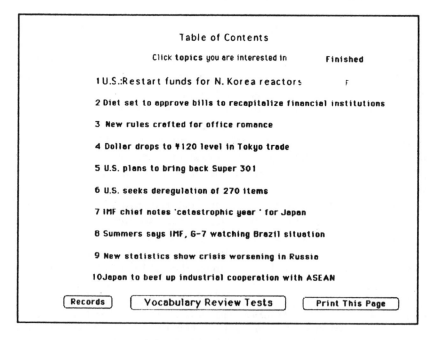

FIG. 9.1.   Table of contents.

passage. They listened to the passage read aloud by an English native speaker, reading along with the voice for pronunciation practice or reading the passage by themselves after listening several times. If they needed assistance in understanding the passage, they clicked on Notes to access support material. Figure 9.2 shows a reading passage with L1 definitions of key terms. When the students felt they understood the passage, they clicked a button to advance to two true–false questions about the passage contents. After completing this activity they checked their answers. If the answer was correct, 1 point was added to the score field of their record page (a score sheet) at the end of the unit. The students could also access additional support material for further study before attempting the true–false questions.

The next activity was a cloze passage (Fig. 9.3) with four content words deleted from the reading passage, and the words listed randomly below. The students dragged each word into the appropriate blank. After completion, they clicked the evaluation buttons at the end of each line containing a blank, these showing either OK or X (incorrect) after the answer. If the

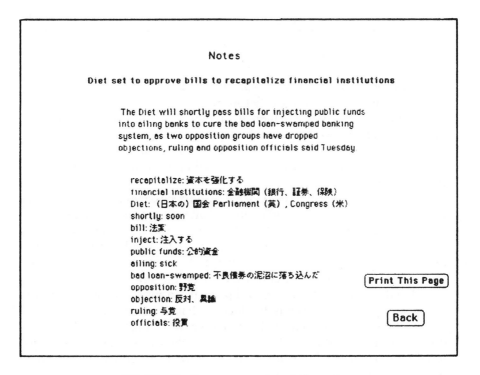

FIG. 9.2. Reading passage and vocabulary notes.

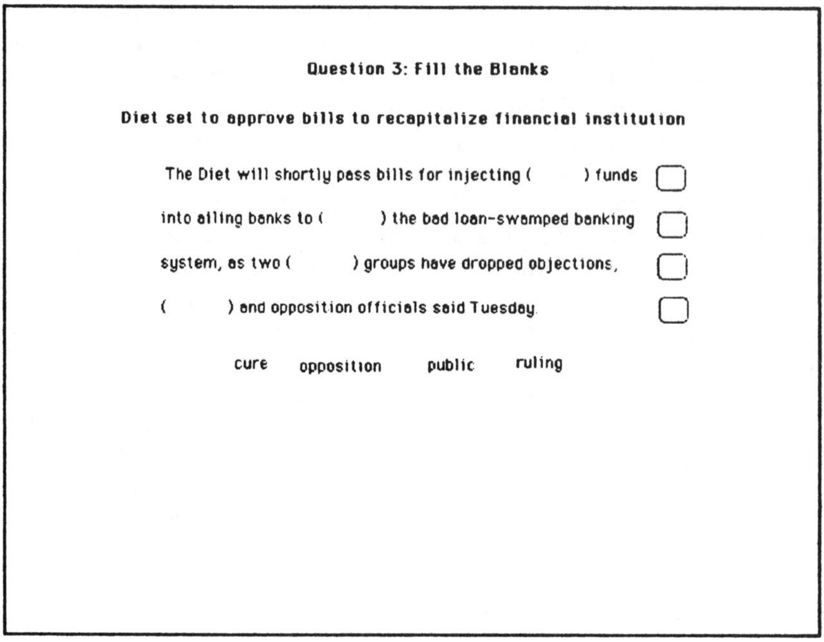

Question 3: Fill the Blanks

Diet set to approve bills to recapitalize financial institution

The Diet will shortly pass bills for injecting (   ) funds   ☐

into ailing banks to (   ) the bad loan-swamped banking   ☐

system, as two (   ) groups have dropped objections,   ☐

(   ) and opposition officials said Tuesday.   ☐

cure   opposition   public   ruling

FIG. 9.3.   Cloze activity.

word was correct, a success page appeared presenting the paragraph with the blank filled in with the correct word.

The final activity was a sentence-arranging task highlighting the students' intersentential comprehension of the reading passage. The students rearranged four phrases so that a correctly ordered sentence appeared (Fig. 9.4). The answer check was performed in the same way as the fill-in-the-blank exercise.

After the students completed all 10 reading passages and activities for the topic, they returned to the table of contents and clicked the vocabulary-review-tests button. Here they matched up the L2 content-based vocabulary used in the reading passages and cloze tests with their L1 translations. When all terms were matched, the students checked each answer. If the answer was correct, OK appeared beside the word and 1 point was added to the score field of the record page. If the answer was incorrect, an X appeared. The program was designed so that all passages and tests for a unit had to be completed, and when they were finished, students advanced to the record page (Fig. 9.5), where their finishing time was entered automatically. The students then printed out and submitted the record page to their instructor.

Question 4: Drag phrases into a sentence

Diet set to approve bills to recapitalize financial institutions

① ▢

② ▢

③ ▢

④ ▢

system, as two opposition groups have dropped objections,

into ailing banks to cure the bad loan-swamped banking

ruling and opposition officials said Tuesday.

The Diet will shortly pass bills for injecting public funds

FIG. 9.4. Phrase arranging activity.

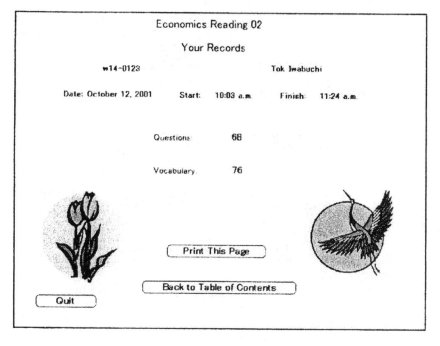

Economics Reading 02

Your Records

w14-0123   Tok Iwabuchi

Date: October 12, 2001   Start: 10:03 a.m.   Finish: 11:24 a.m.

Questions: 68

Vocabulary: 76

(Print This Page)

(Back to Table of Contents)

(Quit)

FIG. 9.5. Reading courseware record page.

Vocabulary Courseware Overview

Our second set of materials was created with Macromedia Director Version 7. Authentic L2 reading material was again collected to provide five different passages for each of the 20 target vocabulary words. Like the reading material, the vocabulary-based reading passages had a listening practice section and a cloze-type exercise to give the students practice in listening to discourse-level English on course-related contents and to develop their intersentential comprehension skills. This was a meaning-based approach reinforcing vocabulary items taught in the classroom. Each unit also had two sets of review tests and a record page.

To use the courseware, the students again typed in their numbers and names and clicked the start button. A table-of-contents page appeared, displaying the 20 words, and the students clicked on a word, which then appeared in various designs and sizes accompanied by an English native speaker's reading for listening and pronunciation practice. The students then clicked the go-ahead button and a reading passage including the word at least once appeared, also read aloud by an English native speaker. By clicking the listen-again button, the students could listen to the passage repeatedly. They could also click the notes-and-translation buttons to access support material and an L1 translation.

The next screen presented the students with a cloze test with one blank in the reading passage, and possible words arranged randomly at the bottom of the screen. The students listened to the passage read by an English native speaker and typed in the correct word. Here, the target vocabulary item was used only in the meaning-focused context because the test item was another word. The material was thus structured so that the students encountered multiple communicative usages of the target term, as well as other content-related terms, at the discourse level.

The students then checked their work by selecting a fill-the-blank-and-click-here button. If the answer was correct, they proceeded to the right-answer page automatically and 1 point was added to their scores on the record page. If the answer was incorrect, a "Try Again" message appeared and they remained on the same page, until they entered the correct answer. After the students completed the passage and its activities, they repeated the process for the remaining reading passages containing the target word. When they were finished, they returned to the table of contents to study another word.

After the students completed all activities for the 20 words in the table of contents, they clicked the review-tests button and completed vocabulary-matching tests for the target words. Again, they matched the L1 and L2 terms, and after finishing and checking the tests, they proceeded to the record page. As with the reading courseware, this page displayed the students' number, name, date, starting time, finishing time, and cloze test and vocabulary test scores. Again, the students printed out the page and turned it in to the instructor.

SLA THROUGH NOTICING
AND INSTANTANEOUS FEEDBACK

Research suggests that after L2 students' awareness of target items has been raised through formal instruction, they often go on to notice the items in subsequent communicative input if the items are encountered frequently. Such continued awareness of a target form appears to be important in initiating the restructuring of the students' implicit system of linguistic knowledge (Fotos, 2001a, 2001b). From this perspective, CALL activities that raise the students' awareness of target forms—either by explicit instruction or by repeated communicative exposure allowing them to become aware of the form—can assist them to acquire these forms eventually. On the first CD-ROM, students worked with grammar structures, vocabulary, and concepts that had been taught previously in the classroom. These items were embedded in communicative contents and comprehension was supported by L1 notes and translations. On the second CD-ROM, the students encountered previously instructed vocabulary words in five authentic language contexts and listened to an English native speaker read each word and passage aloud, which also helped them notice the target word. In addition to the target words, the students were exposed to other content words in the passages and support material, so those words might have also remained in their memory, especially if they encountered the words in other communicative contexts. We therefore suggest that this procedure helped the students to notice the material that was presented in the classroom, promoted continued awareness of the material, and thus facilitated its acquisition (see Biber & Reppen, 2002; Ellis, 2002; Fotos, 2001b; Gass & Mackey, 2002).

In addition, the instantaneous nature of the feedback on the correctness of the activities and tests and the provision of supplementary material to aid further study are also suggested to facilitate learning. Research on student response to CALL feedback on the correctness of their grammar and vocabulary usages, particularly when the error is clarified through support modules, and when they can obtain the correct answer quickly, indicates that students: (a) attend to such feedback and correct their output; (b) use the support modules such as dictionaries and explanations; and (c) appreciate being able to access quickly the correct answer as a way to decrease frustration (Heift, 2001; Kaltenböck, 2001; Pujola, 2001).

Finally, following the software design considerations mentioned earlier, the CD-ROMs contained attractive colors, animation, and graphics. Following the model of popular video games, we suggest that the use of animations and graphics in CD-ROM courseware can help maintain the students' interest and can motivate them to practice on their own.

FOREIGN LANGUAGE STUDENT ATTITUDES TOWARD THE COURSEWARE

In the classes, 160 students used the two CD-ROMs and were asked to comment on their experience by answering a simple 11-question survey administered in their L1 at the end of the course (see the Appendix for the English translation and response frequencies). Most reported that the CD-ROMs were their first experience with CALL courseware, and 80% said that they enjoyed the freedom to interact with materials at their own pace. Also, 40% found the authentic material interesting, and 47% said they had learned the vocabulary words presented on the CD-ROMs and recognized them in other readings. In addition, 58% reported liking English more than before, and nearly 50% commented that they were now more interested in studying current affairs and economics through English. Moreover, 43% percent observed that the longer they worked with the programs, the easier it was to understand the passages, and 30% reported positive results from listening to the English native speaker readings. Almost 90% reported that the notes and translation support materials helped them a great deal, a finding that indicates the need for teacher-developed courseware to provide such support.

In the open-ended section of the survey, many students said that they felt relieved because there was no pressure for quick and accurate production, as there is in a teacher-fronted classroom. In fact, several students reported that they became "addicted" to the materials—as though they were playing a video game—and could not stop studying them until they finished the last unit. The high level of enthusiasm for the courseware was very gratifying.

FOR THE TEACHER: TEN STEPS TO DEVELOP COURSEWARE

The following 10 steps are a guide for teachers who want to design course-specific CALL material:

Step 1. Determine the purpose of the course, including the goals and objectives, assessment procedures (such as a record page), and the nature of the proficiency gains to be made. Consider student variables including age,

L2 proficiency, previous experience with CALL, special content and language needs that should be addressed, and ways to create motivation to use the courseware outside of class to provide extra interaction with the target language.

Step 2. Determine the specific learning and assessment activities that the students should perform, based on their proficiency level and the course requirements.

Step 3. Choose authentic L2 reading materials from newspapers and other media that meet the course purposes and are not beyond the students' proficiency level, yet provide them with challenges and new material. Be careful of copyright considerations.

Step 4. Outline the material to be used and determine the order of presentation, the order of activities related to the materials, the tests, record sheets, other assessment activities, and support materials. Because nearly 90% of the students using the two sets of courseware described here appreciated the translation and grammar explanation support materials, and because research has repeatedly indicated their value, such materials should be a strong component of the program.

Step 5. Copy portions of the selected L2 reading materials with a word processor.

Step 6. Insert the copied material into a multimedia authoring program by making text fields on specific screens.

Step 7. Write programs for each behavior following the instructions of the authoring program. Choose attractive illustrations from clipart CD-ROMs or shareware Web sites (enter *clipart* in any search engine to find these sites) and insert them on the screens.

Step 8. Test each part of the program carefully for design and content features, keeping in mind the features of successful courseware mentioned previously (Boling & Soo, 1999, p. 443) and making changes if necessary. The following seven features may also be used for the evaluation process (Tsutsui, 2002, p. 31):

1. Simplicity: In general, operations should require only a click of a mouse or a key stroke to complete.
2. Naturalness: Operations should match natural hand and eye movement.
3. Directness: Operations should require a minimum amount of thought and not have confusing commands, buttons to click, and so on.
4. Spontaneity: Operations should be in accord with common sense and use familiar colors, phrases, and symbols.
5. Flexibility: In general operations should provide multiple paths for completion of the task.

6. Mistake-Free: The possibility of making mistakes using the software should be minimized.
7. Recoverability: If a mistake or misoperation is made, it should be possible for the user to recover without having to restart the program.

Step 9. Change the finished materials into movies and burn them onto CD-ROMs.

Step 10. Evaluate the software by asking students to complete a survey on their experience and to comment on aspects of the software that they found problematical or felt could be improved.

CONCLUSION

Language teachers have traditionally developed their own materials for generations and are now increasingly using multimedia authoring software to develop interactive hypermedia for course-specific needs. It has been suggested that teacher creation of practice material both enhances students' learning of target skills, because the material is tailored to their needs and the course requirements, and contributes significantly to both teacher and student autonomy. Although the ability of courseware to provide corrective feedback is more limited than in a classroom, this very fact has been found to encourage students to develop the ability to self-assess and self-monitor (Wachman, 1999). Here, the CALL students responded positively to the instant nature of CALL feedback and appreciated the provision of support modules explaining the correct answer and providing additional information on target structures.

Current multimedia authoring programs are not difficult to use and do not require any special hardware. All that is needed is a large gigabyte hard disk, which is now available at a very low cost, and a CD-ROM burner. Although pen-and-paper materials are still important, we would like to especially encourage foreign language teachers to create CD-ROM courseware as supplementary material that students can study on their own time, increasing their exposure to the L2 and becoming more autonomous learners, a frequently noted benefit of working with CD-ROM programs. Although it is true that material development is time consuming, we would like to emphasize that language teachers will find great satisfaction from developing their own courseware and will receive appreciative student feedback after its use.

ACKNOWLEDGMENT

This project was supported by a grant from the Senshu University Research Assistance Fund, 2001.

REFERENCES

Ashworth, D. (1996). Hypermedia and CALL. In M. Pennington (Ed.), *The power of CALL* (pp. 79–96). Houston, TX: Athelstan.

Biber, D., & Reppen, R. (2002). What does frequency have to do with grammar teaching? *Studies in Second Language Acquisition, 24*(2), 199–208.

Boling, E., & Soo, K. S. (1999). CALL issues: Designing CALL software. In J. Egbert & E. Hanson-Smith (Eds.), *CALL environments: Research, practice and critical issues* (pp. 442–458). Alexandria, VA: Teachers of English to Speakers of Other Languages.

Chapelle, C. (1999). Theory and research: Investigation of "authentic" language tasks. In J. Egbert & E. Hanson-Smith (Eds.), *CALL environments: Research, practice and critical issues* (pp. 101–115). Alexandria, VA: Teachers of English to Speakers of Other Languages.

Chapelle, C. (2001). *Computer applications in second language acquisition.* Cambridge, England: Cambridge University Press.

Chapelle, C., Jamieson, J., & Park, Y. (1996). Second language classroom research traditions: How does CALL fit? In M. Pennington (Ed.), *The power of CALL* (pp. 33–53). Houston, TX: Athelstan.

Chesters, G. (2001). Editorial. *ReCALL, 13*(2), 145.

Chun, D., & Plass, J. (2000). Networked multimedia environments for second language acquisition. In M. Warschauer & R. Kern (Eds.), *Network-based language teaching: Concepts and practice* (pp. 151–170). Cambridge, England: Cambridge University Press.

Cummins, J. (2002). Learning through target language texts. In K. Nakajima (Ed.), *Learning Japanese in the networked society* (pp. 105–122). Calgary, Canada: University of Calgary Press.

Dunkel, P. (1991). Research on the effectiveness of computer-assisted instruction and computer-assisted language learning. In P. Dunkel (Ed.), *Computer assisted language learning and testing* (pp. 5–36). New York: Newbury House.

Egbert, J., Chao, C., & Hanson-Smith, E. (1999). Computer-enhanced learning environments: An overview. In J. Egbert & E. Hanson-Smith (Eds.), *CALL environments: Research, practice and critical issues* (pp. 1–13). Alexandria, VA: Teachers of English to Speakers of Other Languages.

Ellis, N. (2002). Frequency effects in language processing: A review with implications for theories of implicit and explicit language acquisition. *Studies in Second Language Acquisition, 24*(2), 143–188.

Fotos, S. (2001a). Structure-based interactive tasks for the EFL grammar learner. In E. Hinkel & S. Fotos (Eds.), *New perspectives on grammar teaching in second language classrooms* (pp. 135–154). Mahwah, NJ: Lawrence Erlbaum Associates.

Fotos, S., (2001b). Cognitive approaches to grammar instruction. In M. Celce-Murcia (Ed.), *Teaching English as a second or foreign language* (3rd ed., pp. 267–284). Boston: Heinle & Heinle.

Gass, S., & Mackey, A. (2002). Frequency effects and second language acquisition: A complex picture? *Studies in Second Language Acquisition, 24*(2), 249–260.

Heift, T. (2001). Error-specific and individualized feedback in a web-based language tutoring system: Do they read it? *ReCALL, 13*(1), 99–109.

Higgins, J. (1988). *Language, learners and computers: Human intelligence and artificial unintelligence.* Harlow, England: Longman.

Hubbard, P. (1996). Elements of CALL methodology. In M. Pennington (Ed.), *The power of CALL* (pp. 15–32). Houston, TX: Athelstan.

Kaltenböck, G. (2001). Learner autonomy: A guiding principle in designing a CD-ROM for intonation practice. *ReCALL, 13*(2), 179–190.

Kern, R., & Warschauer, M. (2000). Introduction: Theory and practice of network-based language teaching. In M. Warschauer & R. Kern (Eds.), *Network-based language teaching: Concepts and practice* (pp. 1–19). Cambridge, England: Cambridge University Press.

Levy, M. (1997). *Computer-assisted language learning: Context and conceptualization.* New York: Oxford University Press.

Marzio, M. (2000). Getting "real" with video and CD ROM: Real English at the Marzio School. In E. Hanson-Smith (Ed.), *Technology-enhanced learning environments* (pp. 67–84). Alexandria, VA: Teachers of English to Speakers of Other Languages.

Pujola, J. T. (2001). Did CALL feedback feed back? Researching learners' use of feedback. *ReCALL, 13*(1), 79–98.

Taylor, R. (Ed). (1980). *The computer in the school: Tutor, tool, tutee.* New York: Teachers College Press.

Tsutsui, M. (2002). Developing CALL software. In K. Nakajima (Ed.), *Learning Japanese in the networked society* (pp. 25–37). Calgary, Canada: University of Calgary Press.

Underwood, J. (1984). *Linguistics, computers, and the language teacher: A communicative approach.* Rowley, MA: Newbury House.

Wachman, R. (1999). Classroom practice: Autonomy through authoring software. In J. Egbert & E. Hanson-Smith (Eds.), *CALL environments: Research, practice and critical issues* (pp. 403–426). Alexandria, VA: Teachers of English to Speakers of Other Languages.

APPENDIX

Translation of L1 Questionnaire on Student Attitudes Toward CD-ROM Courseware
(N = 160 students; the numbers in parentheses show response frequencies for each item)

Key: (1) strongly disagree; (2) disagree; (3) not agree, not disagree; (4) agree; (5) strongly agree

1. When I studied these materials, I came to like English better than before.
   (1) 8   (2) 15   (3) 45   (4) 68   (5) 24
2. It became easier for me to read English-language newspapers.
   (1) 20   (2) 49   (3) 63   (4) 24   (5) 4
3. I am more interested in learning about current affairs and economics in English now.
   (1) 11   (2) 24   (3) 49   (4) 42   (5) 34
4. I learned many new words using the CD-ROMs and noticed the words in other material.
   (1) 3   (2) 16   (3) 68   (4) 41   (5) 32
5. I found the headlines very interesting.
   (1) 5   (2) 14   (3) 76   (4) 35   (5) 30
6. I came to understand English sentence structures better than before.
   (1) 22   (2) 35   (3) 48   (4) 30   (5) 25

7. I enjoyed the freedom to use the CD-ROMs to study at my own pace.
   (1) 2   (2) 6   (3) 24   (4) 68   (5) 60

8. The supplementary notes and translations helped me a great deal.
   (1) 0   (2) 3   (3) 14   (4) 80   (5) 63

9. The English native speaker's readings improved my listening comprehension ability.
   (1) 21   (2) 36   (3) 56   (4) 34   (5) 13

10. The more time I spent using the CD-ROMs, the easier it was to understand the reading passages.
    (1) 16   (2) 35   (3) 40   (4) 40   (5) 29

11. Please write your feelings about using the CD-ROM materials.

III

IMPLEMENTING CALL IN INSTITUTIONAL SETTINGS

Part III is also practical in nature, but here the focus shifts from the use of CALL in classrooms to the implementation of CALL on an institutional and inter-institutional scale. A common theme in the three chapters in this section is the importance of having a clear idea of the requirements of the learners, the teachers and the institution, and the need for careful organization and planning. Again, the chapters present theory and research, describe case studies, and offers guidelines for CALL implementation.

In the first chapter, "Setting Up and Maintaining a CALL Laboratory," Browne and Gerrity consider the issues involved in designing and running CALL laboratories. Noting that a common mistake schools make when creating a budget for a new CALL lab is emphasizing the hardware at the expense of the equally important intangibles of lab design—staffing, software, and training programs—the authors have found that decision makers often fail to adequately assess or meet the needs of their school population or to address the physical learning environment where the technology will be used. Furthermore, teachers who possess experience and information in these areas can often be left out of the decision-making process. This chapter helps bridge the gap between teachers and CALL lab decision makers by providing a list of key issues to consider and practical advice to facilitate decision making.

Written from the point of view of a teacher/course coordinator and the service/consultancy outlook of a courseware developer, O'Connor and Gatton's chapter, "Implementing Multimedia in a University EFL Program: A Case Study in CALL" provides a detailed account of setting up and running CALL in a university EFL setting during a three year period. The authors first review research on institutional CALL, then describe the investment in time and skill on the part of teachers, technical staff and computer lab assistants, as well as the institutional learning curve as their institution adapted and reacted to the new courses, noting that the quality of teaching and learning progressed during the period. The chapter thus serves as a "how to" and a "how not to" manual and offers guidelines for teachers contemplating initiating similar CALL programs at their own institutions.

In the final chapter of this section, "A Collaborative Model for Online Instruction in the Teaching of Language and Culture," Opp-Beckman and Kieffer present a review of collaborative learning in the ESL context to frame their model for collaborative online L2 teaching and learning. Noting that educators now have the capacity to co-develop and co-teach/facilitate courses that span continents and bridge cultures, the authors present a collaborative model in which two or more institutions work together to develop and implement online Web-based courses to build L2 language skills and facilitate intercultural awareness. Addressing issues and concerns at the levels of administration, teaching and learning, they present teachers with: (1) a pre-course inventory, needs assessment and analysis, and master planning, (2) a discussion of phases and considerations in developing, implementing and evaluating course content, and, (3) a list of potential pitfalls and possibilities unique to a Web-based learning environment.

Setting Up and Maintaining
a CALL Laboratory

Charles Browne
Aoyama Gakuin University

Scott Gerrity
University of Victoria

So, you've decided (or more likely have been encouraged by others) to set up or upgrade a CALL facility at your institution. If you are like most CALL lab coordinators, it is not a job that you have either been specifically trained for, or aspired to, but one that came about because of an overlap between your institution's need for technology-based language instruction and your own experimentation and experiences in this area. Unfortunately, the scope and magnitude of a CALL coordinator's responsibilities can be daunting. The decisions you make in terms of hardware and software choices, as well as the planning for the design of the facility itself, can easily involve hundreds of thousands of dollars and directly affect the lives of many people, including students, faculty, school administrators, and especially your own!

Sound intimidating? It certainly can be. The information in this chapter, however, has been gathered from a wide range of sources, including both theoretical and practical, to help you to make informed choices when designing, setting up, and maintaining a CALL facility.

USER INPUT AND NEEDS ANALYSIS

All too often, CALL facilities are initiated (and completed) from a largely top-down approach. That is, "many programs are expected by their administrations, for reasons of competition and prestige, to offer a computer based lab, often before teachers and staff know what to do with one" (Szendeffy, 1997). As a result, purchasing and budgetary decisions are often overly concerned with acquiring the latest, state-of-the-art hardware, rather than with identifying the specific needs of the target population or with providing adequate funding for intangibles such as support, training, and upkeep. When planning a new CALL facility, one suggestion made by many CALL administrators is the need to have as much faculty input as possible during all stages of the process. According to McVicker (1997), this kind of involvement not only helps the CALL administrator to make better hardware and software choices but also leads to teachers' having a greater sense of investment in the facility with the result that it is much more likely to be used.

One useful place to begin when planning a CALL lab is to conduct a needs analysis. This doesn't necessarily have to be a large-scale questionnaire or a formal survey—a good starting point can be to simply ask yourself (or the planners) a series of questions regarding how, and by whom, the lab will eventually be used. The process of answering such questions can often lead to a much clearer sense of what type of a lab you will need to develop. McVicker (1997), for example, suggested the following four general questions as a starting point:

1. Is there a high rate of ownership of computers among faculty and students, or will users see the center as a place to do basic productivity tasks such as e-mail and word processing?
2. Does your institution serve residential students who will want to use the center during evening hours, or commuters for whom the center will function mostly during the day?
3. How convenient will the center's location be for language classes and independent study?
4. Does your institution have in-house training programs for technology, and to what extent can your center take advantage of these programs?

A high rate of ownership of laptop computers, for example, might lead to the development of a lab with a section of empty tables and LAN connections so that students can plug in and work from their own computers. If, on the other hand, you foresee many users needing the lab facilities for basic productivity tasks, special areas might be set aside for precisely this type of computer use (specifying the type of tasks that are allowed at a given station can help to ensure that users who need the lab for specific CALL tasks or software are more likely to have easy access).

Surveying user preferences and determining usage patterns as far in advance as a year before construction is a good idea. This can be done easily within an existing facility by tracking visits and usage, as well as through student surveys. If no facility yet exists, much insight can be gained by consulting with other similar facilities that have established usage patterns and by reviewing the growing body of literature on the topic. Any number of issues will arise when undertaking this aspect of a needs analysis, and it is likely that student preferences will differ considerably from faculty preferences. For example, whereas faculty may tend to emphasize the need for group areas or multimedia-based learning to do class projects, students often prefer individual carrels where they can focus on completing assignments. Typically, students enrolled in language courses visit the CALL facility two to three times per week and stay approximately 50 minutes per visit.

It is not surprising, however, that student usage fluctuates dramatically depending on assignment and test dates. At most universities student usage tends to double during the days directly preceding exam periods. During these times, the vast majority of students want quiet, out-of-the-way stations where they can drill with vocabulary- or grammar-based programs. To this end, many CALL facilities now place "low-end" computer stations around the peripheral areas of the facility and dedicate their use solely to basic textbook-accompanied materials for first- and second-year students. Student surveys conducted into the use of other types of language technology support these usage trends. For example, at Harvard University, students indicated that they prefer working individually with audio at single carrels by a margin of 87% to 12% and working individually with video by a margin of 57% to 37% (Doyle, 2000, p. 19).

Ideas for doing a CALL laboratory needs assessment can also be found online. At http://eduvista.com/claire/needs.html ("Faculty Needs Assessment Questionnaire," 1997), for example, an online faculty needs assessment is available and can be freely printed and distributed. Detailed results of a CALL learning center survey conducted at Temple University can be found at http://temple.edu/icsurvey/ ("Learning Center and Smart Classroom Survey," 2000). A more comprehensive resource for both needs assessment and lab design is the IALL (now IALLT—International Association for Language Learning Technology) Language Centre Design Kit (Ledgerwood, 2001; see http://www.iall.net for further information).

You will also need to pay attention to factors outside of the lab that might affect its use. For example, what is the rate of computer ownership among teachers and students in your population? If it is low, it may be wise to set aside a certain number of stations in the lab for basic activities such as word processing, e-mail, and net surfing. If, on the other hand, laptop ownership is high, the lab should contain a number of empty desks with LAN connections to accommodate their use in class.

Will the lab have enough stations to allow access for all students at all times? If not, what arrangements need to be made to accommodate students who are waiting to use the facilities? If floor space is available, it is often helpful to provide empty tables for individual and group study in the area. This feature is extremely popular with students as it greatly increases the range of activities they can do while in the lab.

SPACE, LEARNING TASKS, AND ERGONOMIC DESIGN

Over the past two decades there has been a growing awareness among business and individuals of the importance of ergonomics in the design of work and study spaces. This has translated into a multimillion dollar industry for ergonomically correct office products. This gives a CALL laboratory planner a great range of options when developing a new facility. With so many choices, where is the best place to start? Again, a needs-analysis-type questionnaire may prove useful. Coleman and Healey (1999) have developed a list of questions to ask, which are focused primarily on ergonomic and task-based factors.

Questions about general ergonomic factors:

1. What kind of lighting (artificial and natural) is provided? How well can it be controlled?
2. What kind of flooring or floor covering is needed?
3. What kind of climate control is needed?

Questions about task-based factors:

1. How does the interpersonal focus of human tasks affect the overall room layout?
2. How do specific staff tasks affect the overall room layout?
3. How does the need of individuals to move around because of what they are doing affect the overall room layout?
4. How do the specific hardware needs involving networking issues (including printing and other peripherals) affect the overall room layout?
5. How do the tasks performed by teachers and lab support staff affect the design of the students' workstations?
6. How do the tasks performed by teachers and lab support staff affect the design of all workstations?

Again, how your faculty, staff, and students answer these questions will have a strong influence on the final design of the lab. Consider, for example, the first three questions related to ergonomic factors. Regarding Question 1, it is very important to have highly controllable light sources, so that specific tasks can be managed and the room as a whole can be dimmed or lit with the highest number of permutations possible. Incandescent lights—called pot-lights, recessed into the ceiling—serve well over multiuse areas such as group seminar tables, study areas, and video-projected viewing areas, both to increase lighting for studying purposes or to dim for viewing purposes. Computer monitors, on the other hand, work best where there are no unnatural hot spots, reflection off screens, and flicker or glare off work surfaces. Diffused, indirect lighting—either recessed or baffled—serves well in this case. A presenter at a recent CALL conference gave a convincing demonstration that diffused, baffled spectrum lights focused downward on the walls causes much less computer glare than any other lighting configuration. Teacher-centered areas, such as whiteboards or podiums, require more focused spot lighting.

In response to Question 2 regarding flooring, a slightly elevated floor, although expensive, can protect and hide the vast amounts of wiring associated with a computer facility. Antistatic carpeting is an excellent floor covering because it both helps protect your magnetic media such as floppy disks and minimizes the amount of dust that will get into the equipment. Good carpeting can also absorb sound in a large room, though it is often not enough. For facilities dedicated to multiple uses, you may want to consider the addition of sound absorbing wall materials (often carpeting) as well as electronic sound dampness. In the University of Victoria CALL facility, the walls have ridged wall carpets that absorb sound through the hard edges of the ribbing. Though no electronic dampness were installed, an infrared audio system allows students wearing cordless, light headsets to listen to audio transmissions without disturbing other lab users.

Regarding climate control, keep in mind that computers last considerably longer and break down less often in temperature- and humidity-controlled environments. Though lacking in natural lighting, CALL facility labs are often located in the basement level of buildings because there is more natural cooling and greater humidity control. Artificial air cooling systems are important as well, especially for busy computer networks and dedicated server rooms. In addition to standard air conditioning systems, air exchange systems that move volumes of air across the room are good for both computer systems and human beings. These systems are supplied by an outside air source, usually from a shaded area directly outside the lab. While in the design phase, consider elevating the air vents and recessing them into the walls, and choose the quietest system possible to help further eliminate ambient noise.

Another ergonomic factor you may want to consider is furniture. There are now many companies that specialize in ergonomic computer furniture. Glass-top desks that hold the computer monitor underneath can free up desk space and allow for better eye contact between students (and teachers) during communicative and group tasks. Movable computer desks allow for different arrangements within the same lab, so long as provisions are made for the necessary wiring. Matte (nonglare) surfaces and neutral colors reduce glare. The size and height of chairs and desks may need to be considered if the lab is to be used with younger learners or for those with special-access needs. Most computers now can be easily set up for wireless use, allowing teachers to wheel in a cart of laptops into regular classrooms that are not prewired for use. If group work is the focus, consider building carrels that accommodate multiple users at individual stations, and partition each from the other with glass or plastic to increase privacy and decrease noise. If the option is available in the design phase, configure the layout of stations in your lab first, then attend to the wiring needs. Always provide more electrical outlets and ethernet ports in your plans than originally deemed necessary. Allowing for adequate time to discuss these and other factors can help you to develop a much clearer picture of what kind of facility you will need.

HARDWARE VERSUS "HUMANWARE" NEEDS

Too often, school administrators and decision makers involved with funding CALL are more concerned with having a lab that is more technologically sophisticated or state of the art than surrounding schools than they are with analyzing and meeting the specific needs of their own school population. One of the most common mistakes schools make when creating a budget for a new CALL lab seems to be an overwhelming emphasis on hardware at the expense of money for the equally important "intangibles" of full-time support staff, software, and training programs. Davies (1996), for example, quotes a dean of faculty's remark as typical of the administrator's perception of the use of technology in mass education: "By next fall we want you to have a complete multimedia courseware up and running for five languages. And could you please tell me how many people I can reduce the language teaching staff by, once these materials are in place" (p. 2).

One important principle then, is to keep a clear focus on teacher and student needs rather than on technology. An error that many people make when they begin to plan for a new CALL facility is to rely too heavily on vendors for advice. This can often be problematic because typically they will try to impress you with how the latest (and most expensive) technology will solve all your schools' problems rather than think about what's best for your particular situation. One difficulty with implementing the latest (and most expensive) technologies that vendors rarely mention is that the majority of teachers and students will not yet be aware of or comfortable with using state-of-the-art hardware.

Try to take the "lowest tech" approach possible when designing and setting up the lab. The higher up the technology ladder you go, the more problems you will have to deal with, not just in terms of underuse by teachers and students because of the steep learner curve required but also because of the greater number of breakdowns and software and hardware incompatibilities that always seem to occur with new technologies.

The next principle relates to paying appropriate attention to human resource factors. When making the budget for your CALL lab, it is extremely important that you emphasize the importance of setting aside money for training and support. Once the lab is completed, students and teachers will need to be introduced to or trained in how to use the various features of the lab. As Davies (1996) pointed out, although the promise of new technology was one of the chief reasons for the growth in the number of language laboratories in the 1970s and 1980s, a lack of training in both the operation of and methodology behind their use was a major factor in the quick decline in their use from the 1980s to the present day. Teachers are often intimidated by CALL labs and are much more likely to use them if there is ongoing training and support available.

STAFFING YOUR CALL FACILITY

As much as the other computing services at your institution would like you to believe otherwise, the CALL lab is not just another computing facility. Your facility will run and support specialized hardware, software, and learning materials. Faculty will turn to the CALL lab coordinator for advice and assistance, and students will prefer studying in the CALL facility to other computer facilities because knowledgeable staff are available to help them with both technical and instructional assistance. In this computing facility, language, culture, and learning are valued and nurtured. A balance lies somewhere between broad, standardized computing practices and the focus on individualized learning, in maintaining the autonomy to press forward with specialized services and to determine pedagogic goals and strategies. Growing and juggling relationships to this end should fall under the lab coordinator's job description.

Unfortunately, there is no real standard for the qualifications or job description of the CALL lab coordinator. The institutional culture and the size and role of the facility often determine the coordinator's duties. Larger facilities (at larger institutions) with adequate staffing may require the coordinator to devote more time to administrative or managerial duties while other staff attend to technical issues and work directly with students. Smaller facilities, however, may ask the coordinator to balance administrative, technical, and service-related duties as needed, often as the sole focal point in the large circle of relationships among faculty, students, administration, and technology. Regardless of the institution's size, the coordinator is likely the one called on to promote the use of CALL instruction and to educate faculty and staff in CALL pedagogy. In many cases, faculty and students will turn to the coordinator for advice in teaching methodologies and its application in both older and newer technologies (Scinicariello, 1997). If in this role, the coordinator should possess ample teaching experience and the appropriate credentials, not only to understand the demands of teaching and learning but also to garner the respect of faculty and administrators (often former faculty) looking for guidance and assistance in these areas.

A panel of language lab directors lists the following qualities (in general agreement of the order of importance) for persons managing a language lab:

1. Language teaching experience and expertise,
2. Organizational management skills,
3. Knowledge of another language or experience with another culture,
4. Technical knowledge,
5. Instructional design expertise,
6. Commitment to research and development, and
7. Commitment to service (Dvorak et al., 1995, p. 32).

The same list of qualities could apply to CALL facility coordinators, though not necessarily in this order. Certainly, administrators and faculty committees creating tailored job descriptions will rank these qualities differently based on the role of the facility and context of the candidate search. For example, a coordinator expected to prepare and give frequent workshops, develop educational materials, and work directly with students using language-learning tools and materials would be served better with a background in language teaching, knowledge of language and culture, and instructional design. In another instance, the coordinator may be in charge of numerous self-access rooms and technical support staff, and would likely perform the associated duties more effectively having strong managerial skills and advanced technical knowledge.

Budgetary considerations in most CALL facilities tend to limit staffing beyond the position of coordinator, and more often than not so-called extra staffing needs are met by using part-time student workers. In general, students make excellent staff because they understand the learning issues facing other students and instructors feel comfortable working with them. Many students already possess high-level computer skills; often those applying to work in the CALL facility do so because they already know and like the environment. However, it is important to keep in mind that student workers in general have different priorities from career employees. Stone (1995) pointed out that students tend to prioritize school and social life above the job, with the result that their job commitment is generally temporary and short term, their schedules erratic. This can be problematic because the burden of training and scheduling the students becomes a time-consuming, never-ending task that invariably falls on the already-busy lab coordinator. Career employees, on the other hand, tend to view the job as a desired choice (or a chosen profession), resulting in work hours that are much more stable and a commitment to the lab and to their job that is longer term and more permanent. Having at least a few full-time employees, especially in the technical support area, will also prove invaluable when (not if) your lab runs into problems. If your network crashes, for example, it might be difficult to rely on a student employee to fix the problem. Whereas students tend to work more effectively with the users than technical support staff—and often in the target languages—they cannot and should not be called on to do work that requires a higher level of commitment or skill than they can offer.

There are other staffing issues to consider as well. One often-overlooked aspect of CALL staff responsibilities are the "invisible," non-CALL-related demands placed on them by faculty and staff throughout any institution. In the past 5 years, the nature of support services has changed considerably as technology has made its way into faculty offices. Faculty members now frequently turn to CALL staff for just-in-time support for everything from e-mail program shortcuts to advanced programming in Java. At times, CALL staff are asked by faculty to do workshops on a vast range of computing topics such as word processing, e-mail, Web page creation, spreadsheets, and more, even though these are not directly related to CALL. Though these topics are normally addressed in workshops sponsored by other groups on academic campuses, faculty are less likely to attend these because of scheduling conflicts or comfort issues. At other times, CALL staff are placed in the role of research assistants or even teaching assistants, when asked to find Web materials, administer online or audiovisual quizzes and tests, or train students to do homework on instructor-authored Web exercises or even to author Web exercises themselves.

TRAINING ISSUES

Though there are a wide variety approaches to providing technology training to instructors, there is a general consensus of the goals (see Kassen & Higgins, 1997). The first is to help users establish a general comfort level with the technology. Introductory workshops help do this, but ongoing support that not only revisits frequent questions and concerns but also builds on previous training has proven to be the most successful approach. Faculty, in particular, need to know that their concerns will be addressed and that continued support is available at the institutional level. Participants are most comfortable, for example, in settings where the facilitator–participant ratio is low and the participants know each other professionally. Coordinators and facilitators frequently emphasize the need for hands-on components in general training sessions to allow participants the chance to explore as well as discuss observations and uses. Participants cannot realistically do this in large settings. The primary goal is both to introduce technology and to have participants familiarize themselves with it.

The goal, in every case, is to stir the individual's creative capacities in finding the best fit among technology, curriculum, and personal teaching style, and to promote reflective thinking on that process. Integration of technology into established course curriculum and the development of critical skills are cited as the goals that best address the issues of fit between the technology and pedagogic concerns. Our experience in training instructors is that workshops addressing the creation and integration of technology into language courses must focus on actual projects or ideas brought to the workshop, where instructors can be guided when needed but also allowed simply to explore the feasibility of their ideas. In many cases, at least for instructors already possessing a high comfort level with technology, developing any idea or project necessitates critical skills. Development happens before integration, but each step from planning to student use involves assessing skill levels, tools, student needs, and fit into the course curriculum. This takes practice and guidance and plenty of reversion to previous training material.

TRAINING AND WORKSHOP IDEAS

The following suggestions are all actual workshop and training practices that have proven to be effective at our institutions. The goal is, in almost every case, to address comfort-level issues, provide examples and training for the integration of CALL into existing curriculum, and generally to stimulate ideas and possibilities for CALL development and use.

1. Demonstrate CALL class materials to all multisectional language classes at the beginning of each term. Train yourself and your staff to do this well, so that students find them interesting, intelligent, and entertaining. Although time consuming, this serves two purposes: It gives control to the center coordinator of all CALL materials presentation, and it profiles the center (and materials) to incoming students.

2. Develop jointly with language faculty a series of workshops aimed at teaching assistants and junior faculty that addresses a broad range of language teaching techniques. If language teacher training already exists, work closely with those administering the programs. These workshops place CALL staff squarely in the loop for ongoing training of newer instructors. In this format, CALL materials can be integrated into the programs and showcased as everyday teaching. We see these types of workshops building confidence in inexperienced instructors by providing them with concrete examples of in-class CALL use.

3. Establish procedure and process lists or routines for various types of CALL use or development and train faculty to use them in real projects. These can be general procedures aimed at critical skills around technology, but procedures that can be applied globally in any development project or program use. We find they serve well as departure points for faculty already at a high comfort level with technology.

4. Develop joint projects with faculty that involve their pedagogic expertise and your instructional design and technical expertise. Once finished, showcase these projects to other faculty and staff, with the active participation of the faculty member. Provide a hands-on session after the presentation, and get participants thinking about ideas for their own projects. Instructors respond best to what their peers are doing.

5. Bring in outside presenters that your faculty would acknowledge as experts in the field. Ask the presenters to develop hands-on workshops that are relevant to the needs of your faculty. Have them create or make available interactive Web-based training exercises as part of the conditions of the honorarium or get permission to do this yourself with their materials. Follow up with ongoing workshops in which faculty can continue developing their ideas and projects.

NETWORKS, SERVERS, COMPUTERS: PURCHASE AND CONSIDERATIONS

It is important to keep in mind that at its foundation your new CALL facility will be a small piece in a greater puzzle that compromises the physical and administrative architecture of the institution. For this reason, any planning, purchasing, implementing, and maintaining will require the active participation of your institution's equivalent of facilities management, networking services, computer user services (or academic computing), purchasing, and accounting services. All of these departments will be able to assist you in assessing space, design, network needs, budgeting possibilities, vendor interactions, tendering bids, policy creation, and procedure or code issues. At the beginning of the planning stages, inform all of these departments of your plans and develop liaisons with individuals who are available at the other end of a phone line for immediate consultation. Once plans are initiated, the construction phase will place the coordinator squarely in the position of general contractor, and decisions will have to be made at the spur of the moment. This requires balancing the disclosure of information; working out specifics in institutional, technical, or legal jargon; assessing power dynamics; and juggling administrative hurdles with the immediate need to get things done.

Network planning necessarily begins by assessing your local network needs and comparing these with state of the institutional networking infrastructure. It is likely that your needs will be greater than those of general academic computing because of the focus on multimedia use in teaching and learning. For example, audio files need greater bandwidth (transmission speed capabilities) than text files; video files need greater bandwidth than audio files; streaming video needs more bandwidth than compressed video files—what will your network do and what do you envision it doing several years from now? Can the current institutionwide network sufficiently support what your facility is designed to do? This is important because your local network will be only as fast and as good as the slowest link in the greater networking chain. When assessing the institutional network infrastructure, read general reference materials, find institutional networking diagrams, and certainly consult with your facilities management and networking services. The proper questions to ask center around the following: network bandwidth capabilities, data routing (what paths your CALL data transmissions will follow getting around as well as to and from campus), system platforms (NT, Linux, Windows 2000) supported on campus, port availability, and network upgrade schedules. Bad decisions due to ignorance of general networking issues can be costly and in many cases can cause problems both in the local network and within the institutional network infrastructure. Planning accordingly is very important.

Big-picture networking issues also require a general understanding of network servers. Servers come in many shapes and sizes: There are file and storage servers, application servers, administrative servers, Web servers, proxy servers, video servers, and more. These terms do not necessarily refer to the physical server box, but to its use. Again, what your facility will do will also determine what type of server (and capacity) is required. For example, storing and serving vast amounts of audio or video files will require a large file or storage server, as well as an appropriate backup system. If your facility works with audio files, it would not be uncommon by today's standards to fill 60 to 80 gigabits of disk space in a 2-year span (depending on the size of your usership and the file formats used to house and serve the material). Video will require much more disk space. Many software applications, as well as Web-based materials, can be served on the same server. However, if your CALL facility also supports a turnkey language lab solution, a dedicated software application server will also be required to run their software. Other considerations involve security issues—in their most basic form a student log-in and authentication system—that may require additional server needs.

As the direct interface between the user and the CALL materials, the individual computer is the most tangible technological consideration. As such, it receives a great amount of attention by administrators financing the purchase and set up of a new facility. Most CALL coordinators, however, will tell you that it rates poorly when placed next to networks, servers, software, and digital materials (not to mention user issues). In our experience we have found that the brand of computer is relatively unimportant because many good clones are available at reasonable prices, and still better ones will be available before this article is even published. The computing capacity is the true measure of the computer's worth, which places it in a line of descending order from networks to servers to computer. The items in the individual computer that affect computing capacity are processing speed, random-access memory (RAM), disk drive, and operating system software. These items have become increasingly important as the focus has turned away from stand-alone software programs to Internet use and digital multimedia, the support of which is tied to bandwidth capacity and the serving, processing, and storage of media files. Replacement cycles of computers run 3 to 5 years, and these upgrades have less to do with the computer's life cycle than its computing capacity. Older computers can either be recycled or simply given more basic duties that they can still perform well. Support and expertise are the more important considerations because configuring computers and networks, creating and making available materials, and training users are usually the biggest indicators of a CALL facility's success or failure.

THE CALL MATERIALS-SELECTION PROCESS

Robb and Susser (2000), in their article "The Life and Death of Software," examined a wide range of literature dealing with software selection, and they came to the conclusion that a large gap exists between the advice given in the literature and what teachers actually do when they select courseware. Any teacher or CALL facility coordinator who has been through this process knows how true this observation is and can likely attest to the confusion around the vast amounts of literature pointing out the many and varied methods of selecting CALL materials. Pedagogic issues are compounded by technical issues, and the line between the two often blurs when one begins to analyze what and how the various features of the software program works. Although more detailed suggestion for evaluating educational software (Reeder et al., chap. 13, this volume), and ESL Web sites (Robb & Susser, chap. 14, this volume) are offered elsewhere in this volume, it is important for the discussion here to consider briefly materials selection in the context of planning and maintaining a CALL facility.

POLICY PLANNING VERSUS MATERIALS ACQUISITION

Deciding on the most appropriate CALL materials for your facility can easily become a complex and burdensome affair. The best outcomes tend to be a mix of practices appropriate to the situation, along with a certain amount of flexibility. An important point, which needs to be made from the start, is that it will be almost impossible for you to have a full selection of software available to students upon opening a new CALL facility. This takes time and sustained effort. Software programs, CD-ROMs, and Internet sources should all be evaluated through trial runs by staff, faculty, and students, and should strive to meet the institution's pedagogic as well as technical goals and requirements.

Even in an existing CALL facility, all materials should be reevaluated periodically, and if deemed necessary, upgraded to complement newer teaching methods, techniques, and tools employed by the faculty, or expectations by the students. For that reason, policy issues around software planning and selection (but not necessarily the software itself) should be dealt with early in any facility-planning process and should necessarily involve administrators and faculty members whose students will use the software on a regular basis. In short, CALL materials decisions are curricula decisions, and a high level of involvement by those determining curricula will assure both better and greater use of the materials selected, and thus better and greater use of the CALL facility as a whole.

As is the case with most budgets, who pays for what and how needs to be addressed at the beginning of the process. Will the materials budget belong to the CALL facility, to the individual language units, or will it reside in a general slush fund for this purpose? Certainly, whoever picks up the tab will influence what the selection process looks like, who does it, and what is selected. A more concrete question related to materials planning is to what extent will the software (and technology) be integrated directly into coursework? An important principle to remember is that the degree to which CALL is viewed as a legitimate pedagogic tool (and used as such) will correspond directly to its level of integration into a given language curriculum.

Where possible, CALL materials should not be selected by individual criteria or brought in piecemeal, but rather should be chosen as part of a well-researched and developed plan in which all aspects of a course (or program) follow a defined teaching and learning strategy. In this case, however, CALL materials selection becomes complex because, as Gillespie and Mckee (1999, p. 452) argues, "There needs to be a specific CALL strategy which is agreed and adopted by all staff on a course (or in a subject) and not left to the efforts of one or two academics and therefore seen as peripheral." Levy (1997) adds that specific teaching strategies can be based on a variety of factors including the use of models of SLA, approaches to language learning, descriptions of teaching methodologies, or theories of instructional design.

EVALUATING AND IMPLEMENTING MATERIALS

In practice, selecting and implementing CALL based on a comprehensive learning and teaching strategy involves identifying target skills and finding CALL materials that address these. Once the target skills are identified (preferably through some sort of needs analysis), the selection process becomes increasingly more streamlined and manageable. Concrete frameworks involving checklists, trial runs, and user input can then be more easily created and tested. Programs vary in scope and presentation, yet the most exciting possibilities today lie in the realm of multimedia—both in the off-the-shelf varieties and in self-authoring tools for creating multimedia-based exercises. Many of these authored materials are already available on the Web, created by language instructors for a wide range of uses. A simple Internet search will bring a wealth of hits for such sites.

Although CALL staff will likely rate technical issues higher and educators will focus on pedagogic features such as learner control, ease of use should receive the highest priority when considering any software selection. The stark reality is that irrespective of how many bells and whistles a program has, it is the programs that are easier to use that get used the most. Training, user demands, and troubleshooting issues (and frustration!) are all reduced when programs are easy to use. Keep in mind, however, that materials that have a strategic place within a language curriculum—especially those to be used in class—require more formal training for both staff and end users. Furthermore, their use will likely require just-in-time support whenever used in a classroom setting on multiple computers. In any learning and teaching setting that is governed by time constraints, the issues related to training, technical support, and ease of use will be most likely determine whether faculty will continue using the materials.

One final consideration focuses on the course-materials-selection process, which is no longer limited to textbooks. Publishers now vie for departmental selections using a whole range of course materials such as drill-and-practice computer programs, interactive multimedia programs, CD-ROMs, course Web sites, chat rooms, arranged e-mail exchanges, online tutoring, and video conferencing. Many institutions are also now supporting online classroom environments such as WebCT and Blackboard. Coordinators need to be aware when these selection committees are being formed and attempt to participate at some level in the evaluation process. Be aware that many faculty, especially those who are more technologically savvy, may not like canned solutions and may prefer instead to customize their own environments.

TECHNICAL CONSIDERATIONS

Technical considerations play a large role in the continued use of CALL. In practice, most CALL materials are selected based on their pedagogic merit but are discontinued because they present too many technical difficulties. Specific issues often mentioned by technical staff include: slow or difficult installation, network bugs, size of program, poor tech support from companies, slow-loading Web sites, and incompatibilities with certain computer operating systems (e.g., Windows 95 vs. Windows 2000). Students and educators, on the other hand, tend to cite difficulties centered around program features such as: an inability to pick up where they left off when revisiting a program, an inability to send results to an e-mail address, a poor navigational structure, or a lack of learner control or customizable options in the program. Again, using evaluation checklists and a defined framework during trial runs certainly helps with these issues, especially around program features. However, we recommend remaining flexible and open to exploration, as checklists can never fully accommodate the full range of pedagogic and technical considerations displayed by a given program or Web site.

Network and version compatibility issues are usually discovered only after continued use. CALL staff meetings should address checklist or framework issues, and honing those aspects of the trial process will happen only with experience and time. Faculty should be made aware that even though a trial run may have been successful, technical difficulties may arise once the program is placed on the network, and the CALL coordinator should reserve the right to discontinue the program at a certain juncture if there are excessive technical difficulties. Many a conflict has arisen over this very issue because educators often do not understand the complexity of computer networks and may not see the problem when using the program. Who does this and how these decisions are made should be addressed and made clear in the planning process.

ONLINE MATERIALS DEVELOPMENT

The evolution of online materials development in most CALL facilities has, in the past, been an organic process, originating out of practical concerns around providing good, supplemental materials to students; addressing overcrowding of the physical CALL space; and granting students greater access to materials from different locations. This trend has only increased. Teachers, for one, have become more intrigued with the learning possibilities for their students as a broad range of self-authoring tools have come available, and as both networks and computers have grown in capacity to support the developed materials once placed on the Web. Studies show that students, as the end users, respond more favorably to materials authored by their own instructors (Pederson, 1988). This explosion in availability of easy-to-use authoring tools, as Levy (1997) pointed out, can be attributed directly to authors' ability to customize materials for their students, in contrast to the commercially produced programs that inherently cannot respond to "significant learner characteristics or major contextual factors" at any given institution (p. 91). Understandably, online learning materials development is perhaps the fastest growing area of CALL, and greater attention should be given it when planning and setting up a CALL facility.

At its foundation, any development process—be it a textbook or a Web site—is a cooperative effort between the author and the medium. In light of the innovations afforded by hypertext and digital multimedia, certain limitations of textbooks, long unrecognized as such, are only recently becoming apparent. Newer technologies, on the other hand, exhibit their own limitations, namely what the programming languages, authoring tools, and computers themselves can and cannot do when developing and delivering learning materials. Language instructors, for example, typically bring to the development process an inclination toward a particular language-learning methodology and likely will choose to support its application when authoring materials. If the instructor supports highly communicative methodologies and wishes primarily to simulate authentic language exchanges via computer, he or she will quickly discover that computers cannot do this and that to approximate this exchange in a practical manner would require vast amounts of time, funding, and programming expertise.

The degree to which the pedagogic goal of the learning materials correspond to the technology's capability to support it is commonly referred to by developers as the fit. The first practical step in determining the fit is to assess and understand which uses of technology best support the pedagogic goal of the project. This is, in truth, no easy task because both the technology and the creative possibilities with it are dynamic and complex, and depend greatly on the level of expertise of those involved with the project. On a relatively simple level, the technology may be a selected software authoring tool, in which case an assessment necessarily involves the range of authoring features provided to the author-to-be as well as the degree of interactivity afforded to the end user once the materials are developed. Making an appropriate selection here is important because the developers of the various authoring tools possess their own pedagogic inclinations— explicitly stated or not, but usually evident through simple evaluation of the program's interface design and the features provided or not provided. For obvious reasons, the instructor will want find an authoring tool whose pedagogic design fits with his or her own inclinations. A good place to start is the *CALICO Review*, http://astro.temple.edu/~jburston/CALICO/index.htm, which offers a wide range of critical reviews on language software and authoring tools.

In another instance, the technology may involve a host of development tools and a highly customized design, the consideration of which is possible because a team of developers with expertise in various programming languages and graphic design is in place for project support. If this is the case, the instructor can think on a different scale for the project—one appropriate to the resources available—and will be afforded much more flexibility in design and face fewer limitations that may compromise the initial conception. The fit here necessarily involves other issues such as time, funding and expertise, all of which instructors rate as the leading impediments to initiating CALL projects (Levy, 1997). The instructor can rely on the experts for the technological assessment and development and can focus his or her energies on the creation of content. Budget permitting, this model is ideal, because team members can do what they do best.

At this point, the notion of fit must be expanded to include the needs and attributes of the users, which when combined often becomes the most crucial element determining the successful use of the project. In many cases, these needs are based on known quantities or conditions, such as a specific learning activity identified by the course instructor, the creation of which is done on a small scale to fill in a particular gap in the curriculum. Even at this level, students generally expect that the learning principles and presentation of the activity will be consistent with those in the textbook or those that are emphasized in the course. Greater attention must be paid to learner attributes in large-scale developments such as comprehensive language tutorials, which tend to address reading and listening comprehension or focus on a variety of grammatical components, usually through a series of multiple-choice, cloze, word-order, and short-answer exercises. For example, lower level learners accustomed to teacher-driven learning may find strong tutorial guidance and rigid parameters helpful, but students with a good command of the language-learning process, as well as the computer-control process, will likely want to employ a wider range of discovery strategies. Discovery strategies range from interesting "hint" options, to glossaries, help menus, and thoughtful feedback from the instructor. Self-evaluation options have also proven to be motivating for students. In summary, students without ways to explore learning possibilities are less likely to complete the exercises and tend either to discontinue using the materials or to use it only mechanically by resorting to the "show answer" components more readily than they should. The vast majority of instructors and CALL developers now seem to recognize that students will learn the material better, regardless of the implicit pedagogic goals, on Web sites they enjoy using.

Having considered the issues, it is also important to review briefly actual practices and models. Project development at some institutions is a highly defined process that coordinates all the steps from initial concept to final product, by identifying and implementing in a structured manner the various elements including needs analysis, task breakdowns, learning objectives, learner characteristics, instructional design, media selection, and evaluation. At other institutions, the development is less formally structured, more spontaneous in nature, and adjusting along the way to the lessons learned at the completion of each stage, with ample consideration given to feedback from students and colleagues (see Levy, 1999, pp. 83–107, for a more detailed discussion of this topic). To one degree or another, the initial development phase after planning involves the creation of a prototype on which to base the project as a whole. Often the prototype is the first unit in a multiunit endeavor, created primarily to help test and evaluate items such as fit, instructional design, navigational structure, number and format of exercise templates, input data routines, and the ever-important user feedback. Much of the creative work is done here, so that the developers can commit themselves with confidence to the remainder of the project. Another practical outcome of this approach is that students and graduate assistants can then use the models, templates, and routines to do much of the subsequent work. Training, supervision of tasks, progress assessment, and management issues then become the primary considerations. Evaluation and testing on computers, servers, and networks, plus further attention to user feedback, is often the last phase of the project and requires the whole team's participation.

VIRTUAL VERSUS PHYSICAL SPACE: WHAT TO DO AND WHERE

Arguments are being made at all levels by both administrators and technology proponents that a wide variety of language-learning needs can be better served in a virtual environment than in a computer classroom. Many campuses now have central fileservers and fast network infrastructure that connect computer labs, classrooms, libraries, and dorms. Web-based interactive grammar, vocabulary, and reading exercises; textbook-accompanied materials; and even assignments based on short audio and video clips can be placed on media servers and served remotely, so that students have no need to attend a dedicated facility. Results of student online assignments (and even online tests) can be sent via e-mail or file transfer protocol (FTP) directly to instructors, thus making required lab attendance obsolete. Publishers now provide Web sites, Web-based exercises, and chat rooms that can be accessed from anywhere by students enrolled in courses. With access limitations removed, students and faculty have greater control of their own schedules and can choose to work from any place at any time, providing the network infrastructure is in place to support this.

For many, though, the very identity of the CALL facility is being threatened. As Garrett (1997) and Yang (2000) both noted, physical space proponents need to be able to articulate their arguments for their continued existence on both technical realities and pedagogic considerations.

Technical realities are, in a sense, easier to articulate because the issues involved appear to be more concrete. First, it is important to realize that many of the previously discussed arguments for a virtual classroom arose out of the simple need to address the overcrowding that often occurs in physical centers. Unfortunately, most virtual classroom proponents tend to overestimate what is possible as they get mesmerized with the promise of what new technologies can offer. For example, the reality of what is possible can change dramatically when user needs enter into the picture. Issues such as configuring computers for special fonts and plug-ins (especially for non-Western languages), the higher quality and speed of audio and video on local networks (vs. remote access via the Internet), and the ongoing questions regarding both technical and instructional assistance all seem to be considerably better supported within a physical center. Furthermore, activities that require team project work (Web-based and other), hands-on training and workshops, research into teaching and learning, and project development with both students and faculty can realistically be supported only within a physical center.

Pedagogic considerations are, by their very nature, less definable and can thus seem less concrete, especially with user outcome studies and other research often showing mixed results. However one views the arguments, though, there does appear to be a general consensus by CALL proponents that the pedagogic value of CALL is best served when CALL is integrated directly into course curricula. Introductions and explanations of materials must be prepared, and communicative exchanges must coordinate with pre- and postcommunicative CALL-related activities. Yang (2000), a physical space proponent who addressed many of the issues discussed here, strongly criticized the majority of current out-of-class Web-based instruction in which the computer program replaces the role of the instructor. He argued that although such programs have many positive uses as teaching tools, which can help fill specific curricula gaps, they should never play the role of an instructor (as they necessarily do in the absence of the instructor). According to this line of reasoning, a physical space would be required for most CALL materials and for any in-class use where a range of activities take place within a given session and where students might need hands-on access to CALL materials (which is the case with any teaching and learning environment).

The most powerful argument for having a physical rather than virtual center is also the least tangible. At issue here is the perception administrators have about CALL centers. The issue is simple: Students do not come to the CALL facility to use technology (as many administrators believe); they come to learn languages. The facility must become a center for it to be successful. Language learning is social interaction (Canale & Swain, 1980; Fillmore, 1979); language learning is community building. In the long experience we have working in and observing CALL labs around the world, one intangible that seems to be consistently true is that CALL labs that cater to the social aspects of learning (both formal and informal) are much more successful than CALL labs that focus more strictly on technological solutions to learning. Observe any CALL lab that provides ample space for individual and group study, student lounges for relaxation, and comfortable seating arrangements, and you will likely find a constant stream of students, using the technology or not, as their preferences and needs dictate. Aside from computing-related activities, they receive tutoring, do language exchanges, study textbooks, and generally enjoy being as immersed as possible in a dedicated learning environment. Actually, planning for this aspect of your center is one of the most important challenges you will face, because, to put it simply, if students do not like it, they will not use it.

The untold truth is that many administrators unfamiliar with the complexities of language learning view virtual labs as a practical solution when faced with the financial commitments required to staff and run a CALL facility or train language faculty. If technology, not learning, is the sole issue, it will be difficult to convince an administrator with a budgetary mindset that a physical center is essential. Try to emphasize the complementary role of virtual and physical spaces, and approach the process with learning and teaching, rather than technology, as the central argument.

TURNKEY LANGUAGE LABS

Turnkey language labs refer to comprehensive language-learning technology systems—also known as solutions—offered by companies such as Tandberg, Sony, and CAN8, to name a few. In the past, these systems were associated with the audiolingual method (discussed, for example, in Richards & Rogers, 1986) and were composed of various hardware components such as a master console and student cassette recorders, linked together via a network of audio cables, that provided a full range of features allowing for multiple configurations for individual, pair, and group work.

To one degree or another, the manufacturers of these systems have now embraced the digital era and are producing what are called hybrid systems because they support both digital and analog technologies, and operate over both standard computer networks (software based) and dedicated audio networks (hardware based). Most of the hybrid systems provide the same range of functions as their analog predecessors but have added databases to assist in class set-up and easy access to materials, tracking devices, and authoring tools. Some manufacturers offer, instead of a complete package, component or modular packages based mainly on whether the lab is teacher driven (classroom) or student driven (drop-in facility). Most provide a range of separate components that deal exclusively with video distribution because the bandwidth capabilities over the majority of computer networks cannot support real-time, simultaneous video distribution to more than a few stations at a time. In every case, however, the new look and feel of the hybrid systems is completely digital because the manufacturers have gone to great lengths to integrate seamlessly the analog components, and both instructors and students see only monitors displaying a virtual master console interface and virtual student recorders.

To our knowledge, all of these systems are designed to run on Windows-based systems only (no Macintosh versions are yet available) and require little more than point-and-click input to operate the features. Across the board, the network specifications regarding bandwidth, RAM, and drive storage capacity are far from demanding, and an average computer can now act as student station, master station, and even the dedicated application server needed to serve the software. All of these systems, however, require a large storage or file server to handle the vast amounts of audio files that accumulate quickly, and the same is true for student station hard drives if students are allowed to store the audio and video files locally. Careful planning, back-up of materials, and scheduled deleting of nonessential files can extend server and storage capacity. Video files can also be transmitted, which as far as these systems are concerned (insofar as the system supports the particular file format) operate like any other file. At this point, the real limitation is the network bandwidth capacity, not the turnkey lab itself.

It may be that the hybrid systems will eventually disappear in this transition period of analog to digital and physical to virtual. This is no small consideration when planning a purchase of this magnitude and commitment. Some manufacturers now claim to have created completely digital systems that do everything their predecessors did, conquering the hurdle of exchanging of two-way audio in real time over Internet protocols (IPs). The IP was not designed to support two-way, real-time audio transmission, and a noticeable lag (and poor quality and at times interference) usually occurs between speaker and receiver, creating an interaction between teacher and student in a classroom setting that most would consider unacceptable. Analog technologies over dedicated audio cables (placed squarely within four walls) still do this far better. Consider, however, that students and teachers communicating from remote locations need not worry as much about this problem, and once quality and stability of voice-over IP improves, possibilities open up greatly for use of turnkey solutions that emphasize remote access capabilities.

The three primary arguments vendors use to sell these systems revolve around simplicity of use, the analog to digital capabilities including media players that support a vast array of file formats, and the synchronous audio-distribution possibilities. Many administrators and educators instinctively gravitate toward this one-system-fits-all approach and are willing to lay out large capital expenses, knowing the solution comes completely installed, with some initial training and ongoing servicing provided, thus requiring relatively low maintenance on top of that already required to support the computer network. There is merit to this, and by and large these systems do deliver technically what they promise.

The question remains, however, whether the large price tag of turnkey solutions is justified and whether such a solution is needed or will be used. First, a close inspection of the vast amount of both hardware and software products on the market shows that many turnkey features can be replicated at a relative fraction of the cost of a complete "solution." This was not the case 5 to 10 years ago. Second, many CALL coordinators and lab directors notice that the majority of turnkey features rarely get used by instructors, primarily because of the lack of ongoing training and pedagogic development around the technology. Time, advancement incentives, and expertise are usually to blame here because creating good materials (beyond simple digitized files) and providing technical training to use them is difficult and time consuming. To complicate matters, instructors are rarely adequately recognized by their superiors for this type of work. The CALL coordinator will need to be able to negotiate features and components to get only the features needed and to avoid paying for expensive items that may never be used, as well as to address the many issues around training and developing materials.

Keep in mind that turnkey solutions now operate solely on Windows-based operating systems, so a computer network (including a knowledgeable technical staff) will be required in addition to the actual turnkey solution. This not only multiplies the cost of the solution but also brings up other issues around scheduled use of facility, training of staff and users, software compatibility, and network maintenance.

A thorough needs assessment of users and an equally thorough product assessment of equipment is the best way to address the many issues around deciding on a turnkey solution. This includes visiting facilities that have these systems in place, consulting with as many users as possible, and providing multiple vendor demonstrations to your faculty and staff (vendors are usually willing to give very in-depth demonstrations as the amount of money involved in the purchase is extremely high). The assessment, planning, and acquisition process is necessarily long, at times tedious, and certainly expensive. After installation, there will be bugs, especially in a newly installed computer facility, and things such as user training, analog-to-digital conversions, and materials development are all ongoing. Be prepared to start a year in advance to hone arguments and make solid recommendations; then be prepared to continue assessing use and training users for the duration of the system's use.

THE DIGITAL DIVIDE: EMBRACE IT WHEN PLANNING

All existing CALL facilities and language labs have legacy libraries consisting of hundreds or even thousands of archived analog audio and video materials, some of which still get used regularly, many of which do not. Future CALL facilities will necessarily have to balance the commitment to both analog and digital resources because analog is still used frequently even as digital becomes the state-of-the-art choice for new media. CALL proponents find themselves squarely in a transition period, complete with the ongoing debate about the quality of each, the conversion process, and the technological as well as pedagogic implications of going digital.

CALL development in the last few years has made its greatest strides in its ability to exploit multimedia for pedagogic use. Greater network capacity; the proliferation of good, simple-to-use authoring tools; and the World Wide Web have made it possible to use multimedia in any number of ways on computer networks. In truth, newer facilities can choose to dispense with analog technology altogether and focus solely on digital multimedia in both its pedagogic development in-house, in purchasing materials off the shelf, or both. In doing so, however, the administrative and technical requirements become substantial. Copyright laws, for example, are often still a grey area when dealing with educational use of materials, digital or not. Materials that must be converted from analog to digital should be assessed beforehand for copyright clearance because converting means changing the form of the media and most likely providing a different method of access for users. Placing audio and video files on the Web, for example, requires security measures, likely based on a course ID number and student username and password, so that only enrolled students can access the materials. Who will digitize the materials, and how? Often, when CALL staff digitize materials, instructors are unhappy with the editing scheme and want things redone to their specifications. Instructors, however, rarely want to spend the time to do it themselves. It is important to work out these issues beforehand, as a great deal of time will be spent digitizing, editing, and developing materials. The digitizing process works in real-time only, so be prepared in terms of staffing for a labor-intensive job, requiring long spans of time sitting at the digitizing station(s).

A fully digital facility is indeed high tech, and high tech requires more planning, development, expertise, and maintenance. More things can go wrong, and troubleshooting issues are substantial. User training needs are high, and there will be more resistance (as well as anxiety) to technology that is not yet widely recognizable. Again, it is wise to maintain a balance between high tech and low tech, between the ideal and the realistic.

CONCLUSION

Still overwhelmed? Although it is true that the issues involved in setting up and maintaining a CALL facility are numerous, complex, and often time consuming, the information and advice offered in this chapter can be reduced to a few key principles as follows:

1. Clearly identify the specific needs of your students and faculty. Not only does this prove beneficial by involving the faculty and students at an early stage in the planning process, it also serves administrators whose job it is to make informed decisions.

2. Devote a large portion of your budget to full- and part-time staff and ongoing training for faculty and students. Given that technology is changing more rapidly than ever, having proper staff and training in place is all the more necessary for the continued life of the facility. A proper needs analysis will bring you to this same conclusion.

3. High-tech solutions are not always best for your institution. More advanced technology brings with it the need for more frequent and complex training, as well as greater user-end and technical support demands. When thinking technically, pay attention to computing capacity rather than computers.

4. Pay attention to ergonomic and task-based factors when designing the facility. These factors often boil down to two issues: comfort and functionality. A comfortable and highly functional facility will bring the users in, keep them there longer, and bring them back again.

5. Focus on the people using the facility rather than technological issues alone—people-friendly labs get used more. Try to create a dedicated learn-

ing environment rather than just a computing facility by adding study spaces, student lounge areas, and special events. Emphasize the complementary role between virtual and physical spaces and how both are needed for a language-learning environment.

6. Plan for transition. Newer facilities can address CALL transition issues more readily than older facilities by paying attention foremost to digital and multimedia possibilities and by considering in-house materials development. Properly assess turnkey solutions and involve faculty and students in the process.

By staying focused on these larger issues, you will be less likely to be sidetracked by the many competing interests that will vie for your time and budget. The potential benefits of a well-run CALL facility for students and faculty are enormous.

REFERENCES

Canale, M., & Swain, M. (1980). Theoretical bases of communicative approaches to second language teaching and testing. *Applied Linguistics, 1*, 1–47.

Coleman, D., & Healey, D. (1999). *Laying out a CALL lab.* New York: TESOL Post Convention Institute.

Davies, G. (1997). Lessons from the past, lessons for the future: 20 years of CALL. In A.-K. Korsvold & B. Ruschoff (Eds.), *New technologies in language learning and teaching* (pp.). Strasbourg, France: Council of Europe.

Doyle, R. (2000). A digital language resource centre. *The IALL Journal, 32*(1), 17–25.

Dvorak, T., Charlotteaux, B., Gilgen, R., Herren, D., Jones, C., & Trometer, R. (1995). Whither the language lab? *IALL Journal of Language Learning Technologies, 28*(2), 13–45.

Faculty needs assessment questionnaire. (1997). Retrieved October 7, 2001 from http://eduvista.com/claire/needs.html

Fillmore, W. (1979). Individual differences in second language acquisition. In C. Fillmore, D. Kempler, & W. Wang (Eds.), *Individual differences in language ability and language behavior* (pp. 203–228). New York: Academic Press.

Garrett, N. (1997). Language media: Our professional future. *IALL Journal, 29*(3), 23–35.

Gillespie, J., & Mckee, J. (1999). Does it fit and does it make any difference? Integrating CALL into the curriculum. *Computer Assisted Language Learning, 12*(5), 441–455.

Kassen, M. A., & Higgens, C. J. (1997). Meeting the technology challenge: Introducing teachers to language learning technology. In M. D. Bush (Ed.), *Technology—Enhanced language learning* (pp. 263–286). Chicago: National Textbook Company.

Learning Center and Smart Classroom Survey. (2000). Retrieved October 7, 2001 from Temple University Web site: http://www.temple.edu/icsurvey

Ledgerwood, M. (Ed.). (2001). *The IALLT language centre design kit* (3rd ed.). St. Paul, MN: International Association of Language Learning Technology.

Levy, M. (1997). *Computer assisted language learning.* Oxford, England: Oxford University Press.

Levy, M. (1999). Design processes in CALL: Integrating theory, research and evaluation. In K. Cameron (Ed.), *CALL: Media, design, & application* (pp. 83–107). Lisse, Switzerland: Swets & Zeitlinger.

McVicker, M. (1997). *Advice for computer center planners.* Retrieved October 5, 2001 from Ohio University Web site: http://www.ohiou.edu/esl/teachers/technology.html

Pederson, K. M. (1988). Research on CALL. In W. Flint Smith (Ed.), *Modern media in foreign language education: Theory and implementation* (pp. 99–133). Lincolnwood, IL: National Textbook Company.

Richards, J., & Rogers, T. (1986). *Approaches and methods in language teaching.* Cambridge, England: Cambridge University Press.

Robb, T., & Susser, B. (2000). The life and death of software: Examining the selection process. *CALICO Journal, 18*(1), 41–52.

Scinicariello, S. G. (1997). Uniting teachers, learners, and machines: Language laboratories and other choices. In M. D. Bush (Ed.), *Technology—Enhanced language learning* (pp. 185–213). Chicago: National Textbook Company.

Stone, L. (1995). *Staff development, Module IV, Administering the learning centre: The IALL management manual.* St. Paul, MN: International Association for Language Learning Technology.

Szendeffy, J. (1997). *Questions and considerations to be addressed before installing a computer-based language lab.* Retrieved from Boston University Web site: http://www.bu.edu/celop/mll/call/install.html

Yang, P. (2000). Should our language centres be completely virtual? *The IALL Journal, 32*(2), 37–46.

11

Implementing Multimedia in a University EFL Program: A Case Study in CALL

Peter O'Connor
Musashino University

William Gatton
DynEd Japan

Current literature on CALL is rich on research into its effectiveness as a teaching method, much of it driven by the assumption that the "most convincing way to demonstrate the language learning potential of a CALL activity is through the study of learning outcomes" (Chapelle, 2001, p. 74). However, before CALL practitioners can begin to approach this sort of understanding, there are even more fundamental considerations to address.

In our experience, once the ideal learner outcomes have been decided, the prerequisites of any effective CALL project must include course organization, courseware selection, and student and teacher orientation. (*Courseware* is emerging as a standard descriptive term for CALL-mediated curricula-based material. It is a subset of the more general term *software*.) Other critical elements are the degree of institutional acceptance of CALL among fellow teachers and the quality of institutional commitment available to this relatively new approach to EFL. Compared with research on the effectiveness of CALL, the literature dealing with these concerns is surprisingly thin.

For many teachers, creating their own CALL materials is difficult, so choosing the right courseware is central to the success of any CALL project. However, there are few guidelines in the current literature that can assist teachers in courseware selection. This is partly because research with a focus on courseware alone tends to date rapidly, given the pace of technical change and related enlargements in the scope of CALL. Some writers feel that courseware designers ignore the full potential of the computer, using it as "little more than a tape recorder" (McCabe, 1998, p. 84), but as with conventional hard-copy textbooks, attitudes to the same course-ware differ wildly.

Course organization and the place of CALL in the EFL curriculum are better served in the recent literature. Redfield and Campbell (2000) showed CALL working effectively and enjoyably in their university, and McCarthy (1999) has stressed the importance of integrating CALL with other language classes rather than as an exceptional area of instruction. Most papers discuss these areas, and this chapter also returns to the issue of integration.

Computers and their use in teaching arouse surprisingly strong feelings. As Palloff and Pratt (1999, p. 60) pointed out,

> Many writers in the area of distance learning and educational technology dis-
> cuss the various types of technology that are available and how to use that
> technology in the process of developing and delivering a course in distance
> mode. What they sometimes fail to consider, however, is that people are inter-
> acting with the hardware, the software, the process, and each other.

In an instructive paper dealing with courseware buying decisions at Kochi Technical University, Hunter (2001) noted that although initial selection criteria centered on the lab design, hardware, and software, he and his fellow instructors soon realized that their first consideration should focus on the L2 learner, what is necessary to promote L2 learning, and how to perform tasks that support that learning.

The attitude of teachers and students to personal computers and their use in language learning is central to the success of any CALL course. The orientation of teachers and of students to CALL comes up frequently in the literature. Rilling (2000) provides a useful introduction to teacher orientation. Averill, Chambers, and Dantas-Whitney (2000) highlight the benefits of systematic faculty involvement in their CALL programs in Oregon, and Dunkel (1991, p. 20) seeks to assuage negative reactions to CALL by moving the personal computer out of the center of perception and urging a less technocentric approach to CALL. Elements of Fisher's (2000) account of teaching the teachers in a Web-based learning environment could well be applied to the CALL experience. Meanwhile, Chun (1998) has identified the acquisition of "interactive competence" as a goal of CALL, an endeavor that could bring a useful focus on standards to CALL practitioners.

Institutional support is not easy to address in research. Where institutional support is strong and consistent, it does not seem to merit discussion. The absence of institutional commitment can be interesting and controversial, but it is not easy to discuss objectively, and there is an understandable reluctance among CALL practitioners to draw attention to the failings of their employer or their colleagues (Hunter, 2001). Few would disagree with Palloff and Pratt's (1999, p. 69) view that "institutions, like their faculty, must engage in good planning in the delivery of online programs and courses and be willing to provide the level of support necessary to make the programs and courses a success." Institutions vary considerably, but one has only to talk to fellow practitioners to learn that the early experience of most institutions in delivering CALL programs has been remarkably similar.

Learning situations differ, of course, and lessons drawn from one learning context may need to be adjusted in other contexts. The most salient difference is that between the foreign language and the L2 contexts. In this case study of EFL learners, the participants experienced the target language almost solely in the classroom context. This contrasts with the ESL setting, where constant exposure to the target language is the norm. Despite this difference, there are still considerable commonalities in foreign language and L2 learning situations.

Such similarities and commonalities feed the assumption that drives this chapter. Our hope is that by recounting our experience as a teacher using CALL (the first author) and a courseware developer providing courseware, consultancy, and service to a CALL project (the second author), we can bring to the surface problems, situations, practices and solutions that fellow practitioners can readily identify. CALL is definitely the wave of the future, but even in the bravest of brave new worlds, it helps to have a hand to hold.

SETTING UP AND RUNNING A LARGE-SCALE PROGRAM

Rationale

The decision to run a large-scale CALL program at the social science faculty of our women's university in Tokyo came with an upside and a downside. The upside was that in 1998 we were a new faculty with something new to say and teach about the social world around us. It seemed a good time to launch a new initiative in language teaching. The downside was that we were slated to teach the program in 4 intensive 7-day vacation slots spread over the academic year: in August and September 1998, and in two courses (one of them elective) in February 1999.[1]

---

[1]In Japan, the academic year begins April 1 and ends March 31 of the following year. August and February are vacation months.

Following a review of courseware, the faculty English committee decided to use the U.S. CALL courseware, New Dynamic English (NDE) (Knowles, 2001). Ostensibly, the reasons for this choice were as follows:

1. Curricula-based multilevel courseware with face validity[2]
2. Interactive with speech recognition and video
3. Courseware can run from CD-ROM or server
4. Student support with bilingual access throughout
5. Administration and record-keeping support
6. Instructors' manuals
7. Developer commitment to support

Why "ostensibly"? Because we did not know in 1998 what we know now and, because we knew how little we knew, our main criterion was number 7, developer commitment. We had a fair understanding of CALL pedagogy and courseware, but our experience was not sufficient to make a buying decision solely based on the first six criteria. If we had known in 1998 what we were to learn over the course of two years, we would have been able to run our program without needing such a high level of support (hourly telephone calls, weekend visits, a hotline to technical support in California) from the company. As things stood in 1998, the developers had just released fully networked versions of their courseware and were eager to work closely with us and see how their material played in the lab.

Course Content

NDE is a four-part series for beginning through advanced students of spoken English. Each level of the courseware is built around listening comprehension activities based on short presentations in context, followed by a variety of exercises that focus on grammar, oral fluency development, reading and writing.

The aim throughout our CALL course was to facilitate long-term acquisition. Ideally, by the end of Level 4, students should be able to listen to and read about the news, summarize a presentation, give instructions, participate in decision making, talk on the telephone, take notes, and express their feelings and thoughts about daily activities with a degree of oral fluency. Thus, all

---

[2]Comparative studies by Redfield and associates (Redfield & Campbell, 1999, 2000; Redfield & Layne, 2000) have shown NDE to be as effective as other learning contexts such as classroom-based language instruction.

courseware presented language in contexts that could be linked and extended into the lives and experience of the learners. The language models were spoken naturally but were contextualized and sequenced to ensure comprehension at each level. Through a listening approach, vocabulary and basic grammatical structures were presented in a syllabus that balanced both communicative and linguistic needs. Students moved from talking about themselves to talking about the world around them.

Each level of NDE comes on two CDs. Each CD is divided into five units, of which the first three are the presentation units. Some of these units introduce characters and present different kinds of information about their life and experience. Other presentation units present information and language on subjects of general interest, such as basic human needs, the seasons, the environment, pollution, and global health issues.

The language models in these units prepared students to communicate about their own life and experiences in greater detail as the course progressed. These units developed a more generalized vocabulary, as well as the ability to understand and express a range of important language concepts. This in turn provided a foundation for students to communicate on a wide range of subjects and to use English for content-based studies within our faculty.

The presentation units include follow-up lessons that focus on information questions, grammar, and oral fluency development. These follow-up lessons were studied on a regular basis, preparing students for the mastery tests. In the review exercises section of each disk, students completed dictations, fill-ins, and speech-practice tasks, helping to reinforce and input language from the previous presentation units. These review exercises provided students with an overview of the entire disk as shown in Fig. 11.1.

As students worked on each lesson, the program monitored their progress. Each time a student answered a question by clicking on a word or picture; recorded a sentence; or completed a fill-in, speech recognition, or other activity, the program updated the student's study records and assessed the quality of her study. The study records for all students were stored in the records manager for access, analysis, and grading by the teacher.

All levels of this course tested comprehension and demanded a degree of critical thinking. There was a focus on meaning consistent with the assumption that language learning is best facilitated when the language is both comprehensible and is input through tasks that require the learner to process the language in sequenced stages, from recognition and comprehension to production, review, and acquisition.[3]

---

[3]A complete NDE course Scope and Sequence is available at http://www.dyned.com/dyned/japan/htm/nde3.htm

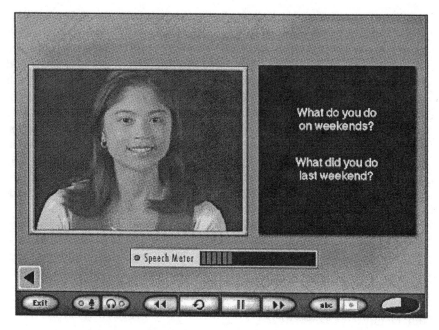

FIG. 11.1. New Dynamic English review lesson with speech recognition.

Integration

Properly organized, integration of CALL with the other elements of a language program adds value to a CALL course and promotes SLA. Integration makes for greater relevance, cuts out slack learning experiences, and makes for more focused teaching and learning.

Since our foundation in 1998, we had been running a unified English program in our faculty. All our language teachers worked with a common text in three defined areas of skill: reading, writing, and speaking. The common text in the four years from 1998 to 2001 was the *Headway* series, with half of our first-year students using *Headway Pre-Intermediate* (Soars, 1996) and the other half using *Headway Elementary* (Soars, 1993).

However, there are clear cultural differences between *Headway* and the NDE courseware. *Headway* teaches British English with frequent reference to British lifestyle and culture.[4] NDE is mostly American English, featuring White, Black, Asian and other Americans in video interactions, and illustrations for European characters in other units. In some ways, it is very American; in other ways, it verges on world English. *Headway* approaches the ele-

---

[4]In 2002, Oxford University Press, publishers of *Headway*, began publishing a multilevel American English equivalent of the *Headway* series we were using, called *American Headway*.

ments of language input in an order different from NDE, but that did not present any problems. So there was no significant conflict between the students' classroom text content and their language-learning software.

In April 2000, with the start of the new academic year, we began teaching compulsory CALL classes alongside traditional classes in term time. The CALL classes and the traditional reading, speaking, and writing classes were well matched in terms of such fundamentals as learning levels and content. These classes were only run for the spring term, and they constituted the tail end of our CALL courses, taught to second-year students who had studied with CALL in their first year. Nevertheless, simply taking space in the regular term-time curriculum was a step in an integrative direction.

In mid-February 2001, a group of our students went to a college in San Francisco for three weeks of language and social studies in a Californian environment. Just before they left, these students took our compulsory intensive course. Given the Californian orientation of the material and the students' immediate destination, we saw the trip as a further step towards the integration of different course elements in our English program.

Course Structure.   In our first academic year as a new faculty, we ran our first intensive CALL week in early August 1998 and mid-September 1998, and other seven-day courses in February 1999 (one compulsory, one optional course), September 1999 and February 2000 (compulsory and optional courses). Each course involved 21 hours of class time: 3 hours a day for 7 days. In 1998 and 1999, all our students were first-year students, but in 1999, we changed the system, switching one of our 4 annual intensive weeks, the August course, to the spring term of 2000, when second-year students took it as a continuation of their September 1999 course. For these 1998–2000 courses, average attendance and timekeeping for a possible 21 hours of class time over each of three compulsory courses and one optional course are illustrated in Fig. 11.2.

Teachers.   Six teachers worked on these courses, each running 7 3-hour classes per course. One teacher took overall responsibility for the course, preparing extra course material, deciding grading criteria and liaising with the publisher and with the IT office in the school. Another teacher helped coordinate with the university offices.

Teaching new material in short 7-day bursts meant that teachers and students had to master the software very quickly. A short orientation course gave teachers enough momentum to overcome initial doubts, but the gaps between courses (September to February to August, then September to February to April) tended to leave us a little rusty. A more comprehensive training session was planned and delivered at the start of the second year.

As a result, at the beginning of each new intensive course, teachers needed to reacquaint themselves with the material. Not all succeeded, and

Course #: Date, Item	# Students	Average Hours per Student	Ave Study Sessions per Student	Placement Technique	Evaluation	Total Records in Set
Course One: Aug–Sep 1998, Courseware	287	18.8	137	None	Rough data analysis	39,224
Course Two: Feb 1999, Courseware	287	12.48	67.8	Mastery Tests	Detailed data analysis	19,465
Course Two: Mastery Tests	287		20.8	Taken on Day One.	Mastery Tests + analysis	5,971
Course Three: Sep 1999, Placement Tests	308		2.1	Placement Tests	Placement Tests	667
Course Three: Sep 1999, Courseware	308	13.7	101	Placement Tests	Mastery Tests	31,127
Course Three: Mastery Tests	308		3.15	Taken after 80% Lesson Completion	Mastery Tests	972
Course Four: Feb 2000	308	12.0	92	Placement Tests	Mastery Tests	28,432
Course Four: Mastery Tests	308		2.04	Taken after 80% Lesson Completion	Mastery Tests	629

FIG. 11.2.   Timekeeping, performance and evaluation, 1998–2000.

there was a certain amount of learning on the job. Nevertheless, by the autumn of 1999 we had begun to approach these courses with less trepidation.

The early problems were predictable. First, the intensive format of the program made it difficult for teachers to integrate the courseware into their normal teaching styles, and teachers struggled with the material. Most teachers were at an early level of understanding of computer-mediated language teaching, and the learning curve was daunting. These problems were made worse by basic insecurities and hostilities regarding computers.

Right from the beginning, the major challenge came from teachers who disliked computers per se and resented being required to use them as a teaching instrument. Teachers who used a personal computer but not in any sophisticated way, rather as a clever typewriter, also had problems and panics, but they at least had a foundation of skill and goodwill on which to build.

Either because of a lack of basic competence or because of an inherent hostility to CALL, there will always be some teachers who will need intensive preparation. Such people are not necessarily "good at computers" or "bad at computers." Two of our best teachers had no experience of using a personal computer and no plans to get one, and yet by simple application, by reading the manuals and getting to grips with the material, they started to manage their intensive class in gifted and exciting ways. This mirrors the process as described by Hunter (2001).

Technical staff members were also new to most aspects of the program. Although they had a good working knowledge of the computer operating systems (Windows and NT in our case) and computing in general, they had difficulty communicating this to those teachers who were new to the vocabulary and concepts.

For at least the first 2 years, these intensive CALL courses were a true battlefield test for our teachers and technical staff. The material answered our needs, but running classes smoothly and delivering measurable results was not easy.

Students.   Few students were familiar with computers, all needed to be taught how to use the network properly (although many forgot), few had any previous experience with language-teaching courseware or CD-ROMs, and none had used speech recognition. Given these constraints, our August 1998 students did not perform too badly.

All the basics of courseware usage were available in the help menus in Japanese, but few students turned to these. Most students became adept at using both the speech recognition and the more general record and playback controls. By the third and fourth days, there was a healthy and constant buzz of students speaking English.

However, by September 1998 the temptation to surf the net, send e-mail, chat, and generally avoid coursework proved too strong for many students. When, at the end of that academic year, a number of students were awarded pass grades despite clear evidence of poor performance, attendance and study hours deteriorated further. One year later, in September 1999, we addressed study standards more firmly, laying down minimum hours for study time and minimum achievements required for a passing grade. Our students applied themselves steadily and we saw a corresponding improvement in their performance thereafter.

Courseware. NDE courseware consists of 4 levels with two CD-ROMs of content per level for 8 modules. Each module contains 3 presentation lessons and a variety of exercise lessons. Each module also contains video segments. The 6 mastery tests per level assess comprehension of material in the main presentation lessons. The levels correspond to recognized assessment tools. The lesson types and interaction modes are driven via speech recognition, video, manipulation of on-screen elements, and more traditional exercise paradigms and are designed to appeal to a variety of learner styles. The course contents were as described previously.

Distribution. We used 2 computer rooms for these intensive courses, one containing sixty-four and the other containing 48 IBM personal computers with 233 MHz processors. To avoid overloading the servers, we decided that the larger (64-machine) room would use courseware contents served from the network and that the smaller (48-machine) room would use CD-ROMs. The developer's new system supported this sort of mixed-mode media—half network, half CDs. This solution allowed all student records, from both networked or CD-ROM-based courseware, to flow over the LAN into the critical tool for CALL class management and analysis: the records manager.

Data Management via the Records Manager. In our intensive courses, around 300 students used both computer classrooms in 3 sets of 3-hour classes running from 8:50 a.m. to 6:10 p.m. The key to the successful management of data generated by such intensive use of the material was the records manager. This central data system records everything students do during their use of the software: every click of their mouse, every log-on and every exit, the intensity and rapidity of their study and mastery of the material, and their achievement as measured by their completion percentage. This standard became a key indicator of progress.

The system is flexible. The records manager can be used to set learner completion feedback to require different levels of difficulty. When a learner reaches the teacher-prescribed target within a lesson, access to a mastery test for that lesson appears. We set the mastery tests to open to students who gained around 80% in their completion percentage. There was also a shuffler level, which could be adjusted to increase or lessen the frequency and difficulty of material.

Development. The nature of this project required that the developer make a commitment to the university. The interaction among teachers, university technical staff and the developer was unusually frequent and close.

Both sides benefited from this agreement. The school gained in terms of almost around-the-clock support and deep analysis of teacher and student use of the program. When teachers came up against a problem, the company gave them rapid feedback and came up with effective technical fixes. The school pointed to weaknesses in the software engine and thereby helped shape upgrades.

The developers also gained in having their new software intensively used. Company engineers and writers in Tokyo and California lived through each vicissitude of the university program over the years 1998 to 2000 and were able to tailor their courseware to real people, real learning problems and real teachers.

COURSE DESCRIPTIONS

Course One: August–September 1998

Day 1. Day 1 of our August–September 1998 course was chaotic. In order to both test the system and to keep all students working in a reasonable order, all 110 students in the two rooms logged onto the system at the same moment. This heavy load caused the server to back up. As a result, some machines froze or dropped students back to the desktop. Fortunately, sufficient technical support staff and developer staff were on hand, and eventually all students began work. This first day taught us useful information about class organization, the server and network streaming.

Grading Criteria. How did we arrive at grades for our intensive CALL students? From the first course, teachers were concerned with the problem of assessing the students based on their performance with the material. The courseware developer, on the other hand, had not expected our assessment to be based on lab performance alone.

The records manager generates a spread of data so rich that in our first year we were at a loss to extract our A, B, C, D, or X grades from it. The developer's slightly purist position was that grading was not their affair, but the system presented a considerable mass of data on the students' performance, from which we somehow had to synthesize our grades. Eventually, we patched together a home-grown set of criteria that gave so many points for timekeeping, so many points for successful encounters, for completion percentages, and so on.

The amount and depth of data created by students using the NDE courseware do not directly point to grading solutions. Both the teachers and the company spent a lot of time discussing the grading issue and arriving at a workable solution. In the first course, teachers were still coming to grips with the depth and complexity of the courseware and records manager system. The developer helped us analyze the data, ranking student performance across the various interactive functions.

Data Analysis. Because data in the first term included numerous entries from the days of chaotic network usage, we decided to eliminate any data that showed usage time of less than 4 minutes. A valid study session had to involve more than simply surfing around a lesson, so no credit could be given for such sessions. Following these excisions, the resulting data set consisted of 39,237 log-on entries.

The grading solution we decided on for the first course utilized the export function of the records manager, which permits all student or class usage data to be handled in Excel, FileMaker or other database programs. Data are generated for every student mouse click. The solution involved evaluation of student usage in the following areas:

- Time spent studying
- Total questions attempted
- Total questions answered correctly
- Total speech recognition tasks attempted
- Total speech recognition tasks completed on first attempt
- Level reached
- Score

These and other factors such as the extent to which students used support options such as translation into the first language, text windows, use of glossary, and record or playback, were weighted and the students ranked. This produced a rough scheme for grading students, but we needed something better. The first stage of this improvement came with the mastery tests.

Course Two: February 1999

Using the rough grading solution we arrived at for our August–September courses was extremely time consuming, and our teachers and the company finally agreed on a workable formula using a newly developed mastery test.

We decided that to get into the running for grading in the September 1999 intensive CALL (Course Three) students would have to put in a minimum 5 out of 7 days and a minimum 10 out of a possible 21 hours. Students would then be graded on the average of their performance in the mastery tests.

Why the mastery tests? Because to get into the mastery tests students needed a minimum 80% completion percentage in the relevant study unit; thus, the mastery tests took into account class performance. And when they took the mastery tests, students had to get a minimum 80% before they could move on to the next set of material. Thus, the mastery tests were good indicators of all-around performance and progress.

Adding Mastery Tests. The new mastery tests evaluate language acquisition in the three main presentation lessons on each CD-ROM (courseware module), providing a progressive evaluation tool throughout the course. There are 6 mastery tests for each NDE level, 24 mastery tests for the entire course. Access to the tests is controlled by the teacher through the records manager. Each test takes from 6 to 12 minutes and consists of between 20 and 50 test questions. Test scores can be viewed by the student through the options/student record menu and by the teacher through the record manager. In each test, test items are grouped, but the individual order of test questions is randomized to ensure variation for each student and from one test to another.

A student's test score is indicated at the bottom of the test screen and in the student study records (if the records are networked). The best possible score for each test is always 100. Generally, a score of 80 or more is an indication that a student has mastered the target language of a unit sufficiently to move on to the next unit. Because all the test items are taken directly from the lessons, students who have focused on the lessons with any sustained effort should be able to score at least 80 provided they have been able to complete the tasks in each of the lessons of the unit being tested.

The mastery tests were installed to the server and run over the network in early 1999. At the beginning of Course Two, all students took mastery tests and their results were used for placement. The summary of the mastery test data for the first course data is in Fig. 11.3.

As the mastery tests were initially used for placement, all students took the first test for Module 1-1 (Level 1, Disk 1). Student scores for progressively more difficult mastery tests indicate a useful degree of validity. As Fig. 11.3 shows, more and more students found themselves unable to reach an acceptable score in Level 2 tests. Students retook mastery tests as they completed a successful amount of study in each lesson of a module. The results were included in grading.

Test No.	Total time (h:m:s)	Average time/student per test session	Total questions	Average questions/student per test session	Total questions correct	Average questions correct/student per test session	Count of students per test	Ave Score	Count as % of total test takers
1	47:26:00	0:08:45	12,090	37.20	10,002	30.78	325	0.83	1.000
2	48:06:00	0:09:01	11,501	35.94	9,474	29.61	320	0.82	0.985
3	61:41:00	0:11:33	24,539	76.68	19,719	61.62	320	0.80	0.985
4	47:04:00	0:09:01	11,292	36.08	9,291	29.68	313	0.82	0.963
5	52:37:00	0:10:13	10,120	32.75	7,504	24.28	309	0.74	0.951
6	59:32:00	0:11:45	13,297	43.74	9,382	30.86	304	0.71	0.935
7	58:54:00	0:12:08	12,945	44.48	9,714	33.38	291	0.75	0.895
8	76:16:00	0:16:10	15,579	55.05	10,136	35.82	283	0.65	0.871
9	62:28:00	0:13:49	15,196	56.07	10,054	37.10	271	0.66	0.834
10	42:15:00	0:10:13	8,501	34.28	5,653	22.79	248	0.66	0.763
11	39:02:00	0:10:10	8,140	35.39	5,393	23.45	230	0.66	0.708
12	36:10:00	0:09:57	7,340	33.67	4,888	22.42	218	0.67	0.671
13	0:25:00	0:08:20	94	31.33	64	21.33	3	0.68	0.009
14	0:38:00	0:09:30	133	33.25	88	22.00	4	0.66	0.012
15	0:32:00	0:10:40	105	35.00	67	22.33	3	0.64	0.009
17	0:01:00	0:01:00	1	1.00	-	0.00	1	0.00	0.003
18	0:06:00	0:06:00	23	23.00	18	18.00	1	0.78	0.003
19	0:02:00	0:02:00	7	7.00	2	2.00	1	0.29	0.003

FIG. 11.3.   Course 2 mastery test data: summary.

212

Enhancing Student Records. Teachers had recommended to the developer that, because students often checked their individual student record while studying, it would be useful to capitalize on their curiosity and turn the data they generate into a motivating factor. To achieve this, the developer prepared a completion percentage formula and added it to all record keeping. Our students were now able to check their own progress in considerable detail on a new function called student record.

The completion percentage is a relative measure of the quality and depth of study in each unit of the course as compared with a hypothetical baseline student. It sets completion goals based on a student's sentence repetitions, sentence recording attempts, speech recognition attempts, use of the glossary, and the number of correctly answered questions. Fundamentally, a student's completion percentage score indicates how thoroughly he or she has studied each lesson. To reach an 80% completion percentage, students needed to go through each part of each lesson several times, focusing on the language in different ways.

Course Two Implementations: February 1999. The main courseware additions at this stage were the mastery tests and the completion percentage. Up to now, we had used 1 lab, with 64 machines, with network-served courseware, and another lab with 48 machines using the same courseware on CD-ROM. In February 1999, we decided to run our new mastery tests from the server alone. This stretched server capacity to the limit, but there were few problems.

The chief problem involved student access. One control option for the teacher when setting up a class in the records manager is to have mastery tests lock automatically after students take them, which discourages students from going back to try to "improve" their score. However, some students logged on incorrectly, and others hit the wrong buttons or exited prematurely. These errors automatically locked these students' tests, and this became a problem as teachers had to use the records manager to unlock mastery tests. Teachers who had not studied the records manager became a little disoriented by this requirement.

Teachers. Teachers continued to fret over the technology. One teacher in the CD-ROM room realized (as a result of using the mastery tests) that the courseware could be accessed via the network for that room as well and had the students abandon CD-ROMs and run real-time on the network. There were immediate problems to which the developer responded, and an ensuing search for a technical fault was conducted. It was only later that we realized that this teacher had broken the usage protocol.

Course Two Conclusions and Data Results

Mastery Tests.   The second course contained 2 data sets: the mastery test data (5,200 log-ons) and the regular NDE courseware data (29,000+ log-ons). We ran the mastery tests as a placement test to find the students' level. This worked fairly well, although in one class a teacher placed all students at the same level whatever the outcome of their test performance.

Grading Solutions.   Once again, the sheer mass of data (some 75,000+ records) made grading difficult. In addition, this was the first time for everyone to interpret the mastery tests. However, the same schema of ranking student usage across a series of weighted factors generated a framework for final grading. Teachers took this responsibility seriously and spent many long and frustrating hours adjusting the schema to the local grading system. The lesson completion percentage introduced this term was not retroactive for first-term data and so was of limited use. However, by the third course, the grading scheme would reach a new level of maturity.

Course Three: September 1999

Placement Test.   In August 1999, the developer released new placement tests, which were installed in the server at our university. These placement tests come in 2 parts. Part 1 places students into Levels 0.0~1.0 and determines whether a student should take Part 2 of the placement test, which places students into the higher levels of the courseware, 1.5~3.0.

The placement tests also helped determine where students were in terms of the language progression found in the courseware. Although these were not proficiency tests (though there is a clear correlation with some standard tests), they worked as a useful indicator of competence, especially at the lower levels.

The placement test provided a quick evaluation of a mix of language skills, with an emphasis on listening comprehension and grammar. Though some reading was required, there were no extended passages. Rather, the focus was on basic, sentence-level comprehension.

The placement test is computer adaptive, responding and adjusting to the student's rate of successful responses. When a student is doing well, the test moves more quickly to items at a higher level. In the best case, the test will continue until the student has completed 65 items for each part of the test, or 130 items for someone taking both Part 1 and Part 2. For students at a lower language level, the test moves more slowly.

Implementation.   For the 1999 academic year, we shifted the August course to weekly slots in the 2000 spring term. This lengthened the gap between courses, and we realized that when we came to teach Course Three in mid-September 1999, we were likely to have forgotten what we had learned from Course Two, run in February 1999. We therefore set up a training day to renew our acquaintance with the basic material and to come to grips with upgrades. Those attending were the course teachers, technical support staff from the university who received separate training in sorting data using the records manager, and developer staff. Besides the training they received, faculty and staff received a student checklist for use on Day 1 and an explanation of minimum timekeeping and attendance standards for the course, both in Japanese.

Perhaps the most obvious benefit of the training day lay in the successful application of all 300+ placement tests on Day 1 of the course. Students quickly knew from their test what they needed to achieve. This focused their attention on the program at a critical point and showed that testing and courseware could be successfully integrated. The training day also resulted in a Day 1 guide that most teachers found helpful.[5]

For the first time, the system was fully implemented. The placement test ensured that study began at a challenging level. The mastery tests were used to motivate, evaluate, and provide a gatekeeper function. A final placement test was used to check progress.

Running Issues. Before upgrading, the developer advised the university that not all the university machines had been maintained in a timely way. This had caused problems with sound level, machines freezing, and so on, some of which were incorrectly blamed on the courseware.

During the intensive course, we learned more about how the tests unlocked. Student data upload to the server at the end of a study session. Therefore, if a student reached 80% and tried to access the test, she would find it still locked. Students had to exit to let the computer register their 80% completion percentage and unlock the mastery test. Nor would mastery tests unlock if a teacher had a student's record open on the records manager. Besides this basic error, there were the usual mistakes taking tests, which meant that teachers had to unlock them again for students.

By now, we were building on previous experience and diagnosing start-up problems without panicking. Once Day 1 was out of the way, most students began concentrated study of the material.

Grading. In Course One in 1998, we ran the August and September weeks as one course, but in 1999, we had only the September week to teach, having shifted what would have been the August week to 2000. Final grading for our Course Three/September 1999 course would be held over until

---

[5]See student checklist at http://www.dyned.com/dyned/japan/htm/supdoc.htm and training day agenda at http://www.dyned.com/dyned/japan/htm/supdoc.htm

the spring 2000 term ended in July 2000, when we would combine student performance data for the two courses to get final grades.

This September 1999 course was our most successful in terms of teaching skills and in terms of our students' application to the material. Average timekeeping was well up on previous courses. The fact that, even though they were putting in longer hours, our students moved at much the same rate of progress through the material, or an even slower rate, told us that students were working more thoroughly. Had we chosen to grade our students on their performance in the mastery tests in the September 1999 course alone, the broadest band would have been between 70% and 80%, around the B level. This indicated that this CALL course had worked well for the broad mass of students.

What Is a Class?

One question with immediate relevance to grading and general relevance to any large-scale CALL program is: In CALL terms, what is a class? In our CALL courses, we had between 300 and 320 students working on slight variations of the same material in 6 groups or classes with 6 teachers in daily 3-hour sessions over 7 days. Given these similarities, what did the 6 classes signify? From our students' performance, we could work out averages per class and we could work out averages for the entire 300-odd student body, but which data set should be used—the class data or the entire student data?

Our instinct was to go for the average for the entire student body as it synthesized the widest set of data, but we remained unsure. On the final day of each course, the students took the placement test a second time. The results of the before and after tests indicated an average raw score increase of thirty-one points: 228 students increased their scores, 9 scored the same, and sixty-nine scored lower on the second testing, as can be seen in Fig. 11.4.

Ideally, if common teaching standards are agreed on, there should not be that much difference between the way each class is run. When there is little difference, the relationship between a student's performance and that of her "classmates" (the students working on machines around her) and the relationship between the student's performance and that of the entire body of students on the course are going to be much the same.

Any teaching group trying to improve its performance can gain by looking at the variations between a student's ranking in a given class and her overall ranking, and by reviewing the class and trying to learn from the data. The upgraded records manager provided such a ranking, and this tool played a significant role in the next course.

Class	Pre Test	Post Test	Change
1	124.7	165.35	40.65
2	108.75	151.41	42.66
3	118.17	138.93	20.76
4	118.96	151.56	32.60
5	105.00	145.61	40.62
6	132.32	161.25	28.89
All data average	119.27	151.87	32.60

FIG. 11.4.   Course Three placement test: raw score comparison by class.

The raw score data showed substantial variations between the progress of groups that started out at roughly the same level, but we would not recommend using raw scores as data for evaluating students. The average placement level for all students was 0.6 and, after the course, 0.7. Of the individual students that took both tests, forty-six decreased in level, 102 had no change, and 155 increased in level.

Course Four: February 2000

Course Four, our fourth consecutive compulsory intensive course, took place in February 2000. Once again, students undertook 7 days of intensive study, working 3 hours a day. These first-year (1999) students had completed the September 1999 intensive course, but 5 months had passed since they last used the material and it was necessary to refresh their memory—and our own.

On the day before the course started, teachers reviewed the material and key areas such as grading. We decided to continue with the following standards and practices:

- Minimum timekeeping and attendance standard of 10 hours and 5 of 7 days
- Grading based on 80% minimum completion percentage and 80% minimum mastery test score
- Running a placement test on the first and seventh days as a progress check

Day 1.   Rather than use the test to place students on the course, we decided to start students at a point following their last successful mastery test in the Course Three September intensive. This took time, as students had to go back into the September 1999 (Course Three) records to locate their previous study point, then their last successful mastery test. Managing this exercise and running the Day 1 placement test used most of the first ninety minutes of Day 1. Other complications related to placement and seating arrangements on Day 1 and Day 7 meant that we were down 12% on study time compared with September 1999.

Placement Test Results.   On Day 2, 306 new students began study in our fourth intensive course. The first action was to orient the students using the checklist we had prepared and then to run the placement test (which we were using to measure progress, not to place students). Happily, the placement test ran smoothly and there were only a few questionable or false test scores.

Data Results.   Despite all the problems and the rush of Days 1 and 7 and consequent loss of study time, we managed to improve student activity over the 7 days by a large margin. There were fewer nonperformers this time around, and most students got over the 10-hour hurdle.

On the final day of each course, the students took the placement test again. The results of the before and after tests indicated an average raw score increase of 25 points. Of the 294 students who took both tests (on Days 1 and 7) 211 increased their scores, 6 scored the same, and 83 scored lower on the second testing.

Running Issues.   Most of the problems during this course had to do with poor organization and basic maintenance: wrongly assigned students, machine troubles and so on. One issue was easily solved. During the session, teachers noticed that students were taking a longer time to build lesson completion percentages in one lesson. Checking student data from other lessons and courses confirmed that the lesson grading for this material was set at too steep a gradient, and a simple internal edit solved the problem.

SUMMARY OF THE PROGRAM

We began this course as a new faculty in 1998. We had now completed two full years of intensive CALL courses and we seemed to be getting it right. Looking at the placement test data over the past 2 years, we could see real improvements. The following year we would begin to tackle the problem of scheduling by moving one of our courses out of the vacation and into main term time.

We had maintained our upside as a new, adventurous faculty and to some extent eased the downside of running courses in the vacation. For most teachers and most of our students, our CALL program was up and running well. What had we learned?

FOR THE TEACHER

In a little over twenty years, CALL has become a fact of life wherever languages are taught and studied. The exciting possibilities raised by phenomenal advances in information technology to focus and improve the language-learning process have enthused many language teachers. E-mail, the Internet, speech recognition, bit-stream video, and a growing range of delivery systems have been adapted and developed into an exciting portfolio of simulations, problem-solving activities, drills and learning games. Clearly, CALL has arrived in language education and it is here to stay.

Although CALL in any situation may have unique issues relating to institutional and pedagogic problems, most of our problems, we are sure, have occurred in some form in the early stages of most CALL programs anywhere. Here's what we have learned from them.

Get Organized

Running a CALL program needs a coordinated approach from both the teaching and the technical side, with clear, uninhibited lines of communication. At least one teacher should take responsibility for the program and liaise with the technical support staff and with the software company. On the technical side, at least one technical staff member or computer teacher should take charge of local technical issues. Ideally, if there is a computer committee in the school, there should be some liaison between that committee and these two representative figures. Without considerable, regular, and open liaison among teachers, technical staff and general administration, the educational purpose of the program will soon get bogged down in technical and administrative concerns, turf wars and so on.

Maintain Your Machines

Following on from this, the school needs to set and stick to good standards of machine and system maintenance. Otherwise, school system problems lead to teaching problems, and new courseware takes the rap for faulty hardware.

The system also needs protection from users. Students will log on incorrectly. They will alter machine settings if they can, or think they can. Some schools use hardware locks to override changes made by users. Teachers will also make mistakes. One of our teachers deleted his class data set. Although a backup had been made and no student data were lost, the lesson was to develop access to all menus for teacher systems such as the records manager in either the native language of the computer operating system, Japanese in our case, or in English.

Get to Know Your Courseware Company

It is well worth getting to know the people who develop your courseware, wherever they are based. If you have a valid service and support contract, you can expect a certain minimum from them, but if they are interested in their material and have an ongoing development process, they should jump at the chance to get involved.

In the EFL situation, most foreign educational software companies are represented by agencies. No matter how successful the company is in the United States or Europe, their commitment to your program will not begin to compare to what you can expect from an educational software company with its own local office, however small.

What to Expect

CALL courseware can do a great deal, but there is still a lot of preparatory work involved in running a course. The courseware will generate huge amounts of data, and teachers should look for courseware that sorts data in a discerning and useful way.

All manuals for our courseware were online in Acrobat format, easily accessible, bilingual and ready to be printed, but hardly an easy read. Nevertheless, if the material is there, teachers should try to read it and use it as a basis for peripheral material (checklists, grading criteria) to meet the needs of their course. Putting together these peripherals is time consuming, but once you have them right, they can be used again and adapted to requirements.

Many Are CALLed . . .

At this stage in its development, the institutionwide CALL process is much more specific and grounded and far less intuitive and inspired than traditional classroom teaching. The CALL classroom is a much more open forum than the regular classroom; because the teaching process is recorded and measurable, teaching with CALL is far more open to scrutiny than conventional teaching. Ultimately, teacher effectiveness as well as student performance may itself be a measurable outcome.

Much English language teaching in Japan, as in other foreign language contexts, has not produced communicatively competent speakers of the target language. Part of this failure can be traced to an unwillingness to acknowledge the nature of language in the process of language teaching. Most universities classify language classes as drill classes or the subject as a "skill subject" as opposed to a "specialty subject" such as literature. Here, language is treated as a self-contained, finite skill, to be acquired in the same way as driving or sewing. The idea that the acquisition of language entails more than the acquisition of a skill—that it involves the open-ended acquisition of a system of thought or of a cultural framework involving different ways of seeing and even of being—is not widely accepted.

This unwillingness to acknowledge the full scope of the process of language acquisition has not encouraged the development of a capable institutional approach. Furthermore, the current approach to language and language teaching would probably continue were it not for the crisis of confidence brought about by Japan's recent dismal performance in the international TOEFL. Of the 189 countries in the United Nations, Japan's TOEFL average stands at 180, slightly above North Korea (Inoguchi, 1999).

This figure illustrates the general need for an overhaul of current approaches to foreign language teaching, but how will CALL develop in response to this dilemma? It could go either way. Those who see L2 and foreign language learning as a skill are greatly attracted by the practical, repetitive drills and exercises to be found in most CALL courseware. On the other hand, some of those who see an L2 and foreign language as far more than a skill to be acquired are so repelled by the difficulty of using drill-and-practice-based CALL courseware that they refuse to use its more sophisticated properties.

CALL practitioners have to negotiate a path between these views. It would be a waste to use CALL only for drill classes, and a pity if the potential of CALL to bring light and inspiration to the higher reaches of language teaching were to be ignored. The duality of approaches is natural, but it need not persist. CALL is not a monolith or a fixed entity; it is developing in as many sophisticated directions as there are sophisticated language teachers and inspired program writers. At any stage of its development, CALL requires just the kind of intuitive, perceptive teacher who can appreciate its limitations and get excited by its potential. Superior CALL demands superior teachers.

CONCLUSIONS

Anyone who has taught L2 and foreign languages will know how heavily time can hang on a class when eliciting responses. Closed pairs or groups make better use of class time, but even in closed pairs, a shy student can remain silent and uncommitted.

The great advantage CALL has over conventional classroom-based activities is the sheer quantity of opportunities it offers to students to interact with the target language. These interactions are relatively private, controlled by the student but managed by the courseware curricula, carried by the microphone and headphones, and by whatever is on the screen. For the shy learner, this kind of interface with the L2 is ideal. Once a class is up and running and students are busily interacting with the material, convention demands that students join the general activity and many who would be silent in class are active in the lab.

For all the problems we encountered with our students, for all the frozen screens, for all the confusion, for all the sheer grind of preparation and orientation, by the spring of 2000 most of us were on our way to running CALL with competence and professionalism. Our place on the learning curve is reflected in the use students made of the material. The data tell the story. Figure 11.5 shows a comparison based on student input in all 4 courses, focused on their use of speech recognition.

Figure 11.5 shows students using the speaking opportunities created by courseware with speech recognition. In Course One, students were working with speech recognition but getting few correct answers, hence the skewed ratio. By Course Two, their study habits had improved with fewer attempts, but they were achieving a greater proportion of correct answers (much time was lost on this course following the introduction of mastery tests, not to mention the disabling effects of a lightning strike on Day 1).

Figure 11.5 also indicates the vigor of our students' approach to the speech recognition material. These are students speaking, listening, and responding. As the graph shows, these CALL courses had developed to the stage where they offered the students an excellent opportunity to move forward in ability and confidence. It had taken 3 years and a consid-

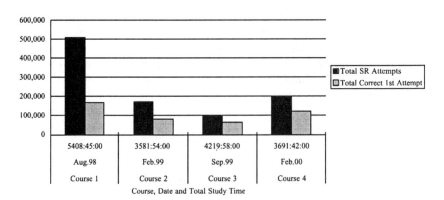

FIG. 11.5.   Four-year course comparison of student interactions: Questions with speech recognition.

erable investment in time and effort to get to this stage, but it was paying off. Thus, for teachers or institutions that are considering setting up and running a CALL program, our advice, and the first message to take away from this chapter, is: CALL can be run successfully, even on a large scale, but it takes time.

Our second message is: We hope that, after reading this chapter, you can deliver your successful CALL program much earlier than we did. If our experience helps you to prioritize course management and to get technicians, administration, and, most important, your fellow teachers working with you, and if you manage to come to grips with your chosen courseware and to orient students clearly and professionally, you stand every chance of getting your program up and running properly almost from the start. Even given the obvious differences between L2 and foreign language learning situations, the lessons derived from this case study have considerable applicability.

Like any major innovation, no large-scale CALL program can succeed unless it is undertaken on a broad institutional front. Attempting to do everything by yourself may be heroic, and it may well be easier and simpler than persuading unwilling colleagues to contribute precious time and energy to the project, but it can also be politically disastrous. Given the high basic cost of CALL courseware, staff orientation and technical time, no practitioner can afford to cut corners when it comes to preparing colleagues and administration for CALL and gaining their support and cooperation, because without a real commitment on a broad institutional and personal front, even the most successful CALL program will lose ground.

REFERENCES

Averill, J., Chambers, E., & Dantas-Whitney, M. (2000). Investing in people, not just flashy gadgets. In E. Hanson-Smith (Ed.), *Technology-enhanced learning environments* (pp. 85–98). Alexandria, VA: Teachers of English to Speakers of Other Languages.

Chapelle, C.A. (2001). *Computer applications in second language acquisition.* Cambridge, England: Cambridge University Press.

Chun, D. M. (1998). Using computer-assisted class discussion to facilitate the acquisition of interactive competence. In J. Swaffar, S. Romano, P. Markley, & K. Arens (Eds.), *Language learning online: Theory and practice in the ESL and L2 computer classroom* (pp. 57–80). Austin, TX: Labyrinth.

Dunkel, P. (1991). The effectiveness research on computer-assisted instruction. In P. Dunkel (Ed.), *Computer-assisted language learning and testing: Research issues and practice* (pp. 5–36). New York: Newbury House.

Fisher, M. (2000). Implementation considerations for instructional design. In B. Abbey (Ed.), *Instructional and cognitive impacts of web-based education* (pp. 78–101). Hershey, PA: Idea Group.

Hunter, L. (2001). CALL labs: Have they run their course? In K. Cameron (Ed.), *CALL—The challenge of change, proceedings of 10th Exeter CALL Conference* (pp. 61–72). Exeter, England: Elm Bank.

Inoguchi, T. (1999). Japan's failing grade in English [Electronic version]. *Japan Echo, 26*(5), Summarized at http://www.japanecho.com/sum/1999/b2605.html#

Knowles, L. (2001). *New Dynamic English* [CD-ROM]. Burlingame, CA: DynEd International.

McCabe, S. (1998). Virtual Manchester. In P. Lewis & T. Shiozawa (Eds.), *CALL: Basics and beyond. Proceedings of the second annual JALT CALL N-Sig conference* (pp. 83–88). Tokyo: JALT CALL N-Sig.

McCarthy, B. (1999). *Integration: The sine qua non of CALL.* CALL-EJ Online (4) 2. September 1999. (ISSN 1442-438X) http://www.clec.ritsumei.ac.jp/english/callejonline/4-2/contents1-2.html

Palloff, R., & Pratt, K. (1999). *Building learner communities in cyberspace: Effective strategies for the online classroom.* San Francisco, CA: Jossey-Bass.

Redfield, M., & Campbell, P. (1999). Introducing computer-aided instruction into the curriculum: A pilot study. *KeiDai Ronshu, 50*(2), 251–262.

Redfield, M., & Campbell, P. (2000). Introducing computer-aided instruction into the curriculum: A pilot study. In *CALLing Asia: Proceedings of the 4th Annual JALT CALL SIG Conference, Kyoto, Japan, May 1999* (pp. 95–99). Nagoya: The Japan Association for Language Teaching Computer Assisted Language Learning Special Interest Group.

Redfield, M., & Layne, G. (2000). Computer aided instruction after one year: A replica study. *KeiDai Ronshu, 51*(3), 203–217.

Rilling, S. (2000). A teacher preparation course for computer-assisted language learning. In E. Hanson-Smith (Ed.), *Technology-enhanced learning environments* (pp. 149–161). Alexandria, VA: Teachers of English to Speakers of Other Languages.

Soars, J., & Soars, L. (1993). *Headway English Course: Elementary.* Oxford, England: Oxford University Press.

Soars, J., & Soars, L. (1996). *Headway English Course: Pre-intermediate.* Oxford, England: Oxford University Press.

A Collaborative Model for Online Instruction in the Teaching of Language and Culture

Leslie Opp-Beckman
Cynthia Kieffer
University of Oregon

INTRODUCTION

In the last decade there has been an explosion in public use of the World Wide Web in commercial, government, and educational domains. Educators now have the capacity to co-develop and co-teach (co-facilitate) courses that span continents and bridge cultures with relative ease. This chapter presents an overview of a collaborative model where two or more institutions work together to develop and implement online, web-based courses that seek to build language skills and facilitate cultural awareness. There are a number of issues and concerns to address at the levels of administration, teaching, and learning. Some primary areas to consider are: (a) precourse inventory, needs assessment and analysis, and master planning; (b) phases and considerations in developing, implementing, and evaluating course content; and (c) some potential pitfalls and possibilities unique to a web-based learning environment.

WHAT DO WE MEAN BY COLLABORATION?

The term *collaboration* is currently in wide use across educational literature and touted as a positive practice in both teaching and learning, in ESOL as well as in other fields, but what does it mean to collaborate in an ESOL and in an online learning context? Researchers in comparative and international education such as Crossley (2000) have drawn attention to the importance of alternative, non-Eurocentric cultural perspectives in informing international educational practices and research, especially in the context of today's increasingly digital and globalized world. Marlow (2000, p. 188) noted that "collegiality and collaboration are recognized by many authors as important components for sustaining partnerships; however, there is little agreement on their definitions and more critically, methods for establishing and maintaining their conditions are not well described." He went on to define collaboration in his own ESOL program as having the following characteristics: the building of strong relationships, the mutual validation of colleagues, shared decision making, shared and individual accountability, and a feeling of caring and a sense of advocacy. In the same vein, Nunan (1992, p. 243) noted that "curriculum development [and, by extension, course development], requires a collaborative approach between the different stakeholders in the educational enterprise including teachers, researchers, curriculum specialists, and program managers and administrators."

Merriam Webster's Online Dictionary tells us that the word collaborate originates from Late Latin *collaboratus*, meaning "to labor together" (*Merriam Webster Online Dictionary*, 2001). It is defined in general terms as meaning the following:

- To work jointly with others or together especially in an intellectual endeavor
- To cooperate with or willingly assist an enemy of one's country and especially an occupying force
- To cooperate with an agency or instrumentality with which one is not immediately connected

The idea that collaboration is grounded in "intellectual endeavor(s)" and can take place in spite of a lack of immediate connection are important characteristics to factor into a working definition as well. On a lighter note, we would hope that academic collaboration could take place with a mutual feeling of trust and goodwill, not with a sense of working with "the enemy."

Salopek (2000) further suggested that digital (online) collaboration additionally encompasses the following dimensions:

Communication is mostly one-to-one or one-to-many. The number of recipients of the communication is theoretically unlimited, and can occur:

- Same time, different place.
- Same time, same place.
- Different time, different place.
- Different time, same place.

In practice, however, digital collaboration is usually many-to-many, but fewer than ten. It is goal-oriented, and can be asynchronous or synchronous (real-time). (p. 40)

However, we would add that, in a teaching and learning context, we have observed that the number of participants is often higher than 10.

In contrast, it can also be useful to consider dynamics that might pose barriers to collaborative processes as Hansen and Stephens (2000) have done, looking at issues related to the role of the teacher as facilitator (vs. "sage on the stage"), learner attitudes and expectations, "learned helplessness" from previous educational settings, and different kinds of learner and instructor evaluation strategies. Hansen and Stephens correctly observed that "collaborative classroom experiences turn negative if group tasks are allowed to deteriorate into low-effort exercises that do little more than pass the time" (p. 44) and they drew attention to the importance of examining underlying assumptions and values ("morals," as they call them) that are inherently part of any teaching–learning relationship.

For the purposes of this chapter then, the kinds of collaborative online ESOL teaching and learning endeavors that we discuss share the following qualities:

- Learning and teaching that is developed and implemented with the human and physical resources of two or more distinct institutions or educational partners. This could be at a district (multi-institutional), campus (institutional), department (intra-institutional), or class level.
- Language and culture-related learning goals. Computer-related technology goals are also often though not always part of the experience.
- Learning and teaching that take place wholly or partly in an online context, primarily through e-mail and the use of the World Wide Web. It can involve asynchronous or synchronous communication.
- Communication and shared learning on student–student, student–instructor, and instructor–instructor levels. It is implied and that collaboration also occurs at an administrative level, though it has been our experience that the instructors have also been the primary developers or administrators of the courses we use as examples.

Most of the learning experiences we describe have been further designed for young adult and adult audiences; however, many of the general principles and methods could be adapted and applied to working with younger learners as well.

PRECOURSE INVENTORY, NEEDS ASSESSMENT AND ANALYSIS, AND MASTER PLANNING

Recent case studies in the literature document the success of instructor collaboration at the departmental level (Knight & Trowler, 2000), with interdisciplinary teacher teams (Crow & Pounder, 2000), and in an even broader context, via the Internet linking two university classes in two countries (Brush & Uden, 2000; Cifuentes & Shih, 2001). This chapter similarly seeks to explore some of the issues surrounding development of a collaborative online learning experience in an ESOL context. We specifically examine elements such as conducting a pre-course inventory, a needs analysis and a master plan in this part of the chapter. As part of this process, we also examine some current benefits and limitations to online teaching and learning (in addition to or in lieu of face-to-face learning), some online planning strategies, and some cross-cultural aspects associated with this kind of endeavor.

Graves (1999) noted that courses typically do not exist independently from the curriculum (the whole program, including its general philosophy and matrix of coordinated courses) that houses them. She further observed that course development includes "planning it, teaching it and modifying that plan, both while the course is in process and after the course is over" (p. 3). This is especially true for computer-dependent, online courses where the number of variables that can lead to planned and unplanned changes are significantly increased.

Though the terms are sometimes used interchangeably, we differentiate between pre-course inventory and needs analysis in this chapter in the following ways. We use the term *pre-course inventory* to describe the process of gathering and analyzing more objective kinds of factual information that might affect the course, for example, country-specific laws or institution-specific policies. We use the term *needs analysis* to describe a more subjective type of assessment from the viewpoint of as many potential stakeholders as possible, for example, a wish list of what an ideal version of the course might look like or an analysis of participants' learning and teaching styles and preferences. These two sets of information then feed into a master plan.

However, the inventory, needs analysis, and master plan do not necessarily need to take place in a linear fashion. We recognize that planning can take place both in a top-down and bottom-up manner. The inventory and needs analysis can be undertaken simultaneously and modified continuously and recursively. In other words, it is possible to have both matrices (checklists) and iterative cycles of analysis and evaluation throughout the course-planning process. At some point, of course, the planners-instructors have to decide that enough infrastructure is in place to take the leap forward and begin teaching the course. We argue that this does not have to mean that all aspects of the course are then "locked in stone" or immutable. Rather, it is possible to have a flexible framework that allows for ongoing adaptations in the master plan in response to changes in the teaching and learning environment.

The following pre-course inventory checklist provides an initial framework for identifying resources for all participating institutions. In our experience, the more matches (similarities) the institutions share, the easier it will typically be to negotiate common learning space and course. Conducting an inventory of this kind entails knowing what kinds of questions to ask. Some cultures and some institutions may be less forthcoming with this kind of information than others. This list can and should, of course, be modified to reflect differences in individual situations.

PRECOURSE INVENTORY

Directions

For each institution involved in the planning and teaching process, the following kinds of information can be useful to have in terms of determining its impact on the proposed program.

Country:

- Laws, for example, related to copyright and fair use, use of the Internet for free speech or pornography, posting of a privacy statement, or student confidentiality regulations
- Belief (values) systems
- Time zone

Institution:

- Degree of learner and instructor access to computers, for example, stationary or mobile labs, or percentage of privately owned computers
- Availability of help desk or support services for faculty and for students (these can differ)
- Academic and weekly calendars
- Policies, both formal and informal (or "understood"), for example, use of synchronous modes of communication such as chat, use of resources to harass others, or permissions that need to be obtained to share e-mail addresses and names of students with others outside the institution
- Decision-making process, for example, identification of all members who control course funding, content, enrollment, and so on
- Evaluation of course, instructors, and students, for example, criteria and reporting
- Budget allocation for this and for other courses

- Materials and resources available with consideration for type, quality, and quantity

Technology:

- Software commonly available to and used by students and instructors
- Hardware commonly available to and used by students and instructors[1]
- Level of connectivity, for example, single or shared dial-up telephone line, digital subscriber line (DSL), ethernet[2]
- Web site hosting, course management servers
- Degree of adherence to accessibility and usability standards[3]

Human resources ("wetware"):

- Instructor time allocated for developing and for teaching, both paid and unpaid
- Clerical support
- Technical assistance personnel, both in-house and external

Suggestion

One way of sorting and analyzing the preceding information is to formulate a table with a column for each institution and to display visually the facts side by side. This can help reveal any gaps in information and help highlight similarities and differences. An abbreviated example might look something like Table 12.1.

A cursory analysis of the preceding information might then lead to the inclusion of related questions in the needs analysis in areas such as the following:

- The investigation of attitudes and practice in web design and the use of others' materials
- Current attitudes and practices toward digitally co-authored works and collaborative endeavors (Blankenship, 1998)
- Agreed-on definitions as to what constitutes copyright, fair use and pornography

---

[1]The U.S. Department of Education also puts out a good publication with more detail on hardware and software issues (United States Department of Education, 1998).

[2]For definitions and information on these and other IT terms, see Webopedia (internet. com Corp., 2001) or whatis?com (TechTarget, 2001).

[3]For more information on web usability and accessibility issues, see Web Accessibility Initiate from W3C (W3C, 2001) and Nielsen (2000, 2001).

TABLE 12.1
Cross-Comparison of Institutions

Institution A	Institution B
Laws, Intellectual Property: Do prohibit the theft of intellectual property; enforced through federal and local court systems along with peer review panels.	Laws:, Intellectual Property: Do prohibit the theft of intellectual property but do not enforce; internationally recognized fair use guidelines are widely disregarded in academic and commercial arenas.
Laws, Pornography: Adult pornography is legal in print and on the Internet (but further restrictions can also be set through local laws), and child pornography of all kinds is illegal; enforced through the court system in a nonsystematic manner.	Laws, Pornography: All pornography of all kinds is illegal; enforced through religious tribunals and courts. Access to pornography as part of the educational process is a major concern of educators and school leaders.
Calendar: 4 terms per year (dates X through Y, and holidays Z); classes Monday through Friday with Saturdays and Sundays off.	Calendar: 2 semesters per year (dates X through Y, and holidays Z); classes Sunday through Thursday with Fridays and Saturdays off.
Hardware: All faculty have desktop computers and about 75% of the faculty also have laptop computers. Learners will use one of many desktop and mobile lab facilities around campus. About half of the students also have home computers, approximately 75% of which are PC (Windows OS), 20% of which are Macintosh, and 5% of which are Linux.	Hardware: Institution provides PC laptops (Windows OS) to new students and to all faculty. Participants will use their own computers.
Software: Standard Web browsers plus plug-ins (Netscape and Internet Explorer), MS Office, and assorted multimedia software.	Software: Internet Explorer, MS Office, and assorted multimedia software.
Connectivity: High-speed ethernet on campus and in student housing; 56K modem and DSL from home.	Connectivity: High-speed ethernet on campus; 56K modem access from home (but both are subject to periodic, unscheduled power outages).
Instructor: Instructor is both the primary developer and teacher. Has a small amount of release time for development, and 6 of her 12 contact hours will be allocated to the teaching of this course.	Instructor: Instructor is both the primary developer and teacher. Has no release time but is receiving an extra stipend for development, and 10 of her 20 contact hours will be allocated to the teaching of this course.
Clerical Support: Limited.	Clerical Support: Nonexistent.

- The relative roles of instructors and students in the course, for example, learner versus student-centered philosophy and practices (Bruer, 1999; Campbell & Kryszewska, 1992; Hansen & Stephens, 2000), and degree of variance in learning and teaching preferences or styles
- Inquiry into mutually desirable and acceptable methods for student–student, instructor–instructor, and student–instructor interactions

Some areas of possible impact that the pre-course inventory might also have on the master plan include decisions related to the following:

1. Shared resolution to honor copyright and fair use guidelines with regard to materials used in and developed throughout this course—model anti-plagiarism practices with students
2. Shared commitment to proactively discourage the use of pornography as part of the class
3. Mutually agreeable dates, days of the week, and scheduled times and deadlines for course start–stop dates and breaks, periodic reports and assessments, and synchronous and asynchronous communication activities
4. Methodical testing of all Web-based course materials on multiple platforms but use of Internet Explorer as Web browser of choice
5. Ability to assume fairly high level and ubiquitous access to computers with fair to excellent connectivity, but with flexibility built into deadlines and coursework to account for power outages
6. Compensatory strategies for lack of clerical support

Needs Assessment

The needs assessment ideally incorporates the needs of as many of the course participants as possible (sample from prospective student population, instructors, cultural and language informants or assistants, decision makers and administrators, technical assistants, etc.). Information can be gathered through a variety means including but not limited to structured, semi-structured or unstructured interviews[4]; focus groups; surveys or polls; analysis of statistical information (budgets, enrollment patterns, attrition and retention rates, test scores, cumulative GPA, etc.); the creation of mind or concept maps; and self-reported or observed behaviors. The idea behind

---

[4]For more on this distinction and for other qualitative kinds of research techniques, see Ely, Anzul, Friedman, Garner, and Steinmetz (1999), LeCompte (2000), and Herndl and Nahrwold (2000).

the needs assessment is to create a profile of all groups of participants, again to identify potential gaps and mismatches that need to be resolved.

Following are two general categories of information that might be useful to collect. The first category, concrete information, loosely represents quantitative or fairly concrete kinds of facts. The second category, relative information, represents information that tends to be more complex and associated with value-laden behaviors or choices. The former is relatively easy and quick to gather, and fairly straightforward to analyze for the purposes of course planning. The latter is more time consuming, certainly more biased in terms of cultural assumptions that are built into the methods and instruments themselves, and more time consuming to deliver and interpret. The importance of carefully handling any kind of confidential information that results from this process is, of course, of utmost importance.

Concrete information:

- Age range
- Gender
- Previous relevant formal, nonformal and informal learning[5]
- Native language(s)· and culture(s)
- Technical expertise
- Proficiency in target language
- Previous exposure to and proficiency in other languages and cultures
- Purpose for designing the course
- Purpose for taking the course
- Interests that might come to bear on the content of the course

Relative information:

- Learning styles or preferences (Christison & Kennedy, 1999; Gardner, 1999; Harper, 2000; Kolb, 1984; Soloman & Felder, 2000; Thornburg, 1997)
- Teaching styles or preferences (Felder & Henriques, 1995; Grasha & Anthony, 1994; Indiana State University, 2002; Special Needs Opportunity Windows, 2002; Zhenhui, 1999, 2001)
- Personality indexes, for example, the Keirsey Temperament Sorter (Keirsey, 2000), the Techno Personality Test (Finley, 1996), or the Color Quiz (2001)
- Communication and decision-making styles (Ahlmark, 1995; Daugherty, 1997; Kreitner, Kinicki, & Buelens, 2001)

---

[5]For more on the distinction in these learning categories, see Merriam and Caffarella (1999) and Smith and Doyle (2000).

- Cross-cultural comparative, world view analysis (Furman, 1998; Inglehart, 2001; Inglehart & Baker, 2001; Pusch, 1979; Summer Institute for Intercultural Communication, 2001; Union of International Associations, 2001; Weeks, Pederson, & Brislin, 1979)
- Affective domains, for example, degrees of extrinsic and intrinsic motivation (Deci & Ryan, 2001; Teleometrics International, 2001a, 2001b) or confidence level (Betz, Borgen, & Harmon, 2001; Skills One, 2001)

Suggestion

As with the pre-course inventory, a visual representation of the profile for each collaborative entity could be represented through a table or grid (see Table 12.2).

As another alternative, ongoing results from the pre-course inventory and needs analysis and ideas for the master plan could be represented in the form of a concept or mind map (Gaines & Shaw, 1995; Plotnick, 1997; Trochim, 2001). Either way, results from the needs assessment would also feed into the master plan. In addition, these results might prompt the planners to revisit the precourse inventory and add or delete categories for consideration.

Master Plan

The master plan for a course will then reflect the information and decisions made related to the outcomes from the pre-course inventory and needs assessment. Some general points that most course planners will want to collaboratively agree on include the following:

Scope and sequence:

- Course timeline and calendar of dates and events
- Number of target languages involved

TABLE 12.2
Pre-course Inventory Example

Institution A	Institution B
Student population profile	Student population profile
Profile of cultural or content informants	Profile of cultural or content informants
Instructor profile	Instructor profile
Profile of administrators or other course planners	Profile of administrators or other course planners

- Number of students, instructors, assistants, guests, and so on who will be involved
- Roles and responsibilities of all involved
- Identification of any participants who have special needs or require assistive technology
- Points of technical compatibility, for example, software and courseware tools, lowest common denominator of connectivity, Web design criteria
- Means of communication, with one or more back-up systems in case the primary mode fails

Content and process:

- Overarching pedagogical principles
- Course goals and learning outcomes for all those involved
- Content topics or themes, organization, and order in which they will be introduced
- Appropriate materials and resources to be used
- Evaluation process, components, and deadlines
- A decision-making process that will work for both institutions
- Shared awareness of areas for potential misunderstanding and mechanisms for working through any that might arise; use of an agree-to-disagree strategy for low-priority and low-impact items

Maintaining motion and keeping perspective:

- Prioritize and divide up tasks to be completed, and set firm deadlines
- Outline any specialized training that needs to occur and time line for completion
- List any donations, purchases, or acquisitions that need to take place, with plenty of time built in for delays and testing
- Develop a sense of fun and adventure and allow each other permission, if possible, to make mistakes along the way and learn from them

PHASES AND CONSIDERATIONS IN DEVELOPING, IMPLEMENTING, AND EVALUATING COURSE CONTENT

Once the initial master planning process is underway, the instructor-developer is ready to proceed with the details of course content. Though more sophisticated tools are technically available (e.g., IP/TV (Internet Protocol

TV), video conferencing), we find that the distance education tools most commonly in use right now for the delivery of content and for carrying out communication are e-mail, discussion tools (discussion or bulletin boards and chat), and Web publishing. This is due in large part to relatively low levels of shared connectivity, especially for international collaboration with developing countries. As content is the focus of this portion of the chapter, we examine some content-related issues for delivery through e-mail, discussion tools and web publishing.

PHILOSOPHY

The interaction hypothesis of SLA states that as learners interact with each other through discourse, their communicative abilities are enhanced (Brown, 2000). One such collaborative course model we have designed maximizes learner interaction to develop language skills and overall communicative competence by matching EFL learners with native speakers to participate in an e-mail exchange and a discussion board (Opp-Beckman & Kieffer, 1997–2001). In this interactive environment, learners receive authentic language input in a real-world context; produce language for genuine, meaningful communication; and write to and for an authentic audience. In other interactive learning-based course models, we have used invited guests to provide additional perspectives and to broaden the scope of materials and kinds of interactions that are possible (Opp-Beckman, 2001a, 2001b). In all cases, the language instructors collaborate to create a climate in which spontaneity can thrive, in which unrehearsed language can be performed, and freedom of expression is given over to learners.

Students are also more likely to learn when they are members of a group that is accepting and allows them to experiment with ideas and actions, and the interpersonal contact that occurs in a classroom often begins this process (Johnson, Johnson, & Stanne, 2000). When instructors use team building and support other efforts to create feelings of community, the social qualities that enhance learning add to the success of the lesson. Learning online necessarily incorporates community building. The number and nature of the interactions that the instructor designs into the lessons are more important.

E-MAIL

Although e-mail may be considered to be a relatively low-tech medium, it can bring effective benefits to the process of learning a foreign language (Gaer, 1999; Ho, 2000; Keogh, 2001; Robb, 1996; Singhal, 1997; Vilmi, 2001; Warschauer, 1996; Warschauer, Whittaker, & Fawn, 1997). One of its most important benefits is that it offers language learners opportunities for authentic communicative interaction in the target language that are not possible in the traditional foreign language classroom (Gonglewski, Meloni, & Brant, 2001). The first stage in one such collaborative model we have participated in entails weekly one-on-one, asynchronous, personal unstructured e-mail exchanges between a native speaker of English and a foreign language learner. The goal of this course is to build communicative competence that consists of organizational competence (grammatical and discourse), pragmatic competence (functional and sociolinguistic), strategic competence, and psychomotor skills. In the e-mail-only phase of the course, the affective goals are to lower inhibitions, encourage risk taking, build students' self-confidence, develop intrinsic motivation, promote ambiguity tolerance, help use their intuition, and develop a positive attitude toward the target language and culture (Graves, 2000). Ideally, e-mail exchanges are integrated into course instruction so that both instructors can link course content and daily class work to the questions that are posed in the correspondence with the native speaker. Following is an example of a collaboration that involves instructors, learners, and language informants.

USING LANGUAGE INFORMANTS

One kind of interaction that can occur in a collaborative course includes structured communication between learners and informants (native speakers that are trained or monitored by the instructor). E-mail exchanges with informants who have less formal language acquisition training than regular instructors but more experience and training than the average person on the street can be highly motivating. In preparation for e-mail exchanges with language informants, the course developer-instructor gathers the necessary information from the aforementioned pre-course inventory and needs analysis to begin designing the course. With the teacher's role no longer at the center of informant–student interactions, two especially important points to consider are: (a) whether the student can get access to e-mail at any time, or if there are only set times and places that allow for communication; and (b) whether the instructor(s) wants to require informants and students to copy messages to them as a monitoring procedure.

With all of this information in mind, the instructor then screens and hires or arranges for the necessary number of native speaker informants to match up with the EFL learners. It is important to take into consideration relative age, gender, culture, education, experience, interest, maturity, reliability, and sense of responsibility. A maximum ratio of one native speaker for every four learners is recommended for one-on-one e-mail correspondence, based on our experience.

Before the first exchange, the instructor-facilitator establishes and clarifies with each informant his or her role and responsibilities as a keypal and cultural-linguistic model, and the parameters of the program. This information should be given to the informants in writing and, ideally, reviewed in a face-to-face meeting. It is very important to establish clear goals. In our series of courses, the informants are trained tutors and the purpose of the exchange is for informants to provide culture information and for EFL students to increase their fluency and comfort in using English. Informants are not to send back corrections on grammar or spelling. If they receive a piece of communication that is unclear, they should model good communication strategies by asking for more information or clarification. They should also use conversational English, but they should model good English by starting sentences with capitals, ending with periods, and using correct spelling.

The instructor-facilitator also designs some kind of tracking system to monitor the exchanges. All participants have non-negotiable deadlines by which e-mails must be sent weekly. On the subject line of the e-mail message, tutors are required to identify the week and general topic, for example, Week 1—Hello. One method of tracking the quantity and quality of participation is for informants to copy all correspondence (including the language learners') to the instructor. This allows tracking of deadlines, monitoring of content, and the collection of data for qualitative and quantitative assessment. This way the instructor finds out in a timely fashion when a message has not been sent or received by the expected deadline. This allows the instructor to contact the informant of the partner instructor to find out if there is a hardware or wetware (human) problem. As the hosting institution, when our informants do not receive a message from their students, they are required to send a short note, inquiring how the student is doing and expressing a desire to hear from him or her to keep the exchange going.

To get the e-mail exchanges going, the instructor provides the informants with the full names of the corresponding students, the students' gender, their e-mail addresses, and a sample letter for the first week that includes a general introduction (age, major, present classes, family, hobbies, questions). To insure that each communication is unique and personal and to avoid confusion through cross-conversations, all correspondence is sent as individual (not as group) messages. We find that it takes approximately 20 minutes per student for a technologically competent tutor to read the latest message and write a response.

In this stage of the collaborative model, personal background information such as family members, hobbies, subjects in school, daily activities, routines, and similar areas of interest such as food, travel, and "neutral" cultural practices are discussed. The students are fully engaged, focusing on meaning and messages, not on grammar and linguistic forms, and they are beginning to appreciate more fully their own competence to use language.

Other kinds of e-mail exchanges are, of course, possible for small groups and for larger communities (usually through an electronic mailing list). See the section "Potential Pitfalls and Possibilities Unique to an Online Learning Environment" at the end of this chapter for more ideas on using e-mail in collaborative courses.

DISCUSSION BOARDS

Asynchronous discussion boards can be an effective way to build on and complement e-mail interactions in collaborative courses. Structured or semistructured, asynchronous discussions are set up on a regular basis. The instructor posts questions, prompts, and readings to which language learners and informants can respond. This provides a more extensive interactive environment than the e-mail exchange in that the participants and the audience is expanded from the one-on-one e-mail interaction to a group discussion, and the conversation changes from personal communication to a discussion of more global issues. In this stage, the communicative goals remain the same and there is more emphasis on learners' communicating their values, feelings, and attitudes on specific issues and topics. The role of the language instructor-as-facilitator is to set the stage, monitor conversation, keep the process flowing smoothly and efficiently, and sum up, as needed.

As with e-mail exchanges, in preparation for this expanded discussion, the collaborating developer-instructors map out the overall goals and process. In addition, they agree on and disseminate directions and information for all participants and identify roles, topics, and prompts. They also decide if the participants should respond to all or some of the questions and if students can post their own questions. One of the advantages of the discussion board is that it provides the facilitator-instructors with the opportunity to employ a variety of materials and activities to engage and prepare students for a profitable discussion. Before responding to a question prompt, to build or activate schemata, students may be asked to read a document, respond to a survey, work on related vocabulary, listen to a sound recording, or view a video clip. These can be made easily accessible through links. The use of such varied resources also addresses individual learning styles and facilitates integrating all language skill areas into the communicative, interactive framework.

Over time, the learners' audience and tasks change. The first discussions are often designed to break the ice, to establish rapport, and to create a sense of community (Ko & Rossen, 2001; Hanna, Glowacki-Dudka, & Conceicao-Runlee, 2000). An easy-to-talk-about topic, (such as holidays, hobbies, or nicknames) in which all participants can be "experts," gives them the confidence to express and exchange information on more complex topics later on. As the interaction progresses, the discussion topics expand to include different dimensions of the target cultures such as social values, depending on their maturity and comfort level (e.g., gender or age differences), attitudes (e.g., in regard to alcohol, smoking, eating, current news events), norms (e.g., ways of greeting, shopping, teaching), and customs (e.g., dating, marriage, child rearing).

Topics can be suggested by participants, both as part of the initial needs assessment and as the course progresses. As the topics are selected, the instructors select questions to stimulate interaction. Certain kinds of questions may discourage interactive discussion; examples of this include questions that don't involve the genuine seeking out and fusing of information, that are vague, or that are too random and don't fall into a logical, well-planned sequence. Successful questions focus on values, feelings, and attitudes, and they require respondents to make inferences, analyze, synthesize, and evaluate. Questions based on a critical incident, a case study, a value statement, or an ethical situation are more likely to stimulate participation.

As the discussion progresses, the instructor and the language instructor closely monitor the discussion and collaborate to make instructional decisions. There are a number of variables that can affect the flow of the discussion, and sometimes it is difficult to predict what topics and questions will engage and sustain it. The discussion design is intentionally flexible so that the language instructors have more than one option at each phase of the discussion. In course preparation, the instructors collaborate to develop a menu of possibilities from which to choose topics, questions, and materials, and the appropriate adjustments are made as they get to know the learners, informants, and context better. The discussion is organic and unpredictable, and it is necessary for the instructors to assess constantly the learners' needs and to make adjustments appropriate to their communicative skills and interests. Ongoing communication and collaboration between the language instructor and any moderator-facilitators or guests is one key to a successful discussion and learning experience for both the language learners and tutors.

Qualitative feedback indicates these types of exchanges motivate learners by providing personal interaction and creating a cultural connection to the target language culture. Through this authentic communication, "communicative goals are best achieved by giving due attention to language use and not just usage, to fluency and not just accuracy, to authentic language and contexts, and to students' eventual need to apply classroom learning to previously unrehearsed contexts in the real world" (Brown, 2000, p. 69). Participants come to recognize their own culture-based values, feelings, and attitudes, and are able to communicate them to others and experientially learn the logic of another cultural system.

WEB PUBLISHING

Hypertext Web publishing is not necessarily part of all collaborative online endeavors but can be a powerful and efficient means of reaching a wide audience. It can be used in a collaborative teaching and learning environment, for example, to help tie the course together. Having one centralized Web address that serves as an anchor for all aspects of the course is a useful reference point for all participants. If the course is bilingual or multilingual, the primary Web page(s) may also be mirrored in other languages, as needed. Course Web sites are commonly created and published (housed on servers) as freestanding works or as part of all-in-one course management systems. This ability to distribute and link to Web-based resources across multiple servers is both the beauty and the bane of Web publishing, however, as the number of Web sites involved tends to be in direct proportion to the amount of time and effort required for monitoring and repairing "link rot" (broken links).

Bear in mind also that with today's roving search engines and archival systems, non-password-protected Web pages automatically become the "public face" of an online course, whether the author(s) intend them to function as such or not. Web sites are often planned, in fact, as a purposeful means of advertising for or disseminating information and materials related to your course. For both of these reasons and for streamlined access to course information by learners, it becomes imperative that all Web pages in a Web site contain the authors' names, accurate contact information, and date last revised, and that their design criteria reflect current international accessibility guidelines (Bailey, 2001; W3C, 2001). The use of an editorial system of checks and balances as well as informal or formal usability testing can also contribute significantly to the quality of a course site (Dumas, 1999; Nielson, 2000; Preece, 2000).

If Web authoring and publishing are also collaborative aspects of the course (it may well be that one or both are the responsibility of just one of the participating institutions or individuals), it is important to agree ahead of time on identical or at least compatible Web-authoring tools, a process for "cleaning up" instructor- or student-authored works before publication, and a set of agreed-on guidelines for copyrighting course materials and fair use of others' materials.

POTENTIAL PITFALLS AND POSSIBILITIES UNIQUE TO AN ONLINE LEARNING ENVIRONMENT

Following are some tips and observations that may help other course developers-instructors avoid some common pitfalls and make the most of some online learning possibilities. There is overlap among them, but for organizational purposes they are grouped in the following categories:

- Course preparation and orientation
- Setting the tone and leading by example
- Creating opportunities for success
- E-mail
- Discussion
- Chat
- Assessment

Course preparation and orientation:

- If you are using a course management system such as Blackboard or WebCT,[6] log into your online course as a student so that you can get the feel of what things look like from the "other side."
- If training materials or tutorials for software or courseware that you plan to use are available, make full use of them well in advance. Find out what product-related help services are available and how to use them so you will be prepared if you need them.
- Allow a period of breaking in and getting oriented at the beginning of the course, especially the first time that you teach it online or the first time that your students take an online course.
- Find another colleague who is teaching online (someone other than your course collaborator) so that you have someone you can share ideas with and consult for advice, as needed.
- Think about what you value in your face-to-face teaching and look for creative ways to incorporate your own personal touch in your online course. Explain your teaching philosophy, how to study for the course and the kinds of assignments you will give.
- Model lifelong learning for your students. Share your own insights about and your reactions to new uses of technology. Let your students know when you are learning along with them.
- Recognize that some students may be apprehensive about the technology that you are using to structure the course and may need extra encouragement, especially if there is no face-to-face aspect to the course. For example, you can acknowledge receipt of assignments right away with a simple "Thank you" and "I'll get back to you by X amount of time" so that they know their assignments have not gotten lost in cyberspace.

---

[6]For more information, see: http://www.blackboard.com/ for Blackboard and http://www.webct.com/ for WebCT.

- Set clear guidelines for the kinds of files you will accept as e-mail attachments or in the digital drop box. Check incoming attachments and drop box files as soon as possible for readability, especially in the beginning of the course so that you can let a student know right away if he or she needs to send it again or in another format.

Setting the tone and leading by example:

- Use technical terms sparingly and provide definitions; do not assume that everyone knows a term or is using it in the same way that you would. Keep the focus on the activities and content.
- Good conversations can happen around technology. Encourage your students to help you, and each other, with technology challenges.
- If you are using an online grading system, make sure students know how to access their individual files.
- Ask students for feedback on a regular basis. Be open to their suggestions and make reasonable adjustments accordingly.
- Be accessible. Encourage regular student–faculty contact. Encourage learners to send private e-mail messages to or to phone the instructor as needed.
- Send regular personal notes throughout the online course to simulate the informal chat that often occurs at the beginning of a traditional class. You can use a template as the core of a message and add individuals' names and personal details.
- Send regular "checking in with you" notes to individuals at regular intervals throughout the course (again, use a template and add in names.) This helps identify and solve little problems before they turn into big ones.
- Send regular reminder notes or post announcements on class business (quizzes, assignments due, etc.).
- Assign individuals or small groups to play the role of "teacher" and of moderator for portions of the course.
- Encourage students to think about computer-based resources conceptually and holistically instead of as a lock-step, linear sets of directions to follow. Show them how to transfer knowledge from previous learning and computer-related work experiences. For example, knowing that other English language learning software has a help or student manual function, it is reasonable to expect that any new online learning coursesite will also have this feature. It might be called something else and there may be differences in quality and interface, but it is a concept that can be generalized across all computer-based learning resources.

Creating opportunities for success:

- Refer students to a frequently asked questions (FAQs) section for common problems. Offer online and print references and help for questions that come out of the online course.
- Encourage cooperation among students. For example, you can set up a mentoring or buddy system that pairs experienced online learners with less experienced learners.
- Build a cushion into deadlines. Online learners often juggle very full work and personal schedules on top of their academic studies. Understand that technical problems and life's problems can cause occasional delays.
- Be alert to delays that are developing into patterns, however. Check the statistics or report option offered by the online learning system frequently. Send private messages to those who are falling behind or who are reading but not writing. If they have not signed on for a week or more, contact them as individuals with a tactful inquiry. Try to help them with their problems or suggest ways in which they might contribute.
- Build redundancy into topics, class announcements, and skills area practice.

E-mail:

- Keep a class roster or electronic address book for the class up to date so you can quickly and accurately send messages to individuals, groups, or the whole class. Send e-mail reminders about deadlines, opportunities, and events frequently.
- Use e-mail to give personal, frequent feedback on performance.
- Develop and keep on hand a "canned" set of messages that you frequently send out so that you can easily slip in students' name, some personal remarks or information, and send them off.
- Set up keypals or e-pals for your learners. Give them engaging guidelines and engaging topics as a foundation for meaningful and directed communication.
- Encourage learners to join appropriate e-mail lists to receive news on topics and take part in topics of interest to them.
- You can use e-mail to have students write collaborative stories or poems.

Discussion:

- Be a process facilitator who makes sure that participants understand and abide by good "netiquette" (Internet etiquette) by not insulting each other or getting way off the course topic. Have the students come up with a set of communication guidelines that they value. Post them and enforce them, as needed. If you notice any inappropriate language ("flaming"), immediately send a private e-mail to the student who sent it. Encourage open and honest dialogue. Model appropriate discussion and expect the same of your students.

- Define the purpose or objective of each discussion. This will help members stay on a specific topic. Encourage reflective thinking and ongoing discussions by offering specific topics while avoiding questions that lead to right and wrong answers.

- Form learning teams. The advantages of cooperative or collaborative learning are well documented (Erven & Zulauf, 1998; Felder, 2001; Felder & Brent, 2001; Johnson, 1992; Ko & Rossen, 2001; Panitz, 2001). Assign a group leader to small-group discussions, and rotate this leader. Share tasks in small groups, and make groups responsible for different parts of an assignment. Have members of the group reflect on the work of other members (Alamprese, 1998; Bulman, 1996; Felder, 2001; Johnson, 1992; Ko & Rossen, 2001; Panitz, 2001; Spooner, Jordan, Algozzine, & Spooner, 1999).

- Contribute no more than one long comment a day, or less if the students are actively contributing. Several short notes are more likely to be read and appreciated more than a single long entry. Write "weaving" comments every week or two, or assign individuals or groups of students to take on this task of summarizing and focusing the discussion.

- Prompt your students to go deeper than mere opinions or surface answers. Have students support their arguments with facts and supportive data when available.

- Be flexible and patient. Guide the conversation but don't dominate it. If a discussion is slow getting off the ground, privately ask one or two students to help moderate or host the topic to get it going. Write privately to individual students who are active participants and ask them to make contact with less active participants. Also, take care that one or two dominant voices do not take up a disproportionate amount of space. Avoid the use of discussions to express course-related concerns or complaints. This can easily escalate into a "flame war" or "mudthrowing contest."

- Create a student cafe or lounge thread where students can freely discuss other class-related issues. Also, consider creating an instructor FAQs thread for common questions to the instructor.

- Invite experts to participate in discussions. Announce to students when the expert will be arriving online. Have students prepare questions or materials in advance, as needed.

- Close and purge or archive "finished" conferences in stages, giving members an opportunity to save any messages they wish to keep.

Chat:

- Use live chat for online office hours. Post specific times in advance and send out reminders.
- Limit chat groups to four to five members each. Assign groups to "rooms" and circulate through them, as needed.
- Allow time at the beginning and end of a chat session for informal, warm-up conversation.
- Speak privately to learners during an active chat session to give sensitive feedback or make inquiries of a personal nature.
- Use chat or discussion to feature an online expert.
- Find another class that is covering the same topic, viewing the same video, or using the same materials that you are. Meet them online for a debate or to compare analyses or opinions.
- Chat can be useful before a final exam or a midterm for students to collectively express and solve problems. Tutors and teacher's assistants can help monitor these kinds of discussions, too.
- Make the activity interesting. If it is a discussion topic, make it one that students have a reason to get engaged in. Appeal to their life experiences, interests, and ambitions.
- Let the students create some of the topics sometimes. Provide an overall academic framework to guide them where you want them to go.
- Invite "mystery" guests for learners to interact with. These can be real people or people who take on other identities. For example, students themselves or visitors can role play the character parts from a story or video that the class is using.

Assessment:

- Learners appreciate and seem to learn much from the responses of other learners.
- Check in with students via e-mail and see how they are feeling about the course. This will tell you if something is off-track and allow you to address it before it becomes a big problem.
- Take advantage of your course statistics or tracking tools to see what parts of the course students are using and when. In classes where learner responses are required, keep track of those who respond and those who do not.

- Take advantage of your course gradebook to automatically input and calculate scores on student work, and to automatically compute surveys and class evaluation statistics; in short, it can really save you time.
- Online learners need frequent feedback and cannot seem to get enough. Feedback (or the lack thereof) is a commonly mentioned concern of online learners.
- Weight the course so that more time is set aside in the beginning weeks or days for technical support. An orientation period sets time aside to assess students in terms of content and technology and allows a buffer of time for everyone to "norm" to the technology tools at hand.

CONCLUSION

Collaboration, a key refrain echoed throughout this chapter, continues to be a core aspect of our online teaching and learning endeavors. We believe that the pros and cons of working in a partnership as instructor-developers merits careful consideration. In our program and in our personal professional endeavors we continue to be strongly committed to instructor-facilitated learning experiences versus self-paced, exam-driven, autonomous courses. In our online courses, instructors teach more than ever "at the point of need" and adjust pacing and content according to students' needs. We want language-related online learning to be a communicative and community-building experience, not isolating for instructor-developers or for students. Precourse planning and work-style compatibility cannot be overemphasized. Talking in advance about learning styles, cultural considerations, and the method of instructional delivery that computer-based technology sometimes dictates helps control attrition rates. Also, attrition decreases when the participants have a local partner or cohort for support and ideas. Ongoing, cyclical assessment of the course and students, coupled with a flexible, adaptable approach around the core content and learning outcomes, is crucial.

On a technical level, we find that doing research in advance to have a clear sense of currently available tools that match our course design and learning outcomes and to have back-up tools for when (not if) things go awry helps us make transitions rapidly and smoothly, as needed. We have also gained new appreciation for the excellent record-keeping systems that our program already has in place so that we can easily keep track of students' work over time for accreditation purposes. With careful planning, core infrastructure, and ongoing communication, the benefits of collaborative endeavors can definitely outweigh potential problems.

We know that we are successful when a student writes, "Thank you again for the course, it's very passionating."

REFERENCES

Ahlmark, T. (1995). *Decision Style Inventory* [Web page]. Retrieved December 11, 2001, from http://www.informatik.umu.se/~tah/dsi.html

Alamprese, J. A. (1998). *Promoting systemic change in adult education.* East Lansing, MI: National Center for Research on Teacher Learning (ERIC Clearinghouse, Information Series No. 377).

Bailey, J. (2001). *Designing web accessibility for people with disabilities* [Web page]. Retrieved December 2, 2001, from http://darkwing.uoregon.edu/~atl/web_acs.htm

Betz, N. E., Borgen, F. H., & Harmon, L. W. (2001). *Strong interest inventory and skills confidence inventory* [Web page]. Retrieved December 1, 2001, from http://www.career-lifeskills. com/products_services/atpr/sii/cpp-86500s.htm

Blankenship, S. E. (1998). *Factors related to computer use by teachers in classroom instruction.* Unpublished doctoral dissertation, Virginia Polytechnic Institute and State University.

Brown, H. D. (2000). *Teaching by principles: An interactive approach to language pedagogy.* New York: Longman.

Bruer, J. T. (1999). *Schools for thought: A science of learning in the classroom.* Boston: MIT Press.

Brush, T. A., & Uden, L. (2000). Using computer-mediated communications to enhance instructional design classes: A case study. *International Journal of Instructional Media, 27*(2), 157–164.

Bulman, T. (1996). *Peer assessment in groupwork* [Web page]. Retrieved December 2, 2001, from http://www.oaa.pdx.edu/CAE/FacultyFocus/spring96/bulman.html

Campbell, C., & Kryszewska, H. (1992). *Learner-based teaching.* Oxford, England: Oxford University Press.

Christison, M. A., & Kennedy, D. (1999). *Multiple intelligences: Theory and practice in adult ESL* [Web page]. Retrieved November 20, 2001, from http://www.cal.org/ncle/DIGESTS/ MI.htm

Cifuentes, L., & Shih, Y.-C. D. (2001). Teaching and learning online: A collaborative between U.S. and Taiwanese students. *Journal of Research on Computing in Education, 33*(4), 456–474.

Color Quiz [Web page]. (2001). Retrieved December 1, 2001, from http://www.colorquiz. com/

Crossley, M. (2000). Bridging cultures and traditions in the reconceptualization of comparative and international education. *Comparative Education, 36*(3), 319–332.

Crow, G. M., & Pounder, D. G. (2000). Interdisciplinary teachers teams: Context, design, and process. *Educational Administration Quarterly, 36*(2), 216–254.

Daugherty, K. (1997). *Decision making styles* [Web page]. Retrieved December 1, 2001, from http://www.leadershipmanagement.com/html-files/decision.htm

Deci, E. L., & Ryan, R. M. (2001). *Self-determination theory: Questionnaires: Intrinsic Motivation Inventory* [Web page]. Retrieved December 1, 2001, from http://psych.rochester.edu/SDT/ measures/intrins.html

Dumas, J. S. (1999). *A practical guide to usability testing.* Exeter, England: Intellect.

Ely, M., Anzul, M., Friedman, T., Garner, D., & Steinmetz, A. M. (1999). *Doing qualitative research: Circles within circles.* Philadelphia: Farmer Press.

Erven, B., & Zulauf, C. (1998). *Key points concerning group assignments* [Web page]. Retrieved December 2, 1998, from http://www.osu.edu/education/ftad/Publications/keypoints. html

Felder, R. M. (2001). *Active and cooperative learning* [Web page]. Retrieved December 2, 2001, from http://www2.ncsu.edu/unity/lockers/users/f/felder/public/Cooperative_ Learning.html

Felder, R. M., & Brent, R. (2001). *FAQs-3. How can I get students to work in teams in a distance learning environment?* [Web page]. Retrieved December 2, 2001, from http://www2.ncsu.edu/unity/lockers/users/f/felder/public/Columns/FAQs-3.html

Felder, R. M., & Henriques, E. R. (1995). *Learning and teaching styles in foreign and second language education* [Web page]. Retrieved December 2, 2001, from http://www2.ncsu.edu/unity/lockers/users/f/felder/public/Papers/FLAnnals.pdf

Finley, M. (1996). *Techno Personality Test* [Web page]. Retrieved December 1, 2001, from http://www.skypoint.com/~mfinley/test.htm

Furman, G. C. (1998). Postmodernism and community in schools: Unraveling the paradox. *Educational Administration Quarterly, 34*(3), 298–329.

Gaer, S. (1999). *Email projects homepage* [Web page]. Retrieved December 3, 2001, from http://www.otan.dni.us/webfarm/emailproject/email.htm

Gaines, B. R., & Shaw, M. L. G. (1995). *Collaboration through concept maps* [Web page]. Retrieved November 19, 2001, from http://ksi.cpsc.ucalgary.ca/articles/CSCL95CM/

Gardner, H. (1999). *Intelligence reframed: Multiple intelligences for the 21st century.* New York: Basic Books.

Gonglewski, M., Meloni, C., & Brant, J. (2001). *Using e-mail in foreign language teaching: Rationale and suggestions* [Web page]. Retrieved October 16, 2001, from http://iteslj.org/Techniques/Meloni-Email.html

Grasha, A. F. (1994). *Teaching Styles Inventory, Version 3.0* [Web page]. Retrieved December 2, 2001, from http://www.fcrc.indstate.edu/tstyles3_instructions.html

Graves, K. (1999). *Teachers as course developers.* Cambridge, England: Cambridge University Press.

Graves, K. (2000). *Designing language courses: A guide for teachers.* Boston: Heinle & Heinle.

Hanna, D. E., Glowacki-Dudka, M., & Conceicao-Runlee, S. (2000). *147 practical tips for teaching online groups.* Madison, WI: Atwood.

Hansen, E. J., & Stephens, J. A. (2000). The ethics of learner-centered education; Dynamics that impede the process. *Change, 33*(5), 40–47.

Harper, W. S. (2000). *Learning-Style Inventory* [Web page]. Retrieved December 1, 2001, from http://pss.uvm.edu/pss162/learning_styles.html

Herndl, C. G., & Nahrwold, C. A. (2000). Research as social practice. *Written Communication, 17*(2), 258–297.

Ho, M. L. C. (2000). *Developing Intercultural Awareness and Writing Skills Through Email Exchange* [Web page]. Retrieved October 18, 2001, from http://www.aitech.ac.jp/~iteslj/Articles/Ho-Email.html

Indiana State University. (2002). *Teaching Styles and Instructional Uses of the World Wide Web* [Web page]. Retrieved December 2, 2002, from http://web.indstate.edu/ctl/styles/tstyle.html

Inglehart, R. (2001). *World values survey* [Web page]. Retrieved March 13, 2001, from http://wvs.isr.umich.edu/

Inglehart, R., & Baker, W. E. (2001). Modernization's challenge to traditional values: Who's afraid of Ronald McDonald? *Futurist, 35*(2), 16–23.

internet.com Corp. (2001). *Webopedia* [Web page]. Retrieved December 1, 2001, from http://www.pcwebopedia.com/

Johnson, D. W. (1992). *Cooperative learning: Increasing college faculty instructional productivity* [Web page]. Retrieved December 2, 2001, from http://www.ntlf.com/html/lib/bib/92-2dig.htm

Johnson, D. W., Johnson, R. T., & Stanne, M. B. (2000). *Cooperative learning methods: A meta-analysis* [Web page]. Retrieved December 2, 2001, from http://www.clcrc.com/pages/cl-methods.html

Keirsey, D. M. (2000). *Keirsey temperament sorter and Keirsey temperament theory* [Web page]. Retrieved December 4, 2000, from http://www.keirsey.com/

Keogh, R. (2001). *Examining Australian and Japanese stereotypes via e-mail exchange, A worksheet and a CALL lesson plan* [Web page]. Retrieved October 18, 2001, from http://www.aitech.ac.jp/~iteslj/Lessons/Keogh-Stereotypes/

Knight, P. T., & Trowler, P. R. (2000). Department-level cultures and the improvement of learning and teaching. *Studies in Higher Education, 25*(1), 69–83.

Ko, S., & Rossen, S. (2001). *Teaching online, A practical guide.* Boston: Houghton Mifflin.

Kolb, D. A. (1984). *Experiential learning: Experience as the source of learning and development.* Englewood Cliffs, NJ: Prentice-Hall.

Kreitner, R., Kinicki, A., & Buelens, M. (2001). *Organizational behavior, chapter 11: Individual and group decision making* [Web page]. Retrieved December 1, 2001, from http://www.mhhe.com/business/management/kreitner5e/student/olc/ch11assess.mhtml

LeCompte, M. D. (2000). Analyzing qualitative data. *Theory into Practice, 29*(3), 146–155.

Marlow, M. P. (2000). Collegiality, collaboration and Kuleana: Three crucial components for sustaining school-university partnerships. *Education, 121*(1), 188–195.

Merriam, S. B., & Caffarella, R. S. (1999). *Learning in Adulthood, A Comprehensive Guide.* San Francisco, California: Jossey-Bass, Inc. Publishers.

Merriam Webster online dictionary. (2001). Retrieved November 25, 2001, from http://www.m-w.com/

Nielson, J. (2000). *Designing web usability.* Indianapolis, IN: New Riders.

Nielson, J. (2001). *UseIt.com* [Web page]. Retrieved December 1, 2001, from http://www.UseIt.com/

Nunan, D. (1992). Toward a collaborative approach to curriculum development: A case study. In D. Nunan (Ed.), *Collaborative language learning and teaching* (pp. 230–267). Cambridge, Cambridge University Press.

Opp-Beckman, L. B., & Kieffer, C. (1997–2001). *Senshu University and University of Oregon distance education and on-site exchange programs* [Web page]. Retrieved December 2, 2001, from http://darkwing.uoregon.edu/~aei/pastsenshu.html

Opp-Beckman, L. B. (2001a). *Computer assisted language learning LING 410/510* [Web page]. Retrieved December 2, 2001, from http://aei.uoregon.edu/ling410/index.htm

Opp-Beckman, L. B. (2001b). *Africa online, English language education: Using web resources to develop classroom content-based materials* [Web page]. Retrieved December 2, 2001, from http://aei.uoregon.edu/safrica/index.htm

Panitz, T. (2001). *Ted's cooperative learning e-book* [Web page]. Retrieved December 2, 2001, from http://home.capecod.net/~tpanitz/ebook/contents.html

Plotnick, E. (1997). *Concept mapping: A graphical system for understanding the relationship between concepts* [Web page]. Retrieved November 19, 2001, from http://www.ericit.org/digests/mapping.shtml

Preece, J. (2000). *Online communities: Supporting sociability, designing usability.* New York: Wiley.

Pusch, M. D. (1979). *Multicultural education: A cross cultural training approach.* Chicago: Intercultural Network.

Robb, T. N. (1996). *E-mail keypals for language fluency* [Web page]. Retrieved October 26, 2001, from http://www.kyoto-su.ac.jp/~trobb/keypals.html

Salopek, J. J. (2000). Digital collaboration. *Training and Development, 54*(6), 38–43.

Singhal, M. (1997). *The Internet and foreign language education: Benefits and challenges* [Web page]. Retrieved October 26, 2001, from http://www.aitech.ac.jp/~iteslj/Articles/Singhal-Internet.html

Skills One. (2001). *Strong Interest Inventory* [Web page]. Retrieved December 1, 2001, from http://www.skillsone.com/%5Cstrong%5Cstrong.html

Smith, M. K., & Doyle, M. E. (2000). *The informal education homepage* [Web page]. Retrieved November 26, 2000, from http://www.infed.org/

Soloman, B. A., & Felder, R. M. (2000). *Index of Learning Styles Questionnaire* [Web page]. Retrieved December 1, 2000, from http://www2.ncsu.edu/unity/lockers/users/f/felder/public/ILSdir/ilsweb.html

Special Needs Opportunity Windows. (2002). *Learning to learn, Teaching Styles Inventory* [Web page]. Retrieved December 2, 2002, from http://snow.utoronto.ca/Learn2/mod3/tchstyle.html

Spooner, F., Jordan, L., Algozzine, B., & Spooner, M. (1999). Student ratings of instruction in distance learning and on-campus classes. *Journal of Educational Research, 92*(3), 132–140.

Summer Institute for Intercultural Communication. (2001). Retrieved December 1, 2001, from http://www.intercultural.org/index.html

TechTarget. (2001). *whatis?com* [Web page]. Retrieved December 1, 2001, from http://whatis.techtarget.com/

Teleometrics International. (2001a). *Management of Motives Index (MMI)* [Web page]. Retrieved December 1, 2000, from http://www.teleometrics.com/mmi02.htm

Teleometrics International. (2001b). *Work Motivation Inventory (WMI)* [Web page]. Retrieved December 1, 2001, from http://www.teleometrics.com/wmi02.htm

Thornburg, D. (1997). *Multimedia encourages new learning styles* [Web page]. Retrieved March 5, 1998, from http://www.tcpd.org/

Trochim, W. M. K. (2001). *Concept mapping* [Web page]. Retrieved November 19, 2001, from http://trochim.human.cornell.edu/kb/conmap.htm

Union of International Associations. (2001). *Integrative concept: Word soul* [Web page]. Retrieved May 18, 2001, from http://www.uia.org/uiademo/kon/c0302.htm

United States Department of Education. (1998). *Technology @ your fingertips, CES 98-293.* Washington, DC: U.S. Department of Education, Office of Educational Research and Improvement, National Center for Education Statistics.

Vilmi, R. (2001). *International writing exchange* [Web page]. Retrieved October 26, 2001, from http://www.ruthvilmi.net/hut/

W3C. (2001). *Web accessibility initiative (WAI)* [Web page]. Retrieved December 1, 2001, from http://www.w3.org/WAI/

Warschauer, M. (1996). *Motivational aspects of using computers for writing and communication* [Web page]. Retrieved October 21, 2000, from http://nflrc.hawaii.edu/NetWorks/NW01/NW01.html

Warschauer, M., Whittaker, P. F., & Fawn, P. (1997). *The Internet for English teaching: Guidelines for teachers* [Web page]. Retrieved October 16, 2001, from http://www.aitech.ac.jp/~iteslj/Articles/Warschauer-Internet.html

Weeks, W. H., Pederson, P. B., & Brislin, R. W. (1979). *A manual of structured experiences for cross-cultural learning.* Yarmouth, ME: Intercultural Press.

Zhenhui, R. (1999). *Modern vs. traditional* [Web page]. Retrieved December 2, 2001, from http://exchanges.state.gov/forum/vols/vol37/no3/p27.htm

Zhenhui, R. (2001). *Matching teaching styles with learning styles in East Asian contexts* [Web page]. Retrieved October 16, 2001, from http://iteslj.org/Techniques/Zhenhui-TeachingStyles.html

IV

EVALUATING CALL

Second and foreign language instructors are often overwhelmed by the sheer number of CALL materials and Web sites, most of which claim to be "leading-edge" or "state-of-the-art." Part IV addresses the challenging issue of how to critically evaluate CALL software and online Web activities through two chapters, the first reviewing criteria for assessing CALL software, and the second suggesting procedures for Website evaluation. Again, the topic is approached through a review of current options, case studies and specific guidelines for the teacher.

In the first chapter, "Toward a Theory of E/Valuation for Second Language Learning Media," Reeder, Heift, Roche, Tabyanian, Schlickau, and Gölz pose a basic question regarding the current generation of CALL software, "Does it fulfill its stated educational purposes?" In their research review, the authors note the lack of evaluative criteria which measure not only learning outcomes but also learning processes. They present an assessment scheme for evaluating the educational effectiveness of new multimedia language learning software by considering both the nature of the software as well as its potential to promote L2 learning in relation to current theories of language learning and teaching. Reeder and his associates conclude by describing a research-based program they term "E/Valuation," a process to assist teachers to ask and answer questions about the educational effectiveness of language-learning software.

The final chapter, "Evaluation of ESL/EFL Instructional Websites," by Susser and Robb, reviews the literature on evaluating online instruction, and then proposes an evaluation method based on four perspectives: 1) the standard literature evaluating ESL/EFL textbooks, 2) the multimedia CALL evaluation literature, 3) evaluations of distance learning and Internet-based training, and 4) Website evaluation based on Web usability theory, interface design rules, and other parameters. The chapter is divided into two parts, with the first introducing the screening and evaluation procedures and describing a framework for evaluating ESL/EFL CALL Websites. In the second part, the authors demonstrate how teachers might apply this framework to any language learning context by using it to make a checklist to evaluate a specific category of Websites. The conclusion offers practical advice for teachers and learners who wish to make use of the Internet for L2 instruction and learning.

Toward a Theory of E/Valuation for Second Language Learning Media

Kenneth Reeder
The University of British Columbia

Trude Heift
Simon Fraser University

Jörg Roche
Ludwig Maximilians Universität

Shahbaz Tabyanian
The University of British Columbia

Stephan Schlickau
Ludwig Maximilians Universität

Peter Gölz
The University of Victoria

Language instructors are bombarded in professional conversations, conferences and publications with glowing reports and demonstrations of "leading edge," "new generation," "must-have" L2 or foreign language software packages. Indeed, with the advent of such interesting and attractive software as A la rencontre de Philippe (Furstenberg, 1994) or Dans un quartier de Paris (Furstenberg, 1999) for French, Berliner Sehen (Crocker & Fendt, n.d.) or Uni-deutsch.de (n.d.) for German, or Ucuchi (Andersen & Daza, 1994) for Quechua, and their ilk, it comes as little surprise that a great deal of discussion, often of a highly technical sort, surrounds these new tools for teaching and learning. A question that many of us in the profession are sometimes reluctant to ask about newer software packages is whether in fact the software has convincingly been shown to fulfill its educational purposes. What do we know about the educational effectiveness of the current generation of multimedia language-learning software? And, underlying that question, how best do we go about finding out?

The present chapter makes a modest claim. The authors, all working as language instructors and researchers in school and university settings and sometime designer-developers of language software, argue that a new approach is needed for the educational evaluation of language-learning software that falls under the rubrics "new media," "multimedia," and "e-learning" as distinct from previous generations of CALL software. We discuss the case for such a new approach by arguing that present approaches to the evaluation of CALL software, though reasonably adequate (but not wholly, we note) for earlier generations of CALL programs, are not appropriate for what we show to be a new genre of CALL software distinguished by its shared assumptions about language learning and teaching as well as by its technical design. We conclude by sketching a research-based program of what we term *E/Valuation* that aims to assist language educators in answering questions about the educational effectiveness of recent language-learning software. We suggest that this needs to take into account not only the nature of the new e-learning software and its potential to promote language learning in novel ways but also, as Chapelle (2001, p. 8) suggests, current knowledge about language learning and teaching processes and principles drawn mainly (but not exclusively) from the field of applied linguistics.

E-LEARNING SOFTWARE FOR LANGUAGE DEVELOPMENT

What distinguishes the design of new generation e-learning media when applied to language learning? Our team has identified three types of L2 or foreign language teaching and e-learning software as the basis for its investigation: microcosm simulations, microethnographies, and online programs (Roche, 2000).

The common pedagogical traits of these programs include their proximity to authentic or simulated linguistic and cultural settings. As a consequence, the programs often promote a high degree of interaction between program and user, promote learning of cultural content and intercultural communication skills using realistic experiences and artifacts, and often share features of immersion language education and content-based instructional approaches. In addition, many of them are based on constructivist assumptions about learning, and consequently the programs often promote autonomous learning. What they tend not to share are characteristics of grammar-translation, audiolingual, or behavioristic assumptions about learning and instructional design such as programmed learning, drill-and-practice sequences, or for that matter, much explicit scope and sequence to syllabus design.

Their common technical trait is that each of the three types of programs makes extensive use of the multimedia capacities of computers, including complex graphic elements such as streaming video or animation and fairly sophisticated sound elements, delivered either from stand-alone media such as CD-ROM or from the World Wide Web, the multimedia manifestation of the Internet, hypertext, or collaborative learning environments. Some make an interesting effort at incorporating artificial intelligence in the form of natural language processing in addition to earlier developments in help systems that are context sensitive or that update themselves according to learners' progress. E-learning media for language development represents the most recent generation of CALL software.

Taken together, these shared characteristics suggest that e-learning software constitutes a recognizable genre of language-learning software whose assumptions about language learning and approaches to instructional design (a) are not adequately taken into account by present approaches to CALL software description and evaluation, and (b) should be taken into account in any comprehensive approach to the description and evaluation of CALL software. We review recent examples of these three categories later when we turn to our modest proposal as to how to go about evaluating the e-learning generation of language software in a more satisfactory fashion.

CURRENT ISSUES IN LANGUAGE SOFTWARE EVALUATION

Recent Practices in Software Evaluation

A critique of recent approaches to software evaluation requires some description of current practices in the field. Generally, there are two main approaches to software assessment: introspective (checklists, reviews) and empirical evaluations. Although checklists are a more or less systematic and structured evaluation that involves the use of a printed form, the typical review includes basic information about the program and the reviewer's subjective description. However, the types of criteria found in a checklist and a review largely overlap (see Hubbard, 1992; Knowles, 1992; Schmueckler & Shuell, 1989). Often the criteria employed in a review vary according to the reviewer rather than derive from a theory of evaluation.

In contrast, empirical evaluations require that the materials have to be used for some time by actual learners in a learning situation, and thus the approach moves away from the introspective approach (see Scholfield, 2000, for a detailed discussion). Our survey of recent evaluation projects of an empirical type, together with some reflection on our own recent practices and experiences with the assessment of our own projects, suggests a lack of methodological rigor or at very least a lack of agreed-on methodological protocols that can create what we term *idiosyncratic assessment.*

An introspective assessment by learners, for example, can prove to be unreliable, producing contradictory results at times. Child's (1997/1998) studies, for example, indicate that even apparently highly interdependent factors vary to a considerable degree. In a multimedia-based language course taught by the same instructor during 1990 and 1995, students were asked to evaluate factors such as "% 'strongly agreeing' course materials are useful"(1991: 71%, 1995: 91%) and "% rating course 'superior' " (1991: 74%, 1995: 65%). Although both factors seem to be highly interdependent, the numeric results show little correlation, raising serious technical questions about both the reliability of measurement and the correlational validity of the measures themselves. We return later to further underlying weaknesses of a less technical nature concerning gaps in the content or construct validity of a great deal of software evaluation.

In the analysis of learning potentials by experts, the material itself is the focus of attention. An expert carefully analyzes all potential effects of the materials. Although this assessment method is fairly accurate in terms of learning potentials, it still does not allow any clear statement on actual achievements by learners. The difference between potential and actual outcomes, however, is of utmost importance because it is widely known that experts and novices employ different strategies when dealing with texts. As a consequence, the competence of the instructors to deal with software is likely to have a significant effect on the achievement levels reached by the learners. However, the competence level of instructors is difficult to measure in itself.

In investigating the main elements found in introspective and empirical evaluations, our research group's survey revealed two main components: product-related components, and instructional design and learning components. We found that assessments of both sorts of components appeared in some cases to lack coherent connections to best practices in language teaching or current understandings of language learning.

Product-Related Components in Software Evaluation

Most of the evaluation approaches we surveyed include an evaluation of the technical or usability features of software. At this level, evaluation is concerned with the general characteristics of the software itself and the ease with which it can be used. This part of the evaluation, which can be done by educational software experts, determines the presence (or absence) of technical features and evaluates the content of the software. Such product-related components can include:

• Technical aspects: Technical aspects include implementation considerations and documentation and packaging. Hardware specifications, cost effectiveness, instructional and operational manual, suggested classroom activities, and the description of the links and branching techniques among data are among the elements evaluated at this level.

• Content considerations: Content considerations include the accuracy and presentation of the material, consistency regarding the level and nature of the content presented, and the general appropriateness of the material for the typical users (Gros & Spector, 1994).

• General use considerations: These often include the quality of the user interface, including menu types, items covered and terminology used in the interface, and support material availability, including adaptability to the Internet. Interaction with and among users is also covered as part of the usability considerations because of the dominance of communicative language teaching (CLT) approaches.

Instructional Design and Learning Considerations in Software Evaluation

• Instructional design: Although the majority of software developers as well as evaluation systems agree on the significance of instructional considerations in the development and evaluation of educational courseware, there is no agreement among researchers and evaluators as to what criteria to use to assess this aspect of language software. Part of this difficulty could be caused by the absence of instructors on software design teams, creating a gap between design, development, and classroom implementation as noted by Hubbard (1992). Moreover, because the instructional needs of any given classroom are context dependent, building accurate evaluative criteria into software evaluation systems presents a serious technical challenge to most software evaluation systems. As Leu, Hillinger, Loseby, Balcom, and Dinkin (1998, p. 204) put it, "Although new technologies are becoming more widely available they are not always appropriated by teachers and systematically integrated into the curriculum." For the same reasons, software designers can remain unaware of instructional concerns of language educators. A notable exception to this rule is reported in Leu et al., in which six elementary school teachers involved in designing software for sixth-grade students proposed features that could accommodate their instructional needs. The researchers and teachers involved in this project identified software design themes that guided their decisions at each stage of the design. Another exception is the design and development plan described by Reeder and Hart (2001) in which a joint university- and school-based instructional design team worked from the outset with an industry-based engineering and production team to develop the Edubba prototype and beta products.

• Learning process considerations: A look at most software evaluation systems reveals the experimental nature of the evaluation approaches. "The prevailing methodology in the evaluation of software in the classroom is based on an experimental paradigm (control group, test, post-test control, etc.)" (Gros & Spector, 1994, p. 38). Lack of a match between course objectives and instructional features included in the design of software seems to be the main reason for the unreliability of most student-gain-based evaluations. Our survey of current evaluative approaches found no examples of formative evaluation of software in which the learning outcomes as well as the learning processes leading to those outcomes were systematically examined. The notable exception was Murray's (1998, 1999a, 1999b) innovative observational study of the learning processes and strategies of dyads who were using the French language multimedia software A la rencontre de Philippe (Furstenberg, 1994). Moreover, Chapelle (1998) pointed out that individual learners might focus on different linguistic aspects and forms during the same task and argued that "to address this fact, a more flexible form of [CALL tasks outcome] assessment is needed—one that tests those linguistic items that the learners choose to focus on" (p. 29). To take the individual students' foci into account, outcome assessment "must be complemented by observing learners as they complete the task" (p. 29).

SHORTCOMINGS OF CURRENT APPROACHES
TO SOFTWARE EVALUATION

In addition to noting the lack of evaluative criteria that measure not only learning outcomes but also learning processes, we identify a number of shortcomings in current evaluative practices in the sections that follow. The question remains as to whether current software evaluation guides can be adapted to address some of these concerns, or whether a qualitatively different approach is needed to address these issues, to the extent that there is agreement that they are real issues for the future of software assessment.

Problems of Validity and Generalizability in Experimental
Evaluation Designs

As most empirical methods tend to aim at some degree of generalizability of their results to a population, they try to ascertain and control the effects of intervening factors. This, in turn, often leads to some experimental designs that consist of a test group, a control group, and some standardized, highly prestructured tools of investigation (e.g., a questionnaire). This type of experimental design, which has been adapted from the sciences, can prove problematic as it can also have a number of weaknesses:

- Difficulty in attributing outcomes validly to the treatment. Instructional and learning processes are of a highly complex nature. It is therefore difficult, if possible at all, to account for all intervening variables. This difficulty normally leads to a design that does not reflect all variables or a lab design that selects a few, but as a consequence, has little if anything in common with a "normal" classroom setting.

- Invalid reduction of complex learning processes. A standardized questionnaire, particularly if poorly designed, will often reflect a highly attenuated or even behaviorist concept of learning if it presupposes an overly narrowly defined set of language-learning issues and translates these constructs into questions with foreseeable "correct" answers. Thus, any learning result that has not been predicted will rarely become obvious in such an investigation. In addition, overnarrowly phrased questions may be so close to the topics discussed or tasks mastered in a classroom that little if any generalizability beyond either the test group or the control group is possible. This in turn argues for the usefulness of complementing such narrowly defined measurement approaches with some more open-ended measures such as open-ended questionnaire prompts or semistructured interviews that can be analyzed with more qualitative methods such as content analysis or discourse analysis. We return to idiosyncratic assessment later in our discussion.

Current Approaches to Software Evaluation Fail to Take Educational Goals Into Account

In numerous cases, evaluative criteria fail to link the design of software to the instructional methodology of the program. Very few of the software evaluation examples we reviewed provide a methodological framework for CALL courseware development and evaluation.[1] A proponent of such a systematic integration of development, evaluation and implementation, and an exception to our general findings, Hubbard (1992), defined a methodological framework as:

A framework for the description and analysis of methods, which are ultimately nothing more than a set of procedures applied in a consistent and reasoned fashion in the pursuit of a given goal, such as learning to speak and understand a foreign language. (p. 41)

---

[1]The software reviews performed by CALICO present an exception to our general findings. Their reviews consistently follow Hubbard's (1992) framework.

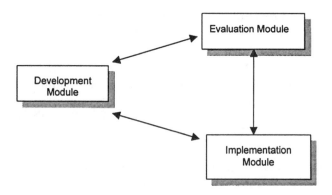

FIG. 13.1.   Hubbard's model of CALL courseware development.

Accordingly, Hubbard (1987, 1992) argued for the application of a curriculum development approach to software evaluation as part of a triangular model for CALL courseware, the other two components being development and implementation. In his model, Hubbard (1992) emphasized the interrelated nature of these components or "modules" as illustrated in Fig. 13.1.

In his network approach, Hubbard (1992) argued for a framework in which the development scheme of software is laid out in the same fashion as a curriculum and instructional scheme. In this way, he argued that software development, implementation, and evaluation can be explicitly related to instructional principles and their related components.

More recently, Chapelle (1998) advanced seven hypotheses derived from SLA research that can be used as design and evaluation bases for CALL software. In her article, Chapelle remarked, "They [the seven hypotheses] are not guaranteed to apply directly to design of CALL activities; but they may provide a valuable starting point to look for principles to apply to CALL" (p. 26).

The Case of New and Multiple Literacies

We are at the turning point of changing understandings of literacy, and particularly of its status in regard to language education, reading, and writing (see the work of the New London Group, edited by Cope & Kalantzis, 2000). Traditional approaches to software evaluation will probably lag behind emerging knowledge and theory about literacy and its relationships to language learning. E-learning media affect the instructional objectives of literacy and language classrooms, which in turn requires evaluating those technologies accordingly. Visual literacy, or the ability to use the graphic elements of multimedia effectively for constructing and conveying meaning, for example, brings about new instructional objectives, which in turn requires new features in software development and, consequently, new criteria for evaluating those features. Perspective changes of this sort require software developers, including teachers, to rethink the design of educational software to accommodate new objectives emanating from those perspectives. In addition to visual literacy, a descriptively adequate approach to software evaluation will often need to deal with dimensions of cultural literacy and critical literacy (Edelsky, 1994; Pennycook, 2001).

Closely related to visual literacy are the cases of visual cultures and popular cultures. The visual culture in which the World Wide Web operates, for instance, depicts a distinctive way of re/presenting meaning through space organization, integration of sounds and images, and so on. Promoted by computer games, virtual communities, and popular youth TV programs, these visual cultures turn into popular cultures which, as Burnett (2002) asserted:

> provide a central if not crucial foundation for the lives of students. Often in not recognizing the centrality of popular culture, teachers may be missing some of the most important elements in students' understanding of their own lives. . . . We need a shared understanding and that will require a profound shift in the ways in which culture is both seen and understood within learning environments. (p. 142)

These popular cultures and their related literacies should be factored into the design and evaluation of any multimedia learning tool including and particularly CALL software, considering the interrelation between language and culture.

The Intercultural Divide in Language-Learning Software Design and Evaluation

Although the development of new information and communication technologies has steadily and rapidly accelerated over recent years, relatively little attention has been paid to the actual use of those technologies by different user cultures (social cultures, gender cultures, learner cultures, national cultures). It is widely assumed that the standardization of the equipment automatically leads to a standardization in its application. Research has shown that ways of communicating cross-culturally vary greatly even among related languages (Kramsch, 1993; Roche, 2001; Schlickau, 2001). However, little is yet known about cultural attitudes toward information and communication technologies (Roche, 2000). As a result, issues of intercultural communication and sociocultural variation among user groups have not been adequately reflected in software assessment. In fact, with a few exceptions, they have not even been considered in the production of language-learning software. For example, this lack of cultural awareness can hardly be better illustrated than by the different versions of the program Who Is Oscar Lake? (Miller & Wickenden, n.d.). The program has simply been translated into different languages, keeping the same name, except for the question word, and exactly the same setting (e.g., the railway station). Only a few items are labeled differently, for example, *gare* or *Bahnhof* for railway station.

However, the significance of intercultural issues is not limited to mere translation of linguistic items. Rather, intercultural mediation involves a complex set of parameters reaching from the linguistic code to cultural values and patterns of viewing and using media. Sometimes, the reluctance to implement cultural awareness in software design is due to different goals and expectations of the software developers. For example, a recent case study of the struggles of language educators to incorporate awareness of intercultural communication and cultural stereotyping issues into the work of a joint university–industry language software development team was documented in Beckett, McGivern, Reeder, and Semenov (1999) in their account of the development of Edubba, multimedia software for academic writing in English (Reeder & Hart, 2001; Reeder, Hooper, Roche, & Shaddock, 2000).

New Media, New Modes of Language Learning

Closely related to the effects of the new curricular assumptions about literacy on technology formation and evaluation is the instructional dichotomy of curricular learning versus free interactive learning paradigms (Lemke, 1998). In contrast to curricular learning, in interactive learning paradigms the instructor and the institution's syllabus take on less central or at least different roles in learning. This is especially evident with new technologies that have enabled collaborative learning environments in the form of synchronous or asynchronous communication. For example, several studies (Berge, 1995; Heift & Caws, 2000; Kelm, 1992, 1996; Wang & Teles, 1998) in CMC have shown that the instructor takes the less dominant role of a facilitator or mediator and that student participation increases (Kern, 1996). The interaction between emerging possibilities offered by new technologies and their effects on instructional paradigms are of main interest. Technological advances create learning situations different from those of mainly text-based traditional classrooms, and these new learning opportunities require new instructional methodology to accommodate them. An efficient evaluative system for language-learning software will be flexible enough to factor in these possibilities.

A RESEARCH AGENDA FOR THE EVALUATION
OF E-LEARNING FOR LANGUAGE DEVELOPMENT

As a first step to extend the reach of CALL software evaluation to take into account the distinct nature of e-learning software and the teaching and learning that can ensue from its uses, we propose a systematic agenda of research and development in this field (cf. Chapelle, 2001, p. 8). We suggest that such an agenda consist of the following four steps, summarized in Fig. 13.2:

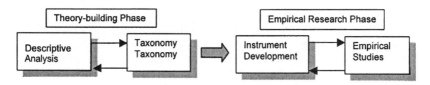

FIG. 13.2.   Steps in an e-learning evaluation.

1. Description: constructing and pilot testing a research instrument to describe e-learning materials for language development in a systematic and consistent manner;
2. Theory building: developing a theoretical framework and taxonomy for evaluation of e-learning media in language learning;
3. Instrumentation: deriving from the theoretical framework a suite of new instruments and guidelines for evaluation of e-learning materials of different types in different development and language teaching contexts;
4. Empirical studies: testing the suite of instruments and guidelines on current e-learning materials in a representative range of instructional settings with a representative range of users.

We discuss each of these steps in turn, in an effort to illustrate the sorts of research and development that might be possible in such a program. Because our work is entering its first phase, we deal in more detail with the descriptive phase of the E/Valuating E-Learning for Second and Foreign Language Learning project, and necessarily in less detail with the remaining phases.

Describing E-Learning Software for Language Development

The three types of software our team has identified as the basis for its research in the descriptive phase of our study are: microcosm simulations, microethnographies, and online programs. The common trait of these programs is their proximity to authentic or simulated immersion settings. Most programs are rooted in communicative teaching approaches, although such roots are often not specified. Undetermined and often unclear is also their footing in learning theory. Nevertheless, some of the more recent developments show traits of constructivist approaches. The three different types of software are all representatives of the most recent generation of programs. We turn to descriptions and recent examples of each main category, by way of exemplifying the sort of work that can be undertaken as a necessary preliminary to any effort to enhance the coherence, validity, and usefulness of the educational evaluation of such learning media.

Microcosm Simulations. Microcosm simulations are programs that attempt to create fictional and nonfictional self-contained worlds reflecting segments of the target culture. These simulations often take the form of stories, ethnographic recordings, and target culture situations. The most common representatives of this type of software are CD-ROMs containing short clips of target culture communications filmed in authentic or pseudo-authentic environments and subsequently adapted for classroom use. Such programming features aim to present authentic communication patterns while providing different help features for learners who need them (e.g., reduced speech rate, vocabulary explanations, reference materials).

• The British program Business Challenges (1996) for instance, presents short video clips of business-related situations and offers context-sensitive help features in several languages. Similar in approach are such programs as Travel Tur (2000) and Einfach Toll! (2000), interactive programs for the teaching of Spanish and German, respectively, that feature a number of conversations and settings involving young adults.

• Edubba, developed by a joint university–industry project at the University of British Columbia, (Reeder & Hart, 2001) supports the development of academic writing for intermediate-level ESL learners. It places the writer-learner in the role as a student reporter for an electronic news organization in a simulated city setting. Writers can explore the city using a variety of means including a taxi tour or maps to file different writing assignments around the theme of an impending water shortage in the city of Edubba and a variety of proposals being debated for its solution. Animated characters are provided with segments of an extensive knowledge base that can be queried by typed interview questions by the student reporter, and characters also reply by means of a simple natural language-processing routine, with distinct opinions and viewpoints about the best approach to the environmental issue. Language skills are therefore acquired by means of content-based instruction in this microcosm simulation.

• A la rencontre de Philippe, developed by Gilberte Furstenberg and her Project Athena team at MIT (Furstenberg, 1994), is among the best known and most sophisticated specimens that use a fictional story as a context for language learning. Filmed on location in Paris by a feature film production crew and scripted by screen writers rather than by educators, the background story follows the misadventures of Philippe, a young man whose girlfriend has thrown him out of her apartment. The viewers-learners are immediately drawn into the action as they are asked to help Philippe find a new apartment in Paris. The ensuing branching storylines involve learners in a variety of search activities and discussions, some of which aim to resolve the conflict between Philippe and his girlfriend. The learners must use the tools at their disposal, of which there are primarily two types: (a) those necessary to solve given tasks (such as maps, directories, an answering machine, and a note pad), and (b) those that facilitate learner comprehension (such as play, repeat and preview functions, search and reference functions, transcriptions, vocabulary glosses, cultural notes, alternative soundtracks, including the original colloquial Parisian speech of the actors, simplified versions, and reduced speech rates).

Microethnographies. This fairly recent category of language-learning software takes advantage of multimedia technology to bridge the gap between (or perhaps even redefine the boundaries between) the learning the language and the learning of culture and appreciation of historical and social contexts of a language and its speakers, often in an interdisciplinary fashion.

• Berliner Sehen, a hypermedia documentary under development by Ellen Crocker, Kurt Fendt, and their MIT team (Crocker & Fendt, n.d.) combines CD-ROMs and other material collections stored on decentralized servers in an attempt to develop a more open learning environment. This program allows students to expand their own archives and to collaborate on the construction over networks of new collections, which can then be made available to other users. Both elements of the program use authentic audio and video recordings taped in a Berlin neighborhood in the late 1990s as well as documentary components from pre- and post-Wall periods, and allow the user to reconstruct and experience the chosen microcosm in different ways.

• Ucuchi (Andersen & Daza, 1994) is a first-year course (two CD-ROM disks, software, textbook, installation/getting started guide, reference guide, VHS version of video) for Quechua, the language of the descendants of the Incas. It was filmed in Bolivia in the village of Ucuchi and in the nearby city of Cochabamba, as an ethnographic documentary. The film was edited to a 2-hour set of 20 scenes of natural speech and interaction. It also contains simple word and suffix references specific to the film content and full transcripts. The transcripts can be displayed in either Quechua or its

English translation, along with optional detailed glosses (see Andersen & Daza, 1994; Kramsch & Andersen, 1999).

- StarFestival (Miyagawa, 1999), a CD-ROM-based fiction-documentary program developed at MIT for the teaching of Japanese (beginners and intermediate), is described at: http://web.mit.edu/fll/www/projects/StarFestival.html

Online Programs.   A virtually infinite amount of material, including sites and links containing authentic audio and video sources in addition to synchronous and asynchronous communication could provide ideal opportunities for language learning and teaching. However, though probably not too difficult at advanced levels of language learning, it remains to be resolved how the largely unstructured and frequently overpowering abundance of information presented in a foreign language can be mediated for beginner or intermediate students.

- Uni-deutsch.de, a large-scale program for the teaching of German for scientific and technical purposes, combines a structured instructional design with the exploratory constructivist options of the Internet. Although focusing on the discourse types and genres that are most relevant for advanced students (e.g., reading scholarly publications, listening to lectures, writing research ·papers, participating in scholarly discussions), the program also offers both basic and advanced assistance and practice on vocabulary and grammar. It contains a large number of exercises that are embedded in the thematic progression of the chapters and address the specific learning conditions of various learner cultures. An intelligent electronic tutor provides feedback on errors and collects acquisition data for research and program development. Online resources such as a news module, a complex communication module, and help and reference modules complete the program.

A comprehensive program of research on e-learning software evaluation would of course need to move beyond detailed descriptions of program features such as those noted earlier to systematic development of relevant categories for the general description of the whole class of software we are concerned with, building on such examples as Hubbard's (1992) CALL software-selection guide and incorporating relevant categories such as learning and teaching assumptions and distinctive characteristics of the new media. The goal would be to develop a descriptively adequate taxonomy sufficient to characterize as many of the educationally important features as possible for any example of e-learning software for L2 and foreign language development. This would be the first step toward a theory of evaluation of this class of software.

Theory Building for Evaluation of New Media in Language Learning

Our group suggests that the research agenda needs to include the knowledge bases from applied linguistics, language pedagogy, and L2 learning at a minimum, if theoretical progress is to continue in the field of language-learning software evaluation. To take one example of a necessary knowledge base, recent views in language acquisition will serve to illustrate the possibility of interdisciplinary illumination of the field. Current thinking about language acquisition as cognitive construction or "meaning making" (Wells, 1986; Wells & Chang-Wells, 1992) implies that for learning media to be effective, they must initiate and support students' active processes of knowledge acquisition, problem solving, and meaning construction. To what extent does the new generation of e-learning software meet these criteria? A rigorous research-based evaluation might reveal that many current programs are insufficiently interactive (e.g., in any open turn-taking activity), leaving inadequate room for learners' creative construction of the L2 or foreign language. Even an overgenerous supply of intelligent help features may pose problems as learners take shortcuts, limiting their opportunities for productive practice and rendering themselves passive. Although contemporary pedagogy argues that learners' energies should be directed to involving them actively in the learning process as opposed to simply clicking buttons or "hotspots" on the computer screen (Davey, Gade, & Fox, 1995, p. 42), it remains to be seen—empirically—whether the latest generation of e-learning software represents a significant improvement in enhancing learning according to such theoretical definitions.

Developing New Tools for the Empirical Study of New Media for Language Learning

The descriptive-taxonomic phase of a program of E/Valuating E-learning Media for Language Learning would be followed by a theoretical phase, during which relevant categories not only for the description but also for the evaluation of e-learning software would be generated. That theoretical work would in turn be followed by an instrumentation phase in which prototype software evaluation tools would be generated from the theoretical model and tested in field settings to determine their validity, reliability, and utility for language teaching.

Tracking Systems for Assessing Learning Processes and Outcomes Associated With E-Learning Software.   In evaluating e-learning software, one of our major goals would be to assess the language-learning process as well as the learning outcomes. Tracking systems in the form of computer logs allow researchers to collect accurate information on student–computer interaction and student progress. Moreover, the data will assist researchers to achieve a higher standardization of measurement in software evaluation.

A computer's access log generally contains just the bare details of timing, path, and input response. A visit to a Web site may be recorded in the server log with the date and time of the request, the originating Internet address, and the system response. Depending on the system and task at hand, additional information is usually available and relevant and therefore worth storing. These logs, particularly when supplemented by analysis and information from a system's components, represent a rich data source for determining the validity and efficacy of pedagogical decisions implicit within the system design and content.

A detailed computer log is necessary for researchers to assess the learning process because studies have shown that learners do not always use every option available in the software, although from an instructor's or software designer's point of view, some features might be very valuable and effective. For instance, Cobb and Stevens (1996) discovered that students did not make use of help options although they knew that such use could improve their learning outcome (see also Bland, Noblitt, Armington, & Gray, 1990; Chapelle, Jamieson, & Park, 1996; Steinberg, 1977, 1989). Moreover, Heift (2001, 2002) found that students showed distinct interaction patterns with the software depending on their language skill level. For example, lower performers made more use of system help options than mid and high performers. Given the outcomes of these studies, an instructor's or designer's judgment of the software cannot measure the learning process as accurately as a computer log. A tracking system can also provide accurate and relevant information on the learning outcome. A detailed computer log on student input will allow researchers to create a student profile over time. This information can then be used to analyze student language skill level.

Complementary and Qualitative Analyses of Learning Processes and Outcomes Associated with E-Learning Software.   Partly to safeguard against the sorts of dangers we identified earlier (reductionism, limitations to generality of findings), we also propose that a comprehensive approach to the evaluation of e-learning software will include research methods of a more naturalistic, observational nature that entail analyses of a "softer," more qualitative nature. Such methods include observational approaches that are structured to a greater or lesser degree.

- *Video observations of users interacting with the program and with one another.* These methods are particularly appropriate for programs that actively promote interaction not only with the program but with a learning partner either in dyadic or small group arrangements. One of the best recent examples of this type of research method applied to e-learning software is Murray's (1998) ethnographic analysis of dyads using the French language program A la rencontre de Philippe. Other video observational methods of the more highly structured type can track users' eye movements, visual lines of regard, or other elements of facial expression or body language to provide data on the users' cognitive and affective engagements with a program (see Pujolà, 2001). Such visual means of research and evaluation seem to us particularly appropriate for programs that contain a high proportion of graphic material.

• *Audio recordings of users.* Hart (2000) studied in detail the ways in which partners collaborated with each other to develop simulated news reports on an environmental issue that was the subject of the animated program, Edubba (Reeder & Hart, 2001). Hart tracked all of the writing partners' conversations using the audio recording capacity of language lab workstations, analyzing these by means of a qualitative discourse analysis approach, and generating a taxonomy of collaborative styles that emerged, dissolved, or advanced throughout the partnerships' development as writers and editors. Those collaborative styles were not of mere sociological interest, for they bore critically on the degree of efficiency with which the learners engaged in the assigned task.

• *Structured and semistructured interviews.* Such methods, though subject to many of the weaknesses we have already identified, can complement the precision afforded by logging and tracking observations and can even capture elements that video and audio observations miss. Their advantage is that they offer opportunities to evaluate in a fairly direct manner specific elements of the learners' intellectual, attitudinal, emotional, or aesthetic responses to their experiences using e-learning software. The major technical challenge for such approaches remains reliability of measurement, but safeguards such as multiple ratings can ensure that data analyses are reasonably consistent from case to case, for example.

Striking a Balance: General Considerations in Designing Research and Evaluation Methods for New Media

The mediation of languages and cultures is influenced by a number of complex and interdependent factors. On the one hand, there are the learners themselves who have been influenced by their former socialization, especially their previous learning experience. According to empirical investigations by Jacobs (1992), learners take advantage of a self-determined learning style if they already have experience in practicing such a style, whereas less independent learners tend to have difficulties when confronted with a lack of clear structures and instructions. On the other hand, there are the learning objectives themselves. The more closely they are defined, the more emphasis there is on an exact reproduction of a given objective. As a result, the deeper the target in the hierarchy of learning objectives, the clearer is the implication of introducing instructionist methods of teaching.

Figure 13.3 takes grammar as an example. Many grammatical structures are rule governed. An example is a word-order rule of main clauses in German. As a formation rule, we can state that the inflected verb is in second position of a sentence. According to the constructivist paradigm, this rule can be learned by discovering it, thus reflecting an inductive approach. On the other hand, studies in instructed SLA have shown that learners can be instructed to learn a given rule by following a cognitive deductive approach. A pure behavioristic approach with pattern drills is less favored in the context of language pedagogy today but would in principle be located as shown in Fig. 13.3. But there are areas of grammar in which a rule requires too much prior knowledge or cannot be reconstructed at all because of its arbitrary nature. For example, with the exception of certain derived words, gender in German or French needs to be memorized and practiced.

Although some decisions clearly depend on the learning objectives, some, however, offer different options. In these cases, characteristics of the learners themselves will influence which teaching method is most effective. As a general tendency, higher level targets in the learning hierarchy have a closer implication for constructivist learning. Learning objectives from a domain such as intercultural communicative competence as it is presently understood will be too complex to be achieved by introducing simple reproductive techniques. Learning objectives in that domain demand an independent learner who is able to act and react in a flexible, empathetic, adequate, and still self-conscious way that cannot be acquired in exclusively instructionist settings. Similarly, autonomous learning cannot be achieved by purely instructionist methods. It requires high metacognitive levels of language-learning awareness as well (see Rüschoff & Wolff, 1999).

In our opinion, these considerations should be taken into account by authors of quality language-learning software, and the approach to teaching, learning, and mediation should be congruent with the type of learning objectives in question. In cases without a clear implication, alternative learning tasks should be offered so that learners depending on their previous learning experience and personal preferences (goals) may choose among different alternatives.

With respect to software evaluation, our research group believes that a widely applicable approach to evaluation design must be flexible enough to encompass a wide range of overall aims of instruction defined by the authors of any given instructional program. This can include broadly defined aims and approaches to language learning, for example, grammatical cor-

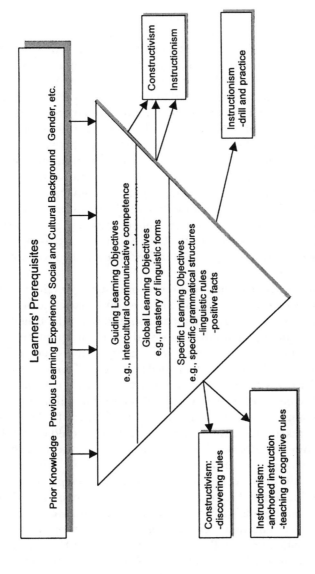

FIG. 13.3.   Relationships among learner variables, learning objectives, and language teaching methods.

rectness versus communicative or intercultural orientations. Consequently, an assessment of learning outcomes will have to take into consideration varied instructional approaches, which in turn define to a large extent specific aims and objectives.

Like many scholars in the field of language teaching and learning today, we do not regard the mere reproduction of facts the central or exclusive aim of instruction. It follows that evaluation materials should not be too closely related in content to the learning materials being assessed. In addition, if the assessment materials are not too closely related to specific teaching materials, they can then be applied to the evaluation of a wider range of course types and hence be of more general utility to the profession. An orientation by global instructional aims would preserve a desirable distance from individual courses but would still be appropriate for use in materials with different detailed learning objectives. Our suggestion, therefore, is to use overall educational objectives formulated in individual language-learning curricula as the basis for evaluating the efficiency of any language-learning software. In cases where those broad objectives or global aims are not explicitly formulated, as in Berliner Sehen, they may be reconstructed from the materials themselves. In Berliner Sehen, for example, listening comprehension and some degree of *Fremdverstehen* may be reconstructed as implicit global aims.

In addition, we propose that the process of designing evaluation instruments be a dialectic process. This, on the one hand, takes into account the rich and varied nature of e-learning materials and is, on the other hand, a necessary consequence of postbehaviorist theories of language learning that do not assume an omniscient or even omnipresent instructor. To illustrate this disposition, let us choose a global aim such as "understanding foreign cultures" as an example. Improvements in ability could be tested by confronting learners with video material from an intercultural encounter that contains some covert or overt intercultural difficulty. The learners, then, could be asked to analyze the encounter, which would elicit relatively little prestructured feedback. As is common in social research, the actual criteria that are taken as indicators of learning results or progress may be developed in dialectic processes on the basis of learners' productions. The basis of the evaluation and comparison of software, then, is formed by sufficiently abstract and empirically constructed categories. However, it is important to keep in mind that these categories remain an open class to provide a suite of evaluation tools flexible enough to deal with new generations of learning software and hypertext learning (e.g., not only naming learning deficits in a comparison with linear texts but also being able to qualify improvements).

An open, minimally prestructured approach to the empirical evaluation of e-learning software is compatible with a constructivist theory of learning.

As noted earlier, such an evaluation approach may be complemented by additional assessment modules perhaps of a more immediately quantifiable nature that focus on specific skills (such as grammar competencies) and make use of the learners' mother tongue as a means of determining comprehension (e.g., using the foreign language to understand and the mother tongue to produce a text that is based on the understanding in the foreign language). A useful and effective balance between the rigorous quantification of language-learning behavior and qualitative assessment tools that allow us to capture subtle learning processes, dispositions, and outcomes can be struck, in our view, by adopting such a dialectical and inclusive approach to the design of empirical tools for e-learning software evaluation.

CONCLUSION

Our research group is preparing such a four-phase research and development agenda on a large scale in an international project currently in its planning stages. The authors, representing four institutions in Canada and Germany, will be joined by colleagues at MIT and Ritsumeikan University (Kyoto, Japan) in a four-nation study of the theory of evaluation of multimedia language-learning software. We anticipate that our project will illuminate not only the distinct characteristics of the new genre for language-learning software we have described here and discover more about the novel kinds of learning it promotes, but also that it will apply very current understandings of language learning and language teaching. We hope that our diverse backgrounds, ranging from computational and applied linguistics to specialists in EFL will assist us to achieve that eclectic, inclusive approach to evaluation to which we aspire.

One of the outcomes we hope to produce is an online, readily updated technical manual of e-learning software reviews in particular, and what we are calling E/Valuation techniques that we hope will be of considerable assistance to the profession. A second outcome we hope to achieve is the founding of an International Institute for Language Learning Software Evaluation. Third, we hope that our project, by building on the pioneering work of Hubbard, Chapelle, and many others cited here, will not only extend our scholarly understandings of learning and teaching with a remarkable new generation of software, but also extend and disseminate professional knowledge about best practices for software integration into our classrooms and labs. Perhaps we will all be in a better position to answer our earlier question, "Is this language learning software effective?" by addressing first the more fundamental question, "How do we go about learning about the effectiveness of new generations of language-learning software?"

ACKNOWLEDGMENTS

This is a greatly revised version of a paper (Reeder et al., 2001) appearing under the title "E/Valuating New Media in Language Development" in *Zeitschrift für Interkulturellen Fremdsprachenunterricht* [Online], 6(2). Available from http://www.spz.tu-darmstadt.de/projekt_ejournal/jg_06_2/beitrag/reeder1.htm. The authors wish to acknowledge the kind cooperation of that journal's editors. Revision of the earlier paper in preparation of this chapter was supported by an award from the University of British Columbia's Humanities & Social Sciences Grants Committee to Kenneth Reeder.

REFERENCES

Andersen, R. W., & Daza, J. L. (1994). Ucuchi: Quechua live and in color! [Computer software]. Los Angeles: UCLA, Authentic Discourse Research and Development Project. Available from http://www.humnet.ucla.edu/humnet/AL//CLRL/media.html

Beckett, G., McGivern, L., Reeder, K., & Semenov, D. (1999). Dilemmas in designing multimedia software for language learners: Action research. *Journal of Research in Computers in Education, 32*(2), 287–297.

Berge, Z. L. (1995). Facilitating computer conferencing: Recommendations from the field. *Educational Technology, 35*(1), 22–30.

Bland, S., Noblitt, J., Armington, S., & Gay, G. (1990). The naive lexical hypothesis: Evidence from computer-assisted language learning. *Modern Language Journal, 74*(4), 440–450.

Burnett, R. (2002). Technology, learning and visual culture. In D. Barton (Series Ed.) & I. Snyder (Vol. Ed.), *Silicon literacies. Communication, innovation and education in the electronic age* (pp. 141–153). London and New York: Routledge, Taylor & Francis Group.

Business Challenges [Computer software]. (1996). Boston: Addison-Wesley.

Chapelle, C. (1998). Multimedia CALL: Lessons to be learned from research on instructed SLA [Electronic version]. *Language Learning & Technology, 2*(1), 22–34. Retrieved December 1, 2002, from http://llt.msu.edu/vol2num1/article1/index.html

Chapelle, C. (2001). *Computer applications in second language acquisition: Foundations for teaching, testing and research.* Cambridge, England: Cambridge University Press.

Chapelle, C., Jamieson, J., & Park Y. (1996). Second language classroom traditions: How does CALL fit? In M. Pennington (Ed.), *The power of CALL* (pp. 33–54). Houston, TX: Athelstan.

Child, J. (1997/1998). Assessing the impact of computer-assisted instruction (CAI) in undergraduate Latin American studies courses. *Computers and the Humanities, 31*(5), 389–407.

Cobb, T., & Stevens, V. (1996). A principled consideration of computers and reading in a second language. In M. Pennington (Ed.), *The power of CALL* (pp. 115–136). Houston, TX: Athelstan.

Cope, B., & Kalantzis, M. (Eds.). (2000). *Multiliteracies: Literacy learning and the design of social futures.* London: Routledge.

Crocker, E., & Fendt, K. (n.d.). Berliner Sehen: A hypermedia documentary integrating the study of German culture and language [Computer software]. Available from http://web.mit.edu/fll/www/projects/BerlinerSehen.html

Davey, D., Gade J., & Fox, J. (1995). Multimedia for language learning: Some course design issues. *Computer Assisted Language Learning, 8*(1), 31–44.

Edelsky, C. (1994). Education for democracy. *Language Arts, 71*(4), 252–257.

Einfach Toll! Version 2.0 [Computer software]. (2000). Boston: Houghton Mifflin.

Furstenberg, G. (1994). A la rencontre de Philippe [Videodisk]. New Haven, CT: Yale University Press. Available from http://web.mit.edu/fll/www/projects/Philippe.html

Furstenberg, G. (1999). *Dans un quartier de Paris: An interactive documentary on CD-ROM for Macintosh computers* [CD-ROM]. New Haven, CT: Yale University Press. Available from http://web.mit.edu/fll/www/projects/Quartier.html

Gros, B., & Spector, J. M. (1994). Evaluating automated instructional design systems: A complex problem. *Educational Technology, 42,* 37–46.

Hart, G. L. (2000). *Collaborative writing strategies of students using multi-media software.* Unpublished master's thesis, University of British Columbia, Vancouver, Canada.

Heift, T. (2001). Error-specific and individualized feedback in a web-based language tutoring system: Do they read it? *ReCALL, 13*(2), 129–142.

Heift, T. (2002). Learner control and error correction in ICALL: Browsers, peekers and adamants. *CALICO Journal, 19*(3), 295–313.

Heift, T., & Caws, C. (2000). Peer feedback in synchronous writing environments: A case study in French. *Journal of Educational Technology & Society, 3*(3), 208–214.

Hubbard, P. (1987). Language teaching approaches, the evaluation of CALL software, and design implications. In W. Flint Smith (Ed.), *Modern media in foreign language education: Theory and implementation* (pp. 227–254). Lincolnwood, IL: National Textbook Company.

Hubbard, P. (1992). A methodological framework for CALL courseware development. In D. Sharp (Series Ed.) & M. C. Pennington & V. Stevens (Vol. Eds.), *Computers in applied linguistics: An international perspective* (pp. 39–65). Clevedon, England: Multilingual Matters.

Jacobs, G. (1992). Hypermedia and discovery-based learning: A historical perspective. *British Journal of Education Technology, 2*(23), 113–121.

Kelm, O. (1992). The use of synchronous computer networks in second language instruction: A preliminary report. *Foreign Language Annals, 25*(5), 441–454.

Kelm, O. (1996). The application of computer networking in foreign language education: Focusing on principles of second language acquisition. In M. Warschauer (Ed.), *Telecollaboration in foreign language learning* (pp. 19–28). Honolulu, HI: Second Language Teaching and Curriculum Centre.

Kern, R. (1996). Computer-mediated communication: Using e-mail exchanges to explore personal histories in two cultures. In M. Warschauer (Ed.), *Telecollaboration in foreign language learning* (pp. 105–119). Honolulu, HI: Second Language Teaching and Curriculum Centre.

Knowles, S. (1992). Evaluations of CALL software: A checklist of criteria for evaluation. *ON-CALL, 6*(2), 9–20.

Kramsch, C. (1993). *Context and culture in language teaching.* Oxford, England: Oxford University Press.

Kramsch, C., & Andersen, R. W. (1999). Teaching text and context through multimedia [Electronic version]. *Language Learning & Technology, 2*(2), 31–42. Retrieved December 1, 2002, from http://polyglot.cal.msu.edu/llt/vol2num2/article1/index.html

Lemke, J. (1998). Metamedia literacy: Transforming meanings and media. In D. Reinking, M. C. McKenna, L. D. Labbo, & R. D. Kieffer (Eds.), *Handbook of literacy and technology. Transformations in a post-typographic world* (pp. 283–301). Mahwah, NJ: Lawrence Erlbaum Associates.

Leu, J. D., Hillinger, M., Loseby, P. H., Balcom, M. L., & Dinkin, J. (1998). Grounding the design of new technologies for literacy and learning in teachers' instructional needs. In D. Reinking, M. C. McKenna, L. D. Labbo, & R. D. Kieffer (Eds.), *Handbook of literacy and technology. Transformations in a post-typographic world* (pp. 203–220). Mahwah, NJ: Lawrence Erlbaum Associates.

Miller, R., & Wickenden, H. R. (n.d.). Who is Oscar Lake? [Computer software]. New York: Language Publications Interactive. Available from http://www.languagepub.com/oscar/oscar.html

Miyagawa, S. (1999). StarFestival [Computer software]. Cambridge, MA: StarFestival. Available from http://www.starfestival.com/index.html

Murray, G. L. (1998). *Bodies in cyberspace: Language learning in a simulated environment.* Unpublished doctoral dissertation, The University of British Columbia, Vancouver, Canada.

Murray, G. L. (1999a). Autonomy and language learning in a simulated environment. *System,* *27*(3), 295–308.

Murray, G. L. (1999b). Exploring learners' CALL experiences: A reflection on method. *Computer Assisted Language Learning, 12,* 179–195.

Pennycook, A. (2001). *Critical applied linguistics: A critical introduction.* Mahwah, NJ: Lawrence Erlbaum Associates.

Pujolà, J.-T. (2001). Did CALL Feedback Feed Back? *ReCALL, 13*(1), 94–128.

Reeder, K., & Hart, G. (2001). Edubba: Multimedia support for academic writing in English. *Zeitschrift für interkulturellen Sprachunterricht, 6*(2). Retrieved May 22, 2003, from http://www.spz.tu-darmstadt.de/projekt_ejournal/jg_06_2/beitrag/edubba2.htm

Reeder, K., Heift, T., Roche, J., Tabyanian, S., Schlickau, S., & Gölz, P. (2001). E/Valuating New Media in Language Development. *Zeitschrift für interkulturellen Sprachunterricht, 6*(2). Retrieved May 22, 2003, from http://www.spz.tu-darmstadt.de/projekt_ejournal/jg_06_2/beitrag/reeder1.htm

Reeder, K., Hooper, H., Roche, J., & Shaddock, P. (2000). Edubba: The language arts program [Unpublished computer software]. Vancouver, Canada: Lunny Communications Group and The University of British Columbia.

Roche, J. (2000). Lerntechnologie und Spracherwerb—Grundrisse einer medienadäquaten, interkulturellen Sprachdidaktik. *Deutsch als Fremdsprache, 2,* 136–143.

Roche, J. (2001). *Interkulturelle Sprachdidaktik—Eine Einführung.* Tübingen, Germany: Gunter Narr Verlag.

Rüschoff, B., & Wolff, D. (1999). *Fremdsprachenlernen in der Wissensgesellschaft: zum Einsatz der neuen Technologien in Schule und Unterricht.* Ismaning, Germany: Hueber.

Schlickau, S. (2001). Praxis und Analyse interkultureller Kommunikation durch Video und Videokonferenz: Lernpotenziale und Anforderungen. *Zeitschrift für interkulturellen Sprachunterricht, 6*(2). Retrieved November 27, 2003, from http://www.spz.tu-darmstadt.de/projekt_ejournal/jg_06_2/beitrag/schlickau1.htm

Schmueckler, L. M., & Shuell, T. J. (1989). Comparison of software evaluation forms. *Journal of Educational Computing Research, 5*(1), 17–33.

Scholfield, P. J. (2000). *Evaluation of CALL software.* Retrieved December 1, 2002, from Department of Language and Linguistics, University of Essex, UK, Web site: http://privatewww.essex.ac.uk/~scholp/calleval.htm

Steinberg, E. R. (1977). Review of student control in computer-assisted instruction. *Journal of Computer Based Instruction, 3,* 84–90.

Steinberg, E. R. (1989). Cognition and learner control: A literature review, 1977–1988. *Journal of Computer Based Instruction, 16*(4), 117–121.

Travel Tur (Version 2.0) [Computer software]. (2000). Boston: Houghton Mifflin.

Uni-deutsch.de [Computer software]. (n.d.) Available from http://werkstadt.daf.uni-muenchen.de/inhalt/html/modules.php?name=werkstadtprojekte

Wang, X., & Teles, L. (1998). Online collaboration and the role of the instructor in two university credit courses. In T. W. Chan, A. Collins, & J. Lin (Eds.), *Global education on the Net: Proceedings of the Sixth International Conference on Computers in Education, Vol. 1* (pp. 154–161). Beijing and Heidelberg: China High Education Press and Springer-Verlag.

Wells, C. G. (1986). *The meaning makers.* Portsmouth, NH: Heinemann.

Wells, C. G., & Chang-Wells, G. L. (1992). *Constructing knowledge together: Classrooms as centres of inquiry and literacy.* Portsmouth, NH: Heinemann.

Evaluation of ESL/EFL Instructional Web Sites

Bernard Susser
Doshisha Women's College

Thomas N. Robb
Kyoto Sangyo University

The World Wide Web is now an established medium for language learning and instruction. Individuals can use a variety of e-learning sites to study foreign languages. Felix (2001, p. 4) listed no fewer than 18 types of language study sites, including courses, grammar-based materials, tools, chat sites, and interactive tasks. Teachers, too, are making much use of the Internet for teaching languages; at least seven books have appeared recently on this topic: Dudeney (2000), Felix (2001), Feyten et al. (2002), Li (2000), Teeler and Gray (2000), Warschauer, Shertzer, and Meloni (2000), and Windeatt, Hardisty, and Eastment (2000). Besides keypal exchanges, MOOing, and home-page creation, teachers assign textbooks such as Gitsaki and Taylor (2000) or Sperling (1999), which bring Internet resources into the classroom for language practice, or have learners exploit Internet sources for reading practice and writing papers.

The vast quantity and variety of Internet resources for language study is welcome but leaves us with the problem of evaluating the quality of what is available. For example, Smith and Salam (2000) conducted a large-scale study evaluating web-based ESL courses, examining 35 sites on criteria such as course length, equipment needed, and access to teacher. Their conclusion lists several positive aspects of EFL "cyberschools," but they report "a significant negative side as well, all [sic] of which currently militates against successful uptake of cyberschooling" (Cyberschool: Threat or promise? section, ¶ 1). To our knowledge, there have not been similar evaluations of other kinds of language study sites.

This chapter provides a method of selecting and evaluating Internet sites for skills practice. There are a great number of such sites, and they might provide students with valuable additional practice to supplement class-room-based learning if instructors had a tool for selecting suitable sites. The selection process consists of two stages: screening and evaluation. Screening is the process through which a manageable number of candidate sites is determined; evaluation is "predictive evaluation," defined as "the assessment of the quality and potential of a software application before it is used with students" (Squires & McDougall, 1996, p. 147). Although this definition refers to software, it applies equally to web-based materials. We use *evaluation*, unless otherwise specified, to mean *predictive evaluation*. This chapter is divided into two parts: In the first, we introduce the screening and evaluation procedures, describing a framework for evaluating ESL and EFL CALL Web sites. In the second part, we demonstrate how teachers might apply this framework by using it to make a checklist to evaluate a specific category of Web sites.

Before starting, we must address a basic issue. As stated previously, we are concerned with evaluation of skills sites, and not with language courses or any of the other types of Internet sites that are or could be used by language teachers. There are hundreds of skills sites, but hardly any of them have advanced beyond the "drill-and-kill" mode that has characterized computer-assisted instruction since its beginnings. Mainstream SLA theory today sees no value in meaningless mechanical drills (Larsen-Freeman, 2001, p. 258); even advocates of "focus on form" emphasize its use in meaning-centered discourse (Ellis, Basturkmen, & Loewen, 2001, pp. 407–412). On the other hand, many CALL practitioners (e.g., Decoo, 1994), not to mention the teachers who took the time to make these drills, believe that such practice helps students to learn the target language. We cannot resolve this problem here but hope that the evaluation model we present will be of use to instructors who choose to use such sites.

SCREENING AND EVALUATION

Teachers who wish to supplement their courses by having students study skills on the Internet must evaluate these sites in the same way they would evaluate any teaching material before having students use it. Given the huge number of ESL and EFL sites on the Internet, the first stage is finding and screening sites to reduce the evaluation pool to a manageable number. This stage is made up of the following steps:

1. Establish rough academic and functional criteria for screening.
2. Find potential sites by using meta sites or published materials such as Felix (1998, 2001) or Li (2000).

3. Visit as many sites as you have time for and use your rough criteria to bookmark a short list of sites for evaluation. Academic criteria include items such as topic, level, type, volume, and feedback. For example, if your false beginner-level students need more work on prepositions, you would look for a site that gave grammar practice on prepositions at that level. What we call functional criteria include such items as cost (normally free of charge), degree of interactivity, level of intrusiveness (how much personal information a user must submit), access and loading time (if you will use this in class), and "face validity" (used by Boshier et al., 1997, p. 330, to refer to the instructor or author's identity, affiliation, and qualifications, and how easily the user can find this information).

One additional functional criterion is the intended mode of access. Robb (2001) proposed four modes for CALL access:

1. Voluntary self-access (the self-motivated student).
2. Guided self-access (the instructor recommends that the student study specific material for general improvement or to offset certain weaknesses).
3. Required self-access (the instructor requires that specific material be studied outside of class as an integral component of the course syllabus).
4. Use in an intact class (the entire class meets in the computer room with the instructor present).

When screening sites, it is important for the instructor to bear in mind the intended access mode. Robb asserted that if the required self-access mode is intended, the site must have some method for tracking student use, either by a built-in record manager or at least by allowing the students to print out or save their work as proof that they have done it.

The next step is evaluation using a modular evaluation framework. This framework is a conceptual scheme made up of several modules; the modules are units covering one aspect of evaluation, each containing a body of principles or criteria for that module's topic. The framework is generative in that the principles in each module serve to generate a set of specific checklist items for each case. This generative aspect is essential to solve the problem pointed out by Squires (1997): Given that learning is situated and highly context dependent, predictive evaluation has "an inherent problem" because "by definition the evaluation is conducted outside the intended context" (Introduction section, ¶ 3). Generative evaluation tools solve this problem by starting from each user's situation and context; this concept has appeared in the literature in several formats: meta checklist (Garrido & Geissler, 1997), integrated evaluation framework (Hubbard, 1987, 1988, 1992, 1996), ELT (English Language Teaching) toolkit (Oliver, 1998; Oliver & Conole, 1998), and generative model (Radzik, 1997). Our framework draws on the insights presented in this literature but focuses on Web-based CALL for ESL and EFL. The framework consists of the following modules:

1. Language acquisition
2. ESL materials design
3. Learner profile and learning styles
4. Courseware and multimedia instructional design
5. Online courseware instructional design

The framework is used to generate a checklist by which the short-listed sites will be evaluated. In theory, the framework states principles or criteria but in some cases the principles must be inferred from the relevant literature. Below we describe the modules and then demonstrate how the framework is used to make a checklist for evaluating sites.

THE MODULAR EVALUATION FRAMEWORK

Language Acquisition

The principles in the first module, language acquisition, are based on Chapelle's (2001) synthesis of language acquisition theories and learner-centered instruction. Specifically, her "criteria for CALL task appropriateness" for promoting acquisition of the target language (p. 55) are a useful summary of important criteria by which language learning tasks should be judged. The six criteria are:

1. Language-learning potential
2. Learner fit
3. Meaning focus
4. Authenticity
5. Positive impact
6. Practicality

Although these criteria obviously apply to classroom tasks in general, Chapelle focused on their application to CALL tasks.

ESL Materials Design

The second module, ESL materials design, applies the criteria established for evaluation of ESL and EFL textbook materials to courseware and web-based learning sites. The emphasis is on the fit between the materials and the curriculum, the students, and the teachers (Byrd, 2001, pp. 416–418). In practice, there is much overlap between the first and second modules, with their respective emphases on tasks and materials, because the former are usually embedded in the latter. We can clarify the difference between the two by borrowing North's (1987) distinction between two kinds of knowledge in composition studies; he contrasts researcher modes of inquiry, which rely on scientific experiments and investigations, with a practitioner mode of inquiry, which relies on experience and lore. Similarly, the principles of the first module are based largely on research studies on SLA, whereas the second module emphasizes evaluation of teaching materials based on teachers' practice; in North's words, "it makes sense in terms of their experience" (p. 45). There is a large literature directed at helping practicing teachers make this evaluation (see the bibliography in Rea-Dickins, 1994, pp. 87–88). Cunningsworth (1984, pp. 75–79), for example, provided a checklist with more than 70 questions covering these areas:

1. Language content, for example, what language skills are taught?
2. Selection and grading, for example, what syllabus does the material follow?
3. Presentation and practice, for example, how are new structures presented?
4. Developing language skills and communicative abilities, for example, what activities are there for integrating language skills?
5. Supporting materials, for example, are there any materials for testing?
6. Motivation and the learner, for example, does the material have variety and pace?
7. Overall evaluation, for example, does the material succeed in achieving its objectives?

Any evaluation of language teaching sites must consider topics such as these.

Learner Profile and Learning Styles

Learner profile and learning styles is the third module. There is some overlap with the learner fit component of the first module, but here the concept is broader. The term *learner profile* comes from Hubbard (1996, p. 22); the points he considered about the learner include the following:

1. Purpose
2. Language level
3. Ability to handle metalanguage
4. Technical ability
5. Receptivity to change

The fit between the instructional material and the learner's language-learning styles and strategies (e.g., Oxford, 2001) also is important but is difficult to carry out in practice with intact classes.

Courseware and Multimedia Instructional Design

The first three modules cover topics that apply to language instruction generally, with only comparatively minor adaptations required for technology. In contrast, the remaining modules refer to aspects of computer-based learning. The fourth module, courseware and multimedia instructional design, draws on the literature evaluating CALL courseware in general, particularly multimedia packages and hypertext software; work strictly on web-based language learning environments is covered in the next module. We discuss briefly some theoretical issues before giving examples of evaluation principles.

Several writers have considered the relationship between learning and the interface. For example, Plass (1998) argued for a user interface design based on a SLA-domain-specific cognitive approach. Domain-specific evaluation criteria are developed through four steps, which include, for example, identifying skills, activities, and cognitive processes, and then assessing "the level of support for these cognitive processes provided by the application and its user interface" (Plass, 1998, p. 41). Watts (1997) insisted that interactive media design must be learner based. For example, one aspect of learner needs is autonomy; this need could be satisfied by allowing "maximum user choice of routes through the activities" (Watts, 1997, p. 5). He likewise provided design rules to meet the requirements for a variety of learning situations (e.g., provision of on-screen instructions) and learner goals (e.g., multilevel formats). Finally, Nelson, Bueno, and Huffstutler (1999) stressed the importance of "a focus on usability principles for educational software design" (p. 284). They found that although students did not always use software in the ways the designers had intended, students did create their own learning strategies "based on the interaction possibilities available in the software" (p. 284); to the extent possible, designers should anticipate this and have the design encourage the development of effective language-learning strategies.

The previously discussed work emphasizes design but by implication offers many valuable suggestions for selection. More to our present purpose, there are many CALL courseware and multimedia evaluation instruments in the literature (Susser, 2001, p. 264) that suggest the criteria we must apply. Tang and Ng (1999), for example, asked not only about objectives and content but also about presentation (layout, use of color and sound, etc.), operation (user friendly, log-in requirements), and even the user's environment (constraints on access, suitability of lab environment for study, etc.). Garrido and Geissler's (1997) meta checklist covered topics that apply to all instructional materials, such as content, learner characteristics, instructional goals, and target language content, but also gave extensive treatment to interface issues (ease of use, navigation, graphics, and sound) and interactivity (feedback and sequence). Specifically, the relevant topic areas they covered are the following:

1. Interface
2. Interactivity
3. Classroom-related issues

Their work was designed for evaluating CD-ROM multimedia but can be applied readily to Web-based materials.

Online Courseware Instructional Design

The fifth module, online courseware instructional design, repeats many topics covered in the fourth module; the difference is that now the criteria are applied specifically to online materials instead of computer-based instructional materials generally. Several writers have provided evaluation criteria for e-learning sites. Roberts and Robson (1999, Scoring Guide) evaluated "web-based pedagogical resources" by the following seven criteria:

1. How well the site employs theories of instructional design.
2. How well the site design facilitates student learning
3. The quality of feedback, record keeping, and other management aspects.
4. Support for human–human and computer–human interactivity.
5. Degree of adaptivity to users' history and preferences.
6. Appropriateness and adequacy of multimedia.
7. Accessibility to persons with physical disabilities.

The Information and Communications Technology for Language Teachers (ICT4LT, 2001) group has an evaluation form for CALL sites. Its criteria include functionality (navigation ease, etc.), media content, linguistic and cultural context, and exploitation and outcomes (value against costs and the usefulness of the page for generating off-line activities). Kelly (2000), also concerned with language teaching, emphasized technological aspects such as designing for rapid loading, easy navigation, and readability.

There are three other related areas of Web design evaluation. One is usability, defined as "the measure of the quality of a user's experience when interacting with a product or system" (National Cancer Institute, 2001, Usability Basics: What Is Usability?, ¶ 1), including factors such as ease of learning and efficiency of use. This area includes also the mechanical aspects of web page design, such as coding and coding errors, browser display issues, dead links, and loading speeds. Nielsen (1994), well known for his work on Web site usability, gave ten usability heuristics for evaluating a site's user interface. These include "user control and freedom," "consistency and standards," and "recognition rather than recall." In each case the ideal is to obtain maximum utility with minimum delay and cognitive load.

A second but related area is accessibility, which deals with the aspects of web page design that may prevent people with disabilities from accessing and using the Internet. The World Wide Consortium has produced a checklist of Web Content Accessibility Guidelines (Chisholm & Vanderheiden, 1999) and the Center for Applied Special Technology (CAST, 2000) has developed Bobby, a software tool that tests pages for accessibility problems by mechanically examining the coding. Examples of barriers that people with disabilities may encounter are a lack of sufficient contrast between foreground and background colors, or the practice of indicating changes only by using different colors. Teachers, who often are not aware of disabilities their students might have, can use this tool to be sure that the pages they assign can be used by everyone in their classes.

The third area consists of the rules and guidelines for designing e-learning sites.[1] Boshier and his colleagues (1997, p. 339) argued that online courses could be evaluated in terms of three aspects: accessibility, interaction, and attractiveness. In her book on creating educational Web sites, S. Horton (2000) covered organization, navigation, Web page writing style, and interactivity. Although her emphasis was on creating sites, her prescriptions are equally useful for evaluating such sites. Finally, Eastment's (1998) "key criteria" for evaluating ELT Web pages are: "aim, accuracy, authority, currency, depth, design, [and] regularity of update" (p. 69).

The application of the preceding guidelines cannot be done mechanically. For example, demands for online CALL courseware commonly in-

---

[1]W. Horton (2000) is a thorough study of Web-based training design; works specifically on academic instruction include Kearsley (2000), Keating and Hargitai (1999), Lynch and Horton (1999), and Sanders (2001). The Ion Resources on "Web Design for Online Courses" (University of Illinois, 2000) are also useful.

clude human–human interaction or the availability of a teacher online. But this depends very much on the situation. Certainly, learners working on writing skills need a human teacher to respond to and correct their work, but learners who need to practice listening skills or review some grammar points may not need anything more than mechanical correction and help messages. Furthermore, there are often trade-offs. For example, hyperlinks on a site are usually represented by a spatial map, which is thought to be the most useful for navigation; on the other hand, research (McDonald & Stevenson, 1999) has found that conceptual maps are more helpful for internal representation of knowledge. In this case, "spatial maps have a positive impact on navigation but a negative one on learning" (Bodain & Robert, 2000, 3.1 Advantages of Hypertext Documents section, ¶ 3). This kind of problem makes site selection and evaluation a challenging task.

As mentioned earlier, these topics are modifications for the Internet of issues that are covered in the fourth module, which covers computer-based learning generally. However, some points are specific to online learning, such as the negative principle of "shovelware." Fraser (1999, ¶ 8) argued that educational content on the Web is mostly "content shoveled from one communication medium to another with little regard for the appearance, ease of use, or capabilities of the second medium." His test is to try to move back; the extent to which the Web-based materials can be moved successfully back to print is the extent to which the designer has failed to make use of the Web's potential. Conversely, the extent to which the materials have "taken advantage of the expanded horizons for communicating ideas with a new medium" (Fraser, 1999, ¶ 17) is the extent to which they are "Web-centric" (the term is from Porter, 2001, p. 47). The distinction between shovelware and Web-centric materials is not absolute but a matter of degree; materials might have some Web-centric qualities, such as interactivity or hypertextuality (from de Kerckhove, 1996) but might lack others, such as community or scalability (from Greenfield, cited in Porter, 2001, p. 48). Web-based learning materials at present offer a range from simple readings or exercises uploaded without any change from print materials (some even directing the learner to print them out for use) to interactive models that cannot be presented in the classroom (such as chemistry experiments "that are too complicated or dangerous to run in the lab"; Davis, cited in S. Horton, 2000, p. 25). The Web-centricness of a site is the extent to which it breaks free from the traditional learning experience and becomes transparent to the principles of the Web.[2] In

---

[2]There is significant disagreement on this point. S. Horton (2000, p. xi) explicitly rejected Fraser's (1999) negative evaluation of making existing materials available on the Web, whereas Sanders (2001, p. 8) agreed with Fraser that there is no point in using new technology unless we take advantage of what it can do.

practice, the degree of Web-centricness required depends on the teacher's or learner's purpose for using the site.

APPLICATION OF THE MODULAR EVALUATION FRAMEWORK

In this section we demonstrate how the framework described previously can be used in practice to construct a checklist for evaluating a specific category of CALL Web site. For purposes of illustration we posit a first-year university EFL composition class in which the instructor wants the students to improve their use of English prepositions by self-study outside of class.

Screening Process

The first step in screening is deciding the academic and functional criteria. The academic criteria might be:

1. Preposition practice (without explanations or metalanguage beyond the students' ability to comprehend)
2. Language at a high elementary or false beginner level
3. Sufficient volume
4. Feedback that provides the correct answer

The functional criteria could be equally basic:

5. Cost: free
6. Tracking that keeps records of scores and time on task that are automatically sent to the instructor

Once the screening criteria are established, the next step is finding potential sites.[3] We used a search engine (Google) with the keywords *ESL*, *prepositions, practice,* and *grammar.* We also used several meta lists for ESL and related fields; two good lists were Krauss's (2001) ESL Independent Study Lab—Grammar (because it ranks sites by level, gives a concise description, and even includes some reviews of the site by learners) and Stevens's (2001) A Web Resource for CALL Lab Managers (because of its detailed descriptions of sites). Some sites useful for finding grammar-based activities are listed in Table 14.1. Of the more than 200 pages we looked at, we found about 80 preposition sites. (The story of this search will have to wait for another paper: the dead links, the "under construction" signs, the misleading titles, the in-your-face advertising, the links that took us around

---

[3]See Husari (2001) for a description of an Internet search for grammar exercises.

TABLE 14.1
Some Useful Sites for Grammar-Based Activities

About.Com http://esl.about.com/
This is probably the best designed all-around ESL site. Click on Quizzes and Tests to go to Quiz Central.
ESL Quiz Center (Dave's ESL Cafe) http://www.pacificnet.net/~sperling/quiz/
There are about 50 quizzes here. They rely on CGI (Common Gateway Interface) technology so students must be online to have their answers evaluated.
E.L. Easton http://eleaston.com/grammarqz.html
This is a metasite, containing no quizzes itself, but finely categorized listings of material available elsewhere.
ESL Blues http://www.collegeem.qc.ca/cemdept/anglais/trouindx.htm
This is well-structured with a diagnostic quiz and autoreferral to appropriate sections. It has grammatical information with many right–wrong examples.
Internet TESL Journal http://iteslj.org/quizzes/
More quizzes than you could click a mouse at.
Passaic County Community College http://www.pccc.cc.nj.us/library/asrc/esl/
Lots of links to categorized grammar activities, each of which takes you directly to an activity on someone else's site!
UVic English Language Centre Study Zone http://web2.uvcs.uvic.ca/elc/studyzone/
Grammar explanations and activities keyed to the University of Victoria's English program.
See Michael Krauss's *Top Picks* for more sources: http://www.lclark.edu/~krauss/toppicks/grammar.html

---

Note. The activities on these sites have a wide variety of material for grammar practice. Whether they will be useful to your students, however, depends on your own evaluation of them. *Caveat clicker.*

in circles, the out-of-control spawning of multiple browser screens, the poor HTML programming that caused our computers to crash—this task is not for the faint-hearted.)

We had no trouble finding sites that met Criteria 1, 2, 4, and 5, but 3 (volume) and 6 (tracking) were difficult. Most sites had only a few relatively short preposition drills; hardly any had tracking in the sense described earlier. The majority of sites consisted of sentences with a blank where the preposition should be; the user had to guess the word mentally, type in an answer, or click on one of the multiple choices provided. Two main content problems were apparent. First, on many sites, an unacceptably high percentage of items were defective because of a lack of context. For example, the feedback for the sentence "The dog jumped _____ the car." might accept only "on" or "into" as correct, but learners might well imagine a scenario in which "out of," "over," "around," or even "under" might be correct. This problem is partially avoided when three or four multiple-choice answers are given, but even in this case we found examples when possibly correct answers were judged wrong. Providing negative feedback to input that might be correct has an extremely adverse effect on learning. Second, very few activities appeared to be based on an analysis of the common errors that students make when using prepositions or on an understanding of why they make those errors. Better designed activities concentrated, for example, on prepositions that are often confused, such as in–on–at in time expressions in English, and practiced them in minimal pairs to help students induce the correct usage. Other content problems included typographical errors and cultural bias and insensitivity.

Technically, most sites were interactive in the sense that the learner could click on an answer or check button and see the correct answer; often the total score (number of correct answers) was displayed. Superior sites recycled missed items or allowed comparison feedback by displaying both the learner's incorrect response and the correct answer(s). Many pages were made with pull-down tabs or Hot Potatoes, with some using Flash or Shockwave for a greater variety of effects and functions. Numerous sites appeared to be professionally done with clear instructions and excellent navigation principles; others suffered from poor proofreading or clumsy design. Some had annoying advertisements, garish colors, and other distracting elements. A few sites could be characterized as completely shovelware: They advised the user to print out the exercises and do them on paper. Many, however, provided feedback and scores interactively and so were web-centric in accomplishing something that could not be done with print media. On the other hand, visually and conceptually they were still shovelware, consisting usually of a screen with a sentence containing a blank. Compared with this, Duber's (1996) Shockwave demonstrations for prepositions are more web-centric because they allow the user to manipulate images on-screen to practice the concepts of "in," "under," and so on. This is conceptually different from what print-based materials can do.[4]

Checklist

Once the screening process has produced a manageable number of sites, the next step is to use the framework to create an evaluation checklist by selectively drawing on only those principles or criteria that are relevant to this situation. The result looks like what is shown in Table 14.2.

CONCLUSION

Some years ago Thiesmeyer (1989) asked a fundamental question about computer-assisted instruction: "Should we do what we can?" Computer technology today lets us do a lot more than we could in 1989, but we are not

---

[4]See Collentine (1998) for a description of technically sophisticated CALL grammar drills in which the computer's multimedia capacity is exploited fully to facilitate acquisition of grammatical structures.

TABLE 14.2
Checklist for Evaluating Preposition Study Sites

Module 1: Language acquisition[a]
  Language-learning potential
  Learner fit
  Meaning focus
  Authenticity
  Positive impact
  Practicality
Module 2: ESL materials design[b]
  Meaningful and contextualized presentation
  Systematic presentation
  Underlying grammar rule is displayed
  Sufficient number of items
  Variety of items
  Items are meaningful
  Items are written well and free of typographical and other errors
  An appropriate variety of English is used
  The vocabulary and subject matter are appropriate for the target audience
  Content is culturally appropriate
Module 3: Learner profile and learning styles[c]
  Purpose
  Language level
  Ability to handle metalanguage
  Technical ability
  Receptivity to change
Module 4: Courseware and multimedia instructional design[d]
  Interface:
    Easy to use
    User can delete entered answers or selected alternatives
    Instructions are clear and simple (the metalanguage is not beyond the intended
      target level of the exercises)
  Navigation:
    Timing is self-paced and flexible
    Clearly marked ways to go back one step or go back to the main menu, etc.
    Help or hint options
    Exits are clearly marked
    Text or images that are hyperlinks are clearly indicated
    The "granularity" (number of links to other screens) is at an appropriate level
    The cursor does not appear when it is not possible to use it
  Text quality:
    Font is large enough and easy to read
    Background color(s) and design are appropriate
    Text is glossed, with pop-up references
    Text inside buttons and other navigational aids is clear and easy to read
    Symbols and icons are obvious or easy to remember after one try
    Symbols are used consistently

(Continued)

TABLE 14.2
(Continued)

Graphics and sound:
    Style and graphics are suitable
    Graphics clarify or enhance the points being made
    Illustrations are clearly labeled
    Illustrations are placed as close as possible to the text to which they refer
    Still images do not interfere with the text
    Sound is intelligible
    Sound constitutes an essential or integral part of the program
Interactivity:
    Feedback is sufficient and of the appropriate type
    Processing time for feedback is sufficiently rapid
    Questions and multiple-choice answers are sequenced or randomized as appropriate
    Does not put learners in infinite loops or send them to dead ends
Module 5: Online courseware instructional design[e]
How well the site employs theories of instructional design
How well the site design facilitates student learning
The quality of feedback, record keeping, and other management aspects
Support for human–human and computer–human interactivity
Degree of adaptivity to users' history and preferences
Appropriateness and adequacy of multimedia
Accessibility to persons with physical disabilities
How Web-centric the site is

---

[a]Chapelle (2001, p. 55).
[b]Most of these items were selected from Cunningsworth's (1984, pp. 76–77) checklist: "presentation and practice of grammar items."
[c]Hubbard (1996, p. 22).
[d]Based on Garrido and Geissler (1997).
[e]Based on Roberts and Robson (1999).

closer to an answer to this question. Just as George Mallory wanted to climb Mount Everest "because it is there" (Bartlett, 1992, p. 593), it may be that language teachers want to use CALL software and Internet sites because they are available and "cutting edge." For this reason we have seen an amazing proliferation of online CALL materials but not so much progress in evaluation methods and tools that will help teachers answer Thiesmeyer's question.

This chapter has presented one tool for evaluating ESL and EFL Web sites. Some may find the framework format too malleable for practical use, but given the wide diversity of tasks, settings, and other variables in language teaching, not to mention the rapid advance in technologies, it seemed to us that we had to sacrifice specificity for adaptability. The function of a framework is to provide "systematic ways of thinking" about one's task (Squires & McDougall, 1994, p. 53). We will be satisfied if we have provided a systematic way of thinking about the task of evaluating ESL and EFL instructional Web sites.

REFERENCES

Bartlett, J. (1992). *Familiar quotations* (16th ed.). (J. Kaplan, ed.). Boston: Little, Brown.

Bodain, Y., & Robert, J.-M. (2000, July). *Investigating distance learning on the Internet.* Paper presented at Inet Japan. Retrieved August 8, 2001, from http://isoc.org/inet2000/cdproceedings/6a/6a_4.htm

Boshier, R., Mohapi, M., Moulton, G., Qayyum, A., Sadownik, L., & Wilson, M. (1997). Best and worst dressed web courses: Strutting into the 21st century in comfort and style. *Distance Education, 18*(2), 327–337.

Byrd, P. (2001). Textbooks: Evaluation for selection and analysis for implementation. In M. Celce-Murcia (Ed.), *Teaching English as a second or foreign language* (3rd ed., pp. 415–427). Boston: Heinle & Heinle.

Center for Applied Special Technology. (2000). *About Bobby: Bobby: CAST.* Retrieved December 9, 2001, from http://www.cast.org/Bobby/AboutBobby313.cfm

Chapelle, C. A. (2001). *Computer applications in second language acquisition: Foundations for teaching, testing and research.* Cambridge, England: Cambridge University Press.

Chisholm, W., & Vanderheiden, G. (1999). *Checklist of checkpoints for web content accessibility guidelines 1.0.* Retrieved December 28, 2001, from http://www.w3.org/TR/WAI-WEBCONTENT/full-checklist.html

Collentine, J. (1998). Cognitive principles and CALL grammar instruction: A mind-centered, input approach. *CALICO Journal, 15*(1-3), 1–18.

Cunningsworth, A. (1984). *Evaluating and selecting EFL teaching materials.* London: Heinemann Educational.

Decoo, W. (1994). In defense of drill and practice in CALL: A reevaluation of fundamental strategies. *Computers and Education, 23*(1-2), 151–158.

de Kerckhove, D. (1996, October). *Webness.* Paper presented at The Future of Communication Formats, International Conference, National Library of Canada. Retrieved December 30, 2001, from http://www.acctbief.org/avenir/webness.htm

Duber, J. (1996a). *A little preposition practice (Preposition practice shocktest).* Retrieved December 28, 2001, from http://www.duber.com/CALL/preptest1.html

Duber, J. (1996b). *A little more preposition practice (Preposition practice: "on").* Retrieved December 28, 2001, from http://www.duber.com/CALL/on.html

Dudeney, G. (2000). *The Internet and the language classroom: A practical guide for teachers.* Cambridge, England: Cambridge University Press.

Eastment, D. (1998). Quality sites on the World Wide Web: Where are the good web pages? [Electronic version]. *Modern English Teacher, 7*(2), 68–78.

Ellis, R., Basturkmen, H., & Loewen, S. (2001). Preemptive focus on form in the ESL classroom. *TESOL Quarterly, 35*(3), 407–432.

Felix, U. (1998). *Virtual language learning: Finding the gems amongst the pebbles.* Melbourne, Australia: Language Australia.

Felix, U. (2001). *Beyond Babel: Language learning online.* Melbourne, Australia: Language Australia.

Feyten, C. M., Macy, M. D., Ducher, J., Yoshii, M., Park, E., Calandra, B., et al. (2002). *Teaching ESL/EFL with the Internet: Catching the wave.* Upper Saddle River, NJ: Pearson Education (Merrill Prentice Hall).

Fraser, A. B. (1999, August 8). Colleges should tap the pedagogical potential of the world-wide web [Electronic version]. *The Chronicle of Higher Education, 48*, B8.

Garrido, P., & Geissler, C. (1997). *A methodology for software evaluation.* Retrieved May 24, 2003, from http://rkenner.concordia.ca/Teslpapers/Methodwebpage/tableofcontents.html

Gitsaki, C., & Taylor, R. P. (2000). *Internet English: WWW-based communication activities.* New York: Oxford University Press.

Horton, S. (2000). *Web teaching guide: A practical approach to creating course web sites.* New Haven, CT: Yale University Press.

Horton, W. (2000). *Designing web-based training: How to teach anyone anything anywhere anytime.* New York: Wiley.

Hubbard, P. L. (1987). Language teaching approaches, the evaluation of CALL software, and design implications. In W. F. Smith (Ed.), *Modern media in foreign language education: Theory and implementation* (pp. 227–254). Lincolnwood, IL: National Textbook Company.

Hubbard, P. (1988). An integrated framework for CALL courseware evaluation. *CALICO Journal, 6*(2), 51–72.

Hubbard, P. (1992). A methodological framework for CALL courseware development. In M. Pennington & V. Stevens (Eds.), *Computers in applied linguistics: An international perspective* (pp. 39–65). Clevedon, England: Multilingual Matters.

Hubbard, P. L. (1996). Elements of CALL methodology: Development, evaluation, and implementation. In M. C. Pennington (Ed.), *The power of CALL* (pp. 15–32). Houston, TX: Athelstan.

Husari, N. (2001). *A personal Internet search: ESL computer tutorial.* Retrieved October 4, 2001, from http://hills.ccsf.org/~esltech/Lessons/Internet/internetsearch.html

ICT4LT. (2001). *ICT4LT project: Evaluation forms.* Retrieved August 9, 2001, from http://www.ict4lt.org/en/evalform.rtf

Kearsley, G. (2000). *Online education: Learning and teaching in cyberspace.* Belmont, CA: Wadsworth/Thomson Learning.

Keating, A. B., & Hargitai, J. (1999). *The wired professor: A guide to incorporating the World Wide Web in college instruction.* New York: New York University Press.

Kelly, C. (2000). Guidelines for designing a good web site for ESL students. *Internet TESL Journal, 6.* Retrieved July 8, 2001, from http://www.aitech.ac.jp/~iteslj/Articles/Kelly-Guidelines.html

Krauss, M. (2001, December 5). *ESL independent study lab—Grammar: Grammar and multi-skill sites.* Retrieved December 25, 2001, from http://www.lclark.edu/~krauss/toppicks/grammar.html

Larsen-Freeman, D. (2001). Teaching grammar. In M. Celce-Murcia (Ed.), *Teaching English as a second or foreign language* (3rd ed., pp. 251–266). Boston: Heinle & Heinle.

Li, R.-C. (2000). *Hunting for ESL treasures on the web: ESL teachers' web resources handbook.* Arlington, TX: Future Horizons.

Lynch, P. J., & Horton, S. (1999). *Web style guide: Basic design principles for creating web sites.* New Haven, CT: Yale University Press.

McDonald, S., & Stevenson, R. J. (1999). Spatial versus conceptual maps as learning tools in hypertext. *Journal of Educational Multimedia and Hypermedia, 8*(1), 43–64.

National Cancer Institute. (2001). *Usability.gov: Improving the communication of cancer research (Usability basics).* Retrieved October 9, 2001, from http://usability.gov/

Nelson, W. A., Bueno, K. A., & Huffstutler, S. (1999). If you build it, they will come. But how will they use it? *Journal of Research on Computing in Education, 32*(2), 270–286.

Nielsen, J. (1994). *Ten usability heuristics.* Retrieved January 8, 2002, from http://useit.com/papers/heuristic/heuristic_list.html

North, S. M. (1987). *The making of knowledge in composition: Portrait of an emerging field.* Portsmouth, NH: Boynton/Cook.

Oliver, M. (1998). *The ELT toolkit.* Retrieved April 4, 2001, from http://www.unl.ac.uk/tltc/elt/toolkit.pdf

Oliver, M., & Conole, G. (1998, July). Evaluating communication and information technologies: A toolkit for practitioners. *Active Learning, 8,* 1–6. Retrieved August 17, 2001, from http://www.ilt.ac.uk/public/cti/ActiveLearning/al8pdf/oliver.pdf

Oxford, R. L. (2001). Language learning styles and strategies. In M. Celce-Murcia (Ed.), *Teaching English as a second or foreign language* (3rd ed., pp. 359–366). Boston: Heinle & Heinle.

Plass, J. L. (1998). Design and evaluation of the user interface of foreign language multimedia software: A cognitive approach. *Language Learning & Technology, 2*(1), 35–45. Retrieved May 24, 2003, from http://llt.msu.edu/llt/vol2num1/article2/

Porter, D. (2001). Object lessons from the web: Implications for instructional development [Electronic version]. In G. Farrell (Ed.), *The changing faces of virtual education* (pp. 47–70). London: The Commonwealth of Learning.

Radzik, A. (1997). *The generative model for CALL development.* Retrieved September 10, 1998, from http://www.geocities.com/CollegePark/Library/8960

Rea-Dickins, P. (1994). Evaluation and English language teaching. *Language Teaching, 27*(2), 71–91.

Robb, T. N. (2001, December). *The importance of "tracking" for the effective use of multimedia.* Paper presented at the LET Kansai Chapter 2001 Multimedia & Internet IS 2001 conference, Kyoto, Japan.

Roberts, R., & Robson, R. (1999, June). *Evaluating web-based pedagogic resources.* Paper presented at the 1999 Ed-Media World Conference on Educational Multimedia, Hypermedia & Telecommunications. Retrieved August 12, 2001, from http://www.eduworks.com/Edmedia99/resources.html

Sanders, W. B. (2001). *Creating learning-centered courses for the world wide web.* Boston: Allyn & Bacon.

Smith, M., & Salam, U. (2000, June). Web-based ESL courses: A search for industry standards. *CALL-EJ Online, 2*(1). Retrieved July 6, 2000, from http://www.clec.ritsumei.ac.jp/english/callejonline/5-1/msmith&salam.html

Sperling, D. (1999). *Dave Sperling's Internet activity workbook.* Upper Saddle River, NJ: Prentice Hall Regents.

Squires, D. (1997, March). *An heuristic approach to the evaluation of educational multimedia software.* Paper presented at CAL97 (International Conference on Computer-Assisted Learning), Exeter, England. Retrieved April 1, 2001, from http://www.media.uwe.ac.uk/masoud/cal-97/papers/squires.htm

Squires, D., & McDougall, A. (1994). *Choosing and using educational software: A teachers' guide.* London: Falmer Press.

Squires, D., & McDougall, A. (1996). Software evaluation: A situated approach. *Journal of Computer Assisted Learning, 12*(3), 146–161.

Stevens, V. (2001, October 16). *ESL_Home: A web resource for CALL lab managers.* Retrieved December 25, 2001, from http://www.vancestevens.com/esl_home.htm

Susser, B. (2001). A defense of checklists for courseware evaluation. *ReCALL, 13*(2), 261–276.

Tang, E., & Ng, C. (1999). A learner generated checklist for evaluating multimedia instructional materials. *Applied Linguistics Forum (TESOL), 19*(2), 4–5.

Teeler, D., & Gray, P. (2000). *How to use the Internet in ELT.* Harlow, England: Pearson Education Limited (Longman).

Thiesmeyer, J. (1989). Should we do what we can? In G. E. Hawisher & C. L. Selfe (Eds.), *Critical perspectives on computers and composition instruction* (pp. 75–93). New York: Teacher's College Press.

University of Illinois. (2000). *ION (Illinois Online Network) resources: Web design for online courses.* Retrieved May 25, 2003, from http://www.ion.illinois.edu/IONresources/webdesign/index.asp

Warschauer, M., Shetzer, H., & Meloni, C. (2000). *Internet for English teaching.* Alexandria, VA: Teachers of English to Speakers of Other Languages.

Watts, N. (1997). A learner-based design model for interactive multimedia language learning packages. *System, 25*(1), 1–8.

Windeatt, S., Hardisty, D., & Eastment, D. (2000). *The Internet.* Oxford, England: Oxford University Press.

V

CONCLUSION

The concluding chapter, "The Language Teacher in the 21st Century," by Chapelle and Hegelheimer, observes that technology is now integral to how language teachers create materials, teach, and conceptualize their profession. Noting that many L2 teachers have developed their knowledge of computer technology by chance, either through contact with other technology-using teachers or students, or through professional development opportunities, the authors suggest that it is necessary to systematically identify the key competencies that L2 professionals now require to effectively and critically engage in technology-related issues. Chapelle and Hegelheimer draw on the topics presented in each of the chapters of this book to summarize the essential areas of professional development for L2 teachers, including: (1) a knowledge of general principles of language teaching and learning, (2) the ability create authentic and interactive materials and tasks, (3) the ability to identify learner needs, (4) the ability to evaluate CALL activities and (5) a thorough knowledge of CALL technology and pedagogy, including Web-based learning, communication tools, and the ability to use language labs, hardware and software effectively.

15

The Language Teacher in the 21st Century

Carol A. Chapelle
Volker Hegelheimer
Iowa State University

Imagine you are Toshiko, an EFL teacher at a school in Japan where proficient speakers of English are not accessible to your class with any regularity. Having read papers and seen conference papers on using Web materials for providing authentic input in the classroom, you and your colleagues have decided to find some listening materials that would be good for adult learners. Your school has access to the Web so you agreed to find the first set—enough to get started with an additional listening activity each day for the next week. "Easy enough," you think, as you turn to the Internet search engine, Google (www.google.com). When you start with a search for "listening," you find that there are plenty of hits, actually 4,860,000.[1] Too many, so you narrow it down to "listening comprehension for ESL learners" (8,480 hits), and then to "listening comprehension activities for ESL learners" (5,850 hits), "listening comprehension activities" (462 hits), and finally "ESL listening comprehension" (41 hits). You spend a couple of hours investigating most of the 41 sites, finding several that seem to fit your need, and then develop a one-page handout to guide the learners through the use of the materials on each site. When the time comes to use the task, you invite two of the other teachers so they can see how it works. The students call up the browser, and type in the address as described on the handout. But within moments confusion breaks out in the lab as each student sees an error message on his or her screen indicating that the plug-in is missing.

---

[1]These searches were conducted November 26, 2001. Because search engines key on words and phrases differently and content on the Web changes constantly, another search would not necessarily turn up exactly the same set of hits.

The chapters in this volume might inform and inspire L2 teachers in a way that may result in their participating in a scenario such as the one just described. These chapters, the teaching activities from which they originate, and the activities they may prompt in the future illustrate the fact that technology has become integral to the ways in which L2 professionals teach, create materials, and even the way they conceptualize the profession in the 21st century. As a profession evolving within a world that is decisively supported and interconnected by technology, what are the key competencies its members should have to effectively and critically engage in technology-related teaching issues? Faculty in the master of arts program in TESL/applied linguistics at Iowa State University faculty have been considering this issue for at least the past decade, and attempting to address it by developing course content within a curriculum that has as one of its objectives preparation of teachers who are able to use technology in their language teaching. This chapter describes some of the outcomes of deliberations on aspects of applied linguistics and technology that L2 and foreign language teachers need for the 21st century, with particular focus on the needs illustrated by the chapters in this volume.

APPLIED LINGUISTICS

Toshiko, the foreign language teacher portrayed earlier, is not working solely with a fixed syllabus and set of materials that can be taught mindlessly. Rather than using what she was handed, she is identifying materials and attempting to construct effective tasks for improving listening comprehension. To play the role of task developer with expertise, the teacher needs to have a firm grasp of fundamental knowledge of the areas of applied linguistics that pertain to L2 teaching. Which of the 41 sites contains materials that would serve as appropriate linguistic input? How can the language on the Web site be contextualized, highlighted, and engaged with sufficient attention and motivation to create an experience that is beneficial for the learners? How can the L2 teacher defend the use of the lab for teaching the class? As task developer, the teacher of the 21st century needs to be firmly grounded in the appropriate areas of applied linguistics, particularly those pertaining to language-learning tasks and language learners.

Language-Learning Tasks

Several of the chapters in this volume (e.g., chap. 12 by Opp-Beckman & Kieffer) demonstrate some of the critical knowledge that teachers need about what students are to learn through working on language-learning tasks. Developing and carrying out such learning tasks require the teacher to hold a view of communicative competence that includes cultural knowledge. In addition, teachers need to have an understanding of the types of tasks that may help learners to learn the target cultural concepts.

Communicative Competence.   Applied linguists have conceptualized and refined the construct of communicative competence over the past 30 years to offer a perspective of language that teachers and other applied linguists could draw on to make decisions about what to teach and assess (Bachman, 1990; Canale & Swain, 1980). These conceptualizations constitute the fundamental and essential knowledge of the profession, but at the same time, today's teachers need to consider the extent to which these perspectives should be reconsidered in view of the electronic contexts in which language teaching and learning as well as language use will take place (Rassool, 1999).

As Warschauer notes (chap. 2, this volume), the language and contexts of cyberspace comprise legitimate and likely settings in which learners will use their L2, and as a consequence, teachers need to be concerned with their learners' communicative competence for chat rooms, bulletin boards, electronic mailing lists, and the array of other opportunities for language use that learners find on the Internet (e.g., Crystal, 2001). These new contexts for language use are of interest because "the language of [CMC] exhibits certain characteristics, and Internet speech communities have incorporated this new medium into their repertoire of language use in particular ways" (Murray, 2000, p. 399). Murray pointed out that members of speech communities make linguistic choices on the basis of what they talk about, with whom they communicate, and what their mode of communication is. This observation can be made at both a general level (e.g., particular speech communities communicate about a range of topics) and more specifically (e.g., Roberta expresses her emotions to Jackie about a lecture through her choice of the expression "I was SOOOO bored!!"). The language of the Internet extends the complexity of a familiar issue in L2 teaching: What is appropriate in spoken and casual language is different from what is appropriate in written and formal language.

Addressing the complexity requires a perspective of language that allows teachers to conceptualize the connections between the contexts of language use and the linguistic choices that learners make. This conceptual infrastructure exists in applied linguistics (Halliday & Hasan, 1989), and recent materials for teacher education have begun to help present and focus these perspectives in a way that is accessible and useful for language teachers (Burns & Coffin, 2001). For example, many foreign language teachers have taken up the challenge of teaching learners to perform in speech communities on the Internet (e.g., McGee, 2001), but all teachers and learners need to be able to understand the forces affecting speech communities, register, and genre if they are to be empowered to understand, select, and ultimately expand their communicative competence to include language varieties on the Internet.

Language Learning. If communicative competence constitutes the "what" of language teaching, language learning encompasses the "how" and "why." How do learners acquire an L2 through the linguistic input and explicit instruction they are exposed to in addition to the interactions they engage in and the linguistic output they produce? Why are these processes believed to foster language development? Selecting and inventing new learning tasks require an understanding of the psycholinguistic and socio-cultural factors involved in SLA. The psycholinguistic perspective has revealed the critical role that input and interaction play in the process of SLA (e.g., Gass, 1997; Long, 1996; Pica, 1994). Teachers need to be aware of what researchers have outlined concerning the characteristics of language-learning tasks in terms of the opportunities they provide for psycholinguistically ideal linguistic experiences. Some of these principles have been articulated in terms of how they would play out in CALL tasks (e.g., Chapelle, 1998). For example, this research would suggest that learners should be given the opportunity and the need to listen repeatedly to and receive help with particular segments of the L2 input that they don't understand the first time. This is an idea that Toshiko could build on when creating the task for listening comprehension.

Sociocultural perspectives, particularly those drawing on the work of Vygotsky, have shown the importance of the social dimension of language-learning tasks, emphasizing the critical role of interlocutors in the interactions (Lantolf, 2000). Sociocultural theory points out that the interlocutor provides scaffolding for displaying and stretching a learner's competence within a social context and that the learner's identity (Pierce, 1995) simultaneously affects his or her willingness to communicate and is influenced by the situation. These perspectives on learning have influenced many CALL activities based on CMC (see Debski, 1997; Warschauer & Kern, 2000), but they also have implications for Toshiko's task design, as she should consider how the learners can work together in the listening activity she plans.

Language Learners

On the other side of the learning task that the teacher designs are the learners, who engage in the task using whatever strategies they have developed for working with learning materials and for interacting with technology. In other words, the teacher can create opportunities for ideal input, interaction, and collaboration, but it is ultimately up to the learner to choose to take advantage of these opportunities. Therefore, in addition to the general principles of language learning and teaching, it seems that the technology prompts us to understand better the strategies that individual learners can and do choose for learning through technology. Hubbard (chap. 4, this volume) argues that learner training is essential for effective use of CALL, and therefore that teaching learners how to learn through technology should be a central part of teacher education. He draws on the work in applied linguistics that underscores the importance of such issues as learner control, interactivity, motivation, strategies, and authenticity of communication (e.g., Oxford, 1990; Skehan, 1998; van Lier, 1996). It is important, however, that he applies the work in this area precisely to the types of technology-supported learning activities for which many learners need training to benefit: tutorial programs and electronic linguistic aids.

Fotos (chap. 7, this volume) develops the role of the language learner in another type of technology-based learning activity: e-mail exchanges. She is concerned that the tasks would spark the learners' motivation in a way that would prove to be a positive force in their language development. The idea that motivation is important for L2 development fits within most people's commonsense notions of learning, but applied linguists have developed a more complex understanding of motivation that encompasses more precisely the issues that language teachers face. In particular, recent research (Dörnyei & Schmitt, 2001) and explanations for teachers (Dörnyei, 2001) has emphasized the importance of the specific features of learning tasks for stimulating motivation. Drawing on this conception of motivation, Toshiko might have considered searching for materials on particular topics that she knew were of interest to the class and considered further how the learners' motivation might be stimulated by the ways in which the activity was introduced and carried out.

Evaluating CALL

All of the considerations about tasks and learners converge as teachers evaluate software and learning tasks for their students. The process of evaluation requires more than a checklist that directs teachers to the good and bad qualities of a product (although such an approach might be used as one part of a broader evaluation). Susser and Robb (chap. 14, this volume) illustrate the issues that might be brought to bear on the evaluation of CALL materials by considering criteria from four perspectives: (a) the standard literature evaluating ESL and EFL textbooks; (b) the multimedia CALL evaluation literature; (c) evaluations of distance learning and Internet-based training; and (d) Web site evaluation using Web usability theory, interface design rules, and other parameters. These perspectives combine judgmental and empirical evidence that might be integrated into an evaluative argument about the quality of a particular CALL activity for the target learners.

The multifaceted evaluation Susser and Robb (chap. 14, this volume) describe highlights one way in which CALL may push the area of materials evaluation to more explicit consideration of the factors involved. To that end, Chapelle (2001) outlined a method for evaluating CALL tasks through consideration of the factors that theory and research suggest should affect their quality: language-learning potential, learner fit (e.g., appropriate level of interlanguage development), meaning focus, authenticity (relative to the registers of language use that learners will participate in), impact (on factors such as motivation), and practicality. Based on these criteria, teachers and researchers can conduct an evaluation of a CALL task for particular learners and can identify areas in which empirical data might strengthen such an evaluation. Empirical data consist of records of learners' performance, think-aloud protocols, and assessment of motivation and linguistic outcomes (e.g., Beauvois, 1998; Borrás & Lafayette, 1994; Chun, 1994; deGraaff, 1997; Lam, 2000; Pellettieri, 2000). Because a full range of quantitative and qualitative approaches to data analysis come into play in evaluating CALL, an understanding of these research methods is also an important component of teachers' knowledge in the 21st century.

These aspects of applied linguistics—communicative competence, learning tasks, and evaluation—represent key areas of knowledge for any language teacher, but as we focus the curriculum on the needs of the technology-using teacher of the 21st century, we tend to select and amplify particular aspects of the broader areas of concern. The need to focus on the essentials is even more profound as teachers require an ever-greater command of the technological skills, which need to be taught as well.

TECHNOLOGY

As the Introduction by Fotos and Browne (chap. 1, this volume) notes, L2 teachers now need a growing number of computer skills to perform their jobs and to stay up to date with the profession. In our computer methods course, therefore, we teach prospective teachers to use all of the following: spreadsheet applications (MS Excel), database applications (MS Access or FileMaker Pro), basic statistics (using MS Excel), and presentation tools (MS Powerpoint), as well as teaching and research applications (e.g., concordancing, screen capturing software). Focusing on the skills needed for classroom activities such as those described in this volume, here we describe knowledge associated with three areas of central importance: the World Wide Web, communication tools, and language laboratories.

World Wide Web

All language teachers need to know how to use the Web as a resource for current authentic language materials in written, audio, and visual media formats and how to find linguistic and other reference materials. This level of "Web literacy," the ability to use Web materials, entails a number of skills as does the higher level of Web literacy required for creating Web materials.

Using Web Materials.   Using the Web encompasses not only searching for information and materials and evaluating Web-based materials, but also the repurposing of materials, which may be a challenge for teachers. A fourth skill involves trouble-shooting to ensure the Web browsers work smoothly.

As Toshiko found out when she started looking for listening materials, searching on the Web is a complex task because of the continuously increasing amount of information available. Teachers and students may be overwhelmed not only by the amount, but also by their varying quality. As several chapters emphasize (in this volume, Reeder et al., chap. 13; Susser & Robb, chap. 14; Taylor & Gitsaki, chap. 8), the Web contains an incredible amount material for teachers to supplement their classes, and for learners to practice. However, locating appropriate materials is a challenge for both teachers and learners. Consequently, knowing how search engines work, performing searches, and letting students engage in canned searches (i.e., searches that have been conducted and their results analyzed) are important areas of expertise. Toshiko's search illustrated techniques that can significantly narrow down searches to make the resulting hit list more manageable, but teachers don't automatically know how to conduct good searches, and therefore in our computer methods course we introduce them to techniques such as those on search tip sites (http://www.searchenginewatch.com/facts/index.html).

Once search techniques have been refined, both teachers and students are more likely to arrive at a manageable number of results. However, because anyone can put up a Web site, materials available on the Web vary dramatically in quality. Knowing which sources to trust and which Web site to choose for students requires the ability to assess the quality, usefulness, and appropriateness of Web materials. Hence, evaluating the wealth of information is a second skill teachers need to possess. Credibility based on authority may be a good approach for evaluating Web sites that teachers are considering for their students to explore. For example, it is arguably easier to advise students on using the Web to locate articles on a given research topic, for example, American foreign policy, by instructing them to use only well-respected newspapers and magazines, such as *The New York Times* (http://www.nytimes.com/), *The Guardian* (http://www.guardian.co.uk/

guardian/), or *Time Magazine* (http://www.time.com/time/). The teacher looking for listening comprehension materials will need to go one step further and listen to all the materials that are to be used in the lesson to avoid inappropriate content. Most Web evaluation guides deal with assessing the accuracy of the content, the authority of the content producer(s), the objectivity of the information provided, and the currency of documents. One example of a page addressing these issues is a Web page published by Cornell University's reference services division (http://www.library.cornell.edu/okuref/webcrit.html).

Once materials have been found and evaluated, a teacher typically needs to repurpose them for student use. Very rarely can high-quality materials be used as is without the teacher carefully considering how the materials are best used for a given set of students, as Pennington observes (chap. 5, this volume). This may involve the creation of a task or worksheet or other materials to help accomplish the objective of a lesson. Taylor and Gitaski (chap. 8, this volume) point out that the real challenge is how to expose the students to online materials that don't conform to a particular language-learning syllabus. In her quest for good listening materials, Toshiko came across numerous listening passages of varying lengths and difficulty levels available online at Randall's Cyber Listening Lab (http://www.esl-lab.com). Although the passages provide students with some instructional materials such as transcripts, in some cases video and audio, and interactive comprehension activities, Toshiko found that these were not at the appropriate level for her students and needed to produce downloadable worksheets to make the activities fit within her objectives for the class. Clearly, Randall's Cyber Listening Lab is an example where EFL learners are targeted. Many times, teachers will have to provide much more than a worksheet to effectively repurpose online materials.

These three skills—searching, evaluating, and repurposing materials—have always been crucial for language teachers even though the Web requires different approaches and techniques. An additional area of expertise is what Toshiko needed when she got to the computer lab and attempted to use the listening materials only to find that her students received messages such as the one that appears in Fig. 15.1.

The fourth skill essential for language teachers who want to use Web materials in their classes is troubleshooting basic browser problems. Because almost all information is accessed through a browser interface, teachers will be expected to be able to address basic browser issues. One frequent problem with the Web involves the use of media that require (browser) plug-ins. Unless plug-ins are installed, media of a given type cannot be displayed. For example, many sites make use of streaming media in RealAudio format (http://www.real.com), Flash (http://www.macromedia.com/flash/),

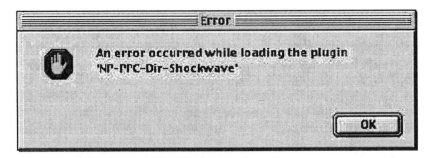

FIG. 15.1. Web browser error message indicating the required plug-in is not installed.

QuickTime (http://www.apple.com/quicktime/), or Authorware (http://www.macromedia.com/authorware). Taking advantage of the media and interactivity in these applications requires the correct configuration of a Web browser. Netscape maintains a Web site with plug-in information, which is a useful resource for teachers (http://wp.netscape.com/plugins/?cp=dowdep2).

Creating Web Materials. To move beyond using others' materials on the Web to creating original materials, teachers need additional expertise that can range from creating basic Web pages on one end of the continuum to programming an online course on the other end. If Toshiko had had this additional bit of knowledge, she could have made a "listening" page for the school containing all of the Web sites that she had found. Two basic approaches can be taken to creating Web pages: working with either an HTML authoring application such as BBedit (http://www.barebones.com/) or a WYSIWYG[2] authoring application, such as Macromedia Dreamweaver (http://www.macromedia.com/dreamweaver). A prerequisite for either approach is knowledge of Web page design and of (Web) server access.

In their chapter on designing and operating a CALL lab, Browne and Gerrity (chap. 10, this volume) mention some of the important Web page design issues such as the need for navigational transparency and a well-conceived layout. More information about these aspects, as well as implementation guidance, is provided by a number of books (Fleming, 1998; Niederst, 2001) and Web sites. Students in our computer methods class have found the *Web Style Guide* by Lynch and Horton (2001) particularly useful. After designing and creating Web pages, they need to be made publicly available by uploading them to a Web server. Server access is necessary

---

[2]WYSIWYG is an acronym for "What you see is what you get."

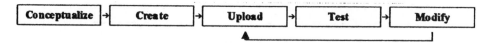

FIG. 15.2.   Schematic overview of fundamental skills involved in Web-page creation.

once a web page has been created so pages can be viewed by others through a Web browser. To make future modifications, it is mandatory for Web authors to know how to download pages, how to make modifications, and how to upload them again as illustrated in Fig. 15.2. Niederst (2001) has provided an overview of these skills.

At a minimum, teachers should be expected to have a basic understanding of Web page design and creation including how to insert hyperlinks and links to media files. Such links are used for basic navigation such as a menu that can take the learners to different topics in addition to supporting reference materials. Additionally, Web page creation entails some maintenance and updating, which teachers need to be able to do as well. After Toshiko creates a Web page containing links to the listening sites she found, she will need to return to that site to add additional links and check that the existing sites still function properly.

More advanced teachers should be able to author materials with the types of interactive components Iwabuchi and Fotos (chap. 9, this volume) discuss. Interactivity on the Web or for courseware can be achieved through the use of a number of software tools such as JavaScript, Applets, Common Gateway Interface (CGI) scripts, Flash, or Shockwave. *Language Interactive*, Bob Goodwin-Jones's guide on creating interactive Web pages (http://www.fln.vcu.edu/cgi/interact.html) offers a starting point, as does Doug Mills's collection of examples showing Web interactivity through JavaScript (http://www.iei.uiuc.edu/JS4LL/). These techniques allow for interactions intended to improve language learning in the way that Iwabuchi and Fotos (chap. 9, this volume) describe.

O'Connor and Gatton (chap. 11, this volume) introduce yet a third level of expertise by talking about possible systematic approaches necessary when considering creation of a companion Web site and freestanding online courses. Both require advanced knowledge not only of Web page creation and design and programming interactivity but also of student record management expertise. Implementation guidance for interactivity and management options are provided by Heinle and Pena (2001) and online at webmonkey (http://hotwired.lycos.com/webmonkey/). These functions are also provided by course management systems such as WebCT and Blackboard, both of which can accommodate most needs of users of varying levels of expertise.

Communication Tools

Teachers attempting to increase learners' communicative competence through CMC need to know how to use communication tools such as chat rooms, bulletin boards, e-mail, and electronic mailing lists. Interesting findings have resulted from the use of these tools in the classroom. First, as Pennington (chap. 5, this volume) observes, the written mode of much CMC allows students to reflect on and plan their language, and therefore tends to engage students who hesitate to contribute during regular class sessions (Peterson, 1997). A second positive effect is cited by Fotos (chap. 7, this volume), who reports increased writing production and increased general L2 proficiency of students participating in an e-mail exchange project. E-mail exchanges, particularly when proficient L2 speakers are involved, can also provide the additional advantage of scaffolding when original text remains embedded in the e-mail messages. Future teachers are familiar with aspects of some or all of these tools, but we provide a balanced introduction of the range of tools they might use in the future, practice using them for teaching, and guidance about how they can be used for research.

The most commonly used communication tools include ICQ ("I seek you," a tool for personal communication) (http://www.icq.com), IRC (http://www.irchelp.org), Java Chat (a Web-based chat, e.g., http://www.parachat.com/ or http://chat.yahoo.com/), MOOs and MUDs (http://www.topmudsites.com/), and instant messaging applications such as MSN Instant Messenger (http://messenger.msn.com/) or AOL Instant Messenger (http://www.aim.com/index.adp). Online resources on these tools are plentiful. For example, the Web site Chatting on the Net (http://www.newircusers.com/) focuses on IRC but provides an overview of Java Chat and Instant Messenger Chat as well. Internet Relay Chat Help (http://www.irchelp.org/) at Duke University, a comprehensive site, includes information on IRC programs, help, and FAQ files, and a directory for communication research, which is of particular interest to teachers and researchers. These tools are particularly valuable because they are available free of charge and they work on various platforms and some (e.g., AOL Instant Messenger) even allow for audio communication.

The key issues for being able to use these tools in teaching are setting up appropriate tasks, providing guidance, moderating the exchanges carefully, and taking advantage of the technical capabilities of the communication tool to be used. Students practice through peer teaching to explore the full range of possibilities, such as role-plays in one-to-one, many-to-many, and one-to-many communication using text, hyperlinks, and audio (only for one-to-one communication). It becomes clear to students that the task that the leader plans is essential for success and that some tasks are more and others are less appropriate for a given communication tool. For example, we engage our students in a role-play that involves a chat room communication exercise with one teacher and a group of four to five (simulated) intermediate learners. The teacher needs to keep the students on task (e.g., discussing a reading passage) without taking over the discussion. Students increase their insight into the use of these tools through discussion of their experience along with findings reported by Donaldson and Kötter (1999), for example, indicating that their students wanted to work independently and thought the teacher should only observe unobtrusively in the background. Another task the class experiments with involves one-on-one communication between a teacher and a novice with the goal of teaching the beginning learners enough to introduce themselves and make a room reservation using text and audio. Healey (1999) discussed skill-building tasks in CALL environments more fully.

Students quickly learn that L2 and foreign language conversation is freely available through access to chat rooms online. AOL Instant Messenger, for example, lists 60 or so community chat rooms on different topics. At the same time, our students become aware that entering a chat room exposes their L2 students to the risk of encountering unmoderated language, which can be shocking, to say the least. In our experience, it is difficult to avoid foul language in public community chat rooms. Hence, teachers need to be aware of that and prepare their students or create a more sheltered environment using a MOO, for example. Donaldson and Kötter (1999, p. 542) reported on a successful use of a MOO for advanced American learners of German and advanced German learners of English. They argued that the structured environment of a MOO, which allowed the learners to communicate with each other while solving tasks, had several advantages compared with e-mail exchanges and chat rooms.

Students also learn first-hand the importance of setting up tasks and providing guidelines that encourage behaviors that would create optimal conditions for language learning such as scaffolding (Fotos, chap. 7, this volume) and others described by Egbert, Chao, and Hanson-Smith (1999). They also learn about options for optimizing communication tools by setting the preferences of the software to allow access to certain individuals or to save a log of recording the conversation for future use.

Recording the learners' written language from these types of exchanges serves as a valuable tool for teaching and research. Examining linguistic output that students produce while working on a task can provide teachers with some evidence of whether certain concepts (e.g., the use of modals to qualify a claim) or vocabulary items have been acquired. Training students to examine their own language and helping them to employ basic technologies that highlight potential problems can aid in recognizing errors and correcting them. For example, students or teachers can copy and paste student output into a Microsoft Word document and go through the built-in grammar and spell checker. Researchers investigating various linguistic features also take advantage of the automated record keeping of various applications. These analytic uses of the records of CMC, for example, are taught to students along with the how and why that they need to use the methods in class.

Language Labs

Why wasn't the plug-in installed in the lab in Toshiko's school? Who was in charge of the language lab? Should the lab manager have known that the teachers would be using software that required RealPlayer? Unfortunately, reliance on a lab manager or lab monitor does not always work. The teacher has to expect the unexpected by knowing basic troubleshooting techniques. Other problematic areas include computer setup, software installation, and language laboratory management. Hence, it is crucial for teachers to be educated about basic computer setup and maintenance, aware of software applications for language-learning research, and actively involved in the decision-making process concerning the language lab. It follows that the teacher of the 21st century should be knowledgeable about the following issues: (a) hardware and software acquisitions; (b) personnel and staffing of a language lab; (c) materials development, display, and exchange; and (d) research and development possibilities (see Liddell & Garett, chap. 3, this volume).

Decisions regarding the hardware and software configurations are based on a number of factors that we discuss with students. With respect to hardware, one factor is scalability: Is there enough room to grow and expand computational capabilities without having to invest in new machines? A second is obsolescence: Will the computers be up to the demands of future applications and networking issues? With respect to software, the questions are: What will meet the needs of the students and how easy is it to obtain information about releases of newer versions and possible upgrade policies? One way to promote the involvement of future teachers is to give them access to fairly up-to-date computer equipment and to encourage them to experiment with computers and software. Although many institutions insist that lab security in terms of configuring computers to prevent anyone from modifying the systems is important, we believe it is equally important to give future teachers the opportunity to "play with" computers, even if it involves occasional rebuilds. We therefore encourage students to download and install trial versions of software in our laboratory, and we have had to develop a system for software maintenance that meets our needs.

The necessary ingredients for future language labs include personnel and commitment as much as equipment. As Browne and Gerrity (chap. 10, this volume) observe, schools that have the financial resources to equip a CALL lab with technology have often focused on hardware needs, thereby neglecting the importance of staffing, software, and training programs. Because staffing is a need that many institutions overlook, we attempt to stress its importance to our students. Effective and efficient use of computer labs presupposes maintenance and support. In fact, the maintenance of computer labs is as crucial as hiring responsible staff who can implement teachers' ideas and play a key role in linking teaching to research by enabling teachers to gather performance data needed to assess students performance. Language laboratory staff also plays an important role in the area of making materials teachers create available.

Bickerton (1999) pointed out that software produced at the local level rarely survives the author's demise. Future language labs need to combat this common occurrence not only by involving teachers in the decision-making process (in this volume, see Browne & Gerrity, chap. 10; O'Connor & Gatton, chap. 11) but also by encouraging collaborative materials development and by inviting other teachers to use these materials, a process that includes the availability of a centralized storage and access facility, for example, a Web server on which teachers can publish their materials and access materials other teachers have created. The benefits to be gained from constant development, usability testing, and modification are evident. On the one hand, materials are used by a wider audience and materials developers can get feedback. On the other hand, as materials become more and more Web-based, future language labs can also substantially contribute to the success and the marketing of their parent organization, which in turn may be necessary for continued funding and a constant influx of students. Instrumental for this success is establishment a Web presence through excellent materials, which increases the online visibility of a language lab. One good example of a language learning lab is The Lingua Center (now IEI English Resources, http://www.iei.uiuc.edu/free.html), an integral part of the Intensive English Program at the University of Illinois at Urbana-Champaign.

Language labs, as Liddell and Garrett (chap. 3, this volume) point out, will continue to evolve to support the pedagogies of the teachers involved with their design and use. Changes will continue to be possible because of advancing computer technology, which, for example, allows for a different room configuration in terms of layout and in terms of the technology available as wireless communication and laptop computers emerge as the standard. Changes will also be motivated by teachers and their needs as areas such as research into SLA processes, the effectiveness of technology-enhanced learning, and (technology-) or Internet-based professional development become more and more important. For example, language labs provide the ideal environment for usability testing and research. Hence, as Liddell and Garrett suggest, future language laboratories will no longer be merely computer labs for student use but will be likely to include hardware and software facilities to conduct research. One example is screen-capturing software (e.g., Camtasia by TechSmith, http://www.techsmith.com/) that allows a systematic investigation into learner–computer interactions by recording each move.

Future teachers need to be aware of the factors involved in setting up and running a language lab to be prepared to influence positively the process of either establishing a language lab or of expanding an existing one. O'Connor and Gatton (chap. 11, this volume) demonstrate that introducing CALL into their university entailed a major innovation for everyone involved in teaching. These broader issues are also evident in Browne and Gerrity's (chap. 10, this volume) observations about initiating and running CALL in language laboratories in general. In view of the need for teachers to have an understanding of the whole system of instruction and how decisions are made beyond their individual classes, work in applied linguistics investigating the systemic nature of language teaching innovations is useful (Markee, 1997).

CONCLUSION

The opportunities afforded the language teacher by technology at the start of the 21st century require a better-than-ever understanding of the principles of language teaching and a broader-than-ever set of skills and teaching practices. Rather than providing teachers with easy answers and prepackaged methods that they can administer to learners, technology appears to be increasing the range of opportunities and options for constructing learning tasks. The need has never been greater for teachers with basic technological skills who understand the capabilities and limitations of technology in teaching and who accept responsibility for critically examining the options and their implications (Franklin, 1999).

As other core areas of applied linguistics are increasingly affected by technology, future volumes are likely to demonstrate more changes in what language teachers need to know. For example, in the special issue of *TESOL Quarterly* on the future of English language teaching, Conrad (2000) suggested changes in our understanding and teaching of grammar that may result from advances in computer-assisted corpus linguistics. In the same volume, Cummins (2000) argued that the technology expands opportunities for critical pedagogy, Cribb (2000) suggested drastic changes in the scope of L2 teaching due to increased reliance on translation technologies, and Warschauer and Kern (2000) painted a picture of a very different world for language teachers as a result of the globalization that is supported by technology. It remains to be seen what the future will bring, but in the meantime, it is evident that the resources offered by today's technologies for learners and teachers provide a valuable opportunity to rethink and perhaps reinvent what constitutes the knowledge base for L2 teachers at the beginning of the 21st century.

REFERENCES

Bachman, L. F. (1990). *Fundamental considerations in language testing.* Oxford, England: Oxford University Press.

Beauvois, M. H. (1998). E-talk: Computer-assisted classroom discussion—Attitudes and motivation. In J. Swaffar, S. Romano, P. Markley, & K. Arens (Eds.), *Language learning online: Theory and practice in the ESL and the L2 computer classroom* (pp. 99–120). Austin, TX: Labyrinth.

Bickerton, D. (1999). Authoring and the academic linguist: The challenge of multimedia in CALL. In K. Cameron (Ed.), *CALL: Media, design, & application* (pp. 59–79). Exton, PA: Swets & Zeitlinger.

Borrás I., & Lafayette, R. C. (1994). Effects of multimedia courseware subtitling on the speaking performance of college students of French. *The Modern Language Journal, 78*, 61–75.

Burns, A., & Coffin, C. (Eds.). (2001). *Analyzing English in a global context.* London: Routledge.

Canale, M., & Swain, M. (1980). Theoretical bases of communicative approaches to second language teaching and testing. *Applied Linguistics, 1*, 1–47.

Chapelle, C. (1998). Multimedia CALL: Lessons to be learned from research on instructed SLA. *Language Learning and Technology, 2*(1), 22–34.

Chapelle, C. A. (2001). *Computer applications in second language acquisition: Foundations for teaching, testing and research.* Cambridge, England: Cambridge University Press.

Chun, D. M. (1994). Using computer networking to facilitate the acquisition of interactive competence. *System, 22*(1), 17–31.

Conrad, S. (2000). Will corpus linguistics revolutionize grammar teaching in the 21st century? *TESOL Quarterly, 34*(3), 548–560.

Cribb, V. M. (2000). Machine translation: The alternative for the 21st century? *TESOL Quarterly, 34*(3), 560–569.

Crystal, D. (2001). *Language and the Internet.* Cambridge, England: Cambridge University Press.

Cummins, J. (2000). Academic language learning, transformative pedagogy, and information technology: Towards a critical balance. *TESOL Quarterly, 34*(3), 537–548.

Debski, R. (1997). Support of creativity and collaboration in the language classroom: A new role for technology. In R. Debski, J. Gaskin, & M. Smith (Eds.), *Language learning through social computing. Applied Linguistics of Australia Occasional Papers Number 16* (pp. 39–65). Melbourne, Australia: University of Melbourne Printing Services.

de Graaff, R. (1997). The Experanto experiment: Effects of explicit instruction on second language acquisition. *Studies in Second Language Acquisition, 19*, 249–276.

Donaldson, R., & Kötter, M. (1999). Language learning in cyberspace: Teleporting the classroom into the target culture. *CALICO Journal, 16*(4), 531–557.

Dörnyei, Z. (2001). *Teaching and researching motivation.* London: Longman.

Dörnyei, Z., & Schmidt, R. (Eds.). (2001). *Motivation and second language acquisition.* Honolulu: University of Hawaii Press.

Egbert, J., Chao C., & Hanson-Smith, E. (1999). Computer-enhanced language learning environments: An overview. In J. Egbert & E. Hanson-Smith (Eds.), *CALL environments: Re-*

search, practice, and critical issues (pp. 1–13). Alexandria, VA: Teachers of English to Speakers of Other Languages.

Fleming, J. (1998). *Web navigation: Designing the user experience.* Sebastopol, CA: O'Reilly.

Franklin, U. M. (1999). *The real world of technology* (Rev ed.). Toronto, Canada: House of Anansi Press Limited.

Gass, S. (1997). *Input, interaction, and the second language learner.* Mahwah, NJ: Lawrence Erlbaum Associates.

Halliday, M. A. K., & Hasan, R. (1989). *Language, context, and text: Aspects of language in a social-semiotic perspective.* Oxford, England: Oxford University Press.

Healey, D. (1999). Classroom practice: Communicative skill-building tasks in CALL environments. In J. Egbert & E. Hanson-Smith (Eds.), *CALL Environments: Research, practice, and critical issues* (pp. 116–136). Alexandria, VA: Teachers of English to Speakers of Other Languages.

Heinle, N., & Pena, B. (2001). *Designing with JavaScript: Creating dynamic web pages* (2nd ed.). Sebastopol, CA: O'Reilly.

Kapoun, J. (1998, July/August). Teaching undergrads WEB evaluation: A guide for library instruction. *C&RL News,* 522–523.

Lam, W. S. E. (2000). L2 literacy and the design of the self: A case study of a teenager writing on the Internet. *TESOL Quarterly, 34*(3), 457–482.

Lantolf, J. P. (Ed.). (2000). *Sociocultural theory and second language learning.* Oxford, England: Oxford University Press.

Lee, L. (1998). Going beyond classroom learning: Acquiring cultural knowledge via on-line newspapers and intercultural exchanges via on-line chatrooms. *CALICO Journal, 16*(2), 101–120.

Long, M. H. (1996). The role of linguistic environment in second language acquisition. In W. C. Ritchie & T. K. Bhatia (Eds.), *Handbook of second language acquisition* (pp. 413–468). San Diego, CA: Academic Press.

Lynch, P., & Horton, S. (2001). *Web style guide* (2nd ed.). New Haven, CT: Yale University Press.

Markee, N. (1997). *Managing curricular innovation.* Cambridge, England: Cambridge University Press.

McGee, J. (2001, August 4). Conversational English and the Internet: A case study of a "Cyber-English" class. Paper presented at the 41st annual Language Educational Technology Conference, Nagoya, Japan.

Murray, D. (2000). Protean communication: The language of computer-mediated communication. *TESOL Quarterly, 34*(3), 457–482.

Niederst, J. (2001). *Web design in a nutshell* (2nd ed.). Sebastopol, CA: O'Reilly.

Oxford, R. L. (1990). *Language learning strategies: What every teacher should know.* New York: Newbury House.

Pellettieri, J. (2000). Negotiation in cyberspace: The role of *chatting* in the development of grammatical competence in the virtual foreign language classroom. In M. Warschauer & R. Kern (Eds.), *Network-based language teaching: Concepts and practice* (pp. 59–86). Cambridge, England: Cambridge University Press.

Peterson, M. (1997). Language teaching and networking. *System, 25*(1), 29–37.

Pica, T. (1994). Research on negotiation: What does it reveal about second-language learning conditions, processes, and outcomes? *Language Learning, 44*(3), 493–527.

Pierce, B. (1995). Social identity, investment, and language learning. *TESOL Quarterly, 29,* 9–31.

Rassool, N. (1999). *Literacy for sustainable development in the age of information.* Clevedon, England: Multilingual Matters.

Skehan, P. (1998). *A cognitive approach to language learning.* Oxford, England: Oxford University Press.

van Lier, L. (1996). *Interaction in the language curriculum: Awareness, autonomy & authenticity.* London: Longman.

Warschauer, M. (2000). The changing global economy and the future of English teaching. *TESOL Quarterly, 34*(3), 511–535.

Warschauer, M., & Kern, R. (Eds.). (2000). *Network-based language teaching: Concepts and practice.* Cambridge, England: Cambridge University Press.

Glossary of CALL Terms

Applescript—A scripting language developed by Apple for the Macintosh Operation System. It helps to automate tasks and customizes the way applications behave.

Applet—A program within another application that usually runs on Java. An applet cannot be executed from an operating system directly.

ARPANET—The precursor to the Internet established by the U.S. Advanced Research Project Agency (ARPA) in 1969.

Artificial intelligence (AI)—A term coined in 1956 by John McCarthy referring to a branch of computer science aiming to create computers that mimic humans. AI includes robotics, neural networks, natural language, expert systems, and games playing.

ASCII—American standard code for information interchange. The seven-bit standard code used to exchange information over computer networks.

Asynchronous communication—Text-based electronic communication that is read after it is written, including private e-mail and e-mail posted (sent) to a bulletin board or e-mail list.

Asynchronous text—Communication in which the data sent do not come in a steady stream but come intermittently.

Asynchronous voice—As with asynchronous text, voice streams in communicative circumstances that are intermittent rather than steady.

Authorware—An authoring tool that allows the user to create documents combining multimedia and hypertext.

Auto summarizer—A Microsoft feature embedded within Microsoft Word that summarizes a document.

Binary—

1. Any base-two system of numbering.

2. The machine-readable code used for transmitting any data other than text, such as pictures, programs, and word-processed documents. In casual use, *binary* refers to a file that uses all eight bits of each byte, as compared with text files that use only seven bits, leaving the eighth bit as 0. E-mail is text based, so binary documents sent via e-mail are encoded into a seven-bit form called MIME.

Broadband—A type of electronic transmission that uses a single medium to carry several channels at the same time. For example, cable TV uses a broadband transmission.

Browser—The program used to access the Internet. The most common browsers are Microsoft Internet Explorer and Netscape Navigator, with Opera a distant third. Early browsers could view only the World Wide Web, that is, nothing more than hypertext documents. Modern browsers do far more: Many support numerous protocols; that is, they can read mail, read the usenet, run ftp, chat, and so on.

Bulletin Board System (BBS)—A collection of downloadable files, personal text messages, or other community resources housed on a computer. Before the advent of the World Wide Web, BBSs were accessed by direct dial-in. In contemporary usage, a bulletin board is simply an electronic message center housed on a Web site.

Captioning—An on-screen text version of the spoken word, usually of a video track, done in real time.

CD-ROM—Compact disc-read only memory. A special type of optical disc capable of storing large amounts of data.

CGI—Common gateway interface. A script that acts as intermediary between a Web Graphical User Interface (GUI) and a Web server. It allows two-way communication, accepting data and returning it to the user.

Chat—Short for "Internet relay chat," or IRC. A type of online, written communication that occurs in real time between two or more users via a computer.

Client—A program or computer using resources provided by a remote machine called a server. Web browsers and e-mail readers are examples of "client-side" programs; online databases and CGI scripts are "server-side" programs.

Computer literacy—The level of expertise and familiarity that someone has in using computers. Individuals who are very computer literate are sometimes called power users.

Computer-mediated communication (CMC)—A term coined by Hiltz and Turoff in 1978 to refer to computer conferencing. It now refers to all electronic communication where the user types on a keyboard and sends the text to other users, including e-mail, bulletin boards, Internet relay chat, MUDs, and usenet.

Computer-mediated ELT—Computer-mediated English language training/teaching. This term refers to English language learning using computers and includes many different forms of CALL activities.

Connectivity—The ability of a program or device to link with other programs and devices.

Cyberschool—A fully integrated learning environment that uses cyberspace (primarily the World Wide Web) as its primary location for learning. It may include, but is not limited to, online courses and their materials, communications between instructors and students, registration, and enrollment.

Cyberspace—The Internet, particularly the World Wide Web. The term appears to derive from the Greek word *kubernates,* meaning governor (*kubernan* = to govern). In the 1940s, the term *cybernetics* was used by an American mathematician, Norbert Weiner, to refer to "the theoretical study of communication and control processes" (*Japan Times,* June 23, 1997, p. 4). In 1984 the term *cyberspace* first appeared in William Gibson's influential science fiction novel *Neuromancer.*

Database application—A program that assists in organizing information in a structured way that makes searching for items efficient and simple; an electronic filing system.

Digital drop box—Digital refers to material based on discontinuous data or events. A drop box is a place or folder where people submit information with "no read" privileges (i.e., suggestion box, submission box); that is, they cannot read what has been submitted.

Discussion board—A Web-based site for sharing information, similar to a physical bulletin board. Here messages are posted (sent to the discussion board) and can be read by anyone.

Distance learning—A type of education where students work on their own at home or at the office and communicate with faculty and other students via e-mail, electronic forums, video conferencing, and other forms of computer-based communication. Most distance learning programs include a computer-based training (CBT) system and communications tools to produce a "virtual classroom."

DSL—Digital subscriber line. This method uses sophisticated technologies and modulation to transfer data through copper wires in a way that is substantially faster than traditional analog systems. It is used to connect to the home or office from a telephone switching station.

E-commerce—Electronic commerce or business interactions that are conducted online, such as buying and selling products and services. E-commerce is conducted using EDI (electronic data interchange) and a virtual payment system such as credit cards, checking accounts, or digital cash.

Electronic journal—A journal placed online to be read via the World Wide Web, usually formatted in hypertext markup language (HTML). Such articles are sometimes coded for password protection so they can only be read by subscribers.

E-mail—Electronic mail. This is a form of computer mediated communication consisting of simple text files sent from one individual to another. The messages are stored in electronic mailboxes and can be opened by the recipients regardless of their geographical location. It is a rapid, inexpensive text messaging service that also permits the transfer of digital "attachments" such as documents, pictures, or music.

E-mail attachment—A file or document "attached" to an e-mail text message. If the attachment is binary, it is encoded into an ASCII-based form (usually MIME—multipurpose Internet mail extensions).

E-mail list—Special interest group where members receive a copy of all mail sent to the group address.

Emoticons—Small icons constructed from keyboard characters and used in e-mail to indicate the emotional state of the sender. For example, the following icon means happy or smiling: :-).

Ethernet—The term refers to both the cable and the protocols used to establish a local area network (LAN), a technology supporting digital transfers of data.

FAQ—Frequently asked questions. This term usually refers to an online document that answers common questions about a specific topic.

Flame—Written abuse or taunting in e-mail or a bulletin board posting. An exchange of insulting e-mail is often called a "flame war."

Freeze (computer)—A freeze occurs when computer programs or operating systems stop functioning and the user cannot input data or control the mouse. The user normally must restart the computer.

FTP—File transfer protocol, a system for moving binary and text files between a local computer and a remote server. Most online software is downloaded from FTP servers.

Gopher—A system for organizing and navigating documents on remote computers, implemented extensively at universities and research facilities in the early 1990s. It was quickly overshadowed by the more usable World Wide Web interface.

Grammar checker—An option provided by word processing programs to check for grammatical inconsistencies in input text. The checker highlights errors in syntax, punctuation, verb tense, and so on that do not conform to its programmed patterns.

Header (e-mail)—An identification line (e.g., To, From, Subject, Date) in an e-mail message that names the sender or recipient, as well as information relevant to the message transmission.

Hits—Retrieval of any item from a Web server (i.e. viewing a page or graphic is called a hit). Also, data-matching criteria (i.e., when search engines list results, the results are called hits).

Home page—The top-level entry point to a Web site. Some home pages serve as a table of contents or a site index and introduce the navigational structure of a site; others consist simply of a "splash page," an introductory screen often presenting advanced graphics, logos, or Flash animation.

HTML—Hypertext markup language. A series of codes or "tags" used to format text to be read by a Web browser. It is one of the primary authoring languages used to display content on the Internet.

HTML tags—Commands used in HTML that direct how the document will be formatted and appear on the Web.

HTTP—Hypertext transfer protocol. The encoding and transmission method used to transfer files from a server to a browser. In a complete URL, such as http://

cnn.com/index.html, the browser is asking the server to transfer the hypertext document called index.html

ICT—Information and communications technology.

1. The Institute of Computer Technology, whose mission is to improve achievement and learning through the integration of technology into education, industry, and the community (http://www.ict.org/).

2. A broad term referring to the use of technology in communication paradigms.

IP—Internet protocol. One of several data transmission protocols that specify the format of data sent over a network. Most networks combine an IP with a TCP (transmission control protocol) to establish the connection between a computer destination and its source. A unique IP address consisting of a series of numbers is assigned to each computer on a network for identification purposes.

Hypermedia—Text linking graphics, sounds, and video elements.

Hypertext—The type of text (or database system) used on Web pages to link specific items (objects, text, pictures, music programs, etc.) together. Users can click on links in the text and maneuver freely from one object or page to the next.

ICQ—I-seek-you. An online type of messaging program used as a conferencing tool to allow individuals to chat online. Users must download the program and can then chat in real time.

IRC—Internet relay chat. A chat system developed by Jarkko Oikarinen in Finland in the late 1980s which has become popular because it enables people connected anywhere on the Internet to join in live discussions through use of special software that allows users to read and write e-mail messages delivered almost immediately.

Instant messaging applications—A real-time text-messaging system that is usually run over the Internet (MSN and AOL each offer popular instant messaging services). Although these systems are typically asynchronous, they nonetheless allow for the rapid sending and receiving of text messages via e-mail.

Interactivity (in CALL programs)—The degree to which a program allows the user to input data, make choices and decisions, and create or customize program content when using the program.

Internet/intranet—A network connecting computers together to allow for the exchange of data. The Internet is a global network consisting of millions of interlinked servers and computer networks. An intranet provides similar services within an organization to those provided by the public Internet but is not necessarily connected to the Internet.

Internet search tool—A tool that performs Internet searches for information based on text and symbols input to execute the search. Topics, titles, lines of text, and terms can be searched throughout the Internet.

Internet telephony—Transmission of traditional voice and fax data over the Internet. The technology is attractive because of the potential savings made possible though bypassing private long-distance carrier networks. At present, the sound quality is not as good as traditional phone networks but improving technology, increasing bandwidth, and the falling price of Internet connections are helping to lessen this problem.

Java—A programming language developed by Sun Microsoft Microsystems that builds on the object-oriented structure of C++.

Javascript—A scripting language to enable Web authors to design interactive sites. Javascript can interact with HTML source code, enabling Web authors to use dynamic content on their sites.

Keypals—an expression referring to Internet "penpals," because a keyboard rather than a pen is used for correspondence, generally via e-mail.

LAN—Local area network. A computer network that spans a small area such as a classroom or a university. Each "node" or individual computer can run its own programs but is also able to access data and devices anywhere on the LAN. Rapid e-mail communication is also possible among users on a LAN.

Listserv—An automatic mailing list server. When e-mail is addressed to a LISTSERV® mailing list, it is automatically sent to everyone on the list.

Log on—A system to authenticate a user for a particular computer or network. In most cases, the log-on (sometimes written as "logon") procedure requires the user to input a username and a password before being granted access to programs or information.

Lurk—To read messages that have been posted (or sent) to an e-mail discussion group, bulletin board, or newsgroup without contributing any messages oneself. The person is called a lurker.

Machine translations—Web sites or software that translate text into various languages. The quality and speed of the translation depends on the complexity of the software's programmed lexicon and its recognition of syntactical patterns.

Mainframe—A very large and expensive computer capable of supporting hundreds, or even thousands, of users simultaneously.

Meaning technologies—Any technological tool or feature in language-learning programs that assists the user in learning the language.

MMLL—Multimedia language learning software. Any computer program that uses multimedia to provide language-learning instruction.

MOO—Multi-user-domain object oriented. A specific implementation of a MUD system developed by Stephen White. MOO is in the public domain and can be freely downloaded and executed.

MUD—Multi-user dungeon (or multi-user dimension). A cyberspace where users can take on an identity (called an avatar) and interact with one another.

Multimedia—The use of computers to present text, graphics, video, animation, and sound in an integrated way.

Multimedia-based ELT—A teaching methodology (or collection of materials) that uses multimedia as its primary tool to teach the English language.

Net surfing—Internet searching done through search engines using keywords to find data.

Netiquette—A contraction of "Internet" and "etiquette," referring to etiquette guidelines for posting messages to online services, lists, and newsgroups.

Netiquette covers rules to maintain civility in discussions (i.e., avoiding flames), and includes guidelines for e-mail, such as use of simple text formats because complex formatting may not appear correctly for all readers.

Network—A group of two or more computer systems linked together.

Network bandwidth—A connection between computers that allows for data transfer within a range of frequencies or wavelengths. In common speech, the term refers to capacity and speed with which data can be transmitted over the computer network. Bandwidth capacity is measured in bits of data transmitted (10 megabits per second, 100 mbps, 1,000 mbps).

Online—A term referring to the period when a computer is linked to a server connected to the Internet. Also a synonym for "ready for use," as in "the program is back online."

Online discussion—A discussion or conversation taking place online either in synchronous or asynchronous time.

Online program—A computer program available online either for downloading to a local computer or for use via a Web site.

Plug-ins—A hardware or software module that adds a specific feature or service to a larger system. For example, there are number of plug-ins for Internet browsers to enable the display of different types of audio or video messages.

Presentation application—Software programs such as PowerPoint created to assist users in formatting, organizing, and presenting content materials, often in a slide show format.

Program—A set of instructions for the computer to follow.

Programming languages—A collection of commands or instructions in a predefined syntax used by a programmer to write a program.

Protocol—A set of rules telling computers how to exchange data, much as rules of grammar enable human data exchange. Examples of different protocols are FTP and HTTP (the Web), POP and SMTP (e-mail), and NNTP (Usenet).

Real time—Taking place in the current time frame; synchronous time.

Real-time conferencing—The act of using computers to interact with other people via audio or video transmission in synchronous time.

Screen capture application—A software program that allows the user to copy what is currently displayed on a screen to a file or printer.

Server—A computer or device on a network that manages network resources or provides data or services to other programs. Servers are often "dedicated," meaning that they perform no other tasks besides their server tasks.

Server log—A file containing information pertaining to server operation. For example, Web servers often keep a server log containing a record of the files requested and the IP address of the requesters.

Shovelware—Content "shoveled" or transferred from one communication medium to another with little regard for the appearance, ease of use, or capabilities of the second medium.

Spam—Third-party large-scale e-mailings, often advertisements, sent to all members of a list, newsgroup or other organizations or individuals.

Speech recognition—The ability of special software to recognize human speech. Sometimes speech recognition software is used to control user interface elements or for automatic transcription (dictation software).

Spell checker—A service provided by word processing software for verifying the correct spelling of words in a document.

Spreadsheet application—A program used to create documents for the storage of numeric or text-string data in a table using rows and column format. The intersection of a row and a column forms a cell, the basic unit of a spreadsheet document.

Streaming—Sound or video sent over a network, typically the Internet, for immediate playback on a user's computer. To allow for a smooth flow, a few seconds worth of video is stored on the user's hard drive (a "buffer"). Unlike downloading, streaming does not allow a user to store a copy of the file.

Synchronous communication—Immediate forms of communication such as real-time video conferencing and online chatting in chat rooms or MOOs, where people are reading and writing text at the same time.

Synchronous text—Synchronous communication in text form.

Synchronous voice—Synchronous communication in voice form, for example, the telephone.

T1 connection—A dedicated (used only for one purpose) communications connection supporting data transfer rates of up to 1.544 megabits per second. The term *connection* in this context usually refers to an Internet connection.

TCP/IP—Transmission control protocol/Internet protocol underlies all other protocols; it is the basic transmission and routing method by which every piece of data is sent on the Internet. A file is broken up into "packets" of data, each of which has the destination address included. Packets might take completely different routes to their final destination. The computer receiving the data then reassembles the packets to recreate a copy of the original file. Transmitting information over phone lines between distant computers is an inherently error-prone process, which TCP/IP makes smooth and reliable.

Technocentric—The notion that a problem is only solvable through technology.

TELL—Technology-enhanced language learning. A project initiated in 1992 in the United Kingdom funded by the Teaching and Learning Technology Program (TLTP) to produce courseware for language learning, including French, German, Spanish, Italian, and Portuguese. The project started in January 1993 and was formally completed in December 1995. See http://www.ukoln.ac.uk/ services/papers/bl/rdr6250/chesters.html

Telnet—A protocol used to log in to a remote server. Although most user interface with the Internet is done via client programs such as e-mail readers or Web browsers, telnet allows server-side access to programs and files.

Thread—A discussion on a particular topic that takes place through e-mail, usenet, Web bulletin board, or another means of CMC. Typically all messages in a thread share the same subject line. A new thread is started by posting a message or sending an e-mail that opens a new topic and is not a reply to another post or e-mail.

Topical database—A database that has been organized into different sections of interest.

Tutorial software—A computer program that gives step-by-step instructions on how to achieve a particular task.

URL—Uniform (or universal) resource locator, the unique address of a document on the Internet. A URL does not need to include the prefix "http://," and many (but not all) URLs also do not need the prefix "www."

Usability—The quality of a user's experience when interacting with a product or system.

Usenet—A giant bulletin board system running separately from the Web using the Network News Transfer Protocol (NNTP). Usenet discussion is divided topically into more than 20,000 separate "newsgroups."

User interface—The on-screen elements which a person interacts with to access a software program.

Video conferencing—The video equivalent of a telephone conference call using TV or, more recently, digital video cameras.

Voicepals—Similar to penpals, except that voicepals communicate via voice instead of by pen and paper. This has recently become popular through the advent of instant messaging programs that handle voice transmission, such as Microsoft's MSN Messenger.

WAN—Wide area network. Similar to a LAN but spanning a large geographic area—for example, a city, province, or country—WANs are usually formed by joining of LANs. The largest WAN in existence is the Internet itself.

Web browser—A software application used to load and display Web pages, for example, Netscape Navigator, Microsoft Internet Explorer, or Opera.

Web-centric—Centered on or pertaining to the World Wide Web. Because of the Web's popularity, the term *Web* is often casually used to refer to the Internet as a whole.

WebCT—A set of Web-based course tools for developing and presenting interactive learning Web sites. The contents are provided by the course instructor.

Webness—This refers to the "essence of any network" and the linking that happens because of it. The term was coined by Derrick de Kerckhove at the University of Toronto in 1996. See http://www.acctbief.org/avenir/webness.htm for more information.

Web publishing—Publishing documents on the World Wide Web instead of on paper.

WELL—

1. Web-enhanced language learning. Using resources on using the World Wide Web to help teach language. For more information on an extensive WELL project sponsored by a group of British universities, see http://www.well.ac.uk/

2. Whole Earth 'Lectronic Link. The earliest—and still active—highly successful Internet community. Started in California in 1985 as a BBS, WELL predated the World Wide Web by many years.

Wetware—The human nervous system, as opposed to hardware or software. The term also refers to the programmers, operators, and administrators attached to a computer system, as opposed to the system's hardware or software. See *The Jargon Dictionary* at http://info.astrian.net/jargon/terms/w/wetware.html

Wireless communication—Sending and receiving information without the use of a physical wire to transmit information. Common wireless communication includes cellular phone or satellite transmission. In computer networks the term refers to networks that use protocols such as Intel's Bluetooth or Apple's Airport technologies.

World Wide Web—The interlinked collection of documents and servers founded in 1991, which transmits documents using HTTP. More generally, and since the advent of browsers that incorporate FTP, usenet, e-mail, and multimedia, the Web has become synonymous with the Internet.

WYSIWYG—What you see is what you get. A term commonly used during the computer printing revolution of the 1980s to refer to the notion that what is on the screen is what is printed on paper. In the mid-1990s, WYSIWYG was used for Web publishing to refer to HTML editors and the appearance of their Web page output.

APPENDIX:
List of CALL Web Sites

This appendix is an annotated list of Web sites related to CALL and L2 teaching and learning activities and research.

Web Site Categories

1. E-Mail Lists and Electronic Newsletters
2. Freeware
3. Journals
4. Keypal/Penpal Sites
5. Meta Sites
6. MOOs and MUDs
7. Online Resources
8. Practice and Drill Sites
9. Professional Organizations
10. Research and Information
11. Testing
12. Tools for Teachers and Students
13. Writing Sites and Online Dictionaries

1. E-Mail Lists and Electronic Newsletters

Edupage

http://www.educause.edu/pub/edupage/edupage.html
An electronic newsletter from EDUCAUSE, a nonprofit association established to advance higher education by promoting the use of IT.

LINGUIST List

http://linguistlist.org/
A linguistics research and conference information service from Wayne State University.

Papyrus News list

https://maillists.uci.edu/mailman/listinfo/papyrus-news
An e-mail news service focusing on topics such as the impact of new technologies on literacy and education.

SLART-L, Second Language Acquisition Research and Teaching List

http://listserv.cuny.edu/archives/slart-l.html
A site containing the archives of the e-mail newsletter of the SLA (Second Language Acquisition) Research and Teaching e-mail list of the City University of New York. There is a link to subscribe to the list.

TESL-L, Teachers of English as a Second Language list and related lists, such as TESLJB-L, TESL Jobs, and employment issues list

One of the first lists for teaching English as an L2 or foreign language. To join related lists, it is necessary to join TESL-L first, by sending an e-mail to listerve@cunyvm.cuny.edu, with "SUB TESL-L first name last name" as the body. Once a member of TESL-L, it is possible to subscribe to the other lists. For those who do not want to receive a number of separate messages, a digest option is available.

2. Freeware

CELIA—Computer Enhanced Language Instruction Archive

http://www.latrobe.edu.au/education/celia/celia.html
A collection of software distributed as either shareware or freeware via a linked FTP site.

A program for the Macintosh computer that produces keyword in context concordances of words in a text.

Half-Baked Software

http://www.halfbakedsoftware.com
Half-Baked Software publishes the authoring suite Hot Potatoes used for creating Web-based exercises for L2 learning, as well as Quandary, an authoring tool for Web-based action mazes. Both titles are shareware although Hot Potatoes can be used for free under some circumstances.

Rolf Palmberg's Downloadable computer programs for EFL

http://vwww.abo.fi/users/rpalmber/download.htm
A selection of CALL programs written for the Windows operating system.

3. Journals

CALL-EJ Online

http://www.clec.ritsumei.ac.jp/english/callejonline/index.htm
A refereed online journal.

The Chronicle of Higher Education

http://chronicle.com
A subscription-based print and online weekly magazine for college and university faculty and administrators. It also includes an extensive list of academic positions.

Educational Technology & Society

http://ifets.ieee.org/periodical/
An online journal publishing articles of interest to educational systems developers and the educators who use and manage the systems; a publication of International Forum of Educational Technology & Society and the IEEE Learning Technology Task Force.

Humanizing Language Teaching

http://hltmag.co.uk
A humanist magazine carrying articles, lesson outlines, and even humor.

Information, Communication & Technology

http://www.infosoc.co.uk

A journal dedicated to the study of information technology's impact on cultures and economies.

Internet TESL Journal (see Meta Sites)

KAIROS

http://english.ttu.edu/kairos/
A refereed online journal with an emphasis on rhetoric, technology, and pedagogy.

Language Fun Farm

http://www.teflfarm.com
An online magazine written in a nonacademic style covering all aspects of TESL.

Language Learning & Technology

http://llt.msu.edu
A refereed online journal for L2 and foreign language educators containing news, reviews, and articles. The site includes a large selection of downloadable documents.

Networks: An Online Journal for Teacher Research

http://www.oise.utoronto.ca/~ctd/networks
A useful site for IT-based activities and pedagogy.

The Reading Matrix: An International Online Journal

http://www.readingmatrix.com/journal.html
A refereed online journal for research in the fields of SLA and applied linguistics.

SIMILE: Studies in Media & Information Literacy Education

http://simile.fis.utoronto.ca
An online journal publishing studies in the new field of IT literacy.

TechKnowLogia

http://www.techknowlogia.org
An online journal of technologies including instructional materials, information technologies, computers, the Internet, and Web-based learning.

TESL-EJ

http://www-writing.berkeley.edu/TESL-EJ/ej19/toc.html
A refereed online journal of teaching English as an L2 or a foreign language known for its reviews of educational texts and resources.

4. Keypal/Penpal Sites

Intercultural E-mail Classroom Connections

http://www.teaching.com/iecc/
A free service to enable teachers and students to engage in cross-cultural e-mail exchanges.

KeyPals Club

http://www.teaching.com/KeyPals/
A correspondence network for educators and students with 50,000 users from more than 70 countries.

PenPal site

http://penpals.englishclub.com/
A free service for e-mail exchange.

5. Meta Sites (sites that contain links to a variety of other sites)

Center for Applied Second Language Studies (CASLS)

http://casls.uoregon.edu
A site with hundreds of links to ESL material on the Web. Users need to be registered to access some parts.

Dave's ESL Internet Cafe

http://www.eslcafe.com
A large site with extensive teacher and student resources, including keypals, chatrooms, Web links, and job information.

DEIL/IEI Center

http://deil.lang.uiuc.edu
The Intensive Language Institute site has an extensive menu of links to resources.

English Club

http://www.englishclub.com
A large site with a great variety of links and activities.

Internet Resources for Language Teachers and Learners

http://www.lang.ltsn.ac.uk/index.aspx
A compilation of annotated links for language students and teachers.

Internet TESL Journal

http://iteslj.org
A monthly web journal with ESL material for both students and teachers, including quizzes, articles, research papers, lesson plans, classroom hand-outs, teaching ideas, and many links.

John M. Murphy's Menus of Links Selected as Helpful for ESL Teachers

http://www.gsu.edu/~esljmm/methods/JMlinks.htm
A site with an extensive menu of links to language-learning resources on the Web.

Kitao, K. And Kitao, S. Kathleen. On-Line Resources and Journals

http://ilc2.doshisha.ac.jp/users/kkitao/online/
A site with extensive information about online resources related to ESL and applied linguistics and a large menu of links.

Kristina Pfaff's Linguistic Funland

http://www.linguistic-funland.com
A selection of language acquisition and linguistics-related links.

The Linguistic Funland TESL Page: Resources for Teachers of English as a Second Language

http://www.tesol.net
A site offering a variety of resources for English teachers, including employment information, software (including downloadable freeware), books, student activities, and teaching materials.

Teaching.com

http://www.teaching.com/

A large nonprofit site for teachers with many activities and links, including ESL links.

Technology in English Language Learning

http://www.eastment.com
A site for links maintained by David Eastment, an IT consultant.

TESL/TEFL/TESOL/ESL/EFL/ESOL Links

http://www.aitech.ac.jp/~iteslj/links/
A site with more than 8,000 links for students and teachers of ESL. It is maintained and updated frequently as a project of *The Internet TESL Journal* (see **Journals**).

ThinkQuest

http://www.thinkquest.org
A site with a number of resources for all students and teachers. ThinkQuest is a nonprofit educational group.

Web Enhanced Language Learning (WELL)

http://www.well.ac.uk
The site for the WELL project sponsored by a consortium of British universities for improved Web-based language teaching.

6. MOOs and MUDs

Connections

http://www.nwe.ufl.edu/~tari/connections/
A site including discussion groups and other kinds of ongoing projects for students, teachers, and educational researchers. Other special projects are also welcome.

enCore

http://lingua.utdallas.edu/encore
A MOO project designed for educational applications.

MediaMOO

http://www.cc.gatech.edu/fac/Amy.Bruckman/MediaMOO/

A professional community for people to explore the future of media technology. It is membership-based and those selected for membership must be involved in media studies.

schMOOze University

http://schmooze.hunter.cuny.edu or http://schmooze.hunter.cuny.edu:8888/
A place for ESL students to meet online and share their ideas with each other, practice their English skills, and use the resources on the page.

TAPPED IN

http://www.tappedin.org
An online virtual community of education professionals, the name referring to Teacher Professional Development (TPD). It is free to join and offers many services, including help with online courses, discussions, focus groups, and Internet tours.

7. Online Resources

The CALL Cookbook

http://www.owlnet.rice.edu/~ling417/
A student project of Rice University providing online activities to enhance foreign language study.

CALL Software Database

http://www.hull.ac.uk/cti/resources/swdb.htm
A site for predominantly U.K.-based software suppliers.

Comenius English Language Center

http://www.comenius.com
Primarily commercial, the Web site has considerable free resources including a monthly idiom with an audio presentation of common English idioms.

English-Zone

http://english-zone.com
Resources for learning grammar, English verbs, idioms, spelling, and conversation.

PageTutor.com—HTML tutoring for the rest of us

www.pagetutor.com
An HTML, Web authoring, and JavaScript Web site with tutorials.

Puzzlemaker

http://www.puzzlemaker.com
A site for the creation of puzzles and games; part of the large Discovery site
for general teaching (http://school.discovery.com).

QUIA

http://www.quia.com
A site for creating games, activities and quizzes. Teachers have also uploaded their own tests and activities.

So You Want to Learn HTML . . .

www.edb.utexas.edu/resta97/aisd/students/turnbull/HTMLtutr/index.
html
A site for instructional technology students who need to complete Web
pages for assignments.

Teaching English

http://www.teachingenglish.org.uk
A site with a range of services, including weekly articles in methodology, activities, and lesson plans.

8. Practice and Drill Sites

DEIL/IEI Linguacenter—Interactive Listening Comprehension Practice

http://www.iei.uiuc.edu/free.html
A site with interactive listening comprehension exercises.

English Practice

http://www.englishpractice.com
A site with more than 40,000 lessons on grammar, listening, pronunciation,
reading, vocabulary, and cultural issues. A chatroom and discussion board
are also provided.

Randall's ESL Cyber Listening Lab

http://www.esl-lab.com
A multimedia listening exercise and quiz site.

StudyCom's English for the Internet

http://www.study.com
A site offering lessons in grammar, reading, writing, listening, and speaking; a placement test is available.

9. Professional Organizations

ACTFL, the American Council on the Teaching of Foreign Languages

http://www.actfl.org
An organization for the improvement of language teaching and learning.

American Association for Applied Linguistics

http://www.aaal.org
An organization for the study of applied linguistics.

CALICO, the Computer Assisted Language Instruction Consortium

http://www.calico.org
A professional organization for education and IT.

EUROCALL, the European Association for Computer Assisted Language Learning

http://www.eurocall-languages.org
An association of language teachers from Europe and around the world for research, development, and practice concerning the use of CALL.

JALT, the Japan Association for Language Teaching

http://jalt.org
An organization of language teaching professionals in Japan; Japan's TESOL affiliate.

TESOL, Teachers of English to Speakers of Other Languages

http://www.tesol.org
A U.S.-based organization with a number of state and international affiliates.

TESL/TEFL/TESOL/ESL/EFL/ESOL Links—TESL Associations

http://iteslj.org/links/TESL/Associations/
A large collection of links to TESL professional associations around the globe; the site is maintained by *The Internet TESL Journal* (see **Journals**)

10. Research and Information

Center for Applied Linguistics

http://www.cal.org
A nonprofit organization conducting research on language-related issues.

ERIC Clearing House on Languages and Linguistics

http://www.cal.org/ericcll
A site operated by the U.S. Center for Applied Linguistics providing detailed resource lists including ERIC/CLL publications, Web sites, organizations, and conferences.

Extensive Reading Pages

http://www.kyoto-su.ac.jp/information/er/
Information and resources relating to extensive reading. The site contains materials such as presentation handouts, classroom models, online research, and instructions on setting up an extensive reading program.

History of Computer Assisted Language Learning Web Exhibition

http://www.history-of-call.org
A Web history of CALL.

Scientific Research on the Internet—WebUse

http://www.webuse.umd.edu
A site presenting Internet-based research.

11. Testing

Dave Sperling Presents . . . The ESL Quiz Center

http://www.pacificnet.net/~sperling/quiz/
An extensive collection of online quizzes on a variety of topics.

E. L. Easton—English—Grammar—Quizzes

http://eleaston.com/grammarqz.html
A testing meta site with links to quizzes and tests across the globe. The site itself has many ESL resources.

English as a 2nd Language

http://esl.about.com
Although this is a general ESL Web site, clicking on "Quizzes and Tests" will take the user to a page of quizzes with links for many more.

ESL Blues(s)

http://www.collegeem.qc.ca/cemdept/anglais/trouindx.htm
This site contains quizzes that, when corrected, will refer students to appropriate quizzes and resources for further study.

ESL Independent Study Lab—Grammar

http://www.lclark.edu/~krauss/toppicks/grammar.html
A meta site with links to quizzes and tests across the globe.

ESL Writing and Grammar Lab

http://www.pccc.cc.nj.us/library/asrc/esl/
A site with links to other site's quizzes.

Self-Study Quizzes for ESL Students

http://iteslj.org/quizzes/
An enormous collection of quizzes.

TOEFL, Test of English as a Foreign Language

http://www.toefl.org
This site explains the TOEFL and provides practice tests. Students may register to take the test online.

12. Tools for Teachers and Students

Blackboard (commercial online course development)

http://www.blackboard.com

Creating Web-Based Language Learning Activities

http://www.cal.org/ericcll/faqs/rgos/webcall.html

Microsoft Office Tutorial

http://www.fgcu.edu/support/office2000/

Software Tools for the Web

http://www.ncl.ac.uk/wwwtools/

WebCT (commercial online course development)

http://www.webct.com

13. Writing Sites and Online Dictionaries

ARTFL Project: Roget's Thesaurus Search Form

http://humanities.uchicago.edu/forms_unrest/ROGET.html
An online version of *Roget's Thesaurus 1911*, Version 1.02.

Computers and Composition Comprehensive Bibliography

http://www.hu.mtu.edu/~candc/bib/bib.htm
An academic bibliography on computers and writing sponsored by the journal, *Computers and Composition* (a journal for teachers who use computers to teach writing).

Free Online Dictionary of Computing

http://www.computeruser.com/resources/dictionary
A dictionary of computer terms.

International Writing Centers Association

http://iwca.syr.edu/IWCA/IWCAOWLS.html
A meta site of English writing centers on the Web.

The Internet Picture Dictionary

http://www.pdictionary.com/
A free, online multilingual picture dictionary designed especially for ESL students.

The Jargon Dictionary

http://info.astrian.net/jargon/terms/a/ASCII.html
An online dictionary of computer terms.

PIZZAZ!

http://darkwing.uoregon.edu/~leslieob/pizzaz.html
A site providing activities for creative writing and storytelling.

Pseudodictionary.com

http://pseudodictionary.com/
A large list of slang, Webspeak and colloquialisms.

TechWeb Encyclopedia

http://content.techweb.com/encyclopedia/
A site with more than 20,000 high-technology terms. IT terms and words are illustrated to help the reader understand the concepts behind the definitions.

Author Index

Subject Index